IT POLICIES & PROCEDURES

Tools & Techniques That Work

George Jenkins ◆ Michael Wallace

PUBLISHERS

1185 Avenue of the Americas, New York, NY 10036
www.aspenpublishers.com

This publication is designed to provide accurate and authoritative information in regard to the subject matter covered. It is sold with the understanding that the publisher is not engaged in rendering legal, accounting, or other professional services. If legal advice or other professional assistance is required, the services of a competent professional person should be sought.

—From a Declaration of Principles jointly adopted by a Committee of the American Bar Association and a Committee of Publishers and Associations

Copyright ©2002 by Aspen Publishers, Inc.
A Wolters Kluwer Company
www.aspenpublishers.com

Permissions
Aspen Publishers
1185 Avenue of the Americas
New York, NY 10036

ISBN 0-7355-3743-7

Printed in the United States of America

2 3 4 5 6 7 8 9 0

Library of Congress Cataloging-in-Publication Data

Jenkins, George Henry; Wallace, Michael.
    IT policies & procedures: tools & techniques that work / George H. Jenkins & Michael Wallace.
        p. cm.
    Includes index.

    1. Management information systems. 2. Information resources management. I. Title.
    T58.6.J465   2002   02-29527
    004'.068'4—dc20   CIP

(*Formerly published by Prentice Hall*)

This book is dedicated to our wives, Patricia Jenkins and Tami Wallace. With them, it was all possible. George would also like to make a dedication to his former teacher and mentor at Purdue University at Fort Wayne, Indiana, the late Conwell Poling.

ACKNOWLEDGMENTS

Our extended thanks to John Hiatt, acquisitions editor at Prentice Hall Direct, who foresaw the need for this manual.

A special thanks, also, to Scott Bushey, Larry Webber, and Chuck Carlos for providing insight into IS operations from their unique points of view.

INTRODUCTION

IT Policies and Procedures: Tools & Techniques That Work is a comprehensive update to *Information Systems: Policies & Procedures Manual, Second Edition.* While many of the basic principles of superior IS operations have not changed over the years—we still have to do backup, service business users, and so on—the Internet and an explosion of connectivity options have added new challenges to running an effective IS organization.

WHAT THIS MANUAL WILL DO FOR YOU

No two information systems operations are alike, but many do share some basic elements, such as hardware, software, and personnel. This manual defines the common threads that link all information systems operations, providing for a variety of situations—not as a one-size-fits-all model, but instead, as an updated guide and decision-making reference that can help you to devise an information systems policy and procedure program uniquely tailored to the needs of your organization.

ORGANIZED FOR QUICK ACCESS

For fingertip access to the information you need on Policy and Planning, Documentation, Systems Analysis and Design, and much more, this ready-reference deskside manual comes with a Policy Manual CD-ROM to help you find what you need quickly and easily. You or your staff can use the CD-ROM or the book itself as a model or a template to create similar documents for your own organization.

"Simplicity is the ultimate design." Often, a multitude of forms is included in policies and procedures handbooks. This manual, however, provides a minimum of forms with the understanding that a well-written memo or e-mail message can take the place of a form and reduce the complexity of an IT operation. As an operation grows in complexity, the challenge to keep it running smoothly grows, and thus the need for a formal system of operations becomes a necessity. IS operations that have a formal systems and procedures manual in place are noticeably more efficient.

ADDED STRATEGIC VALUE

The role of IT management is changing even more quickly than information technology itself. Today the IS operation is no longer found in some obscure corner of the corporate organization. Instead, it plays an interactive role in global systems. This manual will help you to formalize policies and procedures that are needed to formally document the IS operation. Doing so will save both time and effort. This manual and its supplements will help you identify standard operations and procedures, documenting as needed, but still allowing for special needs.

Reality check: End-user computer systems will grow with or without the guidance of corporate IS, but the two working together will provide synergistic dividends. This manual updates the policies and procedures that can expedite your objective.

Our research discovered many well-run information systems operations and some real disasters. The better ones had noticeably good management and practical documentation. Expensive consultants, fad innovations, and cutting-edge technology did not always produce the desired IT results.

IT Policies & Procedures: Tools & Techniques That Work is a compilation of systems policies and procedures—the best practices within the industry—in current use. This manual is a process development tool that any seasoned information systems manager, working in a large or small IS operation, will find useful.

SAVING YOU TIME

To make the manual even more valuable, a CD-ROM is included, containing the manual's forms and text. Because the format of the manual itself follows the structure of a typical looseleaf procedure manual, you can use it as a starting point for developing your own, by importing it into a word processor on a PC. Of course, you can also make needed changes and post the manual on a local area network or even a company Intranet site.

Writing this book has been a challenge because of the explosion of IT technology. By the time you finish this book, technology changes are already being developed for the next supplement.

George H. Jenkins
Michael Wallace

ABOUT THE AUTHORS

As a professional IS practitioner for 23 years, **George H. Jenkins** began his career as an engineering programmer with General Electric, where he wrote an engineering end-user's policy and procedure manual. As a systems analyst with Xerox, he wrote an internal manual, *The Principles of Stock Keeping,* and worked as a DP operations manager with Columbia Record Club of CBS.

As the Administrative Coordinator for Capital Record Club and Capital Record Club of Canada, he wrote a manual on writing policies and procedures. He was also Director for Systems and DP operations for Nicolson File Company and an administrator for Wayne County General Hospital (University of Michigan teaching hospital).

Other accomplishments include: writing one of the first artificial intelligence programs (which designed electric motors for General Electric); designing, programming, and successfully installing the first exponential smoothing inventory control system; installing the second online real-time data collection system for production control; and converting the second-largest business unit record operation to computers.

Dr. Jenkins has been published in the *Journal of Systems Management* and *Data Management* magazine, and is the author of *Data Processing Policies and Procedures Manual.* He has also earned his CDP, CDE, and CSP.

He is currently a Professor Emeritus of Systems Analysis with the University of Findlay (Ohio) where he developed a four-year degree program for systems analysis. Hundreds of his systems graduates have achieved the highest job-placement record of any other discipline at the university.

Dr. Jenkins is currently involved with reengineering systems analysis research, teaching, writing, consulting, etc. He may be reached via e-mail at: jen.acres@buckeye-express.com or by fax at (419) 531-0725.

Michael Wallace has 20 years of experience in the information systems field. He began his career after graduation from Lima Technical College as a mainframe operator for Super Food Services, then moved to a programming position at Reynolds & Reynolds.

He became a consultant after graduating Magna Cum Laude from Wright State University (Dayton, Ohio) with a Bachelor of Science degree in Management Science. For eight years he was President of Q Consulting, a custom application development firm. Mr. Wallace has been an application developer, systems analyst, and technical and business consultant, and recently assisted the State of Ohio in developing statewide IT policies.

Mr. Wallace is currently Application Development Practice Manager at Babbage Simmel, a mid-size consulting and training firm specializing in instructor-led training, Internet application development, business intelligence, infrastructure development, and mobile application development using handheld and wearable devices. Babbage Simmel provides its clients with "the knowledge to stay ahead" through instructor-led training, mentoring, and consulting engagements.

Mr. Wallace is a Microsoft Certified Professional and a past Vice President of the Columbus Computer Society, and has served on the board of directors of various computer organizations. He is presently a member of the Association of Internet Professionals and the Project Management Institute, and is currently enrolled in the Executive MBA program at the Fisher College of Business at Ohio State University.

Mr. Wallace can be reached by e-mail at: michaelw@columbus.rr.com.

CONTENTS

3 SYSTEMS ANALYSIS AND DESIGN: STAYING ORGANIZED   57

4 PROGRAMMING PROCEDURES: SOLID PRACTICES 87

8 MANAGING IT ASSETS: IDENTIFY WHAT YOU HAVE   197

9 POLICIES COVERING PCs: MANAGING THE DESKTOP SYSTEM   233

12 SYSTEMS AND OPERATIONS AUDIT   289

14 IT TRAINING: BUILDING THE TEAM 341

15 VENDORS: GETTING THE GOODS 359

16 MOBILE DEVICES: WIRED FOR SUCCESS   387

17 THE INTERNET   **403**

18 END-USER IT DEVELOPMENT   **427**

1

POLICIES AND PLANS: SETTING THE FRAMEWORK

PURPOSE AND SCOPE: HOW YOU BENEFIT

IT Policies & Procedures: Tools & Techniques That Work offers you examples and templates to follow when setting up comprehensive and vital processes for developing, adopting, and distributing uniform IS policies and procedures to aid in information technology resource management and deployment.

Policies discussed here are general statements of direction and purpose that allow users to exercise good judgment in the daily operation of the business. They promote the efficient use of resources in the organization. Policies explain *what* and *why* things are done.

Setting policy objectives:

❖ Differentiates between the corporate, local area network, and workstation or PC operations.

❖ Provides structure to the interface of various work group information systems, and to the relationship of work groups and stand-alone PC systems with the company's corporate system.

❖ Assigns the responsibility and defines the authority for controlling all computer and network standards, operational standards, and training.

Procedures, on the other hand, are specific statements designed to provide direction in actions necessary to support the policies of the organization. Procedures explain *how* things are done.

This manual provides guidelines for policies and procedures related to information systems functions at the corporate, local area network, and PC workstation levels. It is not intended to replace instructions by various vendors in the operation of their software or hardware. Although the examples used here could be adapted to fit your unique circumstances, there is no "one size fits all" solution.

ORGANIZING A MANUAL

A fundamental step to assigning structure is to develop a policies and procedures manual for quick reference and easy updating. This is true whether you create a paper version or post an electronic version.

Manual Organization: A Living Example

This book is divided into chapters as a "living example" of manual organization and style. The chapters are subdivided into sections. The sections are subdivided into subsections. The manual opens with a table of contents displaying the chapters, sections, and subsections. Contact information for the person responsible for the policies should be included in the front of the manual so that users can request updates or get clarification, if needed.

A TYPICAL STRUCTURE FOR FAST RETRIEVAL

"Nested" Style

The reference index is in the form of:

N. CHAPTER NUMBER

  N.N SECTION NUMBER

    N.N.N Subsection number

      A. First-level subdivision

        1. Second-level subdivision

          a. Third-level subdivision

            (1) Fourth-level subdivision

              (a) Fifth-level subdivision

Type Styles and Page Numbering

Most manuals use type styles to aid in fast information retrieval. For example:

[CHAPTER and SECTION titles will be uppercase.]
[The subsequent text's first character will be uppercase.]

Pages are numbered within each section as page "x–x." For example, if the last page of section six is four, it would be numbered "6–4." The placement of page numbers, headers, and footers needs to be consistent from section to section.

Printing Policies and Procedures

If the policies and procedures manual is printed, use 20-lb. white paper. Temporary policies or procedures should be printed on colored paper—light blue is a good choice—and show the duration time in the "effective date" box at the top of each page (MM/DD/YY–MM/DD/YY).

Page Layout

A clean, uncluttered layout encourages one to read the material. Experiment with different formats to find the one that works best for you.

SETTING THE STANDARDS FOR RESPONSIBILITIES

Information systems policies typically flow top–down from the highest level of authority in the organization that the computer procedures will affect. This person should designate a Policy Manager or Team to develop and oversee the implementation of the policies. Note that imposing policies "from on high" without involving those affected can inhibit acceptance and compliance.

Who Has Management Authority?

For consistency, it's important to designate a single corporate computer systems manager with the authority to implement all company computer systems policies. This person will receive policy mandates from the firm's delegated operations policymakers. These policies will be defined in writing and dated, signed, and forwarded to the corporate computer systems manager who will incorporate these policies, along with his/her own, into the company computer policies.

Financial aspects of the firm's computer systems will require the co-approval of the firm's auditors, both in-house and outside, if applicable. The

EXHIBIT 1-1. Headers and Footers

Headers

Policy and Procedure Manual		Page:	2 of 3
Chapter:	1 Organizational Responsibility	Issued by:	
Section:	2 Manual Organization	Approved:	
Effective Date:	03/01/2001	Supersedes:	

Subject:	Organizational Responsibility	Policy #:	1-2
		Page #:	2 of 3
Covers:	Manual Organization	Effective:	03/01/2001

Footers

Revision #: Revision Date:	Issued by:

Revision #:	Supersedes:	Date:

responsibilities of the corporate computer systems manager are defined in the corporate policies and procedures manual.

Local network manager within corporate IS.   The manager of a work group using a local area network or individual PCs within a corporate information system operation is typically the authority for such systems. If the company has a corporate system with a network or PC policies and procedures manual in place, its maintenance will be the responsibility of the corporate information systems management. Policy enforcement will come under the authority of the manager of the work group whose responsibilities are defined in the corporate information systems policies.

Where the manager of a local area network or individual PCs receives only policy guidance from the head of corporate information systems, he/she needs the flexibility to adapt these policies, as needed, into the PC policies and procedures manual.

Local network manager outside corporate IS.   Managers of local area networks or individual PCs that are not part of the company system are the authority for the systems in their area. The company must create a combined policies and procedures manual formulated to carry out the firm's policies for the company network, local area networks, and stand-alone PCs. The manager of local area networks or individual PCs will be responsible for the procedure development, maintenance, and enforcement within his/her area of authority. The respective responsibilities for the PC policy and procedure manuals will be documented in the *Corporate Policy and Procedures Manual.* Any financial transactions or data access of the company's computer data base systems by local area networks or individual PCs will require the co-approval of the firm's auditors, both in-house and outside, if applicable.

Local network manager with no corporate IS.   Managers of local area networks or individual PCs in a firm that has no corporate information system will be the sole authority of the systems in their area. They are responsible for policy and procedure development, maintenance, and enforcement. The person approving will be so noted at the top right-hand side of each section's first page in the manual. This will be the same person who provides the policies, or a representative.

Policies and Procedures Responsibility

All computer operations, software, supplies, and supporting hardware for the firm will be the responsibility of the head of the firm's corporate computer and/or PC operations. In most organizations, this will be the CIO or the IT Enterprise Architect. The authority to enforce *policies and procedures* is defined in the manual. This person has the responsibility to approve and sign all issued and all temporary policies and procedures and his/her name will be noted at the top right-hand side of each section's first page in the manual. The person writing the policies and procedures will be designated by the head of the company's information system, or may elect to write it him-/herself. The writer is identified at the top right-hand side of each section's first page after the word "By:" and under the name of the person noted as approving.

Firms without a corporate computer and/or PC operations head will require a designated person for the PC policies and procedures responsibility. This person's authority can be defined from information provided on page 3.

COMMENT

The higher up the approval authority, the more likely the policies will be followed. In addition, "buy-in" from users will help policies take root quickly.

Implementation

All corporate and work group managers utilizing the information systems department's management personnel are responsible for ensuring that the provisions set forth in the Information Systems Policies & Procedures Manual are complied with. These management persons:

1 Insure that all application standards are followed in their respective areas.

2 Inform the person in charge of approving the procedures if there are any problems with a procedure or if inputs from other sources do not comply with the defined procedures. This should be done in the form of a memo.

3 Provide new employees with instruction and/or documented procedures that relate to their job descriptions.

All stand-alone PC operations will be covered by a user's procedure manual provided by the supervisor. This manual will contain all procedure information needed for the authorized PC user to be in compliance. Also, the help-desk contact will be identified for any needed assistance.

IS POLICY APPROVAL PROCESS

An official policy creation, review, acceptance and update process should be created so that everyone in the organization understands and participates in the policy process. The life cycle of a policy is:

1 A policy need is identified.

2 A draft is created and reviewed.

3 The appropriate level of management approves the new policy.

4 The policy is distributed.

5 The policy may be revised.

6 The policy may be rescinded.

Policy additions or revisions are communicated using the form shown in Exhibit 1–2, either as a hardcopy form or as a Web page on the corporate intranet. If a Web page is used, a link to a Web page showing the acceptance criteria described on pages 8–9 should be included.

Policy Creation Process

The policy manager identified above is responsible for developing and following a standard process for creating new policies. This process should be similar to the following:

1 **A policy suggestion is made.** Policy suggestions can originate from the policy manager, from users, or from management mandates.

2 **Is there a need for a new policy?** The policy manager works with management to determine whether there is a need for a new policy (see "Policy Acceptance Criteria" on page 8). If the suggestion is rejected, the requestor is notified of the reasons for rejection. Alternatives to a new policy should be suggested to the person making the request.

3 **The policy manager assigns a priority to the policy.** The policy manager works with management input to assign a priority to the development of the new policy.

4 **The policy manager or an assigned policy analyst performs required policy research.** The policy manager or an assigned policy analyst researches the requirements for the new policy. This research includes reviewing existing policies, obtaining examples from outside the company, and conducting interviews with stakeholders affected by the new policy.

5 **A draft policy is created.** The draft policy is reviewed by others in the policy department, if applicable. Some firms have a formal policy review committee for review and change control; for others, this is ad hoc.

6 **The draft policy is reviewed by management.** The draft policy is sent to upper management and important stakeholders for review.

7 **Revisions are made to the draft, if necessary.** Revisions may be made after input is received from upper management and important stakeholders.

8 **Is this a mandated policy?** If management mandated the new policy, then go to step 14. Mandated policies are typically those required by law or requested by upper management.

9 **A copy of the draft policy is sent to selected stakeholders for review.** The draft policy is sent to all affected stakeholders for review and comment. This can be done by hardcopy, e-mail, or placement on the corporate intranet. The quality of the final policy can depend on the number of people who review the proposed policy.

10 **Stakeholder comments are incorporated into the draft, if appropriate.** Incorporating as many suggestions as possible from users will help in gaining acceptance of the new policy.

11 **Determine if additional research is required.** A large percentage of negative comments may suggest that additional research is required.

12 **Revised policy draft is sent to management for review.**

13 **Make any revisions suggested by management.**

14 **Send the new policy to the appropriate person for signature.**

15 **The new approved policy is sent to stakeholders.**

16 **Update the master policy manual.**

Policy Acceptance Criteria

Policy suggestions are made either by filling out the Policy Suggestion Form and delivering it to the policy manager or by filling out a form on the corporate intranet. The form must be filled out completely in order for the policy to be considered. The policy manager will use the following criteria to determine if a suggestion is accepted and a new policy is written or changes made to an existing one. Few suggestions will meet all criteria; the policy manager must balance strengths against shortcomings in evaluating each suggestion. Any of the following criteria may provide an overwhelming reason to either accept or reject a specific suggestion. Policy suggestions made by upper management will be automatically accepted.

A **Purpose.** The purpose of the policy suggestion must be stated clearly and be relevant to the mission, goals, and operations of the organization.

B **Audience.** The suggestion must address and identify the intended users of the policy, and satisfy some real or perceived need of this audience.

C **Authority.** The policy manager must have the authority to issue policy for the area in question.

D **Currency.** The suggested policy must apply to current and/or future activities.

E **Scope.** The scope of the suggestion must match the expectations of the intended audience.

F **Uniqueness.** To avoid needless duplication of effort, the information contained in a new policy should not already be covered in any existing policy.

G **Organizational Impact.** A new policy suggestion should have a positive impact on the operations of the organization. Suggestions with a greater impact will have a higher priority than those suggestions with a lower impact. Impact assessments must address cost-benefit and forecast return on investment.

H **Urgency.** Suggestions with a higher degree of urgency will have a higher priority than those with a lower one. Policy requests mandated by law or upper management will have a higher priority.

Manual Maintenance

Permanent manual revisions will be sequentially identified, after the word "Rev.," at the top right-hand side of each section's first page. Temporary policies or procedures supersede permanent policies and procedures, which will remain in the (three-ring) manual binder; they can only be replaced by the issuance of replacement policies and/or procedures. In the event that a policy and/or procedure is to be discontinued, an order will be issued by the person who originally approved the policy and/or procedure or by a successor or agent in memo form. Requests for temporary or permanent policy and/or procedures will be handled as follows:

A Any user, management person, information systems person, work group head, or manual holder can submit a request for a temporary policy and/or procedure or for a permanent revision to the Information Systems Policies & Procedures Manual.

B Revision requests will be handled in the following manner:

1 Request a revision using the *Header* and *Footer* format on page 4.

2 Submit one copy to the approving authority (or successor) for the policy and/or procedure.

3 The final authority will review the request and approve or deny it, providing a reason for any action taken. The person assigned to investigate the request will be identified. The person assigned to determine the course of action necessary might also be the approval authority. The recommended course of action can result in a feasibility study if the required undertaking is large or expensive enough.

4 If the initial request is denied, the person requesting the change may move up the chain of command to the appropriate level needed for resolution.

C Revised documentation will be issued simultaneously to all affected manual holders using print or electronic means. The person responsible for maintaining the manual and any local area network or stand-alone PC policies will keep a current list of all manual holders with a partial or complete manual. Partial manual holders, who will have identified which sections they receive, will be cross-indexed by those sections. When a particular section is replaced, a list of appropriate manual holders can be provided for distribution. **Note:** The lists may be maintained in a computer database and distribution lists printed as needed.

When permanent revisions are issued, all pages for the given section will be reissued. If corrections to current procedures are required and numbering is not affected, only the affected pages need be distributed. This applies to both temporary and permanent policies and/or procedures. All releases will have a cover memo noting:

1 The person issuing the release

2 The effective date(s) of the release

3 The reason for the release

EXHIBIT 1-2. Policy Suggestion Form

POLICY SUGGESTION FORM

NAME/TITLE: _____

DEPARTMENT: _____   DATE: _____

MANUAL AREA:

CHAPTER: _____   ❏ New Policy

SECTION: _____   ❏ Change Existing Policy

PAGES: _____

SUGGESTED POLICY/CHANGES:

Write the proposed needed revision. Attach any necessary details, along with supporting documentation.

RATIONALE:

Describe the problem and how it is affecting the current operation or will affect future operations. How will the proposed revision resolve the problem?

Signed: _____   DATE: _____

Approved By: _____   DATE: _____

Approved/Disapproved _____   DATE: _____

Date Revision Completed: _____   By Whom: _____

COMMENTS:

IS STRATEGIC PLANNING PROCESS

The IS plan is the major vehicle for articulating the information systems needs of the division and the associated resource requirements. The entire division must be involved in the creation of the IS plan, as it will shape the IS resources available for delivering the business objectives of the division. If left solely to the IS organization without business unit input, it will not provide maximum value to either part of the organization. The plan must reflect the business drivers for the organization, the relationship of those drivers to the intended IS activities, and the resources required to support those activities.

The head of the firm's corporate computer and/or PC operations takes responsibility for developing an effective IS plan for the organization. The corporate IS plan must integrate with the overall business strategies, goals, and objectives. Division-level plans must also be created, showing how the corporate objectives will be carried out. The head of the firm's corporate computer and/or PC operations reviews the division plans, ensuring these objectives are met, and provides support. Plans will also be reviewed to evaluate their technical feasibility and assess achievability of the planned benefits.

Policy and Procedures to Submit a Strategic Plan

Each division prepares an annual information systems strategic plan including strategies, goals, objectives, and performance measures. The division's plan must integrate with the overall business strategies, goals, and objectives. The plan must also consider the overall IS plan, developed at the corporate level.

Submittal Schedule.   Department/division-level IS plans must be submitted at the beginning of each fiscal year to the head of the firm's corporate computer and/or PC operations. Each division should review its plan status quarterly and update corporate every six months.

Submittal Procedure.   The plan must be submitted to the head of the firm's corporate computer and/or PC operations in electronic format, PDF version, with one unbound paper copy.

The sections described below are required, with subsections or appendixes added, if necessary.

1   **Executive Summary.** This is a 1- or 2-page summary that provides a general understanding of the division's IS plan, and a frame of reference for understanding the overall objectives of the plan. It may

also include information on who developed the plan and how the plan was created.

2 **Division Mission.** This section discusses the mission of the division and how it fits into the organization. Each major functional area of the division and its role in fulfilling the division's mission should be discussed.

3 **Goals and Objectives.** This section describes the major goals and objectives of the division and how they will be achieved. Goals are the long-term results that the organization will achieve as it fulfills its mission. Objectives are the near-term results that are attained as the organization meets its goals. Measurements used for determining whether or not the goals and objectives are met should be included in this section.

4 **External Factors.** This section discusses the division's business drivers. The division's business drivers are derived from the mission, goals, and objectives, and define how the division operates. Identify the external forces such as the economy, technology changes, political environment, and so on, that drive the business.

5 **Internal Factors.** This section identifies the factors internal to the division that affect the division's IS activities. This may include organizational structure, personnel capabilities, management strength, facilities, training needs, and financial resources. Describe the organization's strengths and weaknesses and how they affect IS programs and management. Include an IS organizational chart and discuss personnel factors such as recruitment, retention, and training.

6 **IS Architecture.** This section discusses how the division's IS planning supports its business drivers. A diagram showing the division's current architecture, including internal and external linkages, should be included. If there are plans to significantly change the architecture during the current year, a diagram of the proposed changes should be included. This section should also describe how the division's architecture fits in with the overall corporate architecture.

7 **Technology Initiatives.** The major technology initiatives of the division are described in this section. Examples might include e-commerce programs, ERP implementations, wireless initiatives, etc. Business resumption plans and the division's project management methodology should also be included in this section.

8 **Project Plans.** A project plan for each major new or maintenance project should be presented in this section. Minor projects may be grouped together into one or more general support projects. Each project plan should include the following information:

a A brief statement of the project purpose.

b A reference to the goal or objective from the section above that the project supports. This section should describe the scope of the project, the expected benefits, the implementation timeframe, the resource requirements for the project, and the expected impact the project will have on the organizational goals. Also describe the impact on the organization if the project isn't undertaken.

c Describe the success criteria for the project. What metrics (ROI, service level, system performance, and so on) will be used to measure the success of the project?

d Describe the technical approach employed on this project. Include hardware needs, software to be used (including operating system and development tools), and any telecommunications requirements.

e List any additional concerns about the project, such as staffing and training needs, schedule, integration with other divisions, etc.

f Document the estimated costs by fiscal year for staffing, hardware, telecommunications, etc. needed to complete the project.

g Estimate any future maintenance costs for the life of the system once the project is completed.

9 **Project Summary.** Document a summary of each project planned by the division in this section. This should list the project name, estimated costs, projected start and completion dates, and the estimated benefit in dollars.

2

DOCUMENTATION: PUTTING IT ON PAPER

Well-written documentation presents a clear, accurate picture of the process or system documented. The documentation detail depends on the skill levels of the users involved, who should be able to understand a system or operation through this method. This is especially true when users are non-data-processing people. Yet, user documentation is often left until the last minute, written hastily by nonprofessional writers, and most often is considered an after-the-project nicety rather than a requirement of the project itself. For these reasons, company information systems policy requires that documentation be an integral part of any undertaking. This effort will be budgeted and the assigned funds used for documentation only. Users who do not want poorly written instructions or documentation will not be required to "sign off" on them (i.e., accept them).

Documentation of policy often gets short shrift, tacked on as an afterthought, but it is critical as a permanent record of operation methods, development techniques, and organizational policies. Documentation is *institutional knowledge,* a record of procedure development, design, implementation, operation, and revision data that successors can follow. It incorporates policies, rules, and information that must be distributed properly to all users associated with information systems operations so that energies are directed and coordinated correctly.

POLICY AND PURPOSE

IS documentation policy adds formal structure to the documentation of various IS processes within the organization. Among the benefits:

- ❖ Added flexibility to allow for changes
- ❖ The ability to adapt temporary procedures
- ❖ Greater benefits of minimizing cost and confusion, while maximizing the return on investment in software, hardware, and related items

Scope

All processes touching on IS functions within the organization should be documented. Areas requiring policies and procedures documentation include, but are not limited to:

- ❖ Procedure development
- ❖ Computer management operations
- ❖ Computer users
- ❖ Computer user support
- ❖ System analysis
- ❖ Special areas (redefining vendor software, hardware documentation, etc.)
- ❖ Internet and e-mail usage
- ❖ Security procedures

Policy Objectives

User documentation should be written following specific standards defining the content, approach, and objectives. The standards provide a uniform plan for handling every aspect of documentation.

However, information systems policies and procedures are only as good as the effort to correctly maintain and enforce them. User documentation must be kept current or it is useless.

Procedures

A standard three-ring binder, readily updatable, or an electronic file should be used to contain the applicable computer policies and procedures for corporate systems, work group networks, and stand-alone PCs. Work group managers should have ready access to all policies and procedures that affect their area. The person responsible for PC administration and control, or an authorized agent, should maintain a complete information systems policies and procedures manual. If the firm uses an off-site records backup resource, it too should have a current copy of all the information systems policies and procedures. If a separate systems and procedures unit exists, it should keep an appropriate number of printed manuals.

FEASIBILITY STUDY DOCUMENTATION PROCEDURE

A feasibility study is conducted to determine the practicality of changing, developing, or acquiring a system or computer program. Such studies can be omitted when a project is mandated by top management and/or outside regulatory agencies. Each feasibility study, which consists of a small-scale systems analysis and a feasibility report, will require a binder to contain such documentation as memos, correspondence, vendor literature, and detailed information.

The analysis section is a scaled-down study of a current system and a determination of the practicality of the request. The feasibility report contains documented findings as to the request's feasibility. The final feasibility study report is prepared based on these two sections and any other pertinent information.

Feasibility Study Request Memo

Each feasibility study request will be initiated by an authorized person using a printed or e-mail memo form. The firm will identify the individuals authorized to initiate such requests. The memo will state:

- ❖ The nature of the requested system or software
- ❖ The expected tangible and intangible benefits from the new or revised system or software
- ❖ The date by which a reply to the report is needed
- ❖ The contact person for further information about the request

Feasibility Study Binder Contents

If the approving authority denies the feasibility study request, a notification is sent to the person requesting the study, explaining the reason(s) why the request was not approved. Both the requesting and reply memos will be filed in a "feasibility reject file" in the area of the systems and procedures unit. An approved request for a feasibility study will trigger developing a feasibility binder labeled with the title of the study. It will include the following:

❖ An accumulated table of contents or index, as needed
❖ All memos and correspondence related to the study
❖ Vendor correspondence and literature
❖ Accumulated cost data
❖ A log listing the calendar days and hours worked on the study
❖ Documentation of all meetings
❖ A telephone log regarding all phone calls made and attempted
❖ A copy of the final report

The Final Feasibility Study Report

The final feasibility study report will be formatted in the following manner:

❖ Cover page, containing project title, author, and date
❖ Overview of the request
❖ Rationale for initiating the information systems project or for changing an existing system
❖ The body of the final report providing the details of the project/program
❖ Exhibits
❖ Summary, including recommendations, estimated costs, estimated calendar time needed, and estimated man-hours of all persons involved in the project

PROJECT DOCUMENTATION

Project documentation includes instructions, charts, a copy of the feasibility study, correspondence, and other material dealing with a specific project. It provides a permanent description of the undertaking along with the solutions to problems and the methods used to resolve them.

> **COMMENT**
>
> Remember, calendar time and labor time are not interchangeable. If it takes one person 100 hours (12.5 days) to paint a barn, 100 people cannot paint the barn in one hour.

A project binder is created at the start of a project to provide an ongoing record of pertinent information. It should include all related material and vendor information and correspondence throughout the life of the project. It is important to know which document supersedes another. Therefore, each document should be dated before placing it in the binder.

At no time are the contents to be removed from a project documentation binder. If necessary, a copy can be made of any needed part(s) of the binder contents and both the date and the word "copied" posted on each reproduced page.

Identification and Responsibility

In order to stay organized, project number and title are used to identify each project binder. Responsibility for initiating and maintaining the binder rests with the project leader/manager or other responsible person as designated by the information systems head or systems manager.

Project Binder Contents

The binder for a proposed project contains:

A **Table of contents or index.**

B **Project proposal.** The project report may be in the form of a feasibility study or a systems design, or may specify software requirements. The project proposal should contain:

1 **Description of the project.** A brief statement describing the project, its objectives, and a copy of the feasibility study. The responsible person drafts the project description, which may be more detailed than a feasibility study.

2 **Major project tasks.** An outline of the steps necessary to complete the project.

3 **Estimated costs and benefits.** Computed estimated costs for each major task and/or items to be purchased. Costs should be identified as "estimates" obtained at the time the proposal was written and subject to revision. See Exhibit 2–1 for one format for reporting project proposal costs. Consistency of format, once established, is more essential than individual style and saves time when reviewing the contents.

4 **Time estimate for each task.** Estimated dates for inception and completion of each task, based on the needed resources being available as scheduled.

EXHIBIT 2-1. Format for Project Proposal Costs

Description of Project
(Brief description. Use a separate sheet if needed.)

Major Project Tasks (Use only those applicable to this project.)

	START DATE	FINISH DATE	ESTIMATED COST
Preliminary Analysis	xx/xx/xx	xx/xx/xx	$xxx,xxx
Systems Analysis/Design	xx/xx/xx	xx/xx/xx	$xxx,xxx
Programming	xx/xx/xx	xx/xx/xx	$xxx,xxx
Data and File Conversion Costs	xx/xx/xx	xx/xx/xx	$xxx,xxx
System and Program Testing			$xxx,xxx
Training Costs			$xxx,xxx
Hardware Purchase			$xxx,xxx
Software Purchase			$xxx,xxx
Administrative Costs			$xxx,xxx
Miscellaneous			$xxx,xxx
TOTAL COST			$xxx,xxx

Estimated Annual Operation Cost

Data Entry	$xxx,xxx
Processing	$xxx,xxx
System/Program Maintenance	$xxx,xxx
Administrative	$xxx,xxx
Other (specify)	$xxx,xxx
TOTAL ESTIMATED ANNUAL OPERATIONS COST	$xxx,xxx

Project Staffing
(Name the project leader and state the estimated number and competence level of personnel assigned to work on the project.)

Personnel to Contact
(List names of people best able to answer pertinent questions about the various tasks within the project.)

5 **Project staffing.** The FTE (full-time equivalent) personnel assigned to the project by job title and name. Dates of commitment for anyone assigned only for a portion of the project are also listed.

Competence levels of personnel assigned are identified. This is essential when personnel, such as vendors or consultants, are on loan from user areas and outside sources. The caliber of personnel can determine the success of the project.

6 **Project contact personnel.** A list (names and titles) of persons best able to answer pertinent questions about the project. This is most important when dealing with vendors who may be inclined to contact persons in the organization who will benefit them most instead of the project leader or designated person.

C **Systems concept.** A paragraph or more, written for nontechnical, management-level personnel, that provides a detailed overview of the project objectives. For larger projects, the systems concept paragraph(s) specifies the objectives, scope, and methods to be employed. A short descriptive paragraph suffices for smaller projects.

D **Project resource schedule.** After the project proposal worksheet is prepared, a Project Resource Schedule (see Exhibit 2–2) is developed to show the estimated hours per week each task will require. Once the work is completed, actual hours spent on each task are recorded.

Project Progress Folders

Project progress documentation folders, maintained during the life of the project, contain the history of the project and copies of all relevant correspondence filed by date. They also provide a complete historical record, which becomes a source of information when writing a project completion report, and should reflect any agreements between the project group and users or vendors. The folders should include:

A **Correspondence**
   ❖ Memos and letters
   ❖ Project status reports
   ❖ Minutes of status and problem-solving meetings

B **Manpower utilization record.** The estimated hours per task versus the actual hours per task are posted to the Project Resource Schedule (see Exhibit 2–2). Any line-item variations that reflect a cost of over $100 are explained in memo form at the time of the actual expense posting.

EXHIBIT 2-2. Project Resource Schedule

Project Name _____   Project Number _____

Direct Expense	Period 1		Period 2		Period 3	
	Estimated	Actual	Estimated	Actual	Estimated	Actual
Project Manager						
Systems Analyst						
Developer						
Administrative						
Other						
Training						
Total Hours						
Total Dollars						
Cumulative Hours						
Cumulative Dollars						

Project Leader _____   Date _____

EXHIBIT 2–3. Project Documentation Checklist

Project Name _____   Project Number _____

Date Required	Actual Date	Item	Responsibility
		Request Evaluation	
		Design Specifications	
		System Definition	
		System Flowcharts	
		System Inputs	
		System Protocols	
		System Processing	
		System Outputs	
		File/Database	
		System Controls	
		System Test Plans	
		System Audit	
		System Recovery	
		Nomenclature Glossary	
		Software Description	
		Software Controls	
		Software Tests	
		Help-Desk Assignments	
		Operations Instructions	
		System Acceptance	

Project Leader _____   Date _____

C **Project documentation checklist.** To insure that documentation is being completed, a Project Documentation Checklist is used (see Exhibit 2–3). This will be a source for what documentation is to be done.

SYSTEMS DOCUMENTATION

Systems documentation records activities associated with systems analysis and design efforts. It provides proposed system design specifications in a format that management can easily evaluate for approval. It also provides required specifications for software and vendor bidding. Systems documentation and its maintenance are vital to the success of a project and future systems maintenance.

Systems Documentation Binder

A systems documentation binder is maintained for each project, but is distinct from overall project documentation. Forms in this section (Exhibit 2–4 and Exhibit 2–5) are examples of standard formats to be used as needed. This binder is maintained by the lead systems analyst for the project and contains:

A **Title page.** The first or title page contains the project name and identification number, effective dates, and the lead analyst's name and title. Names and responsibilities of all other persons assigned to the project are listed on the second page.

B **Table of contents.** This reflects the specific contents in the systems binder and requires updating as changes and/or additions are made.

C **Revision sheet.** Included in every systems binder (see Exhibit 2–4), it contains columns for:

1 **Number of revisions.** Revisions are numbered sequentially starting with 1.

2 **Revision date.** Effective date of the revision.

3 **Portion revised.** The specific part of the system under revision, including all areas of documentation such as procedures, flowcharts, reports, etc.

4 **Name.** The name of the systems analyst making the revision.

5 **Authorization.** The name of the person authorizing the revision.

EXHIBIT 2–4. Revision Sheet

Project Name _____   Project Number _____

Revision Number	Date	Item Revised	Revised By	Approved By

Project Leader _____   Date _____

Systems Concept

The systems concept is prepared by the lead systems analyst, from specifications provided by the requesting authority. This section will include copies of correspondence or written requests, which outline the requirements of the system. Once approved, it serves as a guide for analysts to design the technical specifications of the system and includes:

A **Approval.** The first page lists the project name, the requesting authority's name, and the title of the person approving the project.

B **Project history.** This section states the background that justifies the project.

C **Project objectives.** The details of project objectives are presented. All functional areas affected by this project are listed, and any problems with overlapping lines of authority are noted so the required coordination can be established. In addition, anticipated results from the successful completion of the project are detailed. To ensure complete understanding of the system by management and users, what the system won't accomplish is also noted.

D **Requirements.** The documentation requirements necessary for proper completion of the project are:

1 A brief explanation of the work to be done during each phase.

2 A schedule for inception and completion dates of each phase and the key tasks within each phase. To help picture the overall schedule, Gantt charting is recommended for key tasks and phases of complex projects.

3 Special requirements for project software from vendors and/or for in-house programmed software.

4 Special requirements for outside acquisitions such as equipment, consultants, contract personnel, and/or vendor services.

5 Current in-house equipment resources that will be committed to the systems project.

6 Man-hour resources, by names and titles, to be committed to the project.

7 Resources expected from the requesting authority, including hardware and personnel assistance, such as training of extra personnel during conversion of the system.

Systems Specifications

Systems specifications provide a means of communication between the designer and the software providers, who may be in-house programming staff or vendors. The systems specifications provide a record of the structure, functions, flow, documentation, and control of the system and include:

A System narrative

❖ Current date

❖ Descriptive title of the system

❖ General requirements with a description of each and with sources cited

❖ Source, expected schedule, and volume of input data

❖ Size and characteristics of the data

❖ Sample exhibits of input documents

❖ Outputs indicating volume and due dates (This may be a monitor display and/or hard copy.)

❖ Sample exhibits of outputs

❖ References to material or organizations that may furnish additional information (This may include vendor-supplied information.)

B System flowcharts. Graphics or flowcharts can identify the processes performed and the steps involved. Each symbol within a flowchart identifies a process as *manual* or *computer*. Each system flowchart is contained on one page. If greater detail is required of any given area of the system, a subsystem flowchart is drawn in a way that both nontechnical management and computer programmers can understand.

C Program specification requirements. These define the environment within a system in which a subsystem or a single program operates. They describe:

❖ Inputs and outputs, including source, format, disposition, retention method, and time period.

❖ Processes controls, functions, and limitations. These specifications, prepared by the systems analyst for the programming staff, need to be confirmed by the person responsible for programming so that they can be accomplished by this staff.

D File/Database specifications. Complete and detailed specifications of the files and/or databases used in the system are identified. If a database is employed for storing data elements, the database administrator maintains a data dictionary, and the systems project should comply with appropriate procedures. This applies to file specifications if they also fall under the jurisdiction of the database administrator. A reference sheet describes the file layout, field definitions, and source references. A sample file layout is shown in Exhibit 2–5. The file layout contains:

❖ File name
❖ File number or label
❖ Current date
❖ File label
❖ Record size
❖ Storage medium
❖ Record length required
❖ Blocking factor (tape only)
❖ Retention requirements (daily, monthly, etc., and the expected currency in the number of days between the cutoff date and the completion of the update). "Monthly 5 days" means the file is updated monthly with 5 days required to complete the update.
❖ Security level
❖ File sequence
❖ Remarks

COMMENT

The ERwin Modeling Suite from Computer Associates is a great tool for designing databases and business processes. It can be used for creating much of the documentation discussed in this section. Computer Associates can be reached at their web site, www.ca.com.

E **Input description.** This is the format for all the data going into the system. It provides the following information for each input record:

❖ Name
❖ Date
❖ Status (raw data or in computer media form)
❖ Each field, identified within a record, its type, and length
❖ Number of records per cycle (day, week, etc.)
❖ Disposition after it is received by the system

EXHIBIT 2–5. File Description

File Name:	
File Number:	Date:
File Label:	
Record Size:	File Size:
Disk: CD: Tape:	Blocking:
Retention Requirements:	
Remarks:	

F **Output description.** The layout of each output should be displayed in monitor or hardcopy format and is part of the systems documentation. Forms designed for this purpose include:

❖ Name of report

❖ Number of report

❖ Location and length of each item within a report layout

❖ Number of copies

❖ Relationship of items in the report to the source of the item information in the input description

SOFTWARE DOCUMENTATION

Software documentation serves various functions. First, program maintenance has become a major expense. The investment and effort required to document software is rewarded by reduced maintenance costs, and possibly management job security. Second, it communicates to the systems analyst or project leader that the programming has been properly done. Program documentation also provides information systems operations and users with the information needed to operate the software. It furnishes the auditors with information about the controls that have been established. Finally, it shows management what exactly has been accomplished with the money spent.

Software Binders

Information about developed programs and purchased software is maintained in "software binders," one for each written program or purchased software package. They contain:

A **General information.** This section identifies the software and its objectives. Each program should have a unique identification number. The programs may be grouped together using any of the following categories:

❖ Low-level written programs

❖ High-level written programs

❖ Reusable code

❖ CASE tools

❖ Operating software

❖ Database software

❖ Network software

- ❖ Purchased mainframe programs
- ❖ Purchased LAN software
- ❖ Purchased PC/workstation software

B **General objectives.** The general objectives include a brief narrative statement of each program's purpose or use.

C **Purchased software.** Any license agreements connected with the programs, including the number of copies purchased and the last date of purchase. Any "Beta" operating software will be so identified, and its agreement information placed in this section.

D **Program's systems specifications.** Vendor-supplied information will also be included.

E **Program flowcharts.** Flowcharts will be drawn by hand or flowcharted using available software that employs the ANSI (American National Standards Institute) symbols (refer to the "Flowcharting Standards" section of this chapter). There are several commercially available software programs that can generate the ANSI symbols and facilitate the drawing of these charts.

COMMENT

Visio from Microsoft is probably the most popular program for technical drawings. The latest version contains different editions for technical and business drawings. Microsoft can be reached at www.microsoft.com.

F **Written program documentation**
- ❖ Source code listings
- ❖ Source of input and format
- ❖ Pre-alpha naming conventions—needed for the database, inputs, outputs, and controls
- ❖ Hardcopy layouts
- ❖ Screen display layouts
- ❖ Screen layouts displaying control buttons, text boxes, and screen labels
- ❖ Database layouts, definitions of field items, and naming references

❖ Table layouts

❖ Data element cross references

❖ Subroutines, sources, and listings

❖ Index of table field names—names used in databases, programs, and input/output locations (useful when programming and doing maintenance later)

Operations Specifications

The programmer or analyst is responsible for preparing operating instructions that can be used by the central computer operations staff, client/server users, LAN systems, end-user systems, or stand-alone PC users. This documentation should contain detailed instructions on how to operate the program and handle any exceptions that occur. It will require the signed and dated approval of the highest authority in the unit for which it is intended. LAN, WAN, or client/server user instructions will require the approval of the head of information systems or his/her designated representative. The types of information to be included are:

A Cover page information

❖ Program number

❖ Program description or name

❖ Name of programmer or help-desk contact

❖ Type of program

❖ Priority requirements

❖ Estimated processing time

❖ Date prepared and revision dates

B Input/output requirements

❖ Keyboard instructions

❖ Scanning instrument instructions

❖ Removable disk and/or CD instructions

❖ External label

❖ Internal label

❖ Other input/output devices not listed

❖ Form number

❖ Number of copies required

❖ Portrait or landscape printing

❖ Report disposition

❖ Printer(s) required

C Magnetic tape instructions

❖ External label

❖ Internal label

❖ Input or output usage

❖ File protection requirements

❖ Tape disposition

D   General operating instructions

E   Restart procedures

Program Test Data

Listings of input used for testing and the resulting outputs are kept in the program test file. Monitor displays are screen-printed or drawn for documentation.

Backup and Recovery

Procedures are written for corporate and other operations for each running system. All changes are noted with the date and the name of the person responsible. Each program must have a recovery procedure in the event of a computer failure. Each backup procedure will be tested after it is placed into operation and every time maintenance is performed. Backup procedures require the following:

❖   When and how the backup was done.

❖   The location where backup programs and data are stored.

❖   The number of backup generations required. If more than one, they should not all be stored in the same location.

❖   If an outside backup facility is available, a complete written procedure is required for its operation.

COMPUTER OPERATIONS DOCUMENTATION

The operating procedures necessary to initiate, schedule, process, control, and restart all phases of the system(s) while it is in operation are maintained in a binder for the operations personnel. All the documentation must be kept current. The project leader is responsible for compiling and validating new systems. Maintenance information systems personnel typically update existing manuals.

The computer operations documentation procedures can vary depending on the configuration of the system's hardware. The corporate computer center operation, with hardware in the form of a mainframe, minicomputer, or PC, is under a corporate computer operations head, who is also in charge of client/server operations. This person is part of the corporate information systems and officially accepts the operations documentation. The acceptance of documentation is noted on the upper right-hand corner of each procedure section's first page.

The head of corporate computer operations can have responsibility for work group systems manual maintenance or this can be the responsibility of the work group management, whichever better serves the users. The authorized person notes the acceptance of documentation in the upper right-hand corner of the first page of each procedure section.

If PC operations, stand-alone or LAN, has a PC manager, this person may approve operator manuals for his/her area of jurisdiction. In the absence of a PC manager, a user area manager will be assigned the task of approving the operation manuals. This task may be delegated by the manager and, if need be, the help-desk person(s) may be consulted or so delegated. The acceptance of documentation is noted by the authorized person in the upper right-hand corner of the first page of each procedure section.

Corporate Computer Center Operation Procedures

This section details the information systems operations procedures for the corporate system, which cover general information pertaining to the overall corporate system(s), backup and recovery, and job procedures.

A **General information.** This includes a narrative description of the overall operation, system hardware, operating system, the purpose of the system, and the methods used to accomplish the tasks. The users of this documentation are information systems operations personnel. Gathering and maintaining the following general information, which could apply to all runs, is the responsibility of the corporate information systems head:

❖ Overview and purpose of operation procedures

❖ Names, titles, and home telephone numbers of all operations personnel

❖ Published shift schedule

❖ Contact person for operating system problems

❖ Contact person for hardware problems

❖ Gantt chart illustrating all scheduled runs

B **Backup and recovery procedures.** Documented by the systems unit in close collaboration with the firm's auditors and corporate computer center operations management, the ongoing maintenance of these procedures by the systems maintenance people is essential to the organization. Off-site backup and recovery emergency procedures are also maintained. The firm's auditors and corporate computer center management must approve all changes. Included in these procedures are:

  ❖ A list of authority hierarchy

  ❖ Backup and recovery on-site procedures

  ❖ Backup and recovery off-site procedures

  ❖ Disaster plan and procedures

C Computer operation procedures. Job instructions should include the following:

  ❖ Job setup instructions

  ❖ The sources of originating data

  ❖ The media used for inputting data

  ❖ The output media

  ❖ Output forms and their disposition

  ❖ Sample of output forms

  ❖ Sample of monitor displays

  ❖ Corrective action to take for error messages

  ❖ Expected job run time

  ❖ External file label instructions

  ❖ Input and output retention procedures

  ❖ Computer log procedures

  ❖ Contact person's telephone number for run problems

D Terminal user procedures. For users who operate terminals and/or client/server PC systems. These users are not always familiar with information systems terms; therefore, operations documentation must be absolutely clear. Possible educational and/or physical limitations of users should be taken into account. User procedures should be simple to read and follow (eighth- to tenth-grade level for nonprofessional personnel). The monitor screen can also be a source of help instructions. Terminal users' instructions should include:

  ❖ Start-up steps, password, etc.

  ❖ Corrective action to take for error messages

  ❖ The proper method to sign off the system

  ❖ Method(s) to obtain hardcopy output

  ❖ Help-desk contact

Work Group Computer Systems

A work group (client/server) computer system can be under the information systems or corporate computer center operations head. It can also be a self-contained unit that may or may not rely on the information systems organization for its policies and procedures documentation. This is a management decision.

The design of work group systems will be under the control of the corporate information head to insure that corporate policies are followed. The design and documentation process can be performed by the information systems unit, contracted out, or undertaken by the work group itself. The corporate information unit will continuously monitor the operational documentation procedures to insure that maintenance procedures comply with the corporate standards. The work group computer system's communication network will follow policies and procedures instituted by the corporate head of computer networking.

A **Work group general information.** Includes a narrative description of the overall work group operation, the system hardware, the operating system, the purpose of the system, and the methods used to accomplish the tasks. The users of this documentation are, most often, more familiar with the efforts of the group than they are with computer technology. The following general information items apply to the work group computer operation and the tasks of the file server computer:

❖ Overview and purpose of operation procedures

❖ Contact person for software problems

❖ Contact person for hardware problems

❖ Start-up procedures for the system

❖ Shut-down procedures for the system

B **Backup and recovery procedures.** When the work group (client/server) system uses and produces financial and/or proprietary information, a close collaboration with the firm's auditors and corporate information systems management is required. Both groups must give their approval to all backup and recovery procedures. The ongoing maintenance of these procedures will also require approval of both groups. If an off-site backup and recovery operation is in place, procedures for this operation are also maintained. Changes to these procedures require the approval of the auditors and/or corporate computer center operations management. Included in these procedures are:

❖ A list of who has what authority

❖ Backup and recovery on-site procedures

❖ Backup and recovery off-site procedures

❖ Disaster plan and procedures

❖ Off-site network access for on-site operations

C **Work group computer operation procedures.** For users of PCs who are networked into a work group system. These users are not always familiar with information systems terms; therefore, operations documentation must be absolutely clear. Possible educational and/or physical limitations of users should be taken into account. User operations should be simple to read and follow (eighth- to tenth-grade level for nonprofessional personnel). The monitor screen can also be a source of help instructions. Operators' instruction procedures can contain the following:

❖ Procedure for turning on the PC (password, etc.)

❖ Accessing program or data from file server

❖ Sample of monitor displays

❖ Corrective action to take for error messages

❖ Expected job run times

❖ Input and output retention procedures

❖ Telephone number for the help-desk

❖ Shut-down procedure

❖ How to access tutorial information

Stand-alone PC Systems

Stand-alone or networked PCs that are not part of a work group or a corporate information system fall into this category. These are PCs throughout a firm that may not have any relationship to other PCs. But, to maintain order, consistency, and a higher level of overall efficiency, their documentation process requires a central source. The corporate information systems unit has the responsibility for companywide "independent" PC documentation, maintenance, policing, and training, as well as help-desk operations for the procedures issued.

A **PC general information.** Includes a narrative description of the overall corporate policies and procedures pertaining to the operation of PCs. Users of this documentation are, most often, more familiar with the duties of their own jobs than with computer technology. Their educational levels will vary widely, from the factory floor to the CEO's office. Therefore, it would be prudent for the writer of this documentation to address more than one reading level. The general information part of this documentation should apply to all users of independent PCs throughout the firm, and should include the following information items:

- ❖ Corporate policies governing PCs
- ❖ Procedure for turning on the PC (password, etc.)
- ❖ Daily PC housekeeping procedures
- ❖ Overview of the operating system
- ❖ Accessing needed programs or data
- ❖ Getting on the network: LAN, WAN, or Internet
- ❖ Shut-down procedure
- ❖ How to access online tutorial information
- ❖ Resources for additional specialized training
- ❖ Frequently Asked Questions (FAQs)
- ❖ Contact person for problems

B **PC operation procedures.** For given kinds of software or special hardware for a particular PC user, this documentation is in module form, one module for each given piece of software or hardware. The PC documentation manual contains the PC general information portion and as many operation procedures modules as required. Copies of vendor information are included whenever it is considered helpful to the user. The following items should be considered for each documentation module:

- ❖ Program or hardware operating instructions
- ❖ Corrective action to take for error messages
- ❖ Backup and retention procedures
- ❖ Telephone number for the help-desk
- ❖ Shut-down procedure
- ❖ How to access tutorial information

FLOWCHARTING STANDARDS

Flowcharts perform several functions in the systems investigation, analysis, design, development, and installation phases. There are several good software flowcharting programs available for PCs. These can be used for drawing organization charts as well.

COMMENT

Most word-processing programs can be used for simple diagrams.

Flowchart diagrams range in complexity from global system flowcharts to procedure step detail flowcharts. The levels of flowcharting are:

A **Global systems.** These interrelate with other computer systems outside the organization.

B **Total systems.** These have an interrelationship with more than one system within the internal organization.

C **System.** This is confined to one area of operation (as in a billing system).

D **Subsystems.** Subsystems may appear at more than one level, with the first subsystem being part of a system flowchart. (See "System Flowchart.")

E **Program or procedure flowcharts.** Both flowcharts depict detail logic or operation steps at their lowest level. Most often, program flowcharts (see "Program Flowcharts") are used for programming instructions, while procedure flowcharts (see "Procedure Flowchart") are used for manual procedure steps.

Global System Flowchart

A "global system" is identified here as an interaction of systems, with one or more systems outside of the organization. One example would be a travel agent's system, interacting with both an airline ticket reservation system and the various credit card systems. The reservation and cost information must be approved before the travel agent can issue a ticket and charge the customer's credit card account. This is a *global* interactive system in operation.

The flowchart exhibit(s) will be on one page. Since there are no recognized standard symbols for global system flowcharts, the manner in which the flowchart is illustrated will depend on the IS technical skills of the viewers. Such charts are most valuable when they are rendered in the simplest terms for the whole group.

Total System Flowchart

A "total system" is identified here as an interaction of two or more systems within the organization, which requires the interaction of all participating systems to function. One example occurs when the production control system interacts with the incentive payroll system of manufacturing, which then interacts with the inventory system for inventory control. The payroll is affected by the worker's scrap rates, which affects inventory and scrap rate report counts. The production unit count credits the worker's pay, but also affects the PM (preventive maintenance) schedule, etc.

The flowchart exhibit(s) will be on one page. Since there are no recognized standard symbols for total system flowcharts, the flowchart should be illustrated in the simplest form.

System Flowchart

The system flowchart shows how the information flows through the system. It is all on one page, allowing the system to be viewed in its entirety. If greater detail is required of any given area of the system, a subsystem or lower level flowchart which illustrates only the desired detail is drawn for that purpose.

System flowcharts are not governed by any national standard. Since they are intended for a diverse audience, from top management to programmers, flexibility is needed to be able to target a presentation appropriately. While programmers can follow a system flowchart drawn for top management, top management may have a problem with one drawn for a project team of systems analysts and programmers because it will often utilize standard programming flowchart symbols.

Systems flowcharts are often viewed by a whole group of people at one time. There is almost no limit to the size of a flowchart and the viewing distance of the audience governs the symbol size. With large groups, it is better to use overhead projection since anything larger than a flip chart becomes a problem to transport and store. Symbols may be used to depict such items as machines and buildings to help top management understand the system, and may, in turn, help sell it. Color is also a good tool to make the system flowchart easier to understand and more interesting to read.

Procedure Flowchart

The procedure flowchart is an excellent method for documenting a manual operation. Placing the flowchart horizontally on a page of quarter-inch graph paper, which comes in rolls of different widths, allows the total procedure to be illustrated on one document. Length presents no problem since the document can be rolled up and stored. The only limitation to length is the space where the chart is displayed for viewing.

Procedure flowcharting is useful for illustrating manual office procedures and is easy to follow, even by people outside the data-processing area. It confirms to the operations personnel that the systems analyst has recorded the procedure correctly. It also gives the systems analyst an easy-to-follow source of information when writing or dictating documentation procedures.

Six symbols are used to draw the procedure flowchart. They represent:

❖   Original information placed on a document

- ❖ Addition of information later to the document
- ❖ The physical handling of the document
- ❖ Document inspection to render a decision
- ❖ Document holding or storage
- ❖ Document leaving the procedure area

These are illustrated in Exhibit 2–6. A Sample Procedure Flowchart is shown in Exhibit 2–7.

If a new, changed procedure contains manual operations, it too can be drawn as a procedure flowchart. In this case, both the old process flowchart and the proposed process flowchart are drawn on the same page for comparison. When preparing a procedure flowchart, the following must be taken into account:

A The direction of flow is left to right.

B Charts are drawn with a number 2 pencil, if done by hand.

C The procedure flowchart is identified in the lower left-hand corner with the following:
- ❖ Project name
- ❖ Project number
- ❖ Date
- ❖ Name of person who produced the flowchart

D All input documents have a receiving point, a starting point, and a disposition. Documents may be sent to a file, disposed of (disposal), or sent to someone else.

E Each line represents a document flow. If a line represents one or more documents, it should be kept at the same level as long as practical.

F Process steps are described briefly by printing the information to the right of the symbol.

G When a multicopy form is originated, the parts are illustrated by the inspection symbol and the form title or number is printed inside the square.

H When the same activity affects two or more documents simultaneously, it is shown by drawing a vertical rectangle around a symbol indicating the activity. The flow lines are drawn to meet the rectangle.

I The charting of one document affecting or creating other documents is shown on the line of the affected action. A "V" line coming from the original document is dropped or inverted to meet the affected document line. After the action shown by a symbol is completed, the last leg of the "V" returns the document to its original level.

Dataflow Diagrams

Dataflow diagrams are replacing the more traditional systems flowchart. Like the system flowchart, they have not been guided by any one national standard. There is more than one proposed set of symbols, but all share the same concept and objective. The four diagramming symbols used in this text are based on work by C. Gane and T. Sarson. Their book, *Structured Systems Analysis and Design Tools and Techniques,* is the source of the concept and symbols represented here.

Dataflow diagrams, which have been around for some time, are familiar in the academic environment. They have many advantages over traditional systems flowcharts when presenting graduated levels of overviews for both current and proposed systems. Because the documentation system is so simple and employs so few rules and symbols, there is little variation between textbooks illustrating its use. Its simplicity provides for a more uniform pictorial presentation of systems that can be followed by systems analysts, programmers, operations personnel, and most users. There are commercially available dataflow diagram templates and PC drawing software. See Exhibit 2–8 for the dataflow symbols. The standard programming flowcharting template may be used with some minor substitutions. The auxiliary operation symbol can replace the dataflow environmental element symbol. The process symbol can replace the dataflow process or procedure symbol. The programming or procedure flowcharting templates can be employed to draw the data storage symbol.

The dataflow diagram illustrates the systems flow and transformation process all on one page, allowing it to be viewed in its entirety. Subsystems requiring greater detail are drawn at the next level, also in their entirety, one per page, with an identification number linking them to their source. This is illustrated in Exhibits 2–9, 2–10, and 2–11. This procedure can be repeated until the final, lowest subsystem level. The complexity and number of subsystems within the undertaking determine the number of levels that may be "exploded." The dataflow diagram levels may be defined as follows:

A   **Context diagram.** The total system concept is drawn as the "large picture," illustrating all dataflows into and out of the system. The processes themselves remain unnumbered and are not described in this general overview. The context dataflow diagram would be the one most likely considered for use in a management presentation (see Exhibit 2–9).

B   **Level 0 (zero) dataflow diagram.** This level represents the total system, numbering and describing each process. Data storage symbols are used to depict the movement of data to or from storage (see Exhibit 2–10).

C **Level 1 dataflow diagram.** This level represents one of the processes or procedures found at the zero dataflow level that has been exploded into its own subsystem detail (see Exhibit 2–11).

D **Level 2 dataflow diagram.** This level represents the further exploding of a given process found at level 1 into its own subsystem detail.

COMMENT

The ease of freehand drawing of this kind of flowchart lends itself well to prototyping. The user working with a systems analyst can easily follow the procedure and the concept of what the four dataflow diagram symbols represent.

Supplemental Dataflow Conventions

The dataflow diagramming procedure can get complex with successive levels of explosions. To help clarify the diagram, each of the four symbols employed can utilize supplemental conventions. Their use is illustrated in Exhibit 2–12. Following are additional conventions that may be of help:

❖ Entity symbols that are duplicated contain a diagonal slash in the bottom right corner. This can reduce the complexity of dataflow lines.

❖ Process symbols contain the process number in the top part of the symbol. When a diagram is exploded, a decimal representing the current level is added to the process number to provide for an audit trail of the related detailed processes (see Exhibit 2–12).

❖ Data storage symbols have a boxed area on the left side of the symbol in which to write the data storage ID. A vertical line drawn to the left of the ID indicates a duplicate data storage location.

❖ When dataflow lines cross each other, one of the lines may use a small crossover bridge to illustrate that the lines do not intersect.

Dataflow diagrams may be drawn by a single person or a group. If prepared by a group, a chalkboard or whiteboard can be used. Or, use a flip chart to keep a record of what was drawn. A board that can reproduce hard copies would be the most ideal instrument.

Using dataflow diagrams is good for both documenting a current system and developing a proposed system.

A Implement dataflow diagram development procedure. Develop a freehand context diagram. This can start with on-hand user input.

   ❖ List the external entities, dataflows, and processes.

   ❖ Determine the scope of the system being charted.

   ❖ Draw the context diagram.

B Develop a level zero dataflow diagram.

   ❖ Apply detail to each process or procedure.

   ❖ Identify and post data storage. Note data storage types such as hard drive, floppy disks, file drawer, etc.

   ❖ Identify process exceptions and post to the diagram.

C Draw the diagrams with the aid of a template. Relabel any symbols requiring more meaningful text and clean up the arrangement of the symbols.

D Explode to the next level and repeat A, B, and C above.

Program Flowcharts

A program flowchart shows operation steps and logic decisions to be followed by the computer for a given program in the processing sequence. All the symbols employed should conform to the ANSI (American National Standards Institute) standards. These symbols are shown in Exhibit 2-13.

Follow these rules in preparing the flowcharts:

A Draw charts on white, $8^{1}/_{2}$- by 11-inch or 11- by 17-inch, 20-lb. paper.

B Draw charts with a number 2 pencil, if done by hand.

C The general direction of flow is top to bottom, and left to right.

D When the flow is not specified or whenever increased clarity is desired, use arrows to indicate the direction of flow.

E Identify each page with:

   ❖ Project name

   ❖ Project number

   ❖ Name of person who produced the flowchart

   ❖ Date

   ❖ Page X of X

F The terminal connector showing that a line is carried to a following page is identified with an uppercase alphabetic character in the center of the connector symbol. The line being continued on the following page starts with a connector symbol and the same character in its center as the departing connector. If that line does not continue on the following page, post the page number to the right of the connector symbol and post the departing page number to the right of the receiving connector.

G Describe process steps briefly by printing the description within the symbol. If necessary, print additional information next to the symbol to clarify a step.

H When changes are made to the flowchart at a later date, the change should be noted, dated, and signed by the person making the change.

Unified Modeling Language™

The latest method being developed for documenting object oriented systems in the Unified Modeling Language™ (UML). Rational Software Corporation developed UML, with contributions from other leading methodologists, software vendors, and many users. UML is based on extensive use of the Booch, OMT, and Jacobson methods to document business processes and objects, and for component modeling. The UML provides the application modeling language for:

- ❖ Business process modeling with use cases
- ❖ Class and object modeling
- ❖ Component modeling
- ❖ Distribution and deployment modeling

The Object Management Group (OMG) is developing UML into an industry standard. OMG is an open membership, not-for-profit consortium that produces and maintains computer industry specifications for interoperable enterprise applications. This standard is still in the process of being developed; for the latest information on UML, go to the OMG Web site at www.omg.org, or the Rational Software Corporation Web site at www.rational.com.

EXHIBIT 2–6. Procedure Flowchart Symbols

Process or Element	Symbol
Original operation, the first time information is placed on a document.	◎
Adding information to a document in a later procedure step.	(hatched circle)
Handling the document, such as sorting, matching, separating or stapling.	◯
Inspection of a document for a decision to be made. Two or more courses of action will follow.	□
Storage of document(s) as inactive, delayed, filed, or held. Also used as a destroy symbol.	▽
Sending or moving the document from one area to another. Also used to show document being sent outside.	◯

EXHIBIT 2–7. Sample Procedure Flowchart

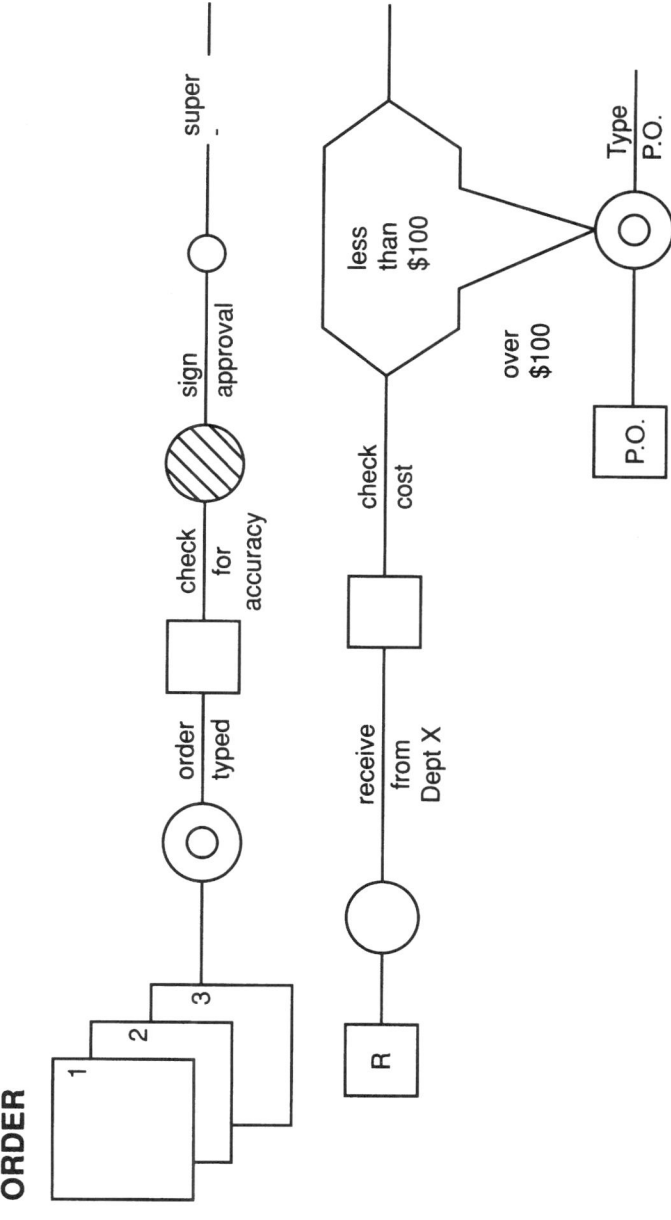

EXHIBIT 2–8. Dataflow Flowchart Diagram Symbols

Process or Element	Symbol
Entity, an environmental element, can be the source or destination of data to or from the system or subsystems.	
Process system or procedures that act on data being received from an external source or an internal file (hard copy or computer database or file).	
Data storage. This can be a computer file or database, hard copy, microfilm or COM, reference lists or tables, even the back of a tablet.	
Data flow. This can be in many forms, such as LAN or WAN systems, direct computer communications, the US mail, UPS, courier or what have you, between the process system (symbols) and data storage or external source. An arrow will be drawn at the contact point of the receiving symbol to denote the recipient of the data.	

The diagramming symbols used for data flow diagrams are based on work by C. Gane and T. Sarson, *Structured Systems Analysis and Design Tools and Techniques,* Prentice Hall, Englewood Cliffs, NJ, 1979.

EXHIBIT 2–9. Context Dataflow Diagram

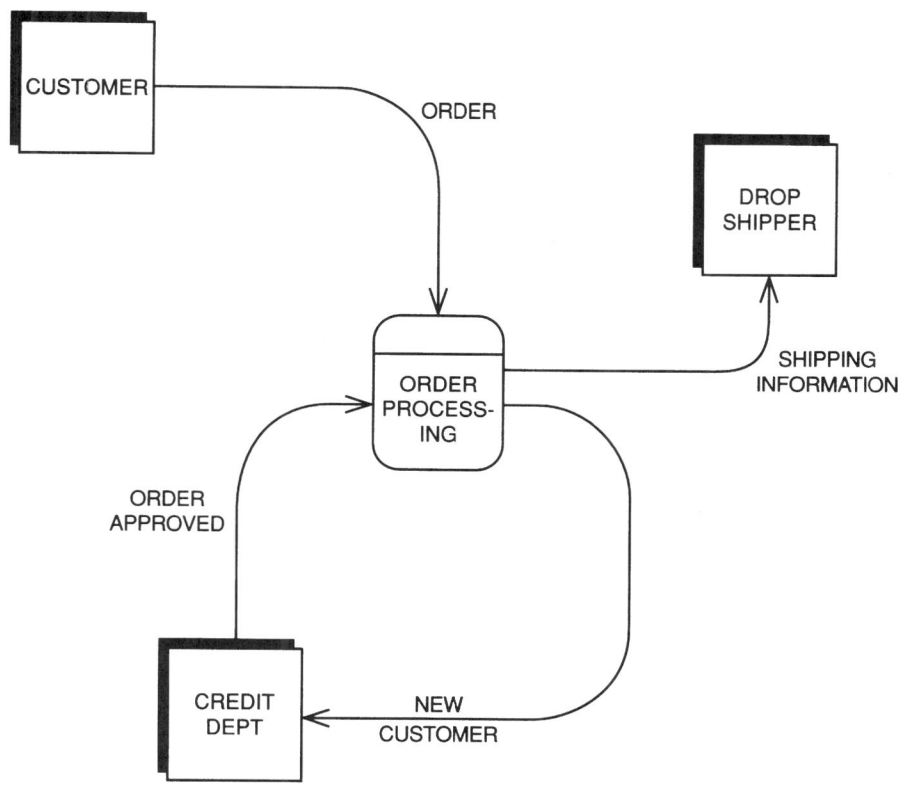

EXHIBIT 2–10. Level Zero Dataflow Diagram

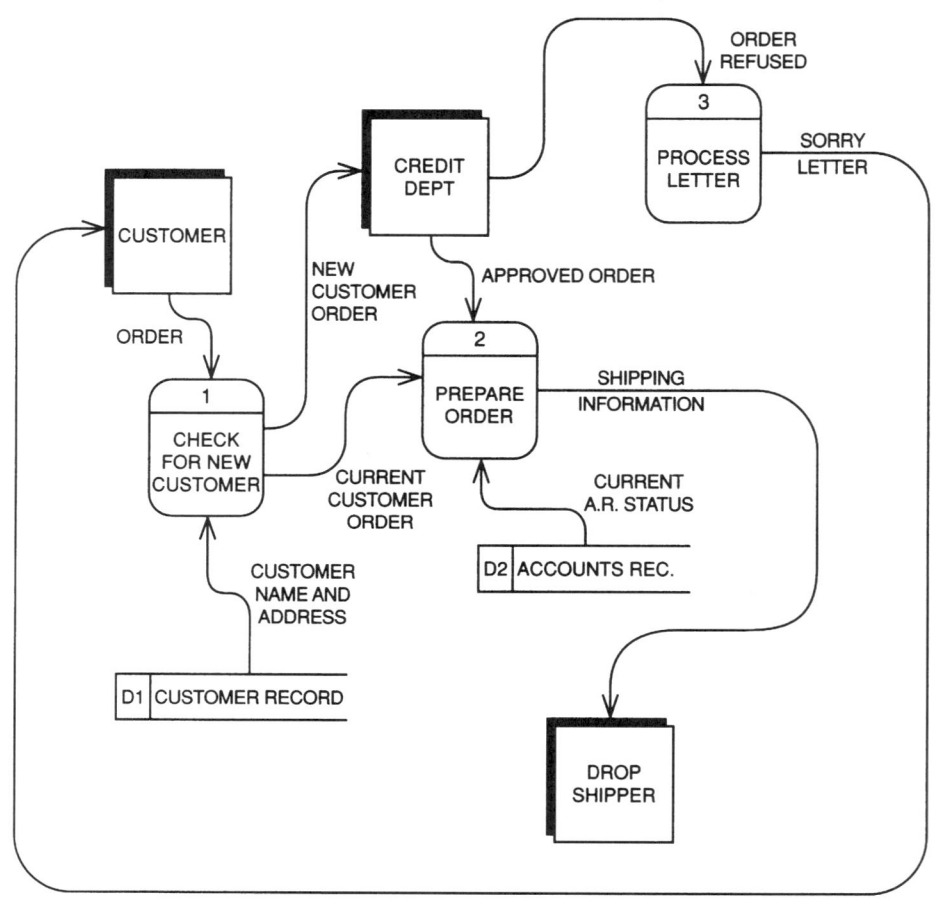

EXHIBIT 2–11. Level 1 Dataflow Diagram

EXHIBIT 2–12. Supplemental Dataflow Conventions

SLASH IN THE LOWER RIGHT HAND CORNER TO INDICATE A DUPLICATE ENTITY.

EXPLODED DIAGRAMS USE DECIMALS TO INDICATE RELATED DETAILED PROCESS.

DATA STORAGE NUMBER.

USE A LINE TO INDICATE DUPLICATE DATA STORAGE.

USE A CROSS ◯ OVER BRIDGE FOR LINES THAT DO NOT INTERSECT.

EXHIBIT 2–13. ANSI Flowchart Symbols

Diskette Input/Output This symbol is used for floppy diskettes of all sizes. (Not ANSI standard.)	
Hard Disk This symbol is for hard disk input or output.	
Magnetic Tape This symbol is for magnetic tape cartridge or reels as input or output.	
Auxiliary Operation This symbol is for an off-line operation such as downloading a magnetic tape to microfiche.	
Preparation This symbol represents the modification of an instruction or group of instructions which change the program itself.	
Manual Operation This symbol is used to show a manual operation which is limited to the speed of a human being.	

EXHIBIT 2–13. (*Continued*)

Process This symbol represents a processing function. It can also represent a system symbol for a central processing unit.	
Decision This symbol represents a decision step, with one or more alternative paths to be followed.	
Input/Output This symbol represents the input or output of data.	
Flow Lines Flow lines are used to connect the symbols and show the process flow.	
Annotation This symbol is used for adding comments to an operation step.	
Connector This symbol is used to exit to or enter from another part of a flowchart, especially when using another page.	
Terminal Point This symbol is used to start or stop a flowchart.	
Communication Link This is used to show data being transmitted over communication channels.	

EXHIBIT 2–13. (*Continued*)

Sort Symbol This is used to represent the arranging of a set of items into a particular sequence.	
Predefined Process This symbol is used to illustrate a sub-routine that is specified elsewhere.	
Document This symbol represents a printed document output.	
Display This is to show output displayed on a CRT.	
Off-line Storage Any storage that is not directly accessible by a computer.	
On-line Storage This symbol is for input or output which uses direct access storage such as hard disk, diskettes and so forth.	
Scanning document This symbol is used for source documents which are to be scanned as input. (Not ANSI standard)	
Manual Input This symbol is used for manual input entered from on-line keyboards.	

3

SYSTEMS ANALYSIS AND DESIGN: STAYING ORGANIZED

PLANNING AHEAD

Most projects begin at the beginning, with an initial project planning stage, and then progress logically through each succeeding phase. However, some projects are not that neat and tidy, and begin later in the process. Either way, it is the responsibility of the project leader or systems analyst to make certain that the project has had the required planning.

A plan is required to manage any project in the most efficient manner. It provides an overall, consistent format to follow in large- or small-scale systems projects. It keeps management informed on the status of each project with periodic progress reports, starting with the first phase, and following through to the end. The plan should aim for those results that are achievable with the resources management allots.

Policy Objectives

The policy governing project development requires the following:

A Organize systems projects into *manageable* major phases.

B Establish a timetable that specifies both chargeable and calendar time.

C   Stipulate the format for progress reporting, which can be arranged by task phases to be completed or by target completion date.

D   An overall plan contains the principal ingredients required for an acceptable undertaking. These are:

1   **Economic feasibility.** Will the new system pay for itself in its expected lifetime?

2   **Organizational feasibility.** Will the system operate within the current organizational structure?

3   **Technical feasibility.** Will the proposed system actually work?

4   **Operational feasibility.** Can the system work within the environment for which it is designed? If applicable, will it successfully operate outside the firm?

Avoiding "Scope Creep"

The scope of a systems project is typically identified by its constrained elements. First, the relevant activities of the project establish limits confined by time, dollar resources, required changes, and/or systems or organizational boundaries. Second, the subject itself can identify and restrict the project scope. If expanded beyond its subject area, the project loses its frame of reference, unallocated resources are likely to be expended, and the objective of the project becomes less clear. Therefore, a policy that contains the scope of a project is essential to its success.

COMMENT

Many IS or systems managers attribute late, over-budget, or uncompleted projects to wandering into unrelated areas of user needs. Objectives and careers are jeopardized if control of a project and resources is not retained. This lack of control may help explain some of the management turnover in the information technology profession.

SYSTEMS DEVELOPMENT AND PLANNING

The system project's organization requires a standard procedure to ensure proper planning, control, and status reporting. These defined procedures provide standards to: (1) assess a project in progress, (2) assess the merits of one project over another, and (3) provide a tool when reviewing employees for merit rewards.

Project Planning

The following tasks are included in project planning:

A Definition of project goals

❖ Systems output

❖ Systems throughput process

❖ Systems control mechanism

❖ Systems requirements

❖ Calendar time needed to complete project

If any of these five areas can be subdivided into measurable milestones for reporting, it should be done. (For example, throughput processing may entail more than one manual procedure or computer program.)

B Project plan preparation. A brief plan and schedule are developed outlining the requisite tasks and timetable to accomplish the project goals. These include:

❖ Identify the work necessary to accomplish project goals. This includes tasks applicable to projects not initially identified as work to be covered in planned goals. These should be divided into measurable units or milestones.

❖ Develop detailed database, file, report, and program specifications.

❖ Establish budgets.

❖ Assign responsibilities.

❖ Prepare workload schedules.

❖ Prepare appropriate project documentation.

❖ Develop Gantt charts from project schedules for planning and reporting the status of project tasks.

❖ Prepare a format and schedule for project status reports.

Analysis of Requirements

The project leader or head systems analyst works closely with the potential user to ensure that the systems requirements are defined and understood, and that the user does not expect system revision in the near future. A number of techniques exist to ensure that all systems requirements are precisely defined. These are:

❖ Determine the capabilities of the project team to achieve given system objectives.

❖ Establish operating parameters.

❖ Organize all pertinent data elements.

❖ Define processing requirements.

❖ Determine output requirements.

❖ Determine required database or file needs.

❖ Determine required data input requirements and the method of input.

To ensure all requirements are defined prior to the systems design phase, use a checklist similar to the one shown in Exhibit 3–1.

Estimating Resource Requirements

A resource estimate, prepared for each project, is used to allocate resources and provide a basis for project financial control. Estimates may also provide a basis for preparing user service charges. The person in charge of planning should:

A Estimate the man-hours required for analysis and programming. This estimate may be revised as programming proceeds. Add a contingency time for each defined task, depending on similar past experience and/or the past performance of the person assigned the task. If the project covers an extended calendar time period, consider contingencies. This can help avoid a possible late or over-budget project. A savvy project head may add extra time for the whole project and call it the "contingency factor." If a project is late or over budget, as most projects are, this budgeted extra time will be welcome. Convert man-hours needed to dollars. If the project finishes ahead of schedule and/or under budget, this can reflect well on the project head.

Prepare Gantt charts for the man-hours required, indicating the calendar time when personnel will be available since not all project personnel are available full time. Set milestones within each Gantt chart to identify the status of each project task. This status can be plotted against the budgeted allotted time to determine whether the task is on schedule.

B Gantt chart the budget allotted for each task or phase. When reporting the project's financial status, plot the actual amount spent on a

EXHIBIT 3–1. Systems Development Checklist

A. Data Input Editing

1. Does editing look for missing data?

2. Does editing include verification of format?

3. Does editing include verification of codes?

4. Will editing be completed in a single process?

5. Will editing procedure vary due to external conditions?

6. What will be the bypass procedure?

B. Database and File Updating

1. How frequently are backups done?

2. Are partial updates done?

3. Must source data be corrected prior to update procedures?

4. Are files purged periodically?

5. Are purged data files transferred to inactive files?

6. Will a transaction backup file be online?

C. Output Preparation

1. Is the output on a monitor?

2. If the output is hardcopy, how many copies are needed?

3. Is the hardcopy output a regular report or only provided on demand?

4. Do the reports contain summaries and intermediate summaries?

5. Will output be made available over a network or the Internet?

D. Error Correction

1. Will the error correction routines require rewriting the source document?

2. Is it possible for uncorrected data to enter the processing system?

3. Can an error be corrected after it has been placed in a file or database? How?

separate chart. Compare the amount spent to date to the budgeted amount at any given point in the project. With these two Gantt charts plotted in parallel, financial problems can be recognized.

C Identify and estimate all equipment, software, and service costs required for the new system. A dollar contingency amount should be added to cover any unforeseen expenses.

Risk Analysis

All IT projects involve some degree of risk. Risk management should be a proactive process, part of the overall project. Risk is not to be avoided, but managed. To manage risk proactively, identify and analyze risk continuously in the normal course of the project. The following steps can be used to manage the risk in a project:

A **Identify the risk.** Discuss risks early in the project. The sooner risks are identified, the sooner solutions can be found.

B **Analyze the risk.** Determine how risk can impact the project. What effect will the risk have on cost, project duration, or the ability of the project to satisfy the user's requirements?

C **Prioritize.** Determine which risks deserve the most attention, and which risks can be safely ignored.

D **Follow up.** Keep track of all risks and what is being done to mitigate their impact.

E **Control.** By making risk management part of day-to-day project management, *you* control the risk, rather than it controlling you.

COMMENT

A CEO study by the Gartner Group reveals that change initiatives are most likely to fail because of such problems as resistance to change, lack of sponsorship, and unrealistic or unknown expectations.

There are several areas of risk that can influence an IT project:

A **Economic.** Economic fluctuation can change the value of the project to the firm or affect funding available for the project.

B   **Government.** Changes in government regulations can impact the cost or utility of the project.

C   **Marketplace.** If the project is meant to support a new product, consumers' acceptance or changing needs can affect the project.

D   **Technology.** A project's technology may not work as advertised or may change during the course of a long project.

E   **Organizational.** Lukewarm management support, changes in management, unrealistic expectations, etc. can all adversely affect the project.

Exhibit 3–2 is an example of a form used to track and manage the risks identified in a project.

SYSTEMS ANALYSIS

Systems analysis analyzes a system that is operational. Of course, if a new system neither replaces nor alters one already in place, there is no need for this analysis. In that case, only the requirements for the new system are needed for the systems design.

Prototyping a new system may not require a thorough systems analysis by the IS design person, but any information he or she can obtain about the user area will be helpful. This information can reduce the time needed for the prototyping development. Also, the user will have more confidence in the systems analyst if he/she "speaks the user's language," which could enhance the final design.

Systems analysis has changed little over the years. Some new to systems analysis and others who do not want to allocate resources and/or costs to this effort, avoid it, or limit its scope. This lack of analysis leads to a process of "code and fix," whereby coding begins before user requirements are fully known, and accounts significantly for new system failures. It is common for established consulting firms to relegate this task to their lower-priced help, with predictable results. There also can be a problem of "paralysis through analysis," spending too much time on this phase. But this is seldom the case.

This section on analysis provides the traditional, proven procedures. Knowing the steps will not guarantee success, but knowing and practicing the procedures can produce the desired results.

Preanalysis Survey

Before attempting to contact the user for an analysis of the current operating system, gather as much knowledge about the unit as possible. A feasibility study is a good place to start.

EXHIBIT 3–2. Risk Analysis Form

ID	Description	Severity	Probability	Value	Plan
1	Database designer with required skills not available when needed.	8	.2	1.6	Work with DBA group to make sure resource is available when needed.
2	Learning curve for new version of report writer steeper than expected.	5	.4	2.0	Send member of team to training before start of project.
3	User resource not available when needed.	9	.5	4.5	Work with senior management to ensure resource availability.

ID—A unique identifier for the risk.

Description—A description of the risk.

Severity—The effect on the project on a scale of 1 (low) to 10 (severe).

Probability—The probability the risk will actually have an impact on the project; 0.0 (none) to 1.0 (certain).

Value—Severity, probability. Used to rank the risks.

Plan—How are we going to deal with this risk?

Identify the unit's head and subordinates, if possible, from an organization chart for large units. One *Fortune* 500 firm employs organizational charts with pictures to go along with the names and titles. Try to remember the names of personnel and their respective titles. Also, know the corporate hierarchy. Any information about personalities and the unit's organization status that can be discovered beforehand can help. Become aware of the unit's corporate politics; these hidden power structures can be a minefield, delaying the system's progress.

Examine current procedural documentation. This provides the systems analyst with the *formal* procedures of the current operation. Later, the analyst will have an opportunity to confirm if the procedures are still valid, and, if not, what has changed. The operating procedures should include forms used. If it does not, obtain copies. They will help you understand their role in the operation.

Initial Unit Visit

Call the unit's head for a first meeting in his/her office. If he/she is not in, leave a voice mail message to return the call.

COMMENT

Prepare for the visit. Dress in a manner appropriate for management. If the area being visited is the manufacturing operation's spray-painting section, do not wear your new $500 outfit.

During your first contact, the art of listening becomes important. It has been said, "You cannot be a listener with your mouth open." Ask about the operation, the unit's problems, and the unit's people. If time and conditions permit, include a little social chatter, along with a cup of coffee. Later, have the person introduce you to the employees. Set up "the best time" for the return visit. If this person cannot see you within a reasonable time, ask to speak with someone lower on the organization chart, or start with the first person in the unit working with the current system.

Information-gathering Interviews

It is wise not to spend too much time on the first visit with any one person. Speaking with a person six times for ten minutes each is better for the systems analyst than a single one-hour visit because the analyst will learn more and also develop a closer relationship with that person. Remember, when conducting an interview:

❖ Start at the beginning of an operation flow.

❖ Interview the person at his/her place of work or meet at a neutral place.

❖ If the person is ill or has a problem, come back later.

❖ Develop listening skills.

❖ Do not repeat rumors.

❖ Interview all the people in the unit, if possible. No one will be seen as a favorite, and more will be learned. Even if several people perform the same job, each may see it from a different perspective. One may contribute something the others overlooked.

❖ Be open with your note-taking. Shorthand pads work well.

❖ Do not jump to conclusions.

❖ Listen carefully for what the person really means.

❖ Leave your information technology jargon at the door.

❖ Be aware of the interviewee's body language.

❖ Look for the content, not the style of delivery of information.

❖ Do not assume anything.

❖ Avoid playing favorites with workers.

❖ Define what tools are employed: hardware, software, files accessed, and such.

❖ Ask questions, but be aware of who may have a stake in or have developed the current system.

❖ Give people time to answer correctly.

❖ Collect copies of documents and ask:

–What is the daily volume of forms, reports, and so on?

–From where do documents come?

–Who originates the first inside document?

–Why is the document used?

–How is the document completed?

–Where are the documents filed?

❖ Other questions:

–Has the worker come up with his/her own procedures to make things work?

–How often and when are backups done?

–What is the security procedure?

–What problems are there with operating instructions?

–Whom do you contact for help?

❖ Conclude the interview by thanking the person.

Document the Interviews

After the interviews are over, analyze the information gathered. Draw (free-hand) flowcharts from the data collected.

Return to the unit and authenticate the flowchart(s) by observing the actual people doing the jobs. If necessary, send a follow-up memo verifying approval of the documented information by the person or persons inter-viewed.

Document present procedures to be included in the final systems report. Prepare the final flowcharts and make necessary copies.

Work-sampling Studies

Work sampling is a tool used by the systems analyst to find out how people spend their time at work. Since labor costs are a significant part of operating cost, it is essential to know how that time is spent. To justify the cost of new procedures or hardware investments, work sampling is used to study a cur-rent operation. It is a simple procedure and, when properly used, can reveal the areas that require further study.

For example, take the question, "Should the company purchase a second copy machine?" The systems analyst performs random observations of the number of people waiting in line to use the copy machine, then turns that number into hours per day of wait time. These hours represent dollars: the cost of an employee waiting instead of working. This cost, plus the price of acquiring a new machine, along with the additional cost of operating a sec-ond machine (floor space, etc.), determines the write-off time cost for the acquisition. This information helps management decide whether to make the purchase.

Another focus of this work sampling information might be the travel time of people who use the copy machine. Ask people who are waiting the location of their work units to help compute this travel time. Perhaps the sec-ond machine could be better located to reduce travel time costs.

This is a very simple example. More complex studies yield other kinds of information. One undercover study in a department of sixteen people revealed that each person was spending 35 percent of the time doing no work at all. The reason was a lack of supervision.

Another study was set up in an engineering support unit of a *Fortune 500* firm to find out how people spent their time, and what new equipment was needed to reduce the heavy overtime. The result of the study showed that employees were not working so hard or so efficiently because they enjoyed the overtime too much. These findings enabled the company to eliminate Saturday overtime costs.

Other information can help address specific problems. In one instance, discovery of a new government regulation that required a ratio of hours to workers that equaled three persons made it possible to cost justify these three people quickly and cheaply.

A work-sampling study involves the following:

A **Observation times.** Observations of the work area studied are performed at random times and dates. Random numbers can be generated by computer software, taken from a random number table in a math book, or drawn out of a hat. It is suggested that two sets of observation times be drawn: a small sample of 50 to 100, and a larger sample later. The specific sample size is dependent on the number of items and people observed. About a hundred observations per item type observed is typical. There are formulas available used by industrial engineers to compute the number needed for the required confidence level.

B **Preliminary observations.** Compose a list of tasks for the preliminary study of the initial observations. Personal time and miscellaneous should always be included. "Out of the area and available, but no work" may in some cases be selected, too. These tasks are posted to the tally sheet for observations (see Exhibit 3–3). The observations are performed only by the systems analyst and no one else, especially not the boss. People are not usually identified by name.

The observations are taken in a split second and tally marked (i.e., a mark is made for each observation; four in a row, with the fifth mark across the other four). The tallies are counted and posted in the total column on the right-hand side. After the tallies are posted, each total value is divided by the total number of observations. For example, with a preliminary observation of 50, divide each task total value by 50 to get the percent of time spent with that task. Added together, the percent values will total approximately 100 percent.

C **New tally sheet.** Using the results of the preliminary observations, add or delete items from the final observation study. Those with less than a 5-percent tally are normally deleted from the final study. When the miscellaneous category is very high—over 20 percent—try to identify a category or categories to be removed and placed under their own tasks. Then construct a new tally sheet for the final study.

D **Final observation study.** The final observation study is made at the random times and dates selected. Complete the tally sheet as explained in step B. Then divide each task total by the total number of observations to get the task percentage. The total number of observations for the final study, as shown in Exhibit 3–3, will be no less than ten times the number of observations in the preliminary study.

Final Report

Place the procedure text and flowcharts in a binder with a cover sheet entitled *Final Analysis Study Report,* and a name to identify the study. The cover memo summarizes the study, including any recommendations and any additional comments the analyst may make. This memo is not placed in the report binder, but sent to the project leader, along with the feasibility study and the report. The dates and hours expended on the analysis should be reported in the format required by the project leader.

SYSTEMS DESIGN

The objective of systems design is to take the systems parameters as defined in the development and planning phase and create a system to the degree allowed, given the allocated resources and timeframe. The defined scope of the project determines the resources and time limitations. If a systems analysis final report is available, use it as an information base in designing the new system.

The systems analyst synthesizes the elements of several design alternatives and compares them with the design criteria. Compare them with each other and with the current system. The system closest to achieving the defined objectives, with the best utilization of resources, is the best choice. This decision is not the systems analyst's alone; management and/or the user will have an impact on the final selection of the "best" solution. The analyst may design the alternative systems, but management and the user have to live with the selection long after the analyst has moved on to other projects.

The procedure steps required to achieve optimal design are:

❖ Establish detailed system design specifications for the selected design.

❖ Determine proper utilization of software, hardware, assigned personnel, and contract services.

EXHIBIT 3–3. Completed Sampling Tally Sheet

Date(s) _1/10 – 1/20/97_ By _Mary Smith_

Unit observed _Billing Support_ Number of people _4_

Task	Tally	Total	%
Filing	~~////~~ ~~////~~ ~~////~~ ~~////~~ ~~////~~ ~~////~~	30	30
Telephone	~~////~~ ///	8	8
Reading	~~////~~ ~~////~~ /	11	11
Writing	~~////~~ ~~////~~ ~~////~~ ~~////~~ /	21	21
Personal	~~////~~/ ~~////~~	10	10
Misc.	~~////~~ ~~////~~/ ~~////~~ ~~////~~	20	20
	TOTAL NUMBER OF OBSERVATIONS	100	100

❖ Prepare a final systems report supported with documentation and system flowcharts.

❖ Gain the acceptance of the proposed system from requesting authorities and users.

Systems Design Specifications

The development of systems design specifications includes any refinements incorporated into the design as requested by users and the requesting authority. Final design documentation will include input, output, database, and software specifications to meet the design requirements. Above all, backup and recovery procedures, along with security requirements, are a must.

A **System specifications.** The details for this phase are determined by what is needed to communicate the system requirements to programmers or software vendors. Following are guidelines for developing these specifications:

1 Develop output requirements, first based on user report or monitor display needs.

2 Develop file specifications. Develop an Index of Table Field Names—the names used in databases, programs, and input/output locations. The specifications include all data elements required for present or anticipated needs, and a data dictionary to provide their specifications.

3 Define the input layouts. This is the format of all data to be captured for use by the system. This input can be source documents coming into the information systems data entry unit or input received as captured data from outside the computer operation. The source of captured data received by the system is input from terminals or other, nonkeyed data, and is of major concern to the systems analyst who must ensure that only the required input gains entry to the system.

4 Develop the processing requirements. Describe in detail the processing operations required by the software. In addition, general guidelines may be required for some functions, such as:

❖ Procedures for entry of corrections

❖ Controls to monitor out-of-balance conditions (e.g., a minus payroll check or inventory balance)

❖ Editing routines for missing or incorrect data entering the system for the first time

❖ Proper restart procedures for the user

B **Manual procedures.** Clerical tasks are included to:
* ❖ Review data to ensure it can be entered.
* ❖ Correct input data.
* ❖ Change data already in the system.
* ❖ Hold or dispose of input data.
* ❖ Distribute printed output.

Utilization of Resources

Essential to preparing the system design specifications is understanding the availability of hardware, software, and personnel resources. Analyze these to determine their adequacy to fulfill the systems objectives. If any of the three is inadequate, changes are required. If the resources cannot be changed, it may be necessary to alter the system's scope or objectives.

Final Systems Report

The proposed system design is documented in the form of a final systems report that defines objectives and states how the proposed system design meets them. The scope of the undertaking is defined, along with a proposed timetable for installing the new system. It contains proposed costs and return expected, in both tangible and intangible benefits, for the resource investment. Its purpose is to inform and gain acceptance of the proposed system, and the report is hand-carried to the proper individuals one to two weeks before the verbal presentation is to be made.

The report contains the following:

A A summary of the full systems study
* ❖ An overview of the events leading up to the study
* ❖ The subject of the study
* ❖ The objectives and scope of the proposed system
* ❖ A statement of recommendations and justifications for the proposed system

B Body of the report
  1 A description of the current system, including:
  * ❖ A brief description of the current system and its use
  * ❖ The purpose of the current system
  * ❖ The problems with the current system (if any) and the rationale for a new system

2 A description of the proposed system, including:

- ❖ An overview of the proposed system
- ❖ The scope of the project
- ❖ Exhibits of all reports and screen displays
- ❖ System flowcharts
- ❖ Systems documentation of the proposed system and any vendor-supplied material that provides additional information
- ❖ A summary of proposed recommendations
- ❖ A list of personnel needs:

  a Manpower required to install the new system

  b Manpower required to maintain the new system

- ❖ A proposed timetable for installing the suggested system and the work hours required to complete the project

3 The financial information section, including:

- ❖ Present system operating cost
- ❖ Proposed system operating cost
- ❖ Installation cost of the new system and its estimated useful life
- ❖ The tangible and intangible benefits of the proposed system

4 Proposed system summary: A positive statement of the rationale for installing the proposed system, the summary also contains any concerns that exist about the timetable, funds, software, hardware, outside contractors, or personnel available for the undertaking.

C Appendix

1 Prior reports

2 Memos and letters

3 Other supporting documents not included in the body of the report:

- ❖ Sample documents and forms
- ❖ Charts
- ❖ Graphs
- ❖ Gantt charts
- ❖ Tables of data
- ❖ Vendor literature

The Acceptance Presentation

Gaining acceptance is the last step before systems implementation. All concerned are brought together for a verbal and visual presentation. Everyone attending should have had enough time to read the report. This presentation is used to confirm that the proposed system will meet its objective and stay within the defined scope. Although not requisite, the presentation to gain final acceptance can be just as important as the final written report that serves as a basis for the verbal presentation. But reading the report itself is not enough. Therefore, a different approach must be adopted to resolve any problems, whether political or technical. It is very important that the presenter know the attitudes, political positions, and status of all those attending the presentation. Not everyone present may be supportive; some may object to possible added demands on their areas, loss of present control, or loss of operations.

Here are some suggestions on how to sell your proposal:

❖   Be relaxed. Otherwise, people may think you are trying to hide something.

❖   Gain approval by seeking support from people before the meeting.

❖   Decide whether you want credit for your innovation or acceptance. You may not get both. This is corporate politics.

❖   Do not expect others to think like you.

❖   Never have surprises at this presentation. People do not like them.

❖   Never expect that people want change or innovation simply because they may have indicated they did in the past.

Well-planned audio and visual aids help to create a positive impression on the audience. Flip charts particularly add visual interest by providing step-by-step information with graphs, flowcharts, and text materials. You can write notes on the edge of each page to assist you.

Overhead transparency projections are easy to use, but require some preparation to look professional. The information to be presented should be readable by all in the audience. Try this experiment. Place the material at your feet and stand up. If you can read it, so can your audience. With the computer graphic software now available for making overhead transparencies, presentations can look professional. Always have a replacement projector bulb available.

In-house graphic arts departments may be of help in producing the visual aids you require. They may have a PC or laptop and a portable projector for running your presentation right off the PC using Microsoft PowerPoint or similar software. Vendors may be a source of visuals, too.

Make sure you are comfortable with whatever materials you use. New, untried hardware or software can spell disaster. Check out the room the day before and have a dry run, if possible. To insure everything is ready on the day of the presentation, arrive no less than half an hour before the presentation. Test any equipment to make sure it works. Your high exposure may not spell a promotion, but a disaster is something you may have to live down.

The presentation should help gain as much support for and acceptance of the new system as possible. In some cases, it may even wrap up its sale. Following is a basic presentation outline:

A Introduction. The introduction consists only of preliminary descriptions: Introduce yourself and the subject. Explain how the system study began and progressed, and how the presentation will be made. Include:

❖ A statement defining the need for a new system

❖ An explanation about how alternative systems were reviewed before selecting the one being presented

❖ An explanation of the format that follows the introduction

B The body. The body is the heart of the presentation. Use terminology familiar to your audience, especially management and users. Those attending will be more interested in what is done than how the technology works. Emphasize the benefits of the new system and not its hardware or software. Have a positive attitude about the benefits (such as faster processing or response time, better accuracy and control, and, maybe, reduced costs). Reliable information and honesty about any drawbacks are necessities. The body should:

1 Briefly describe the current production system.

2 Describe the proposed system and any alternate proposals.

3 Present the economic information:

❖ Current system operating costs

❖ Proposed system operating costs

❖ Cost of installing the proposed system (Be conservative with cost claims.)

❖ Intangible benefits and/or requirements imposed by customers, vendors, or the government

4 Provide recommendations for the proposed selection.

C Summary of the presentation. All the tangible and intangible benefits of the proposed system should be stressed.

D Discussion.

1 Open the meeting and answer questions.

2 Keep discussion going; call on people who support the proposed system for input.

3 Be aware of the attitudes of the people and have a strategy ready to handle any negative comments.

E **Conclusion.** End your presentation on a positive note.

1 Summarize the areas of agreement brought up during the open discussion.

2 Make a positive statement as to what will happen with the project and how those involved will be kept informed of its progress.

SYSTEMS PROTOTYPING

This section covers ideas and procedures for using prototyping to design a working systems model. Prototyping is an analysis and design technique involving end-users in defining the requirements and developing the system according to their needs and desires. It helps define the end-user requirements more quickly than the traditional analysis and design approach. A complex system can involve a number of (modular) prototypes.

Prototypes can be hand drawn (see the dataflow diagrams, Chapter 2, pages 42–52) or developed with computer software tools that are available for PCs. Computer-aided systems and software engineering (CASE) technologies automate the analysis and design process using modeling tools and other techniques.

Another useful technique is JAD (Joint Applications Development). If you plan to use JAD, start with a "safe" project, one that has very little chance of failure because:

❖ The user is skillful and cooperative.

❖ The application is a one-user and/or simple application.

❖ Minimum of hardware/software changes are needed.

❖ A top-quality team is assigned to the project.

❖ There is an adequate budget.

A well-selected user is essential.

The systems analyst working with the user can develop an iterative series of prototypes that can be viewed and revised interactively. This reduces both the calendar and chargeable project time.

Prototyping is best suited for developing systems that are not well defined, or for exceptional, smaller systems applications. It allows for the visualization and conversation required for quick systems development. All too often users request something they cannot define, or they cannot see how changes will satisfy their needs. This type of situation would be a candidate for a prototyping effort.

The characteristics of systems that are likely candidates for prototyping are:

❖ User requirements are difficult to define.

❖ The application has few users—often only one.

❖ The application may be ad hoc or even parochial in nature.

❖ The application has a low volume of input and/or output.

❖ The application requires a minimum of editing controls.

❖ User(s) may only require a stand-alone PC using their own files or database.

Prototype Development

The systems analyst needs to consider what kind of system requires development since not all undertakings are suitable for prototyping. A traditional system that cuts across two or more departments would probably be a poor candidate. Another poor candidate would be an order-processing or payroll system. Rather, single user, novel and/or complex applications, and semistructured or even unstructured applications are all good candidates for this kind of approach.

The systems analysis management must also evaluate the environmental conditions where the systems analyst will operate. The political climate and the user's personality play a major role in the success or failure of this kind of undertaking.

The lead systems analyst maintains a prototype project folder, containing all papers related to the project, and an activities diary for which a shorthand pad can suffice. The diary should be hand posted while the information is still fresh and should contain such information as the day's activities, time spent on each activity, and any other information the analyst deems relevant. The diary is not for publication; it is only a reference record to be placed in the prototype project folder after the effort is completed.

The procedure for prototyping is as follows:

A **Estimate project expense.** Both direct and indirect costs are computed. This includes the chargeable time of systems analysts and programmers, along with other development costs. Software and hardware costs are generally considered indirect costs, but a one-time-use software package required for the project is a direct cost.

The information system's personnel define the calendar timeframe, as well as the estimated man-hours. If costs and time requirements are agreeable to both user and information systems management, the project will proceed. The costs may be charged directly to the requesting user's budget or applied to an information systems budget for such projects.

B **Develop manageable modules.** Module size is reduced to a manageable level so that each module can be built separately from other system or subsystem modules. Each is also designed to allow other modules to interact with its features. This development is done in concert with the end-user(s) and the systems analyst.

C **Build the prototype.** As the systems analyst gathers information about the user's requirements for the application, he/she assesses user feedback about the developing prototype to better visualize the systems requirements. Successful prototyping depends on early and frequent end-user feedback to the developing process. User changes made early in the development process will reduce costs and total project development time.

The systems analyst illustrates to the user(s) as early as possible how parts of the system actually accomplish their objectives. This early construction of an operational prototype allows early user feedback so the systems analyst can gain valuable insight into the direction of the prototype construction. To develop the prototype as quickly as possible, the analyst uses whatever special tools are available, such as personal, work group or even organizational databases, computer software, and other prototype design tools. Access to databases, other than personal ones, will require the permission of the data administrator and/or the database administrator.

Rapid prototyping development reduces the chance of changes imposed by the user. The longer it takes to develop a system, the more the system is susceptible to changes imposed by the user and/or the operational environment. Rapid prototyping development safeguards against overcommitting resources to a project that could eventually become unworkable.

COMMENT

The saying "strike while the iron is hot" applies here. The hotter the iron is, the easier it is to work. The longer a project is stretched out, the less chance it has to succeed.

D **Modify the prototype.** The prototype will be exposed to an iteration process. Modifications made with each iteration process should move the system closer to what the user(s) says is required. But each modification requires another evaluation by the end-user(s).

As with the initial development, revisions must be done as swiftly as possible to maintain project momentum. The systems analyst's duty is to keep the project moving. The analyst must encourage the user(s) to maintain his/her responsibility to evaluate each revised version for required modifications as soon as possible. The prototyping process requires that the user(s) debug the program as it evolves.

The analyst must also prevent the user(s) from deciding a prototype is operational before it is completed. Here the systems analyst acts more as a facilitator of iteration than a designer.

This whole process requires good people skills on the part of the systems analyst. Listening to the needs of the user(s) is essential, and technical vocabulary should be left behind when communicating with the user.

The systems analyst should prototype in a direction that will require a minimum of skill on the part of the user(s) to operate. The completed system must be easy to understand, learn, and operate by all users. Today, the trend is to provide the user with an online interactive system that uses a display as a source of output.

If a chain of interactive prototypes is required for the completed system, the interaction between each prototype module must be operational for the project to be finished. This kind of prototype development could have multiple users, a potential for user disputes that should be resolved as soon as possible.

E **Complete the prototype.** The prototyping is complete when the user has what he/she wants and the systems analyst is willing to sign off on the prototype. The sign-off can take two forms:

1 Scrap the prototype when the user(s) is not satisfied with the finished product or the requirements are beyond what can be reasonably provided.

The systems analyst is the representative of the systems department, the database administrator, and the data administrator. These areas require limited access by the end-users. The systems analyst is required to police the needs of users so that they do not violate any policies or procedures that are in place for these areas.

2 Accept the prototype. Operationally completed prototypes require sign-off by both the user(s) and the systems analyst. This might be a joint memo from both to the user's management and the head of the systems department. The user(s) by this time will have been trained in the operation of the prototype system, and an operation manual will have been completed and in place. This training and documentation is the responsibility of the lead systems analyst assigned to the project.

A final project memo is sent by the lead systems analyst to the systems manager within a week after the prototype has been signed-off. This allows for follow-up to confirm that all went as planned. The memo is a summary report on the effective utilization of information systems resources on behalf of the prototype effort. The report may end with an editorialized summary by the analyst responsible for the prototype. The prototype project folder and its diary are sources of information for this report.

Types of Prototyping Methods

Due to different needs, a single "all in one" prototype model is not realistic. However, there are four tools available to the systems analyst. All four follow the same prototype development procedures as outlined under "Prototype Development." They are:

A **First-of-a-series prototype.** A pilot prototype is developed as a full-scale system, can be made up of subsystems, and is a "true" prototype, i.e., one that is developed and debugged at one site. The following prototypes are modified to further improve the system. The first-of-a-series is volume tested after it is debugged, insuring that the prototype can be replicated at other sites with a minimum of effort and problems.

B **Modular prototype.** This prototype does not contain all the attributes that the final system version will have. This allows for the rapid development of less complex prototypes. After the first has been developed, another similar-featured one is developed and joined to the first to construct a finished product. There can be any number of designated prototypes connected to complete a final version.

C **One-shot prototype.** This prototype does not have to be efficient because it will be used only once. (It could be used later, but seldom is.) Such a prototype can afford to be inefficient, as long as the development cost is less than what would be gained from a more efficient operating model. The retrieval, storage, and computation can be primitive, if workable. If this type of prototype were popular, time and effort to develop a "user/request" form would make sense. This form would save time for both the user(s) and systems analyst or programmer analyst.

COMMENT

Using such a form for one-shot programs is not a new idea. George developed one for a General Electric Engineering department some years ago.

D **Input–output prototype.** This is a scale model prototype, without an operating program, used to save the cost of developing an expensive process program. This prototype has well-defined input and output formats, like those used for a model car. Management may gain enough information from this scale model to determine that the cost of the process development is worth it. A software tool used for this prototype could simply be a good word-processing program. Of all the prototype methods, this is the one least used.

COMMENT

The last input–output prototype observed by this writer was one constructed by a group of students working on a systems project. The students were to write a COBOL program that would produce a printed report. Instead of having the program perform the calculations, they hand calculated the results from input test data, and then used WordPerfect to print the report. There was no operating program, just an output prototype.

SYSTEMS IMPLEMENTATION

This section covers the procedures governing implementation of the proposed system. This is the most challenging task of any information systems undertaking.

Implementation Prerequisites

The following must be completed before a system is implemented and approved as operational.

A Systems documentation conforming to the standards defined in Chapter 2

B A system walk-through

　　1 **Purpose.** The purpose of a systems walk-through is to prove the logic of the system with another systems analyst or with users. It must be proven that data records are compatible between operations and/or programs. "Index of Table Field Names" is referenced, updated, and corrected at this point. The walk-through starts with input and is followed through to the required output.

　　2 **Input requirements.** Input requirements for walk-throughs include:

　　　　❖ Raw data or machine-usable input

　　　　❖ Batch or online input

　　　　❖ Control totals or record counts

　　　　❖ Database elements chosen or generated to provide realistic test data

　　3 **Anticipated processing.** This includes the process steps required to provide output of data or update of the database or files.

　　4 **Anticipated outputs.** These are normally classified into categories and followed through ensuring all the data elements are available in the forms required. The following actions are taken:

　　　　❖ Total record counts, units, dollars, or other data are checked against expected values.

　　　　❖ The contents and format of monitor displays and reports are checked against stated requirements and precomputed results.

❖ Errors are identified for those items expected to be rejected by the system.

❖ Output data elements that will become input to other systems are checked for compatibility.

Implementation Procedures

The following actions are taken as part of the implementation phase:

❖ Develop implementation plans, estimates, and conversion procedures.

❖ Review and update systems specifications to reflect requirements developed during programming.

❖ Develop test data for program and systems testing.

❖ Evaluate results from program tests, systems tests, volume tests, and any parallel testing operations. This is done with users to ensure that test specifications and system requirements have been met.

❖ Update schedule changes.

❖ Develop training procedures for systems operations and user personnel.

❖ Confirm that all operational procedures and manuals are in place.

❖ Confirm that all operational personnel have been trained.

❖ Request systems operations and/or user sign-off.

❖ Perform any tests that the auditors have requested.

SYSTEMS MAINTENANCE

Before a request for any maintenance is approved, the system is examined to determine if it should be modified or redesigned. The presence of three factors tends to favor redesign instead of modification:

A The cost of maintenance of a project exceeds 30 percent of the actual development costs.

B The existing system has been patched extensively or modified over a period of two to three years.

C The existing system lacks proper documentation and there is sufficient factual information to justify redesign of the system.

Types of Maintenance Projects

Maintenance efforts may originate from one or more of the following sources:

- ❖ Change in policy
- ❖ Change in procedure
- ❖ Change of system flow
- ❖ Change of program instructions
- ❖ Change of operation requirements
- ❖ Change of operating system
- ❖ Hardware changes

Requirements and Responsibility

The systems head defines the responsibility for coordinating requirements for system maintenance and establishes tasks to be performed.

A **Review and estimate of work required.** The standard task list is reviewed to determine which tasks are necessary to satisfy the maintenance request.

- ❖ Identify the problem to be solved by the maintenance project.
- ❖ Define the scope and the limitations of the maintenance effort.
- ❖ Rewrite operational procedures as required.
- ❖ Redesign input–output documents, files, or database requirements, and monitor displays or reports as required.
- ❖ Correct the Index of Table Field Names, as needed.

COMMENT

The results of a programmer's decision NOT to test a "too-simple revision": It cost the programmer his job and the firm over one million dollars. *Always* test revised programs.

- ❖ Designate programs and procedures that require modification.
- ❖ Make needed program changes.
- ❖ Test revised programs.
- ❖ Document the revisions.
- ❖ Perform system tests.

B **Management and/or user approval.** Management and users are responsible for the following tasks:

❖ Approve the intent and objectives of the system modification.

❖ Help develop test data for the system modification.

❖ Review and approve the test results.

❖ Make operational personnel available for any retraining required.

Control

Control checkpoints are established for each maintenance project. Their purpose is twofold: to ensure the quality and completeness of the maintenance project, and that the changes made to the system do not alter policy or degrade the system's present performance.

Minimally, controls should be at the following points:

❖ Completion of program testing

❖ Completion of system testing

❖ Completion of changed documentation

❖ End of maintenance (for confirmation that policies have not been changed)

Revision Conventions

These revision practices are followed:

❖ All binders for the revisions are updated at the same time to avoid any documentation conflicts.

❖ A revision information cover page, with a revision number and date, is completed and inserted into each binder.

❖ Obsolete documentation is labeled "obsolete," the date posted, and the documentation filed or destroyed according to the records retention procedure.

❖ Each procedure or policy affected has the revision number posted at the top right-hand side of each new page of documentation.

4

PROGRAMMING PROCEDURES: SOLID PRACTICES

SOFTWARE POLICIES

Business software must reflect the business user's needs in its changing and complex operations if it is to provide useful information and functionality. Creating or buying software is more than a question of resources and cost. It is also a question of remaining competitive in order to stay in business. There is a need on the policy level to provide direction for software development, purchase, and maintenance.

Creating computer software is expensive, and a company that employs its own programming staff has invested a considerable amount of money into *processes* to support its business. Ideally this provides the company with an operating efficiency or other business advantage. To protect this investment, the company must have a clearly defined policy that stipulates that all programs written using company resources (such as time, equipment, utility software, books, and so on) are the company's property. Without this protection, a company may find its internal software processes being used by a competitor or generally available in the marketplace.

Software and programmers have traditionally not been subject to organizational policies. However, organizations have recently become aware of the costs and risks associated with a lack of such programming and software

87

policy. The move toward interactive processing, client/server development, Internet applications, and PC users makes clear the necessity of policy development.

Proprietorship of Computer Software

All software developed during work hours by programming personnel paid by the hour is the exclusive property of the employer. Salary-exempt personnel have no proprietary interest in programs they develop. All programming effort and documentation is the exclusive property of the employer as long as the hardware/software used belongs to the firm. Additional programs and software policies apply to purchased and unauthorized software.

Purchased Software. Purchased software and software documentation may only be copied as specified by the vendor. No versions of any purchased software are permitted beyond the number the firm has purchased. This applies to all organization personnel.

> # COMMENT
>
> When you purchase licensed software, you are buying permission to use a product under the conditions detailed in the license. If you violate the terms of this license by making more than the stipulated number of copies of the software, then you have violated the license agreement. This may result in a lawsuit for damages as well as the possibility that you may lose the licenses for which you have paid.

Unauthorized Software. Personnel may not purchase or write their own software for use in the organization without authorization. They may not bring to the organization any software, in any form, that is not the property of the organization. The downloading of any unauthorized software to company-owned hardware at any company site is also not permitted. Any violation of this policy subjects the offender to immediate discharge and/or the reimbursement of all costs associated with such action.

COMMENT

Computer technicians appreciate the difficulties of keeping all of the loaded systems software in "agreement" so that one program does not "crash" another. The introduction of additional software not previously tested and approved for company use exposes stable systems to the potential of a destabilizing influence. Other issues include the ability for the unapproved software to exchange files with other systems as well as the ability of the company to provide cost-effective support to users.

Uniform Programming Practices

The head of computer programming is the authority both for setting standards for computer programming throughout the IS organization, and for allocating the resources for new programming development.

Uniform programming practices are maintained throughout the organization as defined in the company policies and procedures manual; only approved documentation procedures are used. Individual coding styles are not allowed, and only one style of programming is used for any one authorized computer programming language. The "Procedural Coding" section, on page 94, will be a further extension of the procedure policies that govern program development.

Program Languages

Adoption or discontinuation of any program language can have serious and long-range consequences; therefore, these actions, as well as any upgrades of any given language, must be approved by the head of information systems.

Any purchase or upgrading of operating or network systems software will require the approval of the head of information systems. This policy applies to all corporation systems: corporate, work group, or PC-based.

Beta Software

Beta acquisition must be a concern at the policy level for the information systems of the entire company. It is the responsibility of information systems management to formulate this policy and its required procedures. Top management of the organization will be kept informed about the policy and its rationale. The IS management will be the only party that can approve the company's involvement in any Beta testing and the degree of that testing. Any employee involved with unauthorized Beta testing can be subject to immediate discharge.

There can be more than one level of involvement in Beta testing at any given time. But the degree of each Beta involvement will be decided by IS management. By the nature of its responsibility, management is required to have the essential information needed for such commitments. Beta testing can affect different levels of obligations, from the strategic interest of the company to postponing an upgrade.

Audit Review

As an organization becomes more dependent upon computer technology, the need for systems and programming audits becomes greater. Audits are necessary to assure that the system continues to run properly.

Management bears the ultimate responsibility for having an IS audit policy that can assure them of the validity and integrity of financial and reporting programs. Auditors determine the actual audit procedures, and either internal or external auditors perform the actual audit.

COMMENT

Computer-related fraud is now an everyday possibility. Because of the disturbing rise in unauthorized access to databases, computer fraud, mismanagement, and lawsuits, IS managers and auditors have to be more security-minded than ever before.

Auditors approve and oversee financial programs, but also oversee the data's accuracy. A savvy IS manager requires the auditor's approval to confirm reliability of financially related systems and programs. Audit reviews seek to:

1   Review all corporate computer programs under development or have maintenance performed to assure adequate and reliable audit controls are built into the system and program software.

2 Determine that specified controls are actually reliable within operational system programs.

3 Confirm that access to operating programs and databases by remote access or any sort of network access is continually governed by the current state of security to prevent unauthorized access.

4 Confirm that established accounting standards have been met and employed by all information systems using them.

PROGRAM DEVELOPMENT

The longer it takes to develop software, the greater the chance that problems will occur. "Creeping user requirements" can be legitimate. It's simple. User needs do change. Anyone responsible for software development or who is an IS head should read Capers Jones's book, *Assessment and Control of Software Risks* (Englewood Cliffs, NJ: Prentice Hall, 1994).

After an extensive study of IS projects, Mr. Jones has identified no fewer than 50 major problems affecting software development. He notes, "Few projects have more than 15 software risk factors at any time, but many projects have half a dozen simultaneously." He points out the "five most frequently encountered risk factors for large IS shops":

❖ Creeping user requirements

❖ Excessive schedule pressure

❖ Low quality

❖ Cost overruns

❖ Inadequate configuration control

Application overload and the deterioration of programming quality play havoc with programmer productivity. The prudent IS head not only has effective programming policies and procedures in place, but makes certain they are observed.

COMMENT

All developers are encouraged to read *Code Complete, A Practical Handbook of Software Construction* by Steve McConnell. The sections on commenting code and code reviews are particularly important.

Review of Software Specifications

The initial step in program development is a review of the system's software specifications to ensure there is no misunderstanding of specification requirements between the systems analyst or user and the programmer(s).

General review.   With the purpose and scope of the programs understood, the next step is determining their relationships in the total system. When reviewing each program:

1   Review the program's place in the system.

2   Check the functions of the programs preparing the input for the program under review. Include the sequence of the input elements and contents of the element sets. In addition, check the purposes of the program(s) that will use the output of this program.

3   Resolve any questions regarding the system or programming requirements.

Detailed review.   In order to ensure a complete understanding of the requirements for the program(s), consider the following items:

❖ **Data element specifications.** These determine the precise record formats for files and the data dictionary specifications for database systems. For example, are the "year" data elements four-numeric character fields, or is there some other solution that was used to resolve the year 2000 problem?

❖ **Processing specifications.** These determine calculations and comparison tests of data.

❖ **Systems specifications.** These are reviewed to resolve any ambiguities or problems.

Program Organization

Before the detailed logic of a program is developed, the programmer organizes the major logic functions needed to accommodate the requirements of the programming language or software selected.

Program logic.   This is represented using program block diagrams as logical modules for structured programming. These reflect the relationship of the logical modules and the detailed processing that occurs within each structured module. By using structured programming, the problem's solution can be divided into logical parts or routines, so each may be programmed as soon as possible. This permits complex problems to be broken down into simpler sections. Each module routine becomes a separate entity.

A building block module is created and controlled by a single routine called the main line, which provides the master control that ties all individual processing modules together and coordinates their activity.

Modification of module routines is simplified. Changing or adding new routines is accomplished by changing the main-line routine. This transfers control to the new routine.

To design a modular program, determine the program parameters. List the requirements, elements, and functions of the program as they are developed, with no attention to logical order. Next, review and revise them to determine the logical order of the processing routines and design the main line of the program. Then an overall flowchart can be drawn. Since this flowchart can reveal errors in logic, pay careful attention to it.

In preparing and using the "modular" structured programming method, the following criteria are used:

❖ **Structured flowcharts.** A structured system flowchart gives an overall picture of the major component elements of the routine. Program flowcharts then progress to any desired level of detail, depending on the complexity of the routine. The program coding should be referenced throughout. In this way, the programmer can easily compare the chart to the actual coding for the purposes of debugging.

❖ **Comprehensive narration of each routine.** The narration of each structured routine states its purpose, describes data it processes, and generally explains the program logic as portrayed by the structured flowchart.

❖ **Programming conventions.** The use of standardized nomenclature conventions and standardized program documentation techniques permits someone unfamiliar with the program to readily understand its content. This is very helpful for later maintenance programming.

Program efficiency. Efficiency results from proper use of an existing structured routine to build balanced and flexible programs. Efficient programs require the following:

1 Programming so that a minimum of effort is required later for maintenance programming.

2 Fully utilizing available software and hardware.

3 Using peripheral devices to maximize the capacity of the whole system.

Reusable Component Identification

Reusable components are those having identifiable commonalities across programs of a given project. The project must be large enough or consist of several smaller projects in the same general domain to justify a reuse strategy. For reuse to pay off, a specific plan must be developed before program coding starts. Reuse planning prior to coding a new system will help organizations avoid the error of thinking about reuse too late.

A taxonomy system is needed to identify modules for reuse. No single taxonomy system will apply to all reusable component libraries.

Program module commonalities include common data, common constants, common formula process, common tables, and/or reiteration processes. Because models are built prior to coding the actual program modules, potential reuse is greater.

One word of caution: Make sure the module works. There is nothing worse than having reusable code that has a bug placed into your library. A list should be maintained of each module location in case errors are detected later, as well as for future update requirements.

Procedural Coding

Standard techniques are used to code program instructions. These are the source-code instructions whose procedural language the compiler uses to generate the executable program.

Source coding. All coding documentation requires the programmer's name, the program name, date, and other pertinent information as determined by the project leader or programming supervisor.

Coding requirements
❖ Use techniques identified with the language selected.
❖ Use clear, descriptive comments for explaining complicated or tricky techniques. (Remember that someone may need to make changes in the program at a later date.)
❖ Follow standard coding procedures.

Desk checking. The next step in program coding is desk checking, which is performed after the source program is written but prior to any program compiling. Desk checking includes:

❖ **Verification of program logic.** The programmer traces the flow of the program through each possible path.

❖ **Construction of decision trees.** Decision trees are constructed for both desk checking and object program testing at a later time. These trees represent data points to test for all program exceptions, as well as normal conditions.

Testing

The purpose of testing a coded program is to detect syntax and logic errors. Syntax errors are detected while compiling a source program into an executable program, and commonly occur when program-coding rules for the language being used are not followed. Syntax error messages are produced by the compiler following the statement that contains the error. In some cases, an executable program is not generated because of syntax errors. After all syntax errors are corrected, an executable program is generated by the compiler for testing program logic.

Use the test data prepared in *desk checking* (reviewing your code) to generate input data to test the program's functions. Several types of errors are often made by programmers and can be detected and corrected with the proper testing procedures. These errors are classified as:

A Clerical errors

B Logical errors

C Interpretation or communication errors (These occur due to misinterpretation or misunderstanding of the program requirements.)

After testing is complete, the auditors may provide test data to be run to confirm that auditing standards have been met. Testing is not an afterthought, but should be considered early in the developmental stage of programming.

Documentation

The purpose of program documentation is to allow other programmers to perform program maintenance at some later date. It also defines the manner in which the program is to be run, outlines the controls necessary, and provides information for operations personnel. Additionally, it provides management with a means of obtaining information about the program's operation, complexity, and costs.

Programming documentation is noted here because it is a byproduct of the preceding steps. Details are provided in the "Program Documentation" section of Chapter 2.

Nonprocedural Coding

When using a nonprocedural 4GL, one tells the computer *what* to do, *not how* to do it. Computer-aided software engineering (CASE), one form of 4GL coding, is a very helpful tool for systems development. 4GLs employed in prototyping require a different set of procedures than procedural coding. The time span over which 4GLs are used dictates a different approach for their utilization and documentation. Before and/or during the employment of 4GLs, pay careful attention to the naming conventions, error routines, monitor screen displays, and data dictionaries.

The use of RAD (Rapid Application Development) offers a menu of precoded samples of monitor screens or hardcopy reports to select from. On-screen prompting takes the user and programmer through selecting a database and on to specifying output content. Since this is a shell product, the programmer may need some procedural code or 4GL to custom-code the final RAD product. This procedure may also involve pulling reusable modules of code to complete the task.

Both CASE tools and RAD are used to develop programs in a manner totally different from the procedural approach. Testing, although still performed, is less time-consuming. Documentation is a byproduct of most of this effort. The following can be done for the programmer:

- ❖ Pull-down screen menus
- ❖ Pop-up screen windows
- ❖ Scrolling "help"
- ❖ Screen list boxes
- ❖ Color screen highlighting
- ❖ Dataflow diagrams
- ❖ Data modeling
- ❖ Program specifications
- ❖ Code generation
- ❖ Documentation

PROGRAMMING CONVENTIONS

There may be a different format coding convention for each programming language used. RAD and CASE tools conventions, depending on the vendor, may not be similar to procedure language software. In any case, conventions should be used consistently.

Coding Conventions

Program coding

❖ Coding format is restricted by compiler language specifications.

❖ All program source code should have the programmer's name, program title, page number, and date at the beginning of each source module.

Character representation

❖ Special care is exercised in coding to distinguish alphabetic uppercase O and numeric zero (0).

Comments or notes

❖ Comments or notes are used to explain special mathematical or programming techniques at that point in the program where these techniques appear.

Names used in programming

❖ Data element names and variable names are related to the type of data being stored.

COMMENT

One popular naming convention is "Hungarian notation," invented by Microsoft's Chief Architect Dr. Charles Simonyi, and widely used by Microsoft. It became known as "Hungarian notation" because Simonyi is originally from Hungary and the prefixes give the variable names a non-English look. Documentation on the use of Hungarian notation can be found on Microsoft's Web site at http://msdn.microsoft.com/library/techart/hunganotat. htm.

❖ The size of names used is limited by the naming conventions of the language.

❖ Procedure names used for programming correspond to the names of those procedures used in the program flowcharts.

Controls

It is the programmer's responsibility to incorporate into the program the controls specified by the program supervisor, systems analyst, or auditor. Programmers identify any additional controls necessary for proper processing of data through the system. These controls may focus on such details as:

* ❖ Specifying the use of standard labels
* ❖ Sequence checking input files
* ❖ Validating vital input elements not checked by a previous program
* ❖ Showing specific control totals to be accumulated within the program

PURCHASING SOFTWARE

The decision to purchase software is made when in-house development cost is prohibitive or programming talent is unavailable in the timeframe required. Also, it is totally impractical to write software already available as an off-the-shelf, shrink-wrapped package. One type of packaged software, known as *horizontal software*, is widely available for PCs, such as word processors, spreadsheets, or personal database programs. This software is used universally by many institutions. The other type of packaged software, *vertical software*, has a much more limited market. It is used for specific procedures by organizations that have common needs, such as a billing system for hairdressers. This type of software is more available now for PCs, minicomputers, and mainframes.

When software cannot be programmed in-house, you will have to look elsewhere. If a shrink-wrapped program is not available, you can contact outside software contractors for bids. If possible, request three bids. Contractors can work at their facilities or yours. How much control the company wants over product development will govern where the contractors work. Different procedures for requesting a purchasing order and for payment of the invoice will be required, depending on where the work is done. (See Chapter 8, *Managing IS Assets,* for more software procedures.)

IS Purchased Software

IS purchased software is requisitioned against the information systems budget for software. Someone will be delegated as the coordinator for requisitioning IS purchased software, by the head of information systems, who also furnishes the software budget information. Included are the total dollars budgeted for software, a list of authorized personnel who may request the purchase of software, and the kind of software they may requisition. A dollar limit per order will also be noted. Any request for software that exceeds this limit requires the approval signature of the head of information systems.

IS software requisition procedure.   The coordinator of IS software purchasing is sent a memo listing the software requested, the reason for the request, and the date by which the software is needed. The coordinator checks the approved software purchasing lists by *name* and *kind of software.* The coordinator then prepares a purchase requisition. If the coordinator can approve the requisition, information will be extracted for the monthly software report before the requisition is sent to purchasing. If not, it will be forwarded to the information systems head for his/her approval.

The information systems head will approve or deny the request, note the decision on the requesting memo, sign and date it, and return it to the software coordinator.

The coordinator will take the approved requests and issue purchase requisitions. Information will be extracted for the monthly software report before the purchase requisitions are sent to purchasing. If corporate policy mandates that the information systems head sign the requisitions, that signature will be needed before they are sent on to purchasing. The unapproved requisitioning memos will be answered by the IS head, providing any information as to why the request was denied. The original requesting memos, requisition copies, and reply memos will be filed in the form of hard copies or scanned into a computer data file.

IS monthly software report.   The software coordinator will report the following information to the head of information systems by memo on a monthly basis:

❖ Cumulative expenditures to date for software

❖ Balance of the budget to date

❖ The name and cost of software purchased

❖ The total amount spent to date by kind of software purchased

❖ The name of software purchased by each organizational unit and dollars spent

❖ The total spent to date by each unit

Payment of invoice.   For purchase orders to be paid, the IS software coordinator has to confirm the software has been received. If there are any problems, the coordinator should notify accounts payable to hold up payment to the vendor. If the software is returned, purchasing and/or accounts payable should be notified. If the vendor will not accept the returned software, and there is a problem with it, this information should be given to the systems head. If the vendor requires a rewrapping charge, the original purchase order is cancelled and a new requisition written for the rewrapping charge, which will have to be applied to the software expense list and identified as such.

Other Unit Software Requisition Procedures

Other units that have their own budget for software will use the same procedures as for other purchases. The information systems unit will publish and distribute a list of approved software that they support. Questions will not be answered and help will not be offered by anyone in the information systems unit, including the help-desk, for any software not on the list.

The small print on a software package lists restrictions in force unless the vendor guarantees something else in writing. Documentation should be reviewed before the seal is broken on the program disk container since it is usually impossible to return opened software. If the seal is broken and the software does not perform as expected, ask the purchasing department to contact the vendor. Send a memo to accounts payable instructing a hold on payment of the invoice until the problem is resolved.

Contract Programming

Purchasing contract programs or software is governed by the organization's policy for contracting outside services. The purchase order should contain a statement describing an acceptable program as noted in this chapter's section on "Beta Software Testing and Evaluation" (see page 103).

The vendor will provide the source code, as part of the software documentation, which will be converted to executable code and tested. These results will be compared with the vendor's test output to insure it is the same. The vendor will be provided with test data that has been approved and/or generated by the user, and a copy will be used for the final (in-house) source code test.

Once the software has been purchased, there is little leverage to get corrections made (assuming the firm is still in business when corrections are needed). Therefore, the wise IS manager sends the contract and/or purchase order specifications to the organization's legal department before signing any commitments.

Contract Programmers

Contract programmers may or may not work in-house, but are paid by the hour to work on assigned projects. Their work is paid for by accounts payable. When contract programmers start, the person they are reporting to should give them a short introduction to the staff, a tour of the facilities, and information about the company's established rules of programming and documentation. Giving them samples of previous project efforts to review would be helpful. Contract persons working at the firm's IS site should be provided with a desk and required tools. Other information about working with contract programmers is provided in Chapter 15, *Vendors: Getting the Goods*. The contract person should be monitored closely during the first week or two to assure proper job performance, in addition to the regular progress reports filed weekly by all programmers. Any personality problems with staff or users should also be noted and addressed promptly.

Evaluation of Packaged Software

There are some major issues to address when purchasing packaged software, which can apply to almost any type of software supplier. They are:

❖ Will the vendor be in business next year?

❖ What warranty will be provided?

❖ Will the software integrate with other software used by the company?

❖ Will the software adapt to the company's information systems standards?

❖ How flexible is the software package?

❖ Is the current company hardware compatible with the proposed software?

❖ Will the documentation provided be user-friendly?

❖ What type of training is offered?

❖ What other expense will be required?

❖ Can the vendor provide modifications to the software?

❖ Is there an upgrade planned in the near future?

❖ Is there a vendor help-desk?

❖ Will the vendor supply a copy of the purchase contract?

❖ What is the vendor's reputation?

❖ How many will use the software?

❖ Is there a users' support group?

❖ Will the vendor supply the names of current users? If the answer is yes, contact them and ask them for other users to contact!

❖ What is the major business focus of the vendor?

To discover how difficult or easy it will be to implement the proposed software, the following issues should be addressed:

❖   How complex is the installation procedure?

❖   Will the vendor provide installation assistance?

❖   How easy is the software to maintain?

To evaluate vendor-supplied software, ask current or former users the following:

❖   Would they buy from the same vendor again?

❖   Did the software perform as promised?

❖   Was the training of value?

❖   Was the documentation easy to follow and complete?

❖   Were there any implementation problems?

❖   Did installation or operation have any hidden costs?

❖   Would the referenced user allow a visit to his/her site to see how the software is working and talk to operations personnel?

New packaged software must be evaluated, whether for new applications or for placement on the "approved purchase list," especially if this purchase commits the company to buy in volume. Depending on the software considered, use the following procedures.

General use software evaluation.   A person or formal committee will be responsible for general-use packaged software evaluation. A request for such evaluation can come from a user, a systems analyst, information systems management, or the party performing the evaluation. The person or committee responsible will be a source for packaged software information consulting services. Exhibit 4–1, on page 104, is a sample form used for software evaluation.

Whenever possible, more than one vendor should be evaluated for the same kind of software. Computer publications, as well as their advertisements, are good sources of evaluation information. Keep an information folder for each type of packaged software evaluated.

Client/server and vertical software evaluation.   Client/server and vertical packaged software will require a preliminary operations hands-on test followed by controlled client/server or work group prototype operations testing. Users' evaluation will also be required. The time required for each controlled group prototype test will vary with the complexity of the software operation and the number of planned future users. The more users, the safer the software should be, i.e., free of bugs. The time required for testing would also be limited by the vendor, the time limit on returning the software, or when the invoice has to be paid.

Beta Software Testing and Evaluation

Any Beta commitments will require the prior approval of the head of information systems or a designated agent. Any commitments to use Beta testing will be limited to pilot operations not part of the corporate information systems operation. No Beta operations will be planned beyond the time limit specified by the vendor.

Beta testing will not have access to the corporate system or database at any time but will be limited to client/server, work group, or stand-alone PC systems. It will not have contact with any processing or database that is under the domain of the auditors.

All costs associated with a Beta testing operation will be monitored and reported monthly to the head of information systems. In addition, a final report will be submitted after Beta testing is complete. The following will be reported:

A   **Personnel time.** Personnel time will be kept for IS staff, user employees, and other workers. The total time for each group will be reported. If required by the head of IS, the dollar cost by each group, the total cost, and any overtime incurred because of Beta testing will be listed and identified in the report.

B   **Other costs.** Costs, other than personnel, will also be reported. This covers such items as: supplies, postage, long-distance telephone calls, costs of outside services rendered, any charge-back services (computer, copies made, etc.), and expense account reimbursements.

C   **Beta operating problems.** Any Beta testing and/or operating problems occurring during the month will be reported, with the estimated total cost of each occurrence. It should be noted if any problem has occurred before and, if so, how often.

D   **Vendors' contact documentation.** Copies of correspondence sent to vendors, telephone call notes, and e-mail sent or received will be attached to the report. The person writing the report will summarize comments addressing these issues.

E   **User reports.** Copies of Beta testing memos or e-mail concerning the project will be attached to the report. The person writing the report will summarize comments addressing these issues.

F   **Report summary.** The person writing the report will summarize the status of the Beta testing. Any changes the vendor plans to make

EXHIBIT 4–1. Software Evaluation Worksheet

Software Title _____   Version _____

Vendor _____   Software Description_____

_____

Vendor Address _____

Contact Person _____   Phone # _____

Purchase Order # _____   Date_____

Date(s) Software Tested_____   By _____

Software Copied to Server_____   Date_____

Rights Are Assigned/Flagged (list rights) _____

Software Copied to Other Servers (list) _____

_____

Software Evaluation (attach extra pages and documents)_____

_____

_____

_____

_____

_____

Documentation Evaluation (attach extra pages and documents) _____

_____

_____

_____

_____

_____

_____

_____

_____

_____

that would benefit the future use of the software should be noted. Any recommendation as to continuing or discontinuing the Beta testing or any other comments worth noting should be included. Also, the question of whether the Beta shut-down date will create any problems should be addressed.

G **Final report.** A final report will be submitted after Beta testing has been completed. Attached to the final report will be a copy of all completed Software Evaluation Worksheets (see Exhibit 4–1). Benefits derived from the Beta test project should be reported in detail. The report will also include a summarized cost-benefit analysis and what final action was taken based on the Beta testing.

PROGRAM TESTING

Software written by IS programming staff or contract programmers, or contracted with an outside firm will require program testing according to the procedures presented here.

Test Planning

All new and maintenance programs require testing, the magnitude and complexity of which may be determined by the auditors. User acceptance should not be overlooked. Everyone concerned in the company may be happy with the test results, but unless the user is satisfied, operation problems may occur later. A formal test plan should be composed of the following:

- ❖ General information
- ❖ Test plan
- ❖ Approval
- ❖ Test results

General information.   This section contains pertinent information needed to identify program(s) and the project with which it is associated. The following information is included:

- ❖ Project number
- ❖ Program number(s)
- ❖ Date
- ❖ Programmer(s)
- ❖ Scheduled completion date
- ❖ Language the program is written in

Test plan.   This section describes the steps required for testing individual segments of each program's logic. The information includes:

- ❖ Program number
- ❖ Test number
- ❖ Function to be tested
- ❖ Test priority

Approval. This section contains the signature blocks required to approve the test plan and authorize the testing. The program supervisor or project manager will also use this part of the program test to indicate the type of testing to be conducted.

❖ **Unlimited.** The programmer may test until completion without additional review and/or approval.

❖ **Limited.** A specific number of tests is permitted before approval expires and a review to approve further testing is required.

Test results. This section reflects the progress of the program during testing, including date of the first test, systems tests, and volume test. If tests are run for the auditors, the date the auditor's presence is required will be noted.

Test Preparation

To ensure test data is representative, all conditions shown in the program flowcharts must be included. The flowchart can be reduced to a decision tree, showing only the decision points and the conditions for the decisions. This makes it easy for users or auditors to follow the decision conditions.

Another tool for test preparation is a decision table. (See Exhibit 4–2 for a Decision Table Structure.) The box labeled "title" contains the procedure title. The area labeled "condition stub" lists all possible conditions tested. The "action stub" area lists all actions that can take place. Under "decision rules" are listed "condition entries," the actual conditions that determine how the data will be treated, and "action entries," the actions that determine which course to follow predicated on the entry conditions. A sample procedure for credit approval is shown in Exhibit 4–3. A decision table for an "else" rule is shown in Exhibit 4–4.

For best results, someone other than coding personnel should prepare the test data. The coder may conduct preliminary testing, as long as someone else does the final test development. This procedure and use of the decision table enhance the potential for detecting errors.

Test material is retained and kept current for later use in testing systems and program specifications. Following are specifications for preparing test data:

❖ The requirements outlined in the system specifications must be clearly understood.

❖ The logic and major routines requiring testing must be reviewed and the findings documented.

❖ The test data must be filed in the library or project folder. This material is considered part of the documentation and must be maintained during the life of the program.

❖ The analyst or program supervisor responsible must review all system modifications to determine if any changes are required in the test data. When a change is made, the programmer or test preparer conducts tests with the pertinent data to ensure the modifications are correct and have not affected other processing areas.

Test Analysis

The following should be carefully checked to avoid testing errors:

Input/output

❖ Proper heading format, line spacing, spelling, and punctuation of reports

❖ Correct data element size and content

❖ Report output matches expected specifications

❖ Correctly keyed-in data

Problem analysis

❖ Original specifications are understood.

❖ Flowcharting does not have logic errors.

❖ Coding errors are not present.

❖ No software revision errors exist.

Operating Program Maintenance

Only maintenance programmers will have access to the software and be allowed to copy it for maintenance. The maintenance of running programs is forbidden without the approval of the operations manager, and auditor if required. A violation of this procedure is grounds for dismissal.

After the required maintenance is completed, the program(s) should be tested. The procedures described in the "Review and Acceptance of Test Results" section, on page 111, will be repeated in order for the changes to become part of the production system.

EXHIBIT 4-2. Decision Table Structure

TITLE	DECISION RULES							
	1	2	3	4	5	6	7	8
CONDITION STUB	CONDITION ENTRY							
ACTION STUB	ACTION ENTRY							

EXHIBIT 4–3. Decision Table

CREDIT APPROVAL	DECISION TABLE							
	1	2	3	4	5	6	7	8
ON APPROVED LIST	Y	N	N	N	N			
PAST EXPERIENCE OK	—	Y	N	N	N			
APPROVED CO-SIGNER	—	—	Y	N	N			
SPECIAL APPROVAL RECEIVED	—	—	—	Y	N			
APPROVE ORDER	X	X	X	X	—			
RETURN ORDER	—	—	—	—	X			
GO TO TABLE A5	X	X	X	X	—			
END OF PROCEDURE	—	—	—	—	X			

EXHIBIT 4–4. Decision Table with "Else" Rule

EMPLOYMENT	DECISION RULES	
	1	ELSE
COLLEGE DEGREE	YES	—
3 YEARS PROGRAMMING EXPERIENCE	COBOL	—
APPLICATION FORM	GET ONE	
INTERVIEW	SCHEDULE	
DISPOSITION	—	REJECT

SOFTWARE INSTALLATION

Transferring a software program from developmental to operational status follows standard review and approval procedures. These procedures apply to programs developed by IS programming staff or contract programmers, or contracted with an outside firm. Purchased or completed Beta tested software will follow the same procedures whenever possible. The conversion can begin only after the software or system passes all testing procedures.

Installation or conversion is placing into operation the tested software or system, which either replaces existing programs or is completely new. When discontinued software is replaced by a new system, the options are:

1 **Phased.** The new system is installed in modular fashion or in phases. When one phase is identified as operational and accepted, the next part of the installation can begin.

2 **Direct.** Direct installation is a complete, one-time conversion or installation. The old system is replaced completely by the new. Operations has to be totally involved with the installation and operation of the new system software.

3 **Pilot installation.** The new system is installed as a prototype operation in one safe location. After this operation is running properly, it may be installed in other locations. This type of installation is ideal for work groups or independent PC operations.

4 **Parallel conversion installation.** This type of installation is most often used with corporate IS computer operations. It is the safest and most preferred method of installing a new software system, but also the most costly. If, after comparing output results and the database status of both systems, the results are compatible, the new installation is considered complete.

When no existing software is being replaced, new software installation can occur as phased, direct or pilot installation. The other procedures for software installation are the same whether a new system is replacing an old one or not.

Review and Acceptance of Test Results

To ensure that correct results are obtained from extended program testing, a review should be conducted with users, and auditors, if they are involved. Acceptance will be confirmed by memo from involved users and/or auditors directed to the system project manager or the program supervisor. A vendor who is involved with the project will receive this information from the system manager and/or programming supervisor.

Review and Acceptance of Documentation

Documentation should be prepared according to established specifications. Any changes or additions will be conveyed by e-mail or hardcopy memo to the appropriate person in charge of documentation approval. Its acceptance will be conveyed by memo to the heads of programming and systems.

Acceptance of Contracted Software

The installation of contracted software will follow the same installation procedures as in-house developed software programs. Acceptance of purchased software as operational includes informing accounts payable via memo or e-mail that the invoice can be paid. The note should contain the vendor's name, item name and description, and purchase order number. If, on the other hand, the software does not meet the standards specified in the purchase order, a memo or e-mail is sent to the purchasing and/or accounts payable departments so informing them; the purchasing department will then inform the vendor.

Development Programmer Sign-off

After the installation of the software is completed and accepted, the development programmers will no longer have access to the production system software. Their access codes will be removed from the controlled access subroutine in the system software.

PROGRAM MAINTENANCE

Program maintenance tasks, maintenance responsibility, and maintenance conventions are required for program maintenance.

Types of Program Maintenance

1   Program revisions are changes made that do not require a major logic change. Examples are:
    ❖ Updates of constants and other variables
    ❖ Increases in the dimensions of tables, arrays, or work areas
    ❖ Implementation of hardware features
    ❖ Correction of minor processing deficiencies
    ❖ Conformation to programming standards

2 Program modification are changes involving the redesign of program logic or the relationships of the subprograms or components. They are required to accommodate changes in input or output specifications.

Responsibilities and Controls

A The head of computer programming has the authority and responsibility for new programming, while the IS computer operations head has the authority and responsibility for maintenance programming.

B Testing or program maintenance will not be performed on any production software under the control of IS computers or work group systems. This will be done off-line with no access to the production system software.

C Testing or program maintenance should verify that changes have been made properly and that other sections of the program were not affected by the changes.

D The programmer and program supervisor will review the final test output and documentation for correctness and completeness.

E User management or IS computer operations management will require a sign-off before the modified software is placed into production. Once this occurs, the maintenance programmer will no longer have access to it. However, in case of an emergency the programmer may regain access under supervision and with the permission of user management or IS computer operations management.

Conventions

In addition to the conventions outlined below, those established for program development (as found in "Coding Conventions," on page 97) are followed in performing program maintenance.

A **Changes to flowcharts.** Flowcharts are modified in the following manner:

1 For hand-drawn charts, changes are made to the contents of a symbol by erasing the pencil-drawn symbol, redrawing it, and penciling in the new contents. The correction date is posted next to the symbol and initialed. There is no limit to the number of these changes except that imposed by neatness and legibility.

2 If a flowcharting program was used, a new chart is drawn by that program. The changes are noted on the new chart, dated, and initialed by the programmer. Both old and new charts are filed.

3 Additional pages added to flowcharts because of changes require off-page connectors to direct the flow to the inserted pages.

B **Changes to reports.** Always retain one copy of the original report layout in the documentation.

1 Report layouts are to be redrawn if lines are altered.

2 Rubber-cemented patches can be used to cover text changes.

3 If reports are generated by report design software, the old design and the new design are to be filed together with changes noted in the new report.

C **Changes in program coding and testing**

1 A source program is copied into a new file before extensive changes are made. After testing is complete and the updated program put into production, the old source program may be erased after 90 days.

2 When testing program changes, the entire program must be checked, not only the routines that were inserted, deleted, or changed. Those segments not changed are tested to insure the program will continue to function properly. The test data becomes part of the program documentation.

5

PROJECT MANAGEMENT: GETTING IT OUT ON TIME

PROJECT MANAGEMENT POLICIES

Project management is the marriage of different technologies; it requires both technical and managerial skills executed in an organized, cooperative fashion. To maximize the performance of the project activities, a project manager's primary responsibility is to allocate personnel who can make significant contributions, based on such attributes as language skills, analytical capabilities, and hardware knowledge.

Most technical professionals lack the administrative and interpersonal skills needed to function effectively in this position. However, project management responsibility is often their first management experience. This chapter puts some basic management procedural guidelines into perspective and establishes a uniform format for managerial procedures to be followed by all project managers.

The IS organization is not limited to one project in progress at a time. Therefore, a central authority is required to act as the focal point for all IS project activities. This authority is the IS systems department manager or a delegated coordinator, who settles disputes over resource allocations, monitors the progress of each project, and attends all project presentations. For the purpose of identification, the person performing this duty shall be called the *projects coordinator.* All project reporting will be directed to the projects coordinator.

PROJECT MANAGEMENT DEFINITION

Each project must have achievable objectives that are defined by management. The success of a project assignment must be measurable, the objectives covering a limited number of activities. Under the coordination of the project manager, the combination of personnel, administrative, technical, and financial resources are optimized to achieve a definable goal within a given calendar time period. A project will have a starting point defined by time and place, and an ending point; when the project can be considered complete.

It will have a defined budget allocation. Assigned personnel will have their time and commitments defined, because knowing the duration of an assignment is essential for proper project management. A schedule must be prepared so that work can be performed in measurable milestone units, the progress of which can be reported. Feedback requirements must be defined to meet the needs of the firm's management and the nature of the project.

The Nature of Project Management

What differentiates project management from general management is that project management has a starting point and a completion point. The calendar time period is determined before the project starts, and the project only exists between these points.

The other main difference is in the way each utilizes personnel resources. Members of a project are associated with it only for the lifetime of the project, or less. Their primary obligations are elsewhere; they may be assigned to the project for a specified number of calendar days, and even allotted specific times during those days. Their loyalty can only be short-lived because all projects have a termination point by definition.

At the project's completion, any unused material resources will have a predetermined disposition. They may be purchased during the project's existence or on loan to the project.

An IS project operates within defined boundaries, and has a specific scope of operation. Resources must be utilized within this committed scope. Any expansion of the scope by the project manager will dilute the effective use of the resources provided.

Project management requires that three important variables be in control: cost, quality, and calendar time. The project manager must ensure project completion, keeping all three within the planned limits. Altering any one variable can affect the others. Generally, to improve quality, higher cost and possibly more time would be required. For example, to deliver better, more effective user operation manuals and training than originally planned and budgeted for would exceed the project allocation. It would also cost more time if extra resources could not be commandeered to meet the project's calendar time deadline.

COMMENT

Lifeboats on ships have two sets of numbers painted on them. One is the identification number; the other is the lifeboat capacity. Lifeboats are resources designed for the project of saving lives, but only for a given scope, or number of people. If too many people board the lifeboat, all can be lost. That's why sidearms are issued to the ship's officers when orders are given to abandon ship.

The project manager has another option. He/she can reduce the scope of the project. However, this action cannot be taken without the approval of IS and user management.

IS Project Types

There are two kinds of projects with different purposes: a feasibility study and a project. The feasibility study is a mini project, used to determine the justification of a full-blown project. Not all projects require this: Some are mandated by top management or by forces external to the company.

A feasibility study informs management whether the proposed project is warranted and provides an estimate of the resources and calendar time required, information that is essential to planning and undertaking the project.

Once the decision is made to go forward, the project is addressed. The person who is responsible for the feasibility study is also a good candidate for the position of *project manager*. Contacts made and familiarity with the area gained through doing the feasibility study provide a solid base when the actual project is undertaken. The skills required to be a project manager evolve through hands-on experience with actual projects. More complex projects require experienced project managers.

IS/IT projects can run from a few days to years and involve a project team, while one person can accomplish a feasibility study in a day or a few weeks. IS/IT projects may include:

- ❖ PC conversions
- ❖ Mainframe conversions
- ❖ Developing a prototype
- ❖ Software implementation (for a wide range of systems)
- ❖ Implementation of new operating system

❖ System development and implementation

❖ End-user system development and implementation

❖ IT projects involving installation of new database, e-mail, Internet, LAN, or WAN system

❖ Business reengineering projects, which entail developing and implementing improved business operations with or without computers

IS Project Components

No project (feasibility study or project) exists in a vacuum. Other components interact with it and permit its existence. One such component, representing management, is the *steering committee*, which is attuned to the firm's strategic goals and prioritizes projects. The committee is kept informed of the progress of each project through status reports, required at least once monthly from each project manager. Feasibility study results are delivered as only a final report. Other components in this scenario are:

A **IS management.** The project's success will require the support of the IS management controlling the IT resources loaned to the project. IT management has a vested interest in the success of the project as well as in its assigned personnel.

B **Project advocate.** This person or group is a party to the request. It could also be the one who requested the undertaking because of a government mandate.

C **User management.** The user management who will utilize the end result has a vested interested, and can also be the project advocate.

D **Other projects.** Other projects will compete for resources. Shared resources require prioritizing and queuing to gain the most overall benefit.

E **Consultants and contractors.** Outside resources budgeted for a specific project can also be involved with more than one project for the firm. It is their responsibility to deliver what they promised by the time specified. The advantage of using consultants or contract people is that they can provide expertise or staffing not available in-house. Their service is utilized only as needed.

F **Corporate technical experts.** These are experts on loan from other areas of the company for a predetermined time. If these people are unavailable, outside experts may have to be employed.

G **The project team.** The project team itself is made up of two parts: the project management and the team members. These two parts must work well together for the project to be successful.

1 **Project manager.** The project manager must possess certain attributes required for a successful project completion.

2 **Project team members.** These are people with the technical skills needed for the project to succeed. They may be available full time or part-time for a given time duration. They could hold any of the following titles:

- Systems analyst
- Systems and procedure analyst
- Analyst programmer
- Programmer
- User specialist

- Project librarian
- Database designer
- Network specialist
- Industrial engineer
- Project secretary

Project Life Cycle

A project life cycle is composed of segments or phases. With the many different types of projects, one life cycle size does not fit all. There is somewhat of a consensus on the elements required, although some can be present for one kind of project but not for another.

The segments can be further defined by the internal elements. Following is a generic list of segment possibilities:

- Recognition of a need
- Request for a feasibility study
- Feasibility study
- Report of feasibility findings
- Request for systems analysis and design
- Systems analysis
- Systems design
- Acquire software (buy or write)

- Acquire hardware
- Install database and/or network
- Complete procedures
- System test
- Complete training
- Install system
- User acceptance
- System follow-up

To aid in reporting project status, the major milestones are the identifiable and measurable segments, which are reported as completed or not.

MANAGING PROJECTS

The management of IS projects starts with the steering committee, with upper-level management heavily represented. The committee members oversee the priorities to determine which projects are selected. They also influence which resources are allocated, and have final say regarding each project's completion date.

The steering committee follows the progress of all projects in process. Members have the authority to change priorities and completion dates of projects under consideration and in process. They also have the authority to cancel a project. The projects coordinator receives reports from each project manager, which he/she reviews and clarifies in a cover memo to each steering committee member. The projects coordinator will maintain a copy of this information. Each steering committee member receives a copy of each project status report with the cover memo from the projects coordinator. It is the court of final resort for user and project management appeals. To make these decisions, the committee has access to information restricted to the higher levels of management. It is not required to explain or justify its actions to the project or user management.

Projects Coordinator

The projects coordinator oversees all projects assigned to the IS organization, coordinating resources and the efforts of project managers and their staffs. He/she also works very closely with the steering committee. This person could be the manager of systems or its appointed projects coordinator—the person to whom the project managers report.

When priorities change, project calendar day slippage occurs, or available personnel changes, the projects coordinator has to resolve the resulting problems with the overall priorities defined by the steering committee. He/she has limited power to create resources; this is mainly under the control of the steering committee. The projects coordinator should allow for slippage due to the unavailability of people, wasted project efforts, vendor delays, etc. If the projects coordinator reports to the IS department manager, he/she is responsible for keeping the systems manager informed and works with him/her on planning for future project staffing and budgeting needs.

The projects coordinator utilizes project management software to oversee all projects. Gantt charts will be used to display the resources assigned to given projects. If people are not needed for a project, the projects coordinator will reassign them. The assignment and reassignment is best done using project management tools.

If the projects coordinator is also the manager of systems, he/she will be responsible for acquiring new systems personnel. If not, the systems manager is responsible. If there is no systems head, the head of IS will be responsible for obtaining new systems personnel and any other IS personnel needed for projects. Whoever is in charge of obtaining new personnel will work with the Human Resources department. The Human Resources department must have the new job requirements to set up interviews and help select new people. The projects coordinator will select the mentor for the new employees when assigning their duties.

The projects coordinator is instrumental in acquiring project consultants and contractors. He/she, *not* the project manager, has the authority to negotiate and sign contracts. This person will follow the procedures spelled out in Chapter 15, *Vendors: Getting the Goods.*

The projects coordinator writes a monthly status report. These reports are sent to the steering committee and to the head of IS. When the projects coordinator is not the systems manager, the systems manager also receives a copy of the report. Each project is reported, even if there is no activity. If there should have been activity, but there was none, the reason(s) must be reported.

An annual report is prepared at the end of each fiscal year by the projects coordinator who provides a narrative of each project, including its successes and problems, the percent of allocated budget spent versus the percent of the project completed, and a recap of the performance of each project manager. It will identify problems arising from a project manager's weakness and recommend improvements. The report should also include the next responsibility of each project manager after the project is completed. The annual report will recommend future projects for consideration, including resource acquisitions. Reports not written by the systems manager will require his/her approving signature before the annual report is sent to the head of IS. The head of IS will review and countersign it before it is distributed to the approved parties.

Project Manager

The project's success depends upon many factors. For one, dynamic and well-rounded people are required. Since all participants are "on loan" to a project—they know it's temporary—they will have vested interests in other areas. The project manager's position may be debased to that of a coordinator: a person with responsibility, but limited authority.

Selecting a project manager is the job of either the systems manager alone or the systems manager with input from the projects coordinator. Choosing a candidate requires knowledge of certain attributes that have been proven to be universally successful. The only testimonial a person really needs is a successful track record with the company. However, a person being selected as project manager for the first time requires special consideration.

New candidates should have demonstrated their abilities by contributing to a successfully completed project in which they were given increasing responsibilities. A first-time project manager's first assignment should be a project of limited scope and duration. After he/she has successfully completed a project, then longer and more complex projects can be assigned.

Keeping the position of project manager temporary is a face-saving decision made for both the project manager and the firm. If the person is unsuccessful, the problem can be more easily corrected than if he/she had been placed into a permanent position. It also provides excellent training for becoming a manager in the IS organization or elsewhere in the firm.

The selection criteria for a project manager are:

A **Maturity.** The person must display an air of maturity. This is required when dealing with senior management and user management. It also lends credibility to the project team.

B **Administrator.** The person must be able to routinely perform day-to-day administrative activities, such as reporting, requisitioning, memo writing, and the ability to follow schedules, meet deadlines, and handle resources and budgets. A proactive, rather than a reactive, administrator is much more desirable.

C **IT skills.** Because IT encompasses such vast areas today, no one person can be an expert in every area, but the project manager candidate must have enough technical skill necessary to gain the respect of the IT assigned staff.

D **Company knowledge.** The person must know the company to insure the project follows the corporate culture, and does not "rock the boat" of senior and user management. The candidate should know both the formal and informal organization to insure the project will progress smoothly.

E **The person who delegates the work.** The person must be able to delegate and recognize that when a team member is successful, that member gets all the credit. When the member fails, this failure is shared with the project manager.

F **Communicator.** The project manager must keep the project team, management, and others with vested interests in the project well informed. This includes informal day-to-day oral communication, written communication, formal presentations, teaching, and chairing meetings.

When chairing idea and work meetings, an effective project manager will urge all members to participate. Under the right circumstances, quieter team members will contribute valuable input. In addition, since the project manager does not want to discourage communication, he/she should never label ideas "bad."

G **Innovator.** The project manager must not be limited to traditional solutions. He/she must be innovative and encourage others to be the same.

H Leader. The project team must be led through the most trying times. The project manager must be able to work under pressure, remain calm, keep the project objective in focus, and still be sensitive to the team, users, vendors, and the corporate culture.

COMMENT

Many new project managers mistakenly believe that merely because they are managers, they can automatically rally the support of all those assigned to them. Most seasoned managers readily subscribe to the adage that respect is earned and not bestowed by title. All too often, the respect of those being led is forfeited because of the lack of basic interpersonal or management skills.

Following is a list of practices through which project managers can establish and retain the respect of the team:

A Have others participate in decision making. Get the whole team involved in contributing ideas to the project. Though the final decision is not theirs, people value the opportunity to comment because it increases their feeling of worth. An environment of participation garners respect for the project manager who creates it.

B Be honest. The project leader who is open and honest creates an example for the team members to follow and creates respect for his/her opinion.

C Keep promises. An effective project manager does not make unreasonable commitments. Failure to keep promises, especially without a justified explanation, will quickly lead to a lack of confidence and respect; the project manager's word should have credibility with the project team and users.

D Practice a strong work ethic. The project manager must display a work ethic similar to, or stronger than what is expected from the project team. His/her work effort must be real, because some people will not do more than required.

E Be consistent. Consistency in the treatment of all members of the team is a must to maintain total team harmony and loyalty. Showing preference only alienates others.

F **Recognize contributions.** Recognition by acknowledging the ideas of all project team members promotes goodwill and loyalty. An effective project manager never takes credit for an idea that originated with someone else.

COMMENT

Recognition of a job well done shows your appreciation. It costs nothing, but can be more valuable than money at times. A show of appreciation for the efforts of team members not only improves their output, but also increases their appreciation and respect for the project manager.

Project Variables

Project variables include the following activities:

A Project inputs

1 Human attributes

a User attitude about computer systems

b User attitude toward other units involved in the new system

c User attitudes toward the firm and their willingness to participate

d User educational level

e Value system of project team and users

f Experience level of user's management

g Age of users and user management

h Top management's commitment

i The experience that the users have had with the current system

2 Project team's attributes

a Respect for project manager

b Social skills of project team

c Communication skills of project group

d Experience level of project group

e Credibility level of project group

3 Project variables

    a Size of project and project group

    b Time length of the project

    c Value of project

    d Having good measurable milestones

    e Budget allocation

    f State of the technology involved in the project

    g Computer program languages to be used

    h The quality of the acquired hardware and software

4 Organization variables

    a Size of the firm

    b Type of industry of the firm

    c Experience with computer systems

    d Span of management control

    e Centralization of operations

    f Financial status of firm

    g How progressive the firm is

    h Number of levels of management

    i Level of management skill

B Throughput process of project group

    1 Information gathering

    2 Information analysis

    3 Comparisons with objectives

    4 Economic analysis

    5 Using systems analysis tools

    6 Technical writing

C Negative entropy

    1 Team effort of group

    2 Goodwill

    3 System capability

D Project feedback

    1 Cybernetic capabilities

    2 Reaction to various designs

E Project outputs

1 Goal of the designed and installed running system
2 Timeliness of the project
3 Maintenance of budget limits
4 Minimum of personnel turnover

PROJECT INITIATION

After the feasibility study has been completed, and its findings are positive, a report is written and forwarded to the steering committee for its evaluation. When the committee approves the project, the project initiation phase begins. The steering committee defines the scope and specifies the start and completion dates of the project. It will assign non-IS personnel to the project, approve the use of any outside vendor support, and provide for a project budget.

From this point IS management takes over to complete the details of the project initiation and appoints a project manager. The projects coordinator and the IS head will select the full- and part-time IS personnel for the project's duration. If any non-IS personnel, outside talent, and user people are needed, they will already have been approved by the steering committee. The assigned project manager is given the task of "confirming" the project's life cycle so that a schedule for tasks and resources can be completed.

Project Life Cycle

The project manager lays out the project life cycle in the form of a CPM chart. PERT and CPM charts look very much alike. The advantage in using CPM charting is that fewer estimated times are required for each leg (task). The charts can be hand-drawn or constructed using one of the many PC programs available.

After the tasks are organized into a CPM chart, the estimated calendar time needed to complete each task is entered. Starting with the finish date and working backward, the calendar start date for the project is determined. It's important to remember to count holidays and any plant shut-down days. If the results indicate that the start date has already passed, the CPM chart is reviewed for any tasks that can be run in parallel. If there is manpower available, the chart is reconfigured and the project calendar start time is recomputed. If there is still a problem, the project manager immediately contacts the projects coordinator or, if he/she is not available, the IS head.

If necessary, the steering committee must resolve the problem. It can change the finish date or provide for resources to reduce the span of the project time.

> ## COMMENT
>
> Don't count on overtime to meet the finish date. That's like starting a football game without reserve players. More than likely, when people are needed the most, they may be unavailable. Any smart IT person knows it is wise to start looking for another job if a lengthy project is going to be shortened by overtime.

Personnel Resource Scheduling

The context diagram further defines the tasks to be performed (see Chapter 2). The time to complete these tasks is estimated in "man-hours" and inputted into the project management system (see section "Project Resources" on page 136). This can be done manually for simple and small projects involving fewer than four people and twelve tasks. Before the project tasks can be assigned, they must be identified and detailed, and the needed skill levels for each determined so they can be matched to tasks.

To a certain extent, skill levels can be determined by job title. But levels will need to be defined within each job title competency. For example, each basic programmer job title (programmer trainee, junior programmer, programmer, senior programmer, and lead programmer) has a level of competency that can be matched to a specific task. Assigning a task to an unqualified person can create problems, while assigning the same task to an overqualified person wastes resources. When time permits, personnel development should be considered, too, by using a project task to teach a person a new skill.

A Gantt chart will illustrate the task schedule in man-hours. This can be hand-drawn or created by using a project management application. The Gantt charts are to be duplicated as part of the project documentation. If this information is not in a project management program already on the corporate network, copies should be posted and provided to the projects coordinator and/or systems manager and IS manager. If there are several projects in process, they need not be provided to the IS head unless specifically requested.

When allocating task man-hours, the project manager should note the worker's past record for finishing in the time allowed. The project manager will check with the project worker to confirm that the time allowed is reasonable. If not, a different time allowance should be negotiated. In addition, contingency time should be added if needed, based on the worker's past performance record. If there is no previous record, time allowed should be more liberal. Ten percent above the original estimate is not unreasonable. The project manager will recompute the project time based on this new information, rearranging the schedule as needed. If a problem persists, the projects coordinator should be contacted. He/she will, if necessary, assign additional manpower to the project, possibly with personnel previously assigned to other projects. When this data has been analyzed by the computer project management program or manually, the project manager will complete the final staffing plan for the project.

Hardware and Software Delivery

Identify the required dates for the project's software and hardware delivery. Place orders in time to have the items in-house when needed. Contact the vendor a week before the due date to insure the item will arrive on time. Take appropriate action if it will be late. Key items will have extra lead time planned for any delays. Delays may be caused by the following reasons:

❖ Custom fabricated hardware

❖ Written computer software

❖ Shipping problems because of distance (Delays are more likely when items are shipped from abroad.)

❖ Items that have to be scheduled for processing, such as custom-printed forms

❖ Plants closed for vacation or because of a strike

At the same time, items should not be delivered too far in advance. If items come in before needed, there could be a storage problem, incurring an unnecessary expenditure. Also, items ordered too far in advance could become obsolete before being used or their prices might be lowered.

PROJECT OBJECTIVES

One main project objective is to deliver a particular result or end product within the scope and timeframe originally established and budgeted by the steering committee in a form accepted by the user as operational. The final product may be in the form of a new complex system, a report, a manual operation, etc. The end result may be tangible or intangible.

A second objective is to utilize the resources of the project team in the most effective manner. These resources, under the control of the project manager, should be expended in an optimal manner during the project life cycle.

COMMENT

Information systems has earned a poor record of project cost overruns and delays over the years. The longer it takes to deliver a product, the less likely it will be acceptable to the users, since needs change over time. Projects are delayed by changes—adding to the scope, which adds to the delay, and debases the final product objective, causing the project to run over budget and be late.

Project Life Cycle Objectives

The project life cycle is comprised of tasks accomplished by the prudent use of resources available. The effort to complete these tasks requires certain managerial, technical, and/or political skills:

A   **Managerial.** The managerial skill of the project manager plays a major role in achieving the project objective. However, the steering committee, systems manager, projects coordinator, and user management can assist or undermine the project manager's effectiveness.

B   **Technical.** The number of people assigned to the project and their technical skill directly affect IT results.

C   **Political.** The project team should minimize its political "campaigning" activities, but relationships between people are not devoid of political overtones. Almost all project tasks require contact with people outside the project team. The results of these contacts can assist or hinder the project objective.

The tasks identified within the systems life cycle are divided into subtasks so that, if necessary, more than one person can work on a task. Even when one person completes the subtasks, this division provides for more convenient milestones with which to report progress.

Project Product Objective

Standards must be set to confirm the project's product meets the product objective. Tangible objective product standards are easier to define and recognize than intangible ones.

The criteria for a project's successful completion must be defined in the feasibility study or in the project approval statement made by the steering committee. All involved management parties will have agreed to these criteria, including user management and the project manager. The project should not start the design phase until the acceptance criteria have been defined and accepted. These should include:

- ❖ The structure of the product
- ❖ The validation criteria
- ❖ The scope of the product

The validation criteria should include the following:

- ❖ User documentation and training required are specified and in place.
- ❖ Follow-up procedures are specified and in place.
- ❖ Technical documentation for maintenance of software is complete.
- ❖ System and volume tests meet standards set.
- ❖ System downtime is not more than agreed-to limits.
- ❖ Data content of the database meets agreement.
- ❖ User support is in place and operational.

PROJECT FORMULATION

Project formulation begins with the feasibility study. Next, the steering committee—or other decision-making authority—sets the project scope and finish date. Finally, project design considerations are added.

The actual finish date and final project cost are based on factors beyond the control of the project manager. The design estimate is also affected by these same essential estimating factors.

Essential Estimating Factors

Estimating completion dates and work hours needed becomes more accurate as the project advances. Unfortunately, this accuracy is needed much earlier in the project, when it can be the most helpful. Even the best project management software needs accurate estimates.

Research has shown that project members who estimate their own performance for completion times are consistently optimistic. For this reason, an independent (unbiased) group should be used on an ongoing basis to do the estimating for far more accurate results. The advantages of using an independent estimator, whether an individual or a group, are:

A **Unbiased opinion.** An independent party will be unbiased.

B **Estimate consistency.** Estimates will be consistent. Any discovered errors can be corrected for the person or group.

C **Performance database provided.** The employee performance can be monitored. This also provides a source of employee information for staffing projects.

Factors affecting the estimate accuracy and ways to minimize this distortion are:

A **Project size.** The project size can affect the time and effort needed for completion. This in turn affects the amount of calendar time needed and the final cost. The longer the project takes, the more the user can justify additional changes. Changes that will be required for a usable product will also take additional time to install, which can justifiably lead to more changes. This is called the "size snowball effect."

To reduce this possibility, the project undertaking should be as small as possible. Changes made after project completion will then be maintenance changes to a system already in operation. This is preferable to making the same changes to a yet untested system.

B **Project complexity.** The more project variables, the more time and effort it will take to complete. The size of a forecasting project may be relatively small, but very complex.

A complex project can require more development and more testing time than estimated. The complexity can be reduced if the project can be broken into modules, which also permits additional people to work on the effort.

COMMENT

Years ago, George wrote an artificial intelligence program for a General Electric engineering department which took eighteen months to complete. It should have taken six to eight months. The debugging of 45,000 machine instructions led to the discovery of a bug in the original formulas provided to the programmer.

C **Personnel productivity.** This is a universal problem with system and programming departments. In the IS data entry unit, the output minus the errors defines the person's productivity. If the source documents are simple input, the system for judging a worker's output is simple and fairly accurate. This is not the case with the systems and programming production estimates.

A systems analyst's past performance can be a gauge for estimating future performance for similar tasks. The difference in output of programmers has been estimated to be as high as 20 to 1 between the best and the worst.

All too often programmers are judged by how hard they work. The lengthy hours spent and lines of code produced all too often are used to determine a programmer's contribution to the company. Yet the hardest working data entry operator, for example, may be the least productive and rewarded as such.

If the project needs one or more programmers, it would be better to bring in proven contract programmers than utilize those of lower caliber in-house. Management is often willing to pay for good contract programmers, but not willing to pay competitive wages for better in-house programmers. A poorly performing programmer can reduce the group's total output.

COMMENT

An IS manager in Ohio has two systems employees whose salaries are higher than his. When asked why, he answers, "They are worth it."

D **Resources available.** Resources must have quality, but they must be available in quantity, too. There is no assurance that the people promised for the project will be available when needed. The longer the duration of the project, the greater this problem can become. People leave, retire, get promoted, or get reassigned to other higher priority projects.

If possible, make sure monies are budgeted to obtain contract help. It is better to have this money in reserve than to have to ask for it when it is needed, and be unsure of getting it.

E **Resource technology.** The physical and technical resources available to the project team also affect the estimate. These items can include:

1 **Work area.** The final work area can affect the productivity esti-mate. Is the project team housed together in a private area, or spread out into different locations without privacy?

2 **Programming tools.** Are the programming tools familiar to the staff? If the tools are new, will training be available in time to be effective?

3 **Computer hardware.** The PCs available can affect the project team's performance. Are laptop computers needed? What kind of networking is there? What about e-mail and voice mail?

4 **Project management software.** If warranted, a project man-agement software package should be used. It can help save time and effort needed to control the project. (See "Project Management Tools"on page 137.)

Factors Affecting Finish Date

There are factors other than incorrect time and cost estimates that affect the finish date, depending on the nature of the project, the user, corporate cul-ture, etc. Some of these factors can be any number of the following:

A **Adding programmer help.** If the project develops a need for one more programmer, it would be better to do without if the person being considered is not a high producer or performs poorly. In addi-tion, the "communication factor," which will slow down the other programmers, along with the new programmer's learning curve pro-ductivity loss, would probably reduce the total programming output. Therefore, it is better to work overtime for more output than to bring in a new person late in a project. Extended overtime will also reduce programmer productivity.

B **Project delays.** Project delays that extend the finish date can cause further delays. This is the "snowball delay effect." One delay creates other delays, which in turn create more delays, etc. Each delay will affect the time window for each succeeding task. People may be need-ed later than scheduled and may not be available. A new schedule must then be drawn up, based on the availability of key people. This can set a project back far enough that the user may now want to make changes, which will create more delays and increase the project's costs.

With a delay pending, an effective project manager will look ahead to anticipate what problems might occur. A project management soft-ware package can be helpful. Only as a last resort should the project team work overtime.

There should be enough money budgeted for overtime. The law requires overtime pay, for hourly people, which can cover programmers. But, when an hourly person makes more money than a salaried worker does, working the same number of hours or more, there will be problems. In this case, the salaried worker should be rewarded with "comp" days off after the project is over or a money bonus. A better reward would include both.

C **Staff turnover.** The loss of project members can have a significant impact on the project. The effect varies with the loss of staff. When new people come in, there is a learning curve to be expected. There will be a loss of work effort from the time a project member departs until the new person becomes fully productive. A problem can occur when a key user employee leaves, too. When anyone closely connected with the project leaves, the morale of the rest of the project members is affected. This may become a catalyst, causing others to quit, especially if problems exist with the project.

When extra effort and overtime are applied because of project slippage, there is an increase in employee turnover. There is a distinct correlation between employee turnover and overtime pressure.

COMMENT

It is within the realm of reason that a two-year project with twenty people could have over a 100-percent turnover before the project is completed—that is, if it is ever completed.

However, staff turnover is a normal thing and it should be anticipated. If there is a 10-percent turnover in personnel, and a two-year project has twenty people, no fewer than four people will leave at one time or another. This does not count company transfers or promotions.

One solution is asking for more people to start the project. Having key players under contract is another. Overtime bonus pay and time off at the project end also encourage salaried people to stay.

D **New technology introduced.** When new technology is introduced to an ongoing project, it takes away available hours of time from the project, which in turn can result in calendar time lost. Training time is required and there is always a learning curve.

COMMENT

If CEOs can get million-dollar bonuses with firms losing money in the U.S., why can't all project members who complete a project be paid a bonus? It could be prorated to the finish date. This is done every day with contracts for outside construction projects. It certainly could be cost justified. Though there is a lack of research for this theory, we are willing to assist any firm willing to try it.

For these reasons, it is best not to introduce any new technology to a project past the analysis phase. If new technology must be added, it would be beneficial to have a new person join the project early who has already mastered the new technology skills.

E   **Administrative paperwork.** With the current trend to downsize secretarial staff, the project manager is now expected to perform these duties, which include word processing, filing, inputting data to spreadsheets, maintaining a project log, etc. This diverts time from the project manager's main function, which is managing the project.

A clerk typist should be assigned to the project and expected to stay until it is completed or abandoned. This person may expand his/her duties to also be of help to other members of the project. If such a person is not available in-house, contract outside part- or full-time help. This position should be listed on the staffing request for the project when the budget is planned.

Project Design

The last phase in the project formulation is the design phase. At this point the feasibility study and project estimation and analysis are complete. In the design phase, details are formulated from which the program or operation will be constructed. The design can provide the criteria for writing or purchasing a computer program, or it can be a scheme for a manual procedure operation or a new report, etc.

The actual construction can begin after the design phase. It is sometimes feasible for the construction to start even before the design is complete, reducing the calendar time when there is a justifiable need.

Tools are now available that can accelerate the design function. They can be used alone or in combinations. The following is a sample of what is available:

❖ Prototyping	❖ Phased delivery
❖ Joint application development	❖ Simulation

Systems maintenance requires about two-thirds of all programming effort at most IS installations. Effort expended in design, construction, and documentation can reduce this time. This planning can help formulate a much more successful system, which will open up more time for new project development efforts.

PROJECT RESOURCES

IS project resources are comprised of people, tools, techniques, and education. These assets have a profound effect on the success of an IS project. IS organizations with continuous ongoing projects should have a source of project resource information. Depending on the size of the system, this could be the systems manager or projects coordinator with the added duties of resource person for project tools, techniques, and education.

People Resources

People are by far the major expenditure for most IS project efforts, and a record of their activities must be maintained. A project file and a project management file must be maintained on a project management system of all current projects and their assigned personnel, as well as contract personnel and all user assigned personnel. In addition, active personnel will be entered on a personnel project display chart.

After a project is completed, data from the project file will be entered in a personnel project history file, which will contain data records of each completed project such as:

- ❖ Name
- ❖ Job title
- ❖ Project ID
- ❖ Planned start and finish dates of project
- ❖ Actual start and finish dates
- ❖ Hours committed to each project task
- ❖ Hours required to finish each project task

❖ Duties involved for each assigned task

❖ Time ratio (hours required divided by assigned hours

❖ Total project time ratio

The project file of all current projects and the project management file will be maintained by the projects coordinator, who is responsible for allocating personnel resources for the projects. These files are part of the project management system used for controlling people for projects.

The projects coordinator allocates human resources by job title. All consultants and contract personnel will be given the same standard internal job titles assigned to IS personnel. A descriptive narration following the job title will be used when needed. The titles are:

❖ Projects coordinator

❖ Project manager

❖ Assistant project manager

❖ Systems manager

❖ Project secretary

❖ Project librarian

❖ Systems analyst

❖ Systems and procedure analyst

❖ Industrial engineer

❖ Analyst programmer

❖ Senior programmer

❖ Programmer

❖ Junior programmer

❖ Business systems analyst

❖ Data manager

❖ Database administrator

❖ Database specialist

❖ Network specialist

❖ Quality assurance auditor

Project Management Tools

There have been over 700 computer software packages produced for mainframe, minicomputers, and PCs. The prices start at shareware levels and go into the thousands of dollars. Today there are some effective packages for Windows-based PCs, Macintosh, and Unix systems.

COMMENT

Microsoft Project is by far the most popular PC-based project management package. There are also numerous Web-based applications available for managing enterprise-level projects.

When selecting a project management package, first look for software that will run on the hardware and operating system already installed. Second, choose the least complex package that will do the job. Other features that must be considered are:

- ❖ User support
- ❖ User friendliness
- ❖ Reliability

The package should contain:

- ❖ Work breakdown structure (WBS)
- ❖ Single-source data entry
- ❖ Calendar support
- ❖ PERT and CPM charting
- ❖ Online tutorials
- ❖ A database information repository for multiple projects

It should be able to:

- ❖ Perform "what if" scenarios.
- ❖ Identify critical paths and compute slack time.
- ❖ Produce graphics.
- ❖ Support capture of resources for allocation to tasks.
- ❖ Compare planned to actual Gantt charts.
- ❖ Plot milestones.

Other features worth considering:

- ❖ Can be networked.
- ❖ Can handle multiple projects.
- ❖ Has resource leveling.
- ❖ Training is available.
- ❖ Has individual resource calendars for vacation and training times.
- ❖ Can show work completed versus budgeted milestones.

Project Techniques

There is a wide range of project planning techniques. Some require a computer and supporting software, while others utilize manual methods. No one technique resolves all project management needs.

A **PERT charts.** PERT charts can display the total project with all scheduled tasks shown in sequence. These can be produced manually or by using computer project management software. The displayed tasks show which ones are in parallel and can be performed at the same time.

PERT and CPM charts look alike. The only difference is how the task times are computed. The CPM method uses one value (most likely time) for determining the time each task will take. PERT requires a calculation as follows:

$$\text{TASK TIME} = \frac{T_o + T_p + 4T_n}{6}$$

T_o = optimistic time

T_p = pessimistic time

T_n = most likely time

The critical path of the PERT/CPM chart computes the project duration. This can be done manually or by using a project management program. The critical path can be worked backward from a finish date or forward from a start date.

The PERT/CPM chart will show the slack times. Slack time occurs when a task takes less time to do than a parallel critical path task. This information can be valuable. For example, suppose the critical path needs to be reduced in total time by two days, and assume a critical path task of twelve days is found which has a parallel slack task of ten or fewer days. Simply have the critical path task work overtime two Saturdays, and the total project time is reduced by two days. This is a very simple illustration; more complex solutions for reducing the total project time can be found by using a project management program.

The PERT/CPM chart can be the input for the Gantt charts. Each leg of the PERT/CPM chart can become a Gantt chart, displaying the scheduled calendar days. The chart can be available on screen from a project software package and/or placed on the office wall.

B **Gantt charts.** Gantt charts are used to show calendar time task assignments in days, weeks, or months. Task progress and milestones can be shown on the chart. The number of days required to complete a task that reaches a milestone can be compared with the planned number. The actual worked days, from actual start to actual finish, are plotted below the scheduled days. This information can give a forewarning that the task is not on schedule, and adjustments can be made.

Gantt charts can also be used to show dollars allocated versus dollars spent. This information can be compared to the status of task work completed.

Tasks can also be broken down into subtasks, and both used to identify the persons assigned. Charts can be produced showing a person's task type assignment by projects. The overall project status displayed allows the project manager to assign or reassign personnel as needed. It also shows him/her when there is a need for shifting project schedules and can warn of future problems.

Gantt charts can be produced on graph paper or magnetic boards, or by computer project management software. If the latter, the charts can be displayed on a corporate intranet for easy access by the entire team.

Project Management Education

There is a wide range of project education resources today, from informal self-paced education to more formal presentations. Sources are available in the following forms:

A **Reading material.** Many books and articles have been written on this subject. The local library will have a periodical index and books-in-print text. Look under "project management" for the most current source selection. Larger town libraries now have computer access to this information. If the library does not have what you need, it can copy periodical articles and obtain books through interlibrary loans.

B **Seminars.** Seminars are offered by professional organizations as well as others, such as American Management Association, Education Services Department, 135 West 50th Street, New York, NY 10020 (1-800-225-3215); SkillPath Seminars, 6900 Squibb Road, Mission, KS 66201-2768; and Project Management Institute, 130 South State Road, Upper Darby, PA 19082 (215-734-3330). Check the library for more names and addresses.

C **Videotapes.** There are commercially available videotapes on project management.

D **College classes.** Colleges offer project management classes, both in engineering and business programs. These classes are often at the graduate level, most with no prerequisite.

E **Project management professional organization.** The Project Management Institute, 130 South State Road, Upper Darby, PA 19082 (215-734-3330) publishes a monthly "Project Management Journal" and holds seminars.

PROJECT PROGRESS

The project progress is tracked in three ways: task completion, progress measurement, and reporting. This tracking begins when the project starts and ends after it is terminated. Not all projects are completed but all are terminated. Those that are not completed but terminated are the ones most often noted as failures.

Task Completion

As task milestones are reached, this information will be entered into the project management program. Completed tasks are assessed for quality, completion effort required, and effect on the project schedule. The hours estimated to complete the task effort will be compared with the actual hours, and this information will be retained for correcting future estimates.

This task completion information will be utilized to identify the project status at different points in time, and will be discussed in status meetings. If projects start to fall behind schedule, solutions will be sought. The following are some of the solutions that can be used to take care of project slippage:

A **Overtime.** Overtime should be used only for completing critical path tasks and only in the short-term. If the need for overtime becomes routine, it can affect the personnel turnover rate. The best time for paid overtime is after Christmas, and the worst time is during the summer months.

B **Assign more people.** Assigning people at the start of a project is less a problem than adding more later on. The worst time is at the end. As more people are added, the communication required between project members reduces the output per worker, and the learning curve becomes a factor, too. As a result, the project effort could end up less effectively completed than if no further people had been added.

C **Farm out a task to a vendor.** This action has merit if the vendor has reliable skills in the appropriate area. For the best results, the vendor should be given advance notice to expect the project.

D **Reduce the project scope.** If the user management is willing to reduce the project scope, this may be an effective solution to project slippage, helping to keep the quality of the remaining project tasks intact.

E **Reschedule module delivery.** Delay modules that may not be required for the finish date. This could be a better solution than reducing the project scope.

F **Request additional funds.** If you're over budget, more money will have to be requested. The sooner this is done, the better, because as the end of the fiscal year approaches, money becomes less available. If the dollars represent people cost, this is not so much of a problem. Salaried people do not require overtime pay, and both hourly and salaried people are budgeted for, whether they are working on a project or at their regular jobs.

Progress Measurement

Items that must be controlled and managed should be monitored for both quantity and quality. It is harder to measure the quality of output than quantity at the time the work is being done, since the quality of the programming effort starts to show up only when the programs are tested and debugged. Therefore, the testing should not be delayed.

Employee time is the greatest cost of the project, and it should be closely monitored to provide information to gauge the results in terms of the effort exerted. Everyone must complete a time sheet, including the project manager and contract workers and/or consultants. Some of the project management packages collect this data online and summarize it in a weekly report, automatically applying the time and dollar values to relevant project tasks.

So as not to intimidate the employees or have them spend too much time collecting this data, do the following:

A **Explain why the data is needed.** Demonstrate the process used to record the time and explain why it is used. Encourage the use of real numbers, not made-up ones or estimates. Stress the fact that the information is for their benefit, too.

B **Simplify the recording.** Do not require too much detail. Let people know they may receive a telephone call from a spouse or go to the restroom. According to the time measurement people, workers are normally allowed 10 percent of their work time for personal time.

Have the time sheets turned in or inputted to the computer daily. Efforts expended on Monday morning are difficult to remember by Friday afternoon. For forms inputted to the computer, use scannable documents. Ideally, have the worker input the data from his/her own workstation.

Do not insist that the time utilized agree with the required time.

C **Use continuous work sampling.** Note this alternative to having the employees keep track of work time would relieve them of this effort and most likely would be more accurate. (However, it would be more costly.)

◻ **Confirmation of estimates.** Inform employees that the time estimates on which the project is constructed need to be confirmed. Estimates are only approximations and should be corrected, if wrong. This cannot be done without keeping track of the actual time spent.

As a byproduct, workers will be more productive if monitored.

Project Reporting

Project members should submit weekly and monthly project reports to their respective project managers, who then forward copies to the projects coordinator. He/she will compile a monthly report of all projects for the head of information systems and the steering committee. The monthly report will also be sent to the systems manager if the systems manager is not the projects coordinator.

The project team should have a brief status meeting late Friday afternoon to summarize the week's work. Any catching up can be done on Saturday, if necessary. From this meeting and the project management program information, the Monday status report will be produced by the project manager and issued to the project team and the projects coordinator. This status report will note the progress made, what tasks are behind schedule, and what effort is being made to catch up. Tasks still to begin will also be reported.

The monthly report will recap the weekly reports and forecast the project's status for the next month. If the current month's status does not agree with last month's forecast the reasons will be given. The monthly report will provide the percent probabilities that the project will meet the finish date and the budget provided. Dollar variances of over 5 percent or more than $500 must be explained. Any future items that may affect the project should be reported (such as people going on vacation, leaving, etc.).

A final report, written by the project manager, will be sent to the projects coordinator recapping the project's major issues. Problems encountered and how to avoid them in the future will be presented. People who did outstanding work will be noted. This report is only for the projects coordinator who will write a completed project report and submit it to the systems manager if he/she is not the project coordinator, the head of information systems, and the Steering Committee.

PROJECT COMMUNICATIONS

The flow of information concerning a project comes in the form of written communications, e-mail, voice mail, and meetings. Each has its advantages and limitations.

A **Written communications.** These are letters, memos, and e-mail. Letters are used for communications that go outside the firm. Memos and e-mail are preferred for written internal communications. A standard format is used for both types.

B **Voice mail.** Voice mail is used to communicate verbal information. This can be sent to more than one receiver.

C **Meetings.** Meetings are very important, but costly. Project managers can spend over 50 percent of their time in meetings. There are two types of meetings: the one-way communications meeting and the two-way meeting. The one-way meeting is a meeting to inform. The two-way meeting is used to resolve an issue.

Following are procedural steps to use as a guide for conducting a meeting:

1 Write an agenda with time limits for each item.

2 Send out copies of the agenda to all personnel invited to attend.

3 Begin and end the meeting on time.

4 Keep minutes of the meeting and include the names of those present.

5 Limit the number of people for two-way communication meetings to ten to twelve.

6 Arrange the seating for the best communication and control.

7 Place important subjects first on the agenda.

8 Discussion procedures:

❖ Keep to the agenda.

❖ Be aware of supervisor and subordinate relationships.

❖ Draw out shy participants.

❖ Give everyone an opportunity to be involved in the discussion.

MULTIPLE-PROJECTS MANAGEMENT

Seldom does an information systems operation have only one project in process. Therefore, multiple-project management must be considered. The systems manager is responsible for the effort, but may delegate this responsibility to a projects coordinator.

All projects must utilize the methodology of reporting, operation, naming conventions, and so on. This standard must be universal so that resources shared will present no problem when being exchanged. The reports received must also be consistent because of the need to combine them when reporting to the system manager if the manager is not the project coordinator, the IS head, and the steering committee. A database of all personnel (including their job titles) who are involved in projects will be maintained. The database will include a list of project titles, dates of assignment, and time spent on those projects. The database will identify any person(s) being assigned more than one task at a time.

Resource Sharing

The projects coordinator is responsible for overseeing the multiple projects and assigning IS personnel to the different projects. If there is a problem with an assignment, the IS head will resolve the problem. This projects coordinator is also responsible for overseeing contract personnel and consultants. Arrangements for others, who can be on loan, are the sole responsibility of the projects coordinator.

The weekly reports will indicate the status of each project and its tasks. The coordination of the people by the projects coordinator makes it possible for resources to be commandeered from one project for another when necessary. Coordination duties also include the authorization to prioritize projects and tasks within projects.

Backup Personnel

When a large number of people (over thirty) are engaged in project activities, it would be prudent to have extra key workers reporting to the projects coordinator to provide for a needed manpower buffer. The type of personnel that would most likely be needed in the buffer pool would be:

- ❖ Project secretaries
- ❖ Programmers
- ❖ Systems analysts
- ❖ Network personnel
- ❖ Database personnel
- ❖ IS trainers
- ❖ Documentation writers
- ❖ Systems and procedure analysts
- ❖ Project librarians

Scope Management

With more than one project in process, there can be problems of boundary management with users. To avoid this problem, the projects coordinator must be aware of projects that have overlapping scopes. Not only can this cause wasted effort if not policed, but company political problems as well. Projects must be viewed in a proactive light to prevent this from happening.

The projects coordinator will have at his/her disposal the repository plans of all projects in process, as well as planned projects. This information should be kept on a database provided by a PC program management system.

COMMENT

Larry Johnson, a project management consultant, did an excellent job of presenting his style of project management in a video production titled *Project Management*. Volume one is *Planning and Organization* and volume two is *Tracking, Control and Follow-up*. The ISBN number is 1-55977-067-8. It is marketed by CareerTrack Publications, 3085 Center Green Drive, Boulder, CO 80301-5408.

Larry noted that when a project is terminated, there should be a party to celebrate. The end of a project does not necessarily indicate that it was completed. A project's termination may also come in the form of a cancellation. Whatever the reason, it still calls for a party to celebrate the occasion.

6

CORPORATE IT COMPUTER OPERATIONS: ENSURING SECURITY AND SAFETY

IT COMPUTER OPERATIONS POLICIES

This section sets down the policies governing an information systems computer center operation. The operations area is restricted to operational and identified vendor support personnel; but because of today's distributed data processing and computer networks, access is not limited to persons physically entering the area. It can also be vulnerable to unauthorized access through telecommunications, so every precaution should be taken.

Security and Safety in the Computer Room

To maintain proper computer room security and safety, the following policies are in place:

A **Restricted access.** Only authorized personnel—those persons needed to operate, supervise, or provide maintenance to the area and its equipment—are permitted entry to the IS computer operation area. Anyone entering or leaving the area must sign a sign-in/sign-out log or an alternative tracking system.

B **Restricted online access.** Online access to the system from outside the computer center is controlled with proper user and ID access codes that are changed no less than twice a year. Codes no longer authorized should be deleted as soon as possible. Telephone access will have caller ID screening.

C **Power supply.**

1 The computer center area has its own power supply connected to the main power source for the building.

2 A backup UPS (uninterrupted power supply) or a fail-safe device is required to prevent a disk crash if the main power fails.

3 A self-starting generator is available to provide emergency power for work lights, room ventilation, and air conditioning.

D **Air conditioning.** The computer center has its own backup air conditioning system.

E **Construction hazards.** The computer room area is not adjacent to any natural gas or liquid-transporting pipes, high-voltage lines, or magnetic radiation sources.

F **Fire precautions.** Fire extinguishers are the safest possible precaution. All materials used in constructing the computer room area are fireproof or fire retardant.

G **Smoke detectors.** Smoke detection equipment is installed and connected to a monitoring center when no personnel are on duty.

H **Data backup.** Database and file backups are kept as current as is reasonable. Off-site data and software backup is maintained. The off-site storage has a fireproof rating for secondary data devices. Vendor contracted backup of online real-time transaction data is recommended as demand may require.

I **Low profile of the computer area.** The computer center area must maintain a low profile. No signs directing persons to the center should be displayed.

J **Safe location.** The actual site of the IS computer center must not be located on a flood plain or within 50 miles of an earthquake fault.

Housekeeping in the Computer Center

The following are policies that apply to housekeeping in the computer center:

A No smoking, drinking, or eating is permitted.

B Operations personnel are responsible for maintaining a clean working area.

C Operators are not to attempt to repair any equipment without the specific authorization of the supervisor or maintenance vendor.

D Operators are not to alter programs without specific authorization of the supervisor.

E The computer is to be used for only assigned operations.

F Temperature and humidity are to be monitored at all times and kept within the recommended ranges for the equipment.

Disaster and Recovery Plans

Well-organized disaster plans help ensure the firm's continued operation in case of an emergency. Likewise, an effective recovery plan in the event of computer hardware or software failure is a necessity. The company cannot be without an IS computer operation for more than a minimal amount of time.

GENERAL OPERATIONS

This section covers general procedures to be followed by the IS computer center personnel and any visitors. Each center is an enclosed shop with operating areas restricted to only those persons required for the center's operation.

Security and Safety

Procedures that apply to the security and safety of the computer center are:

A Lock the computer operations area at all times.

B Restrict access to the computer center to operations personnel, approved vendor maintenance personnel, and/or operations management personnel due to report for duty at a specified time. Tours by visitors, employees, vendors, or customers must be authorized and approved by the head of IS computer operations.

C Use a sign-in/sign-out log or a computer ID card access door-opening system to keep a record of all who enter the computer area including the time of entrance.

D Fire extinguishers and/or their controls must be easily identifiable. Instructions should be posted next to the instruments.

E Operations personnel are responsible for knowing:

1 Location of fire alarms, extinguishers, and controls for firefighting systems

2 Emergency power-off procedures

3 Emergency procedures for notifying the fire department, the programmer on call, and the appropriate management personnel

Housekeeping Standards

Standard measures are required to maintain cleanliness and ensure safety in the computer operations area.

A Eating, drinking, and/or smoking are not permitted in the computer center area. Post signs to this effect in the computer center and on or near the outside door of the computer center.

B Operators under the influence of prescribed sedatives or similar medication are to be given assignments that will not endanger the operator or the operation.

C Operations personnel are responsible for the general cleanliness in their areas. Items removed for use are returned to the area where they belong.

D Personnel will not place their feet on top of desks or equipment. Shoes must be worn at all times.

E Personal radios, TVs, or audio equipment are not permitted in the computer center area.

F Personal phone calls are limited to five minutes.

Downtime Procedures

When there are hardware or software failures, downtime procedures require computer operators to describe and record:

A General conditions at the time of the failure

B Unusual activity observed in any input/output device prior to computer failure

C Information received from outside sources for correcting the problem

Disk Handling

Proper disk handling ensures data availability for jobs and reduces read-write errors.

A Store removable disks in proper containers when not in drives.

B File disk-storage containers in place when not in use.

C   Identify contents of disks by external labels placed on the front of the disk.

Tape Handling

Following are procedures for handling tapes:

A   General tape procedures

❖   Clean hands are a must for operators handling tapes.

❖   Read-write heads should be cleaned in accordance with the manufacturer's recommendations.

❖   Keep tapes in protective containers when not in use.

❖   To prevent accidental recording, read-only tape reels should have their write-protect rings in place and tape cartridges should have their record tabs in place.

B   Tape handling procedures

❖   Tape reels are handled near the hub to avoid crimping tape edges.

❖   Tape should be mounted squarely and evenly on the tape transport.

❖   Tape reels should be checked after use to discover irregular rewinding.

❖   Tape drive doors are closed when tapes are not in the process of being mounted or dismounted.

OPERATING PROCEDURES

Computer room operating procedures are a combination of vendor-provided instruction manuals and programmer's instructions peculiar to each application. If any procedure appears incorrect, confusing, or contradictory, the problem should be brought to the attention of the appropriate operations supervisor.

Process Flow

The flow of source document input and hardcopy output is funneled through a reception area or user input/output counter. This area provides a buffer to the area outside computer center operations.

Source documents are routed to the data entry unit, which enters the data and transmits it to the computer room. For purposes of control, the data entry area is separate from the computer room. As with any part of the computer center operations area, only authorized personnel may gain entry.

Data being carried into the computer room comes from the data entry area or directly from the receiving input/output counter where it is usually in the form of tapes, disks, and turnaround documents. (Turnaround documents are output documents the computer generates and sends out—for example, utility bills, installment payment documents, factory timecards, etc.). When they are returned, their computer-printed information can be read by both computer input devices and the human eye.

Computer operations keeps off-line data in a storage area called the data library, which is controlled by a librarian or computer operator who logs tapes and disks in and out. Entry to the library is through the computer room. In addition to the flow of data between operations and the library, there is a flow of backup data to and from an off-site data storage location.

Computer Operations Procedures

The heart of the IS operation center is the computer. Operation of the computer equipment is the duty and responsibility of the computer operator. His/her duties and responsibilities vary depending upon the computer, and the policies and procedures of each computer center operation. In a small shop, one individual may be responsible for virtually all activities. Regardless of the size of the computer center operation or the computer system used, some duties or tasks are traditionally performed by an operator, although the computer operation may at times be run unattended.

Daily shift duties. The operator beginning his/her shift first checks with the one ending the prior shift to ascertain if there are any problems. Then the operator:

1 Checks for system messages on the display monitor or system message log book.

2 Checks the schedule of the previous shift. If there are any priority jobs not completed, the operator may rearrange the job schedule. If there is a major problem, he/she contacts the operations supervisor.

3 Performs housekeeping tasks such as checking the tape drives, disk drives, etc.

4 Updates the tapes and disks status required for the rest of the shift. Sets aside tapes and disks to be taken to the data library. Goes to the data library to exchange tapes and/or disks.

5 Checks to see if a backup is required and, if so, performs it.

6 Checks the monitor for the status of jobs being run. If the system does not generate its own processing log, the console operator maintains a written one for each shift's operation. The information logged consists of the number of the job completed, the start and finish times, and any remarks.

7 When questions arise about a job being run, the operator checks the operator's manual and related documentation for that particular job. When all else fails, contact the supervisor.

8 If an error causes a job to be terminated prematurely, the operator corrects the problem by following the restart procedure for that job.

Other shift responsibilities.   In addition to general tasks, some other duties and responsibilities for the operator are:

1 Power up/power down the system. The operator may be required to turn the computer system on and perform an IPL (initial program load) procedure.

2 Turn the computer off (power down) if the computer center does not operate 24 hours a day, or for other specified reasons. The operator follows standard power down procedures as listed in the operator's manual.

3 Initiate the processing procedure required if there are any batch jobs to be run. The operator checks, before starting the job, to ensure that all the required data is available.

4 Monitor the batch-processing job being run.

5 Check tapes or disks into the computer center from other sources.

6 Check in any turnaround documents using the job procedures for logging in documents.

7 Transmit messages to online users of the system including down time and its duration.

8 Change the priority of jobs waiting to be printed by accessing the spooling system.

Administrative responsibilities.   The person responsible for the computer operation performs the administrative responsibilities. In a one-person department, this can be the operator. These responsibilities include the following:

1 Order supply items.

2 Order and maintain technical manuals.

3 Distribute technical briefs and standards.

4 Schedule computer maintenance.

5 Design and maintain special forms and logs required for computer center operations.

6 Schedule operators by shift.

7 Train new operators.

Peripheral Equipment Operation Procedures

Computer systems have a host of online and off-line peripheral devices. In a single-operator shop, the operator is responsible for the main computer and all these devices. In a one-person computer center operation, the individual responsible for the entire operation functions as the data entry person, the computer and peripheral equipment operator, the data librarian, and the center administrator. In a larger operation, these duties are assigned to different people.

Depending on the size of the operation, peripheral device operation procedures can be done by one or many operators. These procedures are defined by vendor's manuals or written by a systems analyst. They are defined as duties or tasks required by the operations personnel. Here are examples.

Printers. The computer spooling program controls the printing operations. The operator determines what kind of paper is required for the scheduled printouts. The center may employ more than one kind of printing device, each with its own manufacturer's operations manual. A printer operator might be responsible for any of the following kinds of printers:

❖ Impact printers

❖ Wire-matrix printers

❖ Ink-jet printers

❖ Laser printers

❖ Computer output microfilm

Duties required for printer operations include:

1 Change or add paper to the printer following the manufacturer's instructions.

2 Check print alignment before starting the printer when a job changes.

3 Monitor paper supply and output stacks.

4   Remove paper jams.

5   Check output at the start of each job to determine if it is necessary to change printer ribbons, replace toner or inkjet cartridges.

6   Perform minor preventive maintenance, as designated in the instruction manual, and clean the machine when needed.

Magnetic tape drives.   Tape drives are reel or cartridge. Cartridge drives present less of a handling problem than reel drives, but with either kind, the tape should never be touched. When mounting a reel tape on a drive, care should be taken to avoid letting the tape touch the floor. The following required procedures apply to both types:

1   Tapes are never stacked on top of each other in a flat position.

2   Tapes are never left on top of tape drives.

3   Tapes are always write-protected prior to reading.

4   External labels are checked before mounting tape to ensure that the correct tape is being used.

5   Magnetic tapes are cleaned as needed.

6   A record of all tape read/write errors is maintained: the tape number, drive number, type of error, time and date of the error.

7   A record of scratch tapes is maintained. (Scratch tapes are those that have been previously used for other jobs but the data they contain are no longer needed.) All old external labels are removed.

8   Tape error messages that appear on the monitor are responded to immediately.

Direct-access devices.   Removable direct-access storage can be in the form of disks, Zip disks, or CDs. The operator handling tape drives often handles the direct-access devices, too. Online computer systems are noted for having many direct-access storage devices. Operating procedures for the devices are defined in the manufacturer's manuals, but some duties and responsibilities are common to almost all devices. Following are duties or procedures associated with direct-access devices:

1   Floppy disks, Zip disks, and CDs are retained in their storage containers when not in use.

2   A felt pen is used when writing on disk labels.

3   Disks and Zip disks are not placed on disk drives or close to telephones.

4 Blank disks are formatted in advance and kept, ready for use, in a dust-free container.

5 The insides of disk and CD drives are kept free of foreign objects.

6 Prompt response to monitor messages is necessary. An operator takes corrective action by following the manufacturer's manual or disk operations manual. If instructions to correct the problem are not available, the operator contacts the lead operator or operations supervisor. Some of the more common problems noted by error messages are:

❖ File label errors

❖ Disk drive errors

❖ Duplicate file names

❖ Read errors

❖ Write errors

Other peripheral devices. Computer centers today utilize a large variety of peripherals in addition to standard printers, direct-access storage devices, and magnetic tapes. One may also be available for a specific computer center application. Some of the more common devices are:

❖ COM (computer output microfilm)

❖ Optical readers

❖ Magnetic-ink character readers

❖ Page scanners

❖ Modems

The degree of operator involvement depends on the device. The manufacturer's manual prescribes the correct operating procedure. Any additional instructions should be available in the operations procedure manual for the job being run.

In the event of equipment failure, the operations supervisor is notified. Operator requirements of the more common devices follow:

1 **COM.** The computer output microfilm device is most often a stand-alone off-line device requiring a tape input. Tape-handling procedures have been defined in the tape-handling duties section (see "Tape Handling," page 151). The operator follows the manufacturer's operating instructions in running scheduled jobs. Main duties required for the device are to:

❖ Perform minor maintenance as required by the instruction manual.

❖ Mount tapes for output as scheduled.

❖ Maintain a log of start and finish times by job.

❖ Clear any jams as prescribed in the instruction manual.

❖ Check distribution counts for each job.

❖ Make sure supplies are available before output is started.

2 **Optical readers.** Optical reader input documents can be user-generated documents or the computer center's own turnaround documents. Operation of the device follows the manufacturer's instructions. Input is most often in batch form. The main duties required for operating the device are to:

❖ Perform minor maintenance as required by the instruction manual.

❖ Maintain a log for the run times of each batch of input.

❖ Clear any jams as prescribed in the instruction manual.

❖ Repair or provide replacement documents for damaged documents.

3 **Magnetic-ink character readers.** This input device receives input from users and may have additional information keyed in at the data entry unit. Operating duties are similar to those for the optical readers.

4 **Modems.** The modem is a peripheral device that serves as an online input/output instrument between outside users and the IS computer. For the most part, it runs unattended. If the modem goes down or is known to be out of service, the operator provides users with information about the current or pending shut-down. Pending shut-downs can be transmitted as monitor displays.

REPORT DISTRIBUTION

There are many different types of forms created for printed reports. Forms and reports are not the same. A form is a sheet of paper, containing preprinted information and providing space for additional data. Preprinted information can be logos, headings, lines, boxes, or constant narratives, such as a payroll check. A report is information printed on blank paper.

Forms can be single sheets, as used by laser printers, or continuous, as used by impact printers. Preprinted forms are usually purchased, while flat forms can either be purchased or printed in-house. Reports can also be produced by COM units in the form of microfiche. Procedures for generating reports were covered under the "Peripheral Equipment Operation Procedures" on page 154.

Preparation of reports requires knowledge of how these reports are distributed; this information provides the basis for control of both reports and forms. Therefore, preprinted forms for inventory and control are part of the preparation of reports operation. Their inventory levels are dictated by quantity discount purchases and delivery times.

"Controlled forms"—such as payroll checks, bank drafts, and savings bonds—require special care to ensure their availability and security. They contain printed, usually sequential, numbers to help prevent theft. Close monitoring and storage of controlled forms is required. Discovering there aren't enough checks to meet the payroll is an unnerving experience for any IS operations manager. The report preparation area should have storage space available for both stock forms and controlled forms, with a fireproof, lockable container provided for controlled forms.

Preparation of Reports

Computer operations personnel are responsible for loading the correct forms or microfiche into the printing device when output reports are generated. When continuous forms are used, pin-feed margins and the pages remain attached until the entire job is complete.

Laser printouts and microfiche output require different preparation procedures. COM is usually processed off-line, while impact and laser printing occur online.

Continuous-forms procedures. If the continuous form is a multipart form with carbon paper, the carbon paper remains between the copies. When accounts payable and payroll checks are printed, the checks are not yet signed. Continuous form documents are processed as follows:

1 The printed reports are placed in a decollator. (See the procedure for operation in the manufacturer's instruction manual.)

2 If pin-feed margins are to be removed, the margin slitter on the decollator is turned on.

3 If multipart forms with carbon paper are used, the carbon paper is attached to carbon spindles on the decollator.

4 The forms are run through the decollator and stacked.

5 Forms that require bursting are run through the burster. Single sheet copies are stacked after the bursting operation.

6 Checks requiring imprinted signatures are imprinted with a continuous-form imprinter or during the bursting operation. The procedure used depends on the hardware available.

❖ **Accounts payable.** The accounts payable unit provides the imprinting stamp for writing accounts payable checks. When the checks are delivered to accounts payable, the imprinting stamp is also returned. The beginning and ending check numbers are reported to accounts payable in accordance with its procedure. All damaged checks are marked "VOID" and returned.

❖ **Payroll.** The payroll unit provides the imprinting stamp for writing payroll checks. When checks are returned to that unit, the imprinting stamp is also returned. The beginning and ending check numbers are reported to the payroll department in accordance with its procedure. All damaged checks are marked "VOID" and returned.

When running confidential payroll or expense reimbursement checks, only authorized personnel are allowed in the processing area and signs are posted to that effect.

7 When computer-printed reports have been prepared for distribution, they are moved into the distribution area. Confidential reports are placed in sealed cardboard boxes or envelopes.

Laser output procedures.   The preparation of laser-printed reports for distribution is as follows:

1 Single-copy reports are moved to the distribution area. Reports of more than one page are stapled together in the upper left-hand corner.

2 If more than one copy of each report is required, the pages are collated and stapled in the upper left-hand corner of each report.

3 The reports are moved to the distribution area.

Microfiche procedures.   Microfiche (COM) are processed as follows:

1 The operator checks to see if there is more than one copy of each microfiche document. If so, all copies (up to twenty) are placed in one microfiche envelope.

2 When there is more than one microfiche document to each report output, or multiple copies of each, the microfiche are sorted and then placed in their respective envelopes.

3 The report name is posted on the outside of the microfiche envelopes.

4 The envelopes are taken to the distribution area.

Report Distribution Procedure

The IS computer operations department produces a variety of reports. Some require extensive attention from the time they are printed until they are delivered.

The preparation, processing, and distribution information required for each report is posted to the Distribution Control Form (see Exhibit 6–1) which is completed by the systems analyst or programmer responsible. Procedures for processing these reports are as follows:

Report log maintenance. At the start of each day, a report generation listing is provided by the console or computer operator and forwarded to the report distribution area.

1 The operator crosses off the report on the Distribution Control Form with a yellow marker.

2 The operator posts the time the report was received after the name of the report on the Distribution Control Form.

3 At the end of each shift, the operator going off duty notifies the arriving operator of reports that have not been produced.

Distribution procedure. The person processing the reports checks the Distribution Control Form to be aware of their disposition. If there is any variation from what is expected, that person notifies the computer operator.

Changes to the Distribution Control Form are made only when a memo is received with instructions from the responsible systems analyst or programmer. The memo is held in a file as long as the report is produced.

When the reports are complete, the operator sets them aside for proper distribution. Those requiring maximum security are kept locked until such time as the documents leave the area.

Distribution methods. The distribution method for reports depends on the report's security status and the distance between the user and the data-processing center. The following options are available:

1 **User pickup.** Report users come to the computer center, or a satellite pickup area, to obtain their reports. Bins similar to the boxes used by post offices, but larger, are used for this purpose. Areas that require some degree of security will have locked doors on the bins.

EXHIBIT 6–1. Distribution Control Form

Report Title:

Report No: Security:

Effective Date: Supersedes:

Description:

Form No: Copies: Burst: Decollated:

Copy   Department   Title   Method

1

2

3

4

5

6

Special Instructions:

2   **IS computer operations delivery.** Computer operations center personnel deliver reports to recipients located near the computer operations or who require special equipment for large-volume delivery.

3   **Mail delivery.** The reports are picked up or delivered to the mailroom. Mailing methods are:

   a   **Interoffice mail.** Interoffice mailing envelopes are used for interoffice delivery.

   b   **Outside delivery.** Some computer-printed reports must be mailed through the U.S. Postal Service. These are items such as purchase orders, bills, and government reports. Packing or envelope inserting is done in the mailroom. Large shipments may be sent by UPS or some other agent.

DATA SECURITY

This section covers procedures to insure data security throughout the computer center operation. These procedures are designed to ensure that management and systems operations audit policies will be satisfied and support their enforcement.

Data Security Responsibility

One person is selected to be responsible for data security reports to the head of information systems and to a security committee of three to five members that authorizes the implementation of its policies. This committee will have a majority representation from the firm's audit area enabling the controller to influence policy and verify that the security responsibility is fulfilled in line with the audit and control policies of the firm. This data security responsibility may or may not be a full-time effort. The person may have a title reflecting the status of the position if it is full-time. Otherwise, the task will be undertaken in conjunction with other duties. If the latter is the case, the security position should not be subservient to the other responsibility. Suggested titles for the position are: security officer, security coordinator, supervisor or manager of security, chief of security, data security officer or coordinator, or data administrator.

Span of Data Security

A   Data security begins at the point data is captured for the Information Systems operation. The actual process of receiving and capturing raw data is under the domain of data security.

B The vehicle used to hold captured data will be returned to sender if required. The return will require a confirmation of time, date, title, and data contents. A record log will be maintained of the returns by item, date, and time, with the signature of the receiver. If the return vehicle or raw data documents are to be transported by a third party (UPS, U.S. Postal Service, or some other agent), a signed and dated receipt will be required to confirm the transaction. Receipts will be held for one year.

C Retained hardcopy raw data will be held under the jurisdiction of the data security person or delegated authority in a secure area until there is a disposition of the material. The length of time the material is kept will be predicated on policies for the various items.

Retained instruments used to convey data other than on hardcopy, such as tapes, disk, etc., will be kept in a secure place as other such records are kept. The length of time the material is kept will be predicated on policies for the various items.

The internal disposition of retained data instruments depends on their source. Tapes or disks that can be erased will be erased and returned to service. A log will be maintained of the erased items by day, title, and control identification. Each batch listing of erased items will contain the signature of the operator doing the erasing. The log will be kept for no less than one year. Raw data documents will be shredded. The level of shredding will depend on the level of security required:

1 Confidential data will be finely shredded.

2 Classified data will be cross-shredded.

3 Unclassified data will need only simple, one-way shredding.

A "destroy log" will be maintained of the shredding operation. The log will contain the name and identification of each batch of raw data. Each batch destroyed will list the level of security and the name of the person performing this duty. The log will be kept for no less than one year.

D Released data and information hardcopy will be duly recorded. ("466-1324" is data; "telephone number: 466-1324" is information.) If the report distribution procedure (see page 160) is not employed, a release log will be maintained for the local release of data and information hardcopy. Confidential hardcopy will be contained in a sealed envelope. The release log will record the signature of the person receiving the envelope, the date, the time, and the item description. The log will be kept for no less than one year. Documents or other storage devices released to outside the organization require second-party verification of the release entered into a log that will contain the item name and identification, date, time, method of shipment, the person releasing the material, and the person receiving the material. Otherwise, follow the distributions methods procedure (see page 160).

E Internal data (data on the system) and secondary storage will also be under data security care. If information systems employs a person as database administrator, that person will be responsible for the physical security of data and/or information. Required procedures for the safety of captured data and information and the policy enforcement will be the responsibility of the designated data security head.

Online Processing Data Security

Teleprocessing (LAN and WAN) and online IS computer access standards and protocol are the responsibility of the person delegated to data security. This subsection defines how the online data security system operates.

A **Access authorization for database data.** The data security person in concert with the database administrator will categorize the security access levels. The database administrator will group the records within a given database so that the record elements, as much as possible, have the same level of security. This is to prevent elements of a higher level from being accessed by a person with a lower-level access to the same record.

The database administrator will use the data dictionary to provide the access level of each listed element. A valid security method is to group only like-level security elements into the same record. However, an element of a lesser level may be included to avoid developing other records only for the sake of common security-level confirmation.

To enhance security, the data dictionary will list the programs authorized to access the data elements. This is to limit authorized program access to specific users, identified by the user's password. If the data dictionary does not provide for a given level of access for the user wanting the higher-level data elements, access will be denied. Employing an IS computer terminal may further enhance control by limiting terminals as to program access.

Gaining access to data is one thing, but unauthorized altering of the data is something else. The data dictionary should allow access to individual data elements based on password level, as follows:

1 Read a data element only.

COMMENT

This system is to prevent someone from getting into highly confidential data that should only be available to the controller. There have been cases of some very interesting data turning up on terminals that should not have had access to the data.

2 Change the data element.

3 Remove the data element.

In cases of vulnerable data, a procedure can be instituted to off-load the old data element and to record the time, the occurrence, and the password performing the alteration.

B **Access authorization for files data.** Files must only be accessed by approved user passwords, which should be grouped by access levels. This grouping should be a joint effort of the database administrator and the data security person. If there is no database administrator, the security person alone will classify which files are to be accessed by which password level. The level of the user's password controls his/her level of access to files as:

❖ Read only

❖ Change

❖ Remove

A file access log should be maintained by the computer system to record the time, file identification, and password accessing the files. If files are altered, off-load the changes—only records, as they were before the change, as an audit trail. This file should be under the control of the data security person and kept for no less than one year.

C **Control of password file.** The vendor-supplied passwords and account numbers should be removed before a system is placed into operation. The password control file is the responsibility of the data security official with access through an encrypted authorized password program. To access a listed code, the password will first need to be decrypted. This list will be under lock and key. The encryption instrument will be in a different locked location. A log will be maintained for each access of the password file, listing the reason, code, time, and date.

D **Granting of data set access.** The data dictionary will list the restrictions level for each data set. Access will be granted only to those authorized for access at the given level or higher.

E **Granting of access levels.** The security officer and database administrator authorize the granting of access levels, either for a given time period or an indefinite period. The security officer and database administrator will review the approved access levels no less than once each year. A random review will also be performed at a time known only to the security officer. The results of the review will be documented and filed.

The access level will be commensurate with the person's need, that is, the level determined by the job description, and changeable if a job requires higher access.

F **Termination of employees with restricted access.** An employee should not be terminated until he/she is denied all access to the system, if possible. The employee's password must be removed from that part of the system that accesses any data or program files.

G **Restricted access after voluntary employee termination.** When an employee gives notice, a review of whether to terminate or restrict access to privileged data should take place, and a decision be made within 24 hours of receiving notice.

COMMENT

Run a routine retail credit check on the financial status of a person receiving a highly vulnerable access level before granting the access code. Research indicates that desperate people tend to be much more susceptible to taking advantage of an ill-gotten opportunity than not. Also, a person's credit rating can change for the worse at any time, and it would be wise to be aware of this before it is too late.

Given access levels may require a great deal of protection because of the monetary vulnerability of the data elements. New and transferred personnel will require the appropriate screening for granting of and for determining respective levels of access.

COMMENT

There was a story some time ago of a U.S. government data-processing clerk who spent money like a member of Congress on his yearly salary of $23,000. By the time management started wondering just how he could support his new lifestyle, he had cashed millions of dollars in checks made out to his dummy company.

H **Data entry processing.** Data entry processing must be separate from file maintenance processing to protect the integrity of the system. File maintenance procedure is discussed under "File Maintenance Data Security" on page 168.

I **Security bypass.** Bypassing the security restrictions for online processing is not permitted, except by following the file maintenance procedure noted in the "File Maintenance Data Security" section.

J **Unauthorized access times.** Terminal access at other than authorized times or on unauthorized terminals will require supervisory approval. The supervisor authorizing the access will forward a memo requesting permission to the data administrator/data security person. That person will notify computer operations when granting the request, and this unit will initiate the procedure to allow the access after the following information is provided:

1 Person to be authorized access

2 Information/data to be accessed

3 Date and start/end times of access

4 Reason for access, other than normal conditions

Network messaging, when available, should be employed both to send the requesting memo and to notify computer operations, with the messages or memos saved for no less than 30 calendar days.

K **Online programmer file access.** No access will be permitted whatsoever for online programming or accessing and testing of database or files. This means all live database or files access, including even live archival data. Programmers may access only files copied for their use. Using copied files will require the approval of the database administrator, with the files provided by computer operations. Any such unauthorized access of live data or files will be grounds for dismissal. Strict operations control procedures should exist to prevent such accessing.

L **Data dictionary data protection definition.** The data dictionary will contain information about all the data elements and their respective applications. The level of protection granted or not granted will be noted in the data dictionary by element or data sets. Any corrections or changes to this information should be published and disseminated on or before the correction or procedure is performed.

File Maintenance Data Security

The file maintenance operation is under the jurisdiction of the database administrator. This includes the loading and maintenance of files and/or databases. The data administrator/data security person has the responsibility to establish policy for file maintenance data security, along with its privacy and integrity. File maintenance will be a separate procedure from that of data entry operations and will cover the updating of all files and databases.

❖ File maintenance
❖ Database maintenance
❖ File uploading
❖ Generating a work access file or database for a given programmer for access and the testing of programs

Confidential, classified, and unclassified file maintenance will be performed and documented under supervisory review which will ascertain:

❖ When the maintenance was done (date and time)
❖ Who performed the maintenance
❖ What files were processed
❖ What data elements were affected
❖ What transpired in the maintenance process
❖ What files were reproduced, if any, and the disposition of the files
❖ What audit trails are there to confirm the process, such as transaction files and/or premaintenance files or databases

Very confidential file maintenance procedures require the review of the data administrator/data security person to identify what, if any, maintenance requirements were performed at the supervisory level. This file maintenance will also record the same documentation as in confidential or unclassified file maintenance.

Password Controls

The data security person defines the password policy. The database administrator stipulates the procedure. If the data administrator challenges this, the problem is presented to the data security committee whose decision is final.

Types of passwords.   There may be two kinds of passwords: one assigned by the database administrator or an agent, and one that is self-assigned. A person given a self-assigned password receives a temporary assigned password until it is changed after he/she first signs on. The authorization of user-assigned passwords is limited to only those persons approved by the data security person.

Changing of passwords.   All passwords will be changed from one to twelve times per year by the authority of the data administrator who may call for a password change any time there is a need.

Password display.   Computer systems will suppress passwords and IDs on the monitor screen and all printed output. Passwords are not to be displayed on or near the monitor. A second notice of a violation of this procedure requires a reprimand by the database administrator/data security person. Any serious problem will be referred to the security committee.

COMMENT

How many times have you seen a password posted to the monitor? 3M's Post-It notes were not invented for this purpose!

Password coding.   Passwords will be limited to no more than ten alphanumeric characters. At no time will a person or department/unit name be part of the password. No whole word found in a dictionary will be used.

Password files.   Password files will be encrypted. The database administrator and the data security person will keep the encryption code keys. This information is placed in a fireproof and locked container. A backup copy is enclosed in a sealed envelope and placed in an off-site location. When a new encryption code key is required, the database administrator or the data security person inspects the sealed envelope insuring the envelope has not been tampered with before the contents are destroyed.

Terminal Controls

Access to the system by terminals requires both physical and procedural operation controls for direct access to the main system or a network system. Terminals employing both WAN and LAN systems should require stricter controls than those used by terminals employed in the computer operations areas. Required controls are:

A **Physical location.** The actual physical location of a terminal is a major consideration. Remote or secluded areas invite unauthorized access attempts and are more vulnerable to vandalism and theft. When such a location is unavoidable, the terminal should be in a room that is locked after normal business hours. If not possible, enclosing the unit or using a cable lock should be considered.

B **Terminal locks.** Terminals that can access any databases or that are in remote or secluded areas must have locks. Personnel assigned such a terminal will be responsible for locking the unit when not in the general area for an extended period, such as more than an hour. When more than one person is assigned the use of the machine, the last to leave the area is responsible for locking the terminal and will be reprimanded by his/her supervisor of any infraction. A supervisor not enforcing this procedure will be reprimanded in writing by the data administrator, with copies of the notice sent to the person's immediate superior and all members of the data security committee. All personnel using terminals should be made aware of this policy both in their training and in the written terminal procedures.

Each lock will be different from the rest. In the event a work group is to share a group of terminals, a common key may be used. The person responsible for issuing keys holds duplicate keys under locked conditions. The data administrator, members of the data security committee, and computer center terminal maintenance employees will each be issued a master key. The master terminal keys will never be removed from the firm's premises.

C **Terminal operating system controls.** The computer operating system maintains a log record of each terminal sign-in, consisting of date, timeframe, and password for each access. The same software controls the access using the time-of-day frame and automatic time-outs. Any violations are logged by terminal, password, time, and date. A listing of the violation log, by date, is forwarded to the data security person and the computer operations manager daily.

The database administration software ascertains which terminal, along with the allowable password, can access which file. The data dictionary identifies which users are allowed to initiate transactions. The final control will be exercised by operations program.

The database administrator confirms these controls before they are placed in service. A reconfirmation is required in the event of any program maintenance, before the program is placed back into operation, regardless of what the maintenance effort entails.

D **User ID/password identification.** The computer operating system allows three attempts at entering a user's ID and password identification. If all three attempts are incorrect, it will allow no further access for a given time period which is determined by the data administrator/security officer.

Passwords will be assigned to given terminals. Any attempt to use a password with an unauthorized terminal will be prevented by the computer operating system. The attempt will be recorded as a violation and reported on the listing noted above under C, Terminal operating system controls.

E **Modem access controls.** The same terminal and user ID/password controls apply to modem access. The computer dial-up telephone number(s) are changed periodically, at the discrimination of the data administrator/security officer.

The level of control for the dial-up access is determined by the data administrator, with level 1 the lowest and level 3 the highest:

1   Standard user ID/password and terminal control.

2   Access confirmed by automatic call-back system or caller ID hardware.

3   Access confirmed by data center personnel by physically calling back the listed authorized number.

    A computer record of all unsuccessful attempts to gain automatic access to the system is maintained. The physical call-back procedure has a manually maintained log containing the same information. A daily notice of the unsuccessful access attempts is sent to the data administrator and the computer operations manager by computer operators assigned the task.

Audit Trail Monitoring

A continuous audit trail monitoring program should be in place to police the access and flow of data and information to and from the central computer system. To accomplish this, the program uses the data dictionary, the database administration system, and the operating control systems. It provides for the report listings noted in "Terminal Controls," C. terminal operating system controls, paragraph one, as well as other information:

A **A transaction detail file.** This contains the transaction detail by terminal and user (ID/password), with the date and time of each access. It can be kept on tape or disk and used to reconstruct the most recent backup file necessary to return the database/file to the point of the last transaction. A computer program is available to produce a listing of this file that can be reviewed manually by either the database administrator or the data administrator on demand.

B **Exception reports.** A file is maintained of daily exception reports called for by any source. A weekly report lists each exception report requested, grouped by requesting party, as well as the data accessed, the date, and time. If the computer system time is charged back to the user, the time and/or dollars are also posted.

C **Teleprocessing report.** A teleprocessing network report will be generated weekly by the computer operations manager. It outlines all access to the system and identifies any abnormal occurrences. If needed, an attempt will be made to explain the reported activity. The report is distributed to the data administrator, database administrator, security officer, and IS head.

The data administrator evaluates it and compiles a monthly statistical analysis report from the weekly reports, and from any other sources deemed necessary. This Monthly Statistical Analysis Network Report is sent to the IS manager, the database administrator, the computer center operations manager, and all members of the data security committee. Each monthly report is discussed at the data security committee meeting and the discussion is recorded in the minutes.

Data Entry Controls

User manuals that users understand will be available at each terminal. The user's name, ID, or password will not be written on the manual, which is put into a locked drawer at the end of each workday.

Training material, such as instruction manuals and tutorials, are available for any terminal operator in the language that person understands.

An immediate supervisor is responsible for the operator's proficiency and the data administrator/data security officer for enforcing this procedure. Any supervisor refusing to comply is reported in writing to his/her superior and the data security committee. Data entry procedures are followed to minimize the loading of incorrect data into the database/files:

THE IS AUDIT MANAGER'S
TEN REQUIREMENTS OF A SECURITY PROGRAM
(FROM A *FORTUNE* 500 OIL COMPANY)

1   Establish and enforce policies on acquiring PCs. Establish network guidelines and enforce them, and enforce disciplinary actions for violators.

2.   Perform preemployment checks.

3.   Secure physical access to computer center.

4.   Backup all data and programs, and store at an off-site storage facility.

5.   Insure adequate power, air conditioning, and fire protection.

6.   Develop and enforce documentation and approval standards.

7.   Establish program change controls.

8.   Monitor usage of computer resources.

9.   Control the teleprocessing network.

10.   Evaluate security and control systems.

❖   Computer program instructions edit incoming data for errors before the data is uploaded to files or database. The data may be contained in a buffer file before it is edited. The editing parameters are listed in the data description tables or the data dictionary. Also, they may be developed using data decision tables.

❖   Any overrides to this procedure requires both the operator's supervisor and the computer operations shift supervisor's approval. The shift supervisor notes the time of the override in the shift log. Any temporary computer program patching for an override requires the normal procedure for program maintenance to be followed. In the event of an emergency, the computer manager may be contacted to expedite the maintenance programming required.

Data Communications Backup

The person or group sending data is responsible for maintaining the data backup until notification that the original data is no longer required. This backup may be in the form of:

❖   Source document retention

❖ Captured digital data in the form of batch tape backup or secondary storage random accessed files

Data communications hardware backup provisions should also be considered, depending on the size of the operation and/or security dependency, in the form of:

❖ Backup modems at critical sites

❖ Alternate data lines available for dial-up backup

❖ Alternate dedicated lines available

COMMENT

A *Fortune* 500 company had its alternate dedicated backup line buried in parallel when a backhoe cut them both by accident. This is some sort of message! The backup provisions should be tested, unannounced, by the data administrator or his/her agent. Perform the tests periodically no less than once per year. The test results should be documented in a memo and copies sent to the database administrator, IS manager, and all members of the data security committee.

7

IT SUPPORT: HANDLING DAY-TO-DAY HASSLES

IT SUPPORT POLICIES

The IS computer center area consists of an IS computer operation and support areas. Support areas are restricted; only authorized personnel may enter. The computer room itself requires a higher level of authorization to gain entry. The main purpose in keeping the support areas apart from the computer operation room itself is to insure security.

For better security and to prevent conflict of interest, personnel responsible for the support areas report to the IS corporate computer center manager.

Support Area Environment

The support area must be a clean, air-conditioned environment. On a daily basis, housekeeping personnel may enter all areas except the data library area and the computer room itself. A fireproof, walk-in vault should house the data library or, if the volume of data does not justify this, a fireproof safe in the data library area. An off-site fireproof vault is also required for backup programs and data.

No smoking, food, or beverages are permitted in the support areas. A separate room will be provided for the storage of personal effects, food and beverage consumption, and for smoking.

> ## COMMENT
>
> Fireproof safes must meet the rating requirements for IT off-line storage. Safes that normally house paper documents are rated at a higher temperature than for IT off-line storage. These safes tend to be larger and much heavier than standard safes. Therefore, the support flooring must be a limiting consideration, along with access needed to get the safe(s) in place, when assigning their location. This will be a determining factor for the size(s) and weight(s) of the safes that will be used.

Systems Software Support Policies

Operations personnel, systems software support personnel, and help-desk personnel report to the technical support manager who reports to the IS corporate computer center manager. Software support responsibilities include the operating system, plus utility and compiler software, but not maintenance of any programs written by the systems or programming units. Service of both sides of a client/server system is also the IS computer center's responsibility. No one other than operations programmers or maintenance programmers may perform any maintenance on the operating software unless given special permission by the head of the IS computer center.

Tape Storage Policies

The limited life span of magnetic tapes mandates the close monitoring of their age and condition. It will be policy to copy all tapes to a replacement media, and have them confirmed as operational before the old tape drives are removed from service.

DATA LIBRARY

The data library is perhaps one of the most critical areas of the IS computer center. It contains magnetic tapes and/or disks and is off-line storage for both data and software.

Data libraries are usually enclosed within a fireproof room or large vault. In smaller operations, a properly rated fireproof safe may be all that is required. A duplicate off-site data and software library needs to be located a safe distance from the main site. The storage of the tapes, disks, and microfilm must meet the proper fire-retardant rating for such media.

A data library is responsible for several services, including:

A **Database and file security.** All the activities associated with the protection of data from fire, nature, misuse, and unauthorized access.

B **Data control.** The activities and procedures for backing up, storing, retrieving, and retaining data.

C **Software backup.** Maintaining backup copies of all current operating software.

D **Data file maintenance.** Activities associated with keeping track of the data and software in storage. (If tapes are stored, they should be monitored for condition and reproduced as needed.)

E **Other storage media.** In some cases, the data library houses other items such as:

❖ Computer-generated reports

❖ Policy and procedures manuals

❖ Cancelled checks or other vital documents

Data Library Operations

The data librarian performs the data library operating procedures, but in smaller shops may also have other duties. The primary responsibility is to support the computer center operation. The storage area may also be provided for such noncomputer center storage media as deeds, titles and other valuable documents. Following are the librarian's duties and responsibilities:

A **Receives new disks and tapes.** Upon receiving new disks or tapes, the data librarian:

1 Compares quantity received with original order and billing information. If the quantity is incorrect, he/she notifies the IS computer operations manager/supervisor.

2 Inspects disks or tapes for signs of damage. If any are damaged, the IS computer operation's head is notified.

3 Logs in new tapes or disks and assigns each a consecutive number. The date received and vendor are also posted to the consecutive number log.

4   Notifies the computer operator that the disks or tapes have been received if a disk/tape inventory is maintained for the computer system. If there is no such inventory, the data librarian will maintain a card or PC file for disks and tapes issued to the IS computer center.

B **Maintains an inventory file.** The librarian monitors the disk and tape inventory. Computer disk/tape inventory programs are available or, for smaller operations, a manual card inventory is kept.

1   **Manual card inventory file.** A 3- by 5-inch file card is used for each disk or tape, with the disk or tape number, the file label, date and time created, and the current file name posted to it.

2   **Computer disk/tape inventory program.** A computer program maintains the status of the disk/tape inventory. A report is available from an online file. (See Exhibit 7–1.) The data librarian:

❖   Checks the status of all disks/tapes daily.

❖   Updates the disk/tape inventory file.

❖   Maintains a sign-in/sign-out log for daily movement of disks/tapes to and from the data library and the off-site storage area. (This log acts as an audit trail and is for updating the disk/tape inventory file.)

❖   Updates and checks the status of the off-site data library inventory daily.

❖   Randomly spot-checks offsite storage inventory status.

C **Maintains software backup files.** The data librarian maintains backup copies of operating software at both on-site and off-site storage locations. The duties performed are:

1   Maintains a record of all stored software. (A sample form is shown in Exhibit 7–2.)

2   Replaces old versions of programs with new versions. Authorization to replace programs comes in the form of a memo from the IS computer center operation's head. Unless otherwise informed, the old programs will be sent to the off-site storage.

D   Other duties

1   Maintains and controls the policies and procedures manual inventory.

2   Maintains and controls the "controlled forms" inventory.

3   Maintains and controls any vital records.

4   Keeps the data library area clean and neat.

EXHIBIT 7–1. Disk and Tape Inventory Status

Date: Report No:

Disk No.	File Label	Date	Time	File Name
1	PAYROLL	09/01/01	13:40	Payroll Master
2	ACCT PAY	09/02/01	09:30	Accounts Payable
3	INV	10/30/01	10:15	Plant Inventory
4	A/R	10/01/01	12:45	Accounts Receivable

Tape No.	File Label	Date	Time	File Name
1	MPT	09/01/01	09:40	Master Programs
2	XXX	10/31/01	08:30	Scratch Tape
3	XXX	12/21/00	11:40	Scratch Tape
4	PR-TRAN	10/01/01	14:45	YTD Payroll Transactions

EXHIBIT 7–2. Program Inventory

Program #	Name	Language	Source	Date
PR3	Payroll	COBOL	Smith	01/15/98
INV-6	Finished Goods	COBOL	Jones	07/04/95
STA	Stress Analysis	Visual Basic	Smith	11/14/00

5 Cleans tapes periodically as needed.

DATA ENTRY PROCEDURES

Operating procedures are a combination of vendor-provided instruction manuals and data entry instructions peculiar to each application. If the procedure appears to be incorrect, confusing, or contradictory, the problem is brought to the attention of the IS computer center operations head.

Data Entry

Data entry procedures can cover various input methods. Processing can be done in "batches" or "online." When raw data is to be converted to "captured" data in machine-readable format, the systems analyst or programmer will provide data entry instructions. The instructions should include an example of the raw data source documents from which input information comes. Data entry procedures, with example source documents containing identified data elements for input, are placed in a folder for each job that can be performed in a centralized or decentralized data entry operation.

Both types of operation have advantages and disadvantages. The way an IS computer center handles data entry is somewhat different from a decentralized system. Decentralized data collection can then forward its information to the IS computer center. This data can be as received or altered.

Centralized Data Entry

A centralized data entry organization requires a unit adjacent to the computer center staffed by employees of the IS computer center processing operations. Source documents from any place in the organization (including the mailroom) are forwarded to the data entry section for processing. The advantages of centralized data entry over a decentralized system include:

A Good utilization of machine resources since all data entry equipment is located in one place.

B Skilled data entry operators providing efficient use of equipment.

C A procedure for verifying input data since there should be more than one data entry operator.

D Better controls over the data entry activities. (This is an important consideration since data entry provides an opportunity for dishonest operators to key in unauthorized orders for goods or monies.)

The procedures for data entry processing are:

A Each batch of source data is date- and time-stamped upon arrival in the unit. Batch numbers are sequential.

B Each batch is logged in on the Data Entry Log (see Exhibit 7–3).

C Each batch is identified for verification (if required) and placed with other batches of the same type for data entry by priority.

D When a batch is entered, the operator initials and posts the time and date of completion. Source documents are forwarded to one of the following:

❖ A verification holding area (if required)

❖ A work completed area

E Documents requiring verification are assigned a priority and made available to a different operator from the one who entered the data.

F The verification operator rekeys the data to ensure it is correct. Corrections are made, if necessary. The verification operator initials and posts the date and time on the source document with a blue marker after completing the batch. The batch of source documents is forwarded to the work completed area.

G The batch number, time, and date are posted to the Completed Batch Log after the documents arrive at the work completed area (see Exhibit 7–4). The batch is then filed or returned to the originating department.

H Filing is by source document and disposition date. When source documents are to be disposed of, the standard disposition procedure is followed.

I By the end of each day, the numbers of all entered batches posted to the Data Entry Log will have been crossed off with a yellow marker.

J After the Data Entry Log is posted to the Completed Batch Log, the Completed Batch Log is filed. Each sheet is held for six months, then discarded. The Data Entry Log is filed after all batch numbers have been crossed off. This sheet is also held for six months, then discarded.

Decentralized Data Entry

Decentralization means the data entry is not limited to one location. Most often, decentralized data entry activities are located where they originate. In this situation, responsibility for them is placed on personnel other than computer operations personnel.

Those operating decentralized input devices are usually familiar with the source documents, data, or information associated with the input. There is less need to convert raw data from a familiar format to a different format for

EXHIBIT 7–3. Data Entry Log

Date_____

Source Document	Batch Number	Time Received	Initial

EXHIBIT 7–4. Completed Batch Log

Date_____

Batch Number	Time Completed	Initial

use by a centralized data entry operator because the individual entering the data is accustomed to the information.

The advantages of decentralization over centralized input are:

A   Fewer content errors because of user familiarity with input data.

B   Data preparation is the only step in the data entry process because decentralized data entry is usually online.

C   Time is frequently saved in the preparation of data for the computer system because it is usually converted to captured data as it is originated.

Many firms employ both centralized and decentralized systems for optimal efficiency. The decentralized data entry procedures for batch processing are the same as defined under centralized data entry procedures.

The instruments providing online data to the computer system exist in many different forms; most common is the online monitor with a keyboard. Others are bar code readers, optical or magnetic character readers, and voice input. In addition to online procedures, keyboard input needs to have special computer operating control procedures provided for the system when in use.

The procedures for online monitor/keyboard data entry processing are as follows:

A   All personnel and terminals are identified with the proper codes ensuring that only authorized terminals and personnel enter data. This includes mobile units, too.

B   When the data is displayed on the screen correctly, the operator keys in the proper code to send the data to the computer.

C   All data is edited by the computer system to ensure that correct data is being received. If the computer discovers an error in its input editing routine, the computer will not place the information into its database but will hold the data in temporary storage and notify the monitor terminal of the possible error. The operator can then correct or abort the input.

D   The computer system maintains a log by terminal to identify, by user code, when each user logs on and the type of data entered.

E   At each monitor terminal there should be a binder with general operating instructions, along with procedures for each kind of data to be entered. There will be a name and telephone number of the contact person if there is a problem.

External File Downloading

Files can be downloaded from the firm's distributed systems input, commercial databases, commercial online services, or even the Internet. Each of these downloading procedures requires a computer operations procedure, provided by the programming staff. Except for a firm's distributed system, all downloading will be under operator control.

Except for a firm's distributed system, all downloading will be to an offloadable secondary storage device. Before this information can be placed into the main system, it must be confirmed as "clean"—that it has no embedded virus or distorted data.

Computer operators will maintain a Downloading Log Book. It will record the date, time, operator name, source of input, amount of input, time required, ID of secondary storage device, and any problems encountered.

Data Entry Administrative Duties

Data entry units with more than one person will have a supervisor or lead operator to keep track of batches and assign data entry jobs. The supervisor or lead operator will perform the administrative duties. These duties include:

A Scheduling each batch that enters the unit. If there is a conflict of schedule and workloads, the IS computer center head is to be contacted for permission to use overtime or to change schedules.

B Maintaining up-to-date operator procedures and documentation for each job.

C Checking the documentation of new jobs for possible discrepancies, unfinished work, errors, and/or ambiguity. Providing copies for each operator and a file copy of all data entry documentation procedures. Updating procedure modifications on all copies in the unit.

D Maintaining ongoing communications with systems analysts, programmers, and users to assure a continued understanding of any new or pending changes. This includes source documents, input procedures, volume by day and hour, and schedules.

E Maintaining data entry supplies.

F Maintaining vacation schedules for operators.

G Contacting the repair service in the event of equipment malfunction.

COMPUTER CENTER TECHNICAL SUPPORT

The primary purpose of the technical support unit is to provide technical services to the IS computer center area of operations. Its four sections are communications, database administration, systems software support, and the client/server help-desk.

Communications

The communications section or unit is responsible for the hardware, software, wiring, cabling, maintenance, and leasing of services for the operation of all corporate communications. Also included in this section are LAN and WAN systems. This unit will assist management with any vendor bidding for communication hardware or software. It will keep the IS computer center operations management and users informed of any planned status changes in communications. Users are responsible for informing communications in the event of transmission problems.

The communications section provides written instructions to the systems analysis and programming units regarding communications. Notice to users of operating procedures is done by e-mail or memo.

The unit is responsible for the system of wireless data transfer. This includes both the hardware and software systems. The standards developed by the PCCA (Portable Computer and Communications Association) should be followed whenever possible. With the proper standards, processing wireless microcomputer data can be simplified by connecting existing applications to the wireless environment.

This unit is also responsible for the firm's telephone communications from the switchboard operator to the voice-mail system. The use of scrambled voice message coding is done as needed by this unit. The operation and maintenance of the telephone hardware and software is its responsibility as well. The following reports will be generated:

- ❖ Monthly telephone usage by phone number (see Exhibit 7–5)
- ❖ Monthly telephone usage by department (see Exhibit 7–6)
- ❖ Monthly telephone usage by the company (see Exhibit 7–7)

The usage by phone number report will be sent to the person assigned the telephone or, in the case of multiple users, to the unit's head. The usage by department report will be sent to each department head for his/her respective departments. The usage by company report will be sent to:

- ❖ IS computer center head
- ❖ Corporate CIO
- ❖ Corporate controller

<u>**EXHIBIT 7–5.** Usage by Phone Number</u>

NOVEMBER 2001 TELEPHONE USAGE REPORT
For: John Smith

Phone number: 456-3321   Department: Accounts Payable #4311

DATE	TIME MADE	MIN TIME	NUMBER CALLED	COST
10/23	9:21	23	800-431-7708	00.00
10/23	10:03	4	513-4141	00.10
10/23	14:19	27	422-313-7931	11.22
10/23	16:33	11	456-5362	00.10
10/26	8:46	2	481-6116	00.10

TOTAL TIME 1 Hour 7 Min   TOTAL COST 11.52

EXHIBIT 7–6. Usage by Department

NOVEMBER 2001 DEPARTMENT USAGE REPORT

FOR: Accounts Payable #4311

PHONE No.	USER'S NAME	TOTAL TIME USED	TOTAL COST
456-3321	John Smith	14 Hours 22 Min	47.63
456-3322	Mary Brown	11 Hours 14 Min	48.21
456-3347	Phil Montros	22 Hours 4 Min	67.83
	DEPT. TOTALS	47 Hours 40 Min	$163.67

EXHIBIT 7–7. Usage by Company

MONTHLY TELEPHONE USAGE REPORT
FOR: July 2001

DEPARTMENT	ID NO.	HOURS	DEPT. COST	YTD COST	BUDGETED
Accounts Payable	4311	48	164	1741	2000
Payroll	4321	27	43	421	600
Shipping	3741	63	221	2643	2500
COMPANYWIDE TOTAL		138	438	4805	5100

Database Administration

The database administrator is responsible for maintaining and controlling the data-processing databases. His/her duties are to:

A Select and maintain the database software.

B Identify personnel and control access to the database as to who can:

- ❖ Read specific information
- ❖ Change information
- ❖ Add information
- ❖ Delete information

Not only will access to the database be controlled by a person's ID code, but also by which terminal the user is allowed access. Terminal access will be limited to given "windows of time." (This is to prevent the cleaning person from accessing data at 10:00 P.M., a common problem nationwide.)

C Control and maintain the database data dictionary.

D Maintain procedures for file and database backups.

E Provide consulting service to data-processing departments and users.

F Provide disaster planning procedures, and test them no less than once a year unannounced.

G Locate and set up off-site data and software backup systems.

H Maintain directory services.

I Promote the use of audit trails for the processed data.

Depending on the size of the database administration, this segment can be part of the database administrator's duties or delegated to a directory services manager.

A directory is a collection of information for given applications. It holds all the information relating to each application, such as user-access and user log-on IDs. Its services make it possible for all applications to share the same database of user and network information, reducing the need to replicate the same information throughout the network. Directory services can be used to find numerous objects on a given network. Developers of software systems have a need for an information tracking system for LAN-based keys.

Software to drive this system is made available by several firms, such as Novel's Microsoft and Banyan Systems, both for network and non-network operations.

Directory services are responsible for evaluating software best suited to the firm's current needs. It will install and maintain the system, and will also provide user instruction and procedures for the software's proper usage.

Systems Software Support

This section covers the software support of the operating system. The applications programs—in-house and purchased software—are the responsibility of the systems software support programmers. Maintenance of operating programs is the responsibility of the programming department. But the maintenance of the operating system software is the responsibility of the systems software support programmers who:

A   Make changes to operating system software when informed by memo from the head of the systems software support section.

B   Inform by memo computer operations, programming, and affected users of any changes to the operating system software.

C   Test new operating system software before it is put into use. Also, test for changes to be made to the operating software.

D   Assist the database administrator with programming needs.

E   Write and maintain monitor procedures in the standard procedure format for operating software.

F   Review for approval the operators' instructions provided for operation programs.

G   Assist in volume program testing and auditors' studies.

H   Maintain system controls for accessing the computer system.

I   Assist with monitor operators' training when putting new systems into operation or making changes to the current operating system.

Client/Server Help-desk

There are three basic forms of client/server help-desks: a computer operator for very small operations, a full-time staffed in-house help-desk, and an out-sourced help-desk. Which is chosen depends on the given situation. A computer operator or in-house help-desk is generally for client/server systems. Other user systems tend to employ outsourced help-desks. But, whatever approach is employed, one person must be responsible for a help-desk's existence and maintenance. Following are basic considerations for implementing and maintaining a client/server help-desk.

A   Determine requirements for such an operation, for example:
  - ❖   Current and future expected use of the system
  - ❖   How to evaluate user requirements
  - ❖   How to communicate user requirements to system development or vendors

B   Seek out available vendor systems:
  - ❖   Look at complete packages.
  - ❖   Look for diagnostic and monitoring tools.
  - ❖   Look at Internet services available.
  - ❖   Look at distributive support technology available.

C   Consider user services, such as:
  - ❖   Directory of services
  - ❖   On-site education and training programs
  - ❖   Online tutorials

D   Develop help-desk staff:
  - ❖   Develop job descriptions.
  - ❖   Determine staff requirements.
  - ❖   Prepare help-desk orientation procedure.
  - ❖   Provide a comprehensive training program.
  - ❖   Instill a proper service attitude.
  - ❖   Provide a safety net for stress and burnout.
  - ❖   Provide for performance evaluation and feedback.
  - ❖   Monitor performance and provide feedback.
  - ❖   Introduce help-desk staff to users.

E   Management considerations for help-desk operations:
  - ❖   Develop budget requirements.
  - ❖   Utilize technology to enhance productivity.
  - ❖   Maintain ongoing user communication.
  - ❖   Seek out user information and training needs.
  - ❖   Create and publish monthly and annual reports.
  - ❖   Create an informative monthly user newsletter.

The day-to-day operation of a client/server help-desk is routine, but unexpected events can occur. The required procedure for day-to-day operation is as follows:

A Log in incoming contacts on a PC.

1 Ask user for user ID number and name.

2 Enter ID number to screen prompt.

3 When the name of the user comes up on screen, the computer begins keeping track of the time the user is in contact. If user's name on screen is different, ask for the correct name. If this is not provided, hang up and record the event.

4 Provide user with help needed.

5 When contact with user ends, press enter key on keyboard. Choose kind of service from menu. (Menu may vary from one company location to another.) Type short, one sentence description, if needed, on monitor display. Press designated "log key." Help-desk operator is now ready for next inquiry.

B Prevent fatigue. Help-desk personnel should not be on the system for more than two hours at a time without time off for lunch or a personal break.

C Compile monthly report. The data collected for each contact will be included in a monthly report prepared by each help-desk employee. One copy will be sent to the IS computer operations manager, one copy retained by the help-desk operator, and one copy sent to user management. If there is more than one help-desk worker, a combined report will be sent to both user management and the IS computer operations manager. The report will list:

1 The number of contacts made by each user

2 Time range of all the contacts made

3 The total time used by each user, sorted in descending order by amount of time spent

4 Total time spent with users by each help-desk operator

5 The count by type of service rendered

There are basic pricing options to consider. This may be reviewed in light of outsourcing the task versus in-house. When considerations are made, the following should be examined:

A Per-solution price. With per-solution pricing, users pay a fixed fee for each call answered and problem solved. This fee may have to be adjusted from time to time.

B **Per-desk price.** This is a common option that is selected. The fee is based on the number of users. The price may range from $20 to over $300 per user served.

C **Call-block pricing.** This help-desk service comes in fixed blocks of calls (a given number) at fixed prices. This allows user management to place a usage cap on help-desk outsourced calls.

Vendor-provided help-desk service most often comes from the vendor's site. This remote service is generally less expensive than on-site service and creates fewer problems. Signing up for a vendor's price is a fixed contract cost; estimated in-house service is *just* an estimate. Like most estimates, it is likely to go up, while the service will not be as expected.

8

MANAGING IT ASSETS: IDENTIFY WHAT YOU HAVE

ASSET MANAGEMENT POLICIES AND OBJECTIVES

Asset management policies address both hardware and software assets. Well-defined and maintained asset management policies and procedures will be financially rewarding, will fine-tune the companywide PC information systems operations, and will help avoid embarrassing litigation.

Top management must formally direct the asset management policies and procedures as the duty of the information systems organization. To be successful IS should be required to:

❖ Inform all employees of the directives.

❖ Explain the need for the policies and procedures.

❖ Mandate that only company-owned hardware and software should be utilized by all employees.

❖ Announce that the downloading of company-owned software is not permitted to privately owned computers or secondary storage in any form.

❖ Permit infractions to be noted in the employees' records.

❖ Emphasize that serious or repeated violations of asset management policies will be grounds for dismissal.

The policy objective of resource management, in the simplest terms, is to reduce cost while increasing overall efficiency and to avoid possible litigation. The department management cannot see the forest for the trees, and top management cannot see the trees for the forest. The asset management people should be able to see both.

The second most likely candidate today for the responsibility of computer asset management would be the purchasing unit since it controls the purchase order system. For example, use of purchase orders makes controlling the purchase of office furniture a simple process. There is seldom the problem of people making their own furniture, buying it with petty cash funds, having a "free trial," or even stealing it. Although PC hardware and software aren't easily controlled through a purchase order system, the purchasing unit can still play a role in information systems control.

COMMENT

Bygone mainframe days seldom had asset management problems. The hardware was purchased under capital expense budgets and the software was developed in-house. All this activity came under the domain of the data-processing department. But today, computer hardware is found throughout the company, and often there are no controls over purchase, standardization. or utilization. Software is even more problematic. It can originate from legitimate in-house development or purchase, or from questionable or illegal sources. This anarchy can appear insignificant because of undocumented direct expense, but the indirect repercussions can be great and the cost astronomical.

The burden of asset management for PC hardware and software assets often falls to corporate information systems, often through default rather than proper planning. This writer installed an asset management program some years ago to determine what additional investment was required to "bring the resources level up to satisfy the demand." After the program was completed, it was found that there was already more invested than what was required.

CONTRACT ASSET MANAGEMENT SERVICE

One route for installing an asset management system is contracting out the effort for the entire firm, a given area, or an entire corporate division. This does not remove the IS responsibility for this function. The established asset management policies will be maintained by any such service. The contract can cover the hardware and/or software, or both. It can also provide a system that either the customer or contractor (or vendor) will install and operate. For the acquisition procedures, see Chapter 15, *Vendors: Getting the Goods*.

The output reports as described in this section are generic. Do not expect all vendors to offer identical reports or output formats, although each product contains common features. The last thing to consider in vendor selection is the output format of the reports; it should be based on which service best meets the needs of IS management.

Outsourcing for Full Service

The firm's legal representative with the information systems management will determine the contract terms with the vendor. Needs will be determined and specified so as to fulfill the management policy for asset management of PC hardware and software.

When contracting for full service, the vendor will develop, install, and operate the system. The major issue here is that the corporate culture of both firms is compatible. It is advisable to look at other operations the vendor has developed, installed, and operated. Are their users pleased with the system? How different are the user firms from yours?

One person from the information systems organization will have to be assigned the coordinator's duties. The position title is *computer asset manager*. If not full-time, it can be combined with the responsibilities of the PC coordinator and/or the software coordinator. The person's workload will depend on the PC inventory size and its complexity. The computer asset manager should be involved with the vendor selection because he/she will be the major contact person.

Establishing an asset management service should be treated as a project. Requirements will be provided to the vendor. Project control and reporting will be normal for this undertaking. The Bid Proposal should define the tools and procedures required of a vendor as well as the calendar time needed to accomplish each of the following:

A **Inventory of hardware.** Take the inventory in the shortest calendar time possible. After each unit has been completed, establish an update procedure to maintain a current unit hardware inventory. Augment this procedure by random inventory spot-checks.

Tag hardware items inventoried with a scannable inventory tag placed on the equipment in the same location for each type of hardware. Each new acquisition of hardware will be tagged. The purchase price, department, and the employee responsible for the hardware will be input to the inventory system.

B **Physical inventory of software.** The PC software inventory can be taken either at the same time as the hardware inventory or later. This depends on the vendor's system. The software of each PC and file server will be identified and logged in; unauthorized software will be purged and recorded to identify to what degree, for each area and user, software violations have occurred.

Software data, by each PC (desktop, laptop, and notebook system) and person responsible for that computer, will be input to the PC inventory system. Purchase price, department, and employee assigned responsibility information relating to new PC software added later will be input to the PC inventory system.

C **PC inventory system.** Department heads will utilize the PC inventory system. Employees within departments will maintain an ongoing PC hardware and software inventory. It will generate a physical report by department after each inventory (first and subsequent inventories). The physical inventory report will also be run at the end of each fiscal year and upon demand by the software coordinator. A copy of the Department Software Report will be sent to the department head and to the software coordinator and/or computer asset manager listing the following:

❖ Department name

❖ Date the physical inventory was taken

❖ Name, total quantity, and total cost of each type of software

❖ Total cost of the department's software inventory

❖ Kind and quantity of software removed

A detailed listing of each employee and his/her assigned PC will also be produced. A copy of this Department Users Report, indicating the department name and the date of the inventory, will be sent to the department head and will be available for the software coordinator, if requested. It will also list the following by employee:

❖ Hardware assigned to the employee

❖ Each computer's software

❖ Unauthorized software removed, by computer

❖ Hardware cost by employee

❖ Software cost by employee

❖ Total cost of both hardware and software

A Department Hardware Inventory Report will be run, after the Department Users Report, for each department. A copy listing the following will be sent to the department head and to the PC coordinator:

❖ Department name

❖ Date the report was run

❖ Hardware type, quantity, and total cost of each type

❖ Total cost of the department's hardware inventory

A Total Hardware/Software Asset Report will be run, listing the hardware/software assets by department. There will be four columns across each page: name of the department, number of PCs, total original investment for hardware/software, and average age of department PCs. The bottom line will indicate totals of the same information for the whole company. This report, to be run at the end of the fiscal year and upon demand, will be sent to the head of information systems, the controller, and the computer asset manager.

The vendor is expected to maintain full service of the asset management system for the life of the contract. Any changes to the system during the contract period will be negotiable with the vendor. Any intent not to renew the service, by vendor or customer, must be given in writing three months before the contract's expiration.

Outsourcing for a Turnkey Operation

Information systems management and the firm's legal representative will determined the contract terms with the vendor. Needs will be determined and specified so as to fulfill the management policy for asset management of PC hardware and software. In this case, the needs will determine the asset management system to be developed and provided by the vendor but operated by information systems. The IS head will delegate the responsibility for the turnkey operation to the software coordinator or the PC coordinator, or a new position of *computer asset manager* can be created. Which option is chosen depends on the size of the firm and the physical location of the PC systems.

The vendor who contracts to provide a turnkey computer asset management system will develop and install it. The vendor will also furnish documentation and operational training for its operation, which will be the firm's responsibility. The contract with the vendor should include a help-desk and maintenance provision.

Before the contract is signed, it is advisable to look at other operations the vendor has developed and installed. Are the users pleased with the system? How different are the users' firms from yours?

The person who will manage the system should also be involved with the vendor selection. He/she will work with the vendor, who has been provided with needs (requirements) specifications, and will be the major contact person. Treat establishing an asset management service as a project. Project control and reporting will be expected. The person appointed to manage the system will be responsible for all reporting.

Tools and procedures employed by a vendor should be defined in the Bid Proposal. In addition, the calendar time needed to accomplish each of the following must also be included:

A **Inventory of hardware.** The inventory should be taken in the shortest calendar time possible. After completion by unit, establish an inventory update procedure to maintain a current accounting. Augment the update procedure by random inventory spot-checks.

Tag each hardware item with a scannable inventory tag, which will be placed on the equipment in the same location for each type of hardware. Each new acquisition of hardware, before the system is operational, will be tagged. The purchase price, department, and employee responsible for the hardware will be input to the PC inventory system.

B **Physical inventory of software.** Software inventory can be taken at the same time as the hardware inventory or later. This depends on the vendor's system. The software of each PC and file server will be identified and logged in. Unauthorized software will be purged and recorded to identify to what degree, for each area and user, software violations have occurred.

Software data will be input to the PC computer inventory system by each PC (desktop, laptop, and notebook system) and person responsible for that computer. Purchase price, department, and employee assigned responsibility information relating to new PC software, added later, will be input to the PC inventory system.

C **PC inventory system.** Department heads will utilize the PC inventory system. Employees within departments will maintain an ongoing PC hardware and software inventory. The software system will generate a physical inventory report by department after each of the first and subsequent inventories. The physical inventory report will also be run at the end of each fiscal year and upon demand by the software coordinator. A copy of the department report will be sent to the department head and to the software coordinator and/or computer asset manager. The Department Software Report will list the following:

- ❖ Department name
- ❖ Date the physical inventory was taken
- ❖ Name, total quantity, and total cost by each type of PC software
- ❖ Total cost of the department's software inventory
- ❖ Number of each kind of software removed

A detailed listing of each employee and his/her assigned PC will also be produced. A copy of this Department Users Report will be sent to the department head and will be available for the software coordinator and/or computer asset manager, if requested. It will contain the department name and the date of the inventory. This Department Users Report will also list the following for each employee:

- ❖ Hardware assigned
- ❖ Software on each computer
- ❖ Unauthorized software removed, by computer
- ❖ Total purchase cost of hardware
- ❖ Total purchase cost of software
- ❖ Total purchase cost of both hardware and software

A Department Hardware Inventory Report will be run, after the Department Users Report, for each department. A copy will be sent to the department head, the PC coordinator, and/or the computer asset manager. This report will list the following:

- ❖ The department
- ❖ Date the report was run
- ❖ Hardware type, quantity, and total cost of each type
- ❖ Total cost of the department's hardware inventory

The vendor is expected to produce "clean" printouts of all reports contracted for before the system is considered operational. After the system has been accepted by IS management, it will be maintained by the person appointed to service the asset management system. When the contract has been completed, further assistance or any changes to the system will be negotiable with the vendor.

Contracting for a Consulting Service

The information systems' management and the firm's legal representative will determine contract terms with the consulting service. Needs will be determined and specified so as to fulfill the management policy for asset management of PC hardware and software. In this case, the needs will determine the asset management system to be developed and provided by an in-house team, with assistance from the consulting service. But it will be operated by information systems whose head will delegate the development responsibility for the asset management system to a project team. The responsibility of project manager can be delegated to the software coordinator, the PC coordinator, or a computer asset manager, or a new position can even be created to manage the project. Which option is chosen will depend on the size of the firm and the physical location(s) of the PC systems.

The consulting service vendor who contracts to work on a computer asset management system will provide the software along with the consulting services to help develop and install the system. The consultant will also furnish documentation and operational training, which will become the firm's responsibility. The contract with the consultant should include a maintenance and upgrade provision.

Before the contract is signed, it is advisable to look at other operations the vendor has developed and installed. Are the users pleased with the system? How different are the users' firms from yours?

The person selected to operate the system should also be involved with the selection of the consultant. He/she will work with the consultant, who has been provided with needs (requirements) specifications, and will be the major contact person.

Establishing an asset management service should be treated as a project. Project control and reporting will be expected. The person appointed to the project and designated to operate the system will be responsible for all reporting.

Tools and procedures employed by a consultant should be defined in the Bid Proposal. In addition, the calendar time needed to accomplish each of the following must be included:

A **Inventory of hardware.** The inventory should be taken in the shortest calendar time possible. After each unit has been completed, establish an update procedure to maintain a current inventory. Augment the update procedure by random inventory spot-checks.

Tag each hardware item inventoried with a scannable inventory tag placed on the equipment in the same location for each type. Each new acquisition of hardware, before the system is operational, will be tagged. The purchase price, department, and employee responsible for the hardware will be input to the PC inventory system.

B **Physical inventory of software.** PC software inventory can be taken at the same time as the hardware or later, depending on the vendor's system. The software of each PC and file server will be identified and logged in. Unauthorized software will be purged and recorded to identify to what degree, for each area and user, software violation has occurred. This information will be input to the PC inventory system for each PC (desktop, laptop, and notebook system) and person responsible for that computer. Purchase price, department, and employee-assigned responsibility information relating to PC software added later will be input to the PC inventory system.

C **PC inventory system.** Departments and employees within departments maintaining an ongoing PC hardware and software inventory will use the PC inventory system. The software system will generate a physical inventory report by department after the first and subsequent inventories. A physical inventory report will be done for the fiscal year. The software coordinator and/or computer asset manager can request a report run at any other time.

A copy of the department report will be sent to the department head and to the software coordinator listing the following:

❖ Department name

❖ Date the physical inventory was taken

❖ Name, total quantity, and total cost of software type

❖ Total cost of the department's software inventory

❖ Number of each kind of software removed

A detailed listing of each employee and his/her assigned PC will also be produced. A copy of this Department Users Report, containing the department name and the date of the inventory, will be sent to the department head and will be available for the software coordinator, if requested. It will also list the following by each employee:

❖ Hardware assigned

❖ Software left on each computer after inventory

❖ Unauthorized software removed, by computer

❖ Total purchase cost of hardware

❖ Total purchase cost of software

❖ Total purchase cost of both hardware and software

A Department Hardware Inventory Report will be run, after the Department Users Report, for each department. A copy will be sent to the department head and to the PC coordinator and/or computer asset manager. It will list the following:

❖ Department name

❖ Date the report was run

❖ Hardware type, quantity, and total cost of each type

❖ Total cost of the department's hardware inventory

A Total Hardware/Software Asset Report will be run, listing the hardware/software assets by department. There will be four columns across each page: name of the department, number of PCs, the total original investment for hardware/software, and average age of department PCs. The bottom line will indicate totals of the same information for the whole company. This report, run at the end of the fiscal year and upon demand, will be sent to the head of information systems, the controller, and the computer asset manager.

The consultant is expected to produce "clean" printouts of all reports contracted for before the system is considered operational. After the system has been accepted by IS management, it will be maintained by the person appointed to service the asset management system. After the contract has been completed, further assistance or any changes to the system will be negotiable with the consultant.

IN-HOUSE ASSET MANAGEMENT PROJECT

Developing, installing, and operating an asset management system is a complex effort. The development and installation should be handled as a project, and the installation should provide a well-documented, operating asset management system.

A project manager should be appointed to head up this project. A computer asset manager should be appointed to serve on the project and later to administer the firm's system. In addition, he/she must have the qualities and skills of a good project manager, be familiar with PC hardware and software, and understand software licenses and copyrights.

Developing the Asset Management Plan

The project manager and computer asset manager develop the Asset Management Plan, with the approval of the head of information systems. The plan should contain the following:

A **Asset management project team.** An asset management project team will be formed, the size to be determined by the head of information systems.

B **Preplanning survey.** The project team will develop a hardware and software asset management plan. Before its completion, a survey will be conducted as to current:

❖ Internal hardware controls

❖ Internal software controls

COMMENT

The computer asset manager should contact the Software Publishers Association at 1730 M St. NW, Suite 700, Washington, D.C. 20036-4510, or call 1-800-388-7478 for current PC and client/server information. A copy of the Association's latest newsletter is available on the Internet at www.sta.org, and antipiracy information is available through its home page. It provides information, courses, and membership opportunities. It is advisable to have both the project manger and computer asset manager attend one of its seminars.

❖ Acquisition procedures for hardware and software

❖ PC data and software protection

❖ Software license compliance

❖ Unauthorized PC hardware (including unauthorized Zip or floppy disks)

❖ Unauthorized PC software

This information will define the current status to be used as a control. It will also provide information as to how the asset management system can be installed with a minimum of conflict and effort.

C **Asset management plan.** The plan utilizes the information from the preplanning survey to:

❖ Define components of the proposed system.

❖ Draft a project timetable.

❖ Plan the selection of standard software.

❖ Plan for communication of the implementation.

❖ Plan for the needed controls.

❖ Select a user test area for the system.

❖ Determine project and operation costs.

Plan Implementation

Implementing the plan is a major part of the asset management project. Following are the major areas:

❖ Selecting and obtaining delivery of software

❖ Installing the software

❖ Testing the software

❖ Training operational personnel

❖ Setting up the help-desk

❖ Preparing for a system audit

❖ Asset tagging the hardware and software inventory

❖ Establishing proof of purchase for the software

❖ Taking corrective actions

❖ Developing a continual audit program

❖ Establishing an operating hardware/software acquisition system

❖ Maintaining a PC users' education program

❖ Installing and maintaining a disaster recovery system

❖ Providing network security and an antivirus system

Implementation and Operation

The implementation starts in a prototype area, preferably one that will offer the best opportunity to debug the system. After that area is operational, the system can be implemented in the next best areas for success. Following are steps to be followed to implement and operate the new asset management system:

A **Inventory of hardware.** The inventory should done in the shortest calendar time possible. After each unit has been completed, an update procedure should be established to maintain a current inventory. Augment this update by random inventory spot-checks.

Tag hardware items inventoried with a scannable inventory tag placed on the equipment in the same location for each type of hardware. Each new acquisition of hardware must be tagged before the system becomes operational. The purchase price, department, and employee responsible for the hardware will be input to the PC inventory system.

B **Physical inventory of software.** PC software inventory can be taken the same time as the hardware or later, depending on the system software selected. The software of each PC and file server will be identified and logged in. Unauthorized software will be purged and recorded in order to identify to what degree, for each area and user, software violations have occurred.

Software data, by each PC (desktop, laptop, and notebook system) and person responsible for the computer(s), will be keyed into the PC inventory system. The software information entered will be purchase price, department, and employee-assigned.

C   PC inventory system. Departments and employees within departments maintaining an ongoing hardware and software inventory will use the PC inventory system. The system will generate a physical inventory report by department after the first and subsequent inventories. The physical report will also be run at the end of each fiscal year and upon demand by the software coordinator.

A copy of the department report is sent to the department head and to the software coordinator and/or computer asset manager. The Department Software Report will list:

❖   Department name

❖   Date the physical inventory was taken

❖   Name, total quantity, and total cost of each software type

❖   Total cost of the department's software inventory

❖   Number of each kind of software removed

A detailed listing of each employee and his/her assigned PC will also be produced. A copy of this Department Users Report, containing the department name and the date of the inventory, will be sent to the department head and made available for the software coordinator and/or computer asset manager, if requested. This report will also list the following by each employee:

❖   Hardware assigned

❖   Post-inventory authorized software by computer

❖   Unauthorized software removed, by computer

❖   Hardware total cost

❖   Software total cost

❖   Both hardware and software total purchased costs

A Department Hardware Inventory Report will be run, after the Department Users Report, for each department. A copy will be sent to the department head, to the PC coordinator, and to the computer asset manager. It will list:

❖   Department name

❖   Date the report was run

❖   Hardware type, quantity, and total cost of each type

❖   Total cost of the department's hardware inventory

A Total Hardware/Software Asset Report will be run, listing the hardware/software assets by department. There will be four columns across each page: name of department, number of PCs, total original investment for hardware/software, and average age of department PCs. The bottom line will indicate totals of the same information for the whole company. This report, run at the end of the fiscal year and upon demand, is sent to the head of information systems, the controller, and the computer asset manager.

COMPUTER HARDWARE ACQUISITIONS

Computer hardware acquisitions can come in more than one form. Hardware can be purchased, leased, or provided by a third-party lease. Acquisitions can come from one or more of these sources. The most practiced one is for the outright purchase of hardware. If it is more practical to lease the hardware, but the vendor will not, a third-party lease may be arranged. Vendors encounter this often enough that they may have some recommendations. Some leases cover a buyout at the end of the lease or third-party lease.

Signing a lease will require the firm's legal representative review the documents before any commitment is made. The purchasing department should also be contacted to insure that the company's acquisition policies are followed.

Major Systems Acquisitions

Any projects affecting more than one department and/or without budgeted funds allocated for such a system are identified as a major acquisition by the head of information systems. User managers will send a memo to the head of the information systems unit and a copy to the person to whom the head of information systems reports. This memo addresses the need for a major computer system acquisition. The memo can originate from one or more user management person(s) or the systems analysis unit's head.

The memo will cover the following issues:

- ❖ The area of the firm that will be affected by the new system
- ❖ A defined need for the acquisition
- ❖ Cost savings expected and the expected life span of the proposed system
- ❖ The maximum calendar time allowed for the expected system to be operational
- ❖ A priority ranking provided for this project as compared with others under study or development

A **Analysis of new systems request.** The head of information systems and his/her superior review the requesting memo. Management evaluates the merits of doing a preliminary systems needs study and the status of the total organization's budget situation. The information systems head sends a reply memo to the requesting manager. The information systems head sends a memo giving the reason for the denial or approval for a feasibility study. If approved, a preliminary systems needs study (which is identified as a feasibility study) will be done. A memo to that effect is sent to the head of systems analysis. The memo asks for a feasibility study and provides the following information:

- ❖ When results of the study are to be expected
- ❖ The people and monetary resources provided for the study
- ❖ What user personnel are to be contacted
- ❖ What level of confidentiality is expected of the preliminary systems needs study

B **Feasibility study.** An analysis of the users' areas can assist the feasibility study before it is undertaken. This information would be helpful before attempting to contact the users for a formal study. Gather as much information about the units as possible before conducting a formal study.

Contact the user personnel identified in the requisition memo received for the assigned project. Remembering the names of the unit's personnel and their respective titles would be helpful. Find out who controls the informal unit organization, who at times can be known as the power behind the throne. They can influence the feasibility study, and even more so when and if a new system is in place. Any knowledge of the corporate politics involved can be helpful. The status of units in the corporate pecking order provides insight regarding the proposed computer system's chances of success.

Examine current procedural documentation. Follow up with a study of the actual procedures followed by the unit's employees. The operating procedure study should include input and output documents. All existing files will be documented—these include hardcopy and computer files. Computer files and their sources will be documented, including the following:

- ❖ Data files only on given computers
- ❖ Data files on local area networks
- ❖ The local area network server's databases

❖ Data used from other sources

The current systems operation studied should provide the following information needed for a final systems design to be completed later:

❖ System flowcharts

❖ Dataflow diagrams

❖ Document flowcharts

❖ Data dictionary

❖ Current procedure flowcharts

❖ Any work sampling studies done

❖ Current operation costs (i.e., direct costs and indirect costs)

❖ Generated reports and/or computer monitor displays

An evaluation of the proposed system is made for its justification. The feasibility will be determined by several factors:

1 Operation feasibility. Operation feasibility analysis determines if the solution will meet end-user requirements: Does the solution fit into the end-user operational environment and meet the requirements of an acceptable time schedule? It ascertains meeting the user's human factors requirements and also fits into the organization's social work scene.

2 Technical feasibility. Technical feasibility analysis determines if the solution is technically practical: Is the technology available or soon to be available and can the end-user and the facilities accommodate the solution?

3 Economic feasibility. Economic feasibility analysis determines if the solution meets measurements of cost-effectiveness. It is justified by a cost-benefit analysis. There are situations that may override economic feasibility. This is when government legislation, customer requirements, or union contracts mandate that it will be done.

When it is completed, the feasibility study will be sent to the head of information systems for his/her approval. When the head of information systems approves the feasibility study, he/she writes a cover memo. The memo will be attached to the report and sent to his/her superior and all user managers involved in the original needs request.

If the feasibility study is not approved, a copy will be returned to the authors of the study with recommendations noted on the document. A cover memo will be written and attached to the returned study reviewing why the study was rejected and what is needed for approval. The required changes and/or additions to the study will be done. If needed, a revised study will be resubmitted for the final approval of the head of information systems.

C **Final systems design.** The final approved system design will be one of the following:

- ❖ A turnkey system provided and operated by a third-party vendor
- ❖ A turnkey system provided by a vendor
- ❖ Company-acquired hardware with a third party providing the software
- ❖ In-house-produced software with company-acquired computer hardware
- ❖ In-house-produced software with company-acquired computer hardware with vendor assistance

Whatever system design and installation will be designated by the head of information systems and financial management approval is required for the final systems design and operation.

The priority assigned by management will determine the priority of the project. The new major computer system will determine the resources and timeframe to install it. The systems designer who performed the feasibility study will (at a minimum) be available to assist the project's completion. The head of information systems and the head of the systems unit determine the degree the project is supported by the current resources. A project manager will be appointed to manage the project's completion. See Chapter 5 for more detailed information about project management.

Budgeted Hardware Acquisitions

Computer budgeting can be done several ways. Hardware budgets are allocated for the entire process of designing and placing the computer system into operations. This is a budgeted item that may cover one or more budget years. Other budgeted hardware acquisitions can be found in different budgeting forms. There are several options with which to acquire computer hardware. One or more may be employed by the organization.

A **Information systems hardware committee.** The head of information systems assigns the computer hardware asset management responsibility to the information technology asset manager. An information systems hardware committee is formed. The chairperson of the committee will be the information technology asset manager. The information systems head appoints members from the programming, operations, and systems technology areas. A representative is appointed by the purchasing manager and the CFO. The committee provides information required for the maintenance of the approved computer hardware list.

No less often than monthly, an update of any added or deleted hardware will be made to the asset management hardware database. An asset management hardware status report is issued monthly. The report is made available to committee members one week before the committee meeting. Minutes of each monthly and special meeting are kept. Approved copies of the minutes will be sent to the committee members and the head of information systems by the IT asset manager.

Any hardware that is not on the current approved computer hardware list will be flagged. The approved computer hardware list is a screening device for current computer hardware acquisitions. The information will be current and available via online access or published listings. Past acquisitions not on the current approved computer hardware list still may be authorized by the head of information systems. Current acquisitions are required to be listed. New computer hardware acquisitions will be listed. The approved computer hardware list is updated and distributed by the chairperson of the information systems hardware committee/IT asset manager.

In cases of special one-time hardware needs not on the approved computer hardware list, an acquisition waiver may be granted. A request is sent to the chairperson of the information systems hardware committee. The chairperson brings the request before the information systems hardware committee. The committee replies to the request. The reply memo is sent to the head of information systems for his/her final approval.

Approved memos will be signed by the head of information systems and sent to the person requesting the hardware. The IT hardware person is sent a copy of the memo. Disapproved requests are returned to the committee for follow-up action. These special hardware items are added to the asset management hardware database when placed into service.

B **Corporate lump-sum budget.** Senior management will allocate a lump-sum budget based on information provided by the information systems head. The information systems head may assign the task of collecting information for the hardware needs to the information technology asset manager.

C **IT hardware loans.** The IT hardware person reviews the request in light of other approvals to the same unit. If not approved, a memo to that effect is sent to the person requesting the hardware with the reason for refusing the request. The memo may be in the form of a hard-copy memo or e-mailed to the person. A copy of the memo will be stored with the request file for that unit. The copy may be in the form of hardcopy or a file maintained in a computer database.

If the loan of equipment is available and approved, it will be issued from the reserve equipment stock. Organizations with a computer store will provide for the loan of the hardware. Whichever unit provides the equipment will maintain a follow-up file. Further information, such as recording who signed for the equipment, the unit to which it is to be loaned, and the expected return date information, must be filed by the return date. Expected return dates will be followed up on by the person making the loan. If the computer hardware is borrowed from another department, the information technology asset manager will be informed.

D **Stocked hardware.** If the information systems unit maintains a stock of computer hardware, the IT hardware person will issue the hardware from the stock supply. He/she will update the computer inventory stock file for the items taken from stock. The hardware may also be made available from the company computer store. The store's inventory record will be updated. The IT hardware person posts an approval and dates and signs the memo. He/she also records on the memo the proper item name and tag number of the hardware. The original copy of the memo is filed, a copy returned to the requesting unit manager, and a copy sent to the information technology asset manager.

Purchasing Expendable Computer Supplies

Computer supply items cover all supplies used by computers, computer peripheral equipment, and other office support equipment. These assets are expended most often during the fiscal year. These assets must meet the required standards established by an IT supply standards committee.

A **IT supply standards committee.** The committee will be made up of IT operational, IT systems, and IT planning personnel. The purchasing department manager appoints a representative to this committee. The committee selects supply items and the vendors to be on the approved purchasing supply list. These items and/or vendors may change at the discretion of the IT supply standards committee. The chairperson for the committee will be appointed by the head of information systems. Representatives of the other IT units are appointed by their respective unit heads. The committee will meet monthly and as needed.

The committee addresses all internal correspondence and provides a reply from other correspondence. Vendors may contact the chairperson of the committee to make a presentation to the committee. Other persons within the organization may refer their received correspondence to this committee to be addressed. The committee replies to all correspondence referred to it by other departments. Minutes that will be taken at each meeting will be provided to all committee members. The minutes will be approved at the next meeting. The head of information systems, the asset manager, and any top management person requesting it, receives a copy of the approved committee minutes.

The committee publishes an approved purchasing supply list (expendable assets) and provides copies to the supply department, computer store head, purchasing agents, and all unit supervisors. Any person not on the distribution list may request to receive copies of the approved purchasing supply list. Copies are for company use and no part of the list is to be made available to anyone outside the firm.

B **Maintaining expendable supplies.** Maintaining expendable supply policies and procedures for computer and computer support devices is the responsibility of the IT supply standards committee. This covers the following areas:

1 Maintaining quality standards for IT supply items.

2 The IT supply standards committee sets the supply product items standards, and is responsible for maintaining the consistency of the purchases.

3 Maintaining corporate IT expendable purchasing policies.

4 The IT supply standards committee follows the policies set down by the company purchasing department and/or the material control department.

5 Expendable computer supply policies and procedures.

Policies are recommended by the IT supply standards committee, which require the asset manager's and top management's final approval. The committee approves of the procedures required for the provision, maintenance, and control of expendable computer supplies.

For vendor contracting policies, please refer to Chapter 15. The vendors selected must meet quality standards first, and price, second.

The IT supply standards committee will monitor the quality of all supplies on a continuous basis. User feedback is encouraged with all supply products. Committee members spot-check the use of the supply items within its jurisdiction. Any problem will be studied to ensure that it is not a machine, operator, or environmental problem before the problem is brought to the attention of the vendor. The vendor's reaction will determine if that item will be purchased in the future from the same vendor. It is the sole responsibility of the IT supply standards committee to decide from which vendor the supply items are purchased.

C **Stocking expendable computer supplies.** The IT supply standards committee will be responsible for approving the policies and procedures for stocking expendable computer supply assets before its policy is presented to the head of information systems. The superior of the information systems head will give the final approval for the policies. The information systems head and asset manager give the final approval for the procedures.

A project team approved by the information systems head and the IT supply standards committee writes procedures for the stocking operation. The IT systems unit committee representative is the project team manager for this task. The following will be considered when pursuing this project:

1 **Storage area.** A central location is recommended for the storage and control of the supply items.

2 **More than one location.** If more than one storage location is required, one of the locations will be the major storage location. The major storage location will contain seldom-requested supply items. It also provides for a backup supply for some items. This stock may be items that, if purchased in larger amounts, will have quantity discounts.

3 **Primary storage location.** If there is more than one stock location, the major storage location should have the largest number of stock transactions. Storage areas should be located to provide optimum distance from users.

4 **Security.** Storage locations will be well secured when not in use. They will be provided with the recommended optimum temperature and humidity at all times.

D **Inventory control system.** An inventory control system of all items may be maintained by a PC. Standard inventory control software packages are available on the market. The IT supply standards committee and asset manager will be furnished a monthly usage report. The report will contain the following data:

❖ Monthly usage quantity and cost of item

❖ Total expense of all items taken from stock

❖ Monthly dollars each unit received from stock and the year-to-date dollars for all items received

- ❖ Cumulative usage of each item and its cost to date
- ❖ Percent of dollars of supply items received by unit of the total consumed, by month and year-to-date
- ❖ Budgeted dollars allocated by month compared with the actual used
- ❖ Year-to-date actual dollars compared with budget dollars used

E **Budgeting expendable computer supplies.** Information from the inventory control system reports is used by the IT supply standards committee to plan the budgeting needs. Any unit having an unexpected usage affecting the total budgeted dollars will be asked to explain its needs. This is so more dollars may be requested for the next budget year.

Any excess of actual dollars used as compared with the budgeted inventory total dollars usage is reported, by memo or e-mail, to the head of information systems and asset manager. When this problem arises, the head of information systems should be provided as much advance notice as possible.

The cost of maintaining the stock of expendable computer supplies will be part of the information systems budget. The person responsible for the operation and control of this inventory will also report to the manager of corporate material control or asset manager.

Procurement Process

Company vendor policies are established by the company's purchasing department. The purchasing department provides a service for the entire company, just as the information systems unit provides service to the company. Working with the purchasing department, information systems is the user. Information systems should provide the same cooperation with purchasing it expects from its users. Purchasing will not necessarily be the only contact for vendors. This depends on the type of purchased item.

Purchasing requisitions used by information systems will be the same kind used throughout the organization. If there is no company purchase requisition form available, the systems unit designs a purchasing form. The head of information systems and purchasing are required to approve the form.

A **Purchasing expendable computer supplies.** Computer supply items requiring custom designing will be done by one or more purchasing department representatives. These representatives will be provided with a current copy of the approved purchasing supply list and any changes that will be forthcoming with the next issue of the list. This provides for a more efficient operation. Purchasing's contact source will be known by information systems personnel and vendors. The Purchasing department will, at times, be contacting the same vendor for purchasing noncomputer-related products.

For small-item purchasing, a credit system reduces the time and cost of procurement. Charge limits would be set and payments covering the blanket purchases. The final procedure would be worked out with the accounts payable unit. Credit card companies provide this kind of service, one being American Express, Small Business Services, P.O. Box 31502, Salt Lake City, UT 84131-9956. They will provide an American Express Gold Corporate Card. A list of authorized employees should receive the cards. This is a competitive business, and it is wise to shop around for the best service.

B **Computer hardware purchase acquisition.** All purchase orders will be issued from purchase requisitions approved only by authorized information systems representatives. These purchase requisitions should be funneled to the same purchasing agents each time because of their familiarity with both the vendor and products. These purchases are for standard hardware items under the asset manager's jurisdiction. If the Purchasing department can arrange for early payment to take advantage of payment discounts, do so. Expense records will have to be adjusted to reflect these cost savings.

Small-item assets may be purchased with a credit card system with limits per purchase. Arrangement and procedure requires the approval of the accounts payable unit. There are credit card companies that will provide this kind of service, one being American Express, Small Business Services, P.O. Box 31502, Salt Lake City, UT 84131-9956. They will provide an American Express Gold Corporate Card. A list of authorized employees should receive the cards. This is a competitive business, and it is wise to shop around for the best service.

C **Computer hardware disposal.** The purchasing organization may be asked to assist with the disposal of unnecessary computer equipment. They may sell it or donate it to a charity. The longer one waits to get rid of used equipment, the harder it will be to dispose of. The IT asset manager and capital asset accounting unit should be contacted about the equipment disposal. They also should be contacted for any money collected or donation credit received for the hardware.

The removed hardware will be deleted from the computer hardware database. The IT hardware person removes the tags before the hardware is disposed of. The IT asset manager is notified by memo or e-mail that the hardware has been disposed of.

COMPUTER SOFTWARE ACQUISITIONS

The purpose of a computer software acquisition policy is to formalize a uniform standard for computer software acquisitions throughout the organization. This policy mandates the endorsement and support by the CEO/head of the organization.

The computer acquisition policy covers all computer software used by the organization. An organization can have several kinds of computer software. The kinds of software will depend on its source. Each computer source will require its own software acquisition policy. The sources/kinds of computer software include the following:

- ❖ Company-written software
- ❖ Contract personnel-written software
- ❖ Vendor-written turnkey system software
- ❖ Purchased operating systems
- ❖ Purchased packaged software
- ❖ Leased software
- ❖ Bootlegged software
- ❖ Pirated software

The objective is to provide the guidelines for having uniform programming software, purchased operating systems, and programs. This also covers all proprietary software, including development, writing, and contracting. Sole ownership of the program's source coding ratifies the programs as proprietary. The code is loaded to a compiler. It will generate the operating program. There will be standards for proposing and recommending benchmarks, vendor selection, and contracting. Purchased software is approved for payment after passing the testing criteria. The purchasing of operating program (object-coded) software is limited to its defined purchase agreement specifications that come with packaged software.

Each type of software has its own software policy requirements. These are directives needed, in addition to the general guidelines, for all software.

A **Company-written proprietary software.** All programming will be done in the approved programming language. All programs written using company software, hardware, and any other company-owned resources are company property. Programming documentation and operation manuals will follow established standards.

B **Contract-written proprietary software.** All contracted programmers will employ the same programming standards and procedures as do company programmers. Documentation, test data, and drafted work information are the property of the company. The company is the sole owner of the source-coded programs.

C **Turnkey system contracting.** This is a vendor-developed turnkey system, including development cost and the program's source coding, and belongs to the company. The company has the copyright and/or patent rights to the developed turnkey system software. Top management can approve other contract arrangements. Any third-party add-on software used will be identified. Limitations on the use of the third-party software will be defined. Its warranties, restrictions, and operations will be fully identified.

D **Purchased packaged operating systems software.** There will be standard uniform operating systems software. There will be no more systems in operation than licensed. The information systems committee will identify the authorized system software version.

E **Purchased packaged program software.** Only approved program software is permitted. There will be only properly licensed programs in operation. The information systems software committee will identify the software version to be allowed. Modifications may be done at the vendor's discretion. These modifications will be provided and identified by the version number.

F **Leased software.** Some software is only marketed by lease arrangements. There will be only properly leased programs in operation.

G **Bootlegged software.** Bootlegged software will not be loaded onto any company computer. Repeated violations of this policy are grounds for dismissal.

H **Pirated software.** Pirated software will not be loaded onto any company computer. Violations of this policy are grounds for dismissal.

Proprietary-developed Software

Proprietary-developed software come from several sources. Required software that is not listed on the asset management software database file or available for purchase or lease may need to be developed. When the developed proprietary software becomes operational, this information will be put into the asset management software database file. The information systems software committee decides if the software will be listed on the approved computer software list. The software's source will be identified on the approved computer software list. This allows potential users to contact the developers for information about the software. The company can have its proprietary software developed by more than one method.

A **End-user developed software.** User-developed software follows the firm's policy for software developed. The information systems area resources will be available, as time is accessible from the information technology units. Monies may be budgeted to departments for such development. Some users can develop their own software. Depending on the area of operations, there can be different levels of skills available. Depending on the corporate culture, user activity varies. At times it would not only be faster to accomplish the task, but even possibly at a lower cost. The average information systems unit is overwhelmed by backlogs. It would be helpful to have users reduce the load of the IT units. Department managers may even buy computers and vendor assistance if they are required to, hopefully not because of IS disinterest.

1 **The inception process.** The end-user department head is required to approve user-developed software within his/her jurisdiction. The user's department head should receive a memo, from the requesting party, defining the need for the unavailable software. The department head can also originate the memo. The memo will be part of the project documentation. This is required before any effort is expended developing the software.

User-developed software will be done at the user's own expense. The information technology asset manager will be contacted before end-user-developed software is produced. The user manager will be informed about available software that may assist the project. Also, user management will be informed of what is available from the asset management software database. Not all company-used software is listed on the approved computer software list. Computer programs may be available that can be used as is or with some modification. Information is available about third-party add-on module software. This module software can be part of the program being developed and save programming time. When users are writing their software, they may find a need for third-party software. It is then that the IT asset manager should be contacted for assistance.

2 **End-user resources.** Consulting resources will be provided by the IS organization when time is available. User management determines what kind of assistance is required. The assistance available from the information systems organization, when needed, should be known before pursuing the project. The information systems unit may charge for this service, depending on the company policy for interdepartment service billing. When information systems has no time available, they can provide vendor

sources for user assistance. Payment for this service will be from the user's budget, unless other provisions have been made. The information technology asset manager will assist end-user management with vendor negotiations.

3 **Developing end-user software.** The user will employ an approved software compiler, for example, Visual Basic (a Microsoft product). The user should contact the help-desk with any problems with the compiler software. If the help-desk person cannot help, he/she recommends a referral. Writing user computer programs should follow the procedures for programming methods provided by IS. For more information see Chapter 4, *Programming Procedures*.

4 **End-user software documentation.** A copy of the project, including source codes, software, and supporting documentation, is sent to the chairperson of the information systems software committee. The committee examines and tests the computer software under the leadership of the IT programming representative on the committee. The approved software requires a memo written by the IT programming representative describing the value of the software. The memo will be sent to the head of information systems and the information technology asset manager. They will determine if the new software warrants being listed on the approved computer software list.

5 **End-user software completion.** After testing is completed, all software documentation is brought up-to-date. Test results are part of the documentation. Any operation manual needed for the operation of the software is written and tested by users who do not have any knowledge about the new software. After extensive successful testing has been completed, the user may employ the software within his/her own operation. The manager of the user department writes an authorizing memo permitting the software to be used in his/her department. The memo contains information on the software's performance. A copy of the memo is placed in the documentation folder and a copy sent to the information technology asset manager. The IT asset manager updates the asset management software database using this information.

6 **User follow-up procedures.** The user developer of the software forwards a copy of the project documentation folder and the software—both the source and object-coded programs—to the chairperson of the information systems software committee, who is also the IT asset manager. The copies will include both a hardcopy of the program software and the operating program on disk.

A copy of the operations manual for user operation is sent with the copy of the documentation folder. The information systems software committee may elect to make the user-developed software available companywide by placing it on the approved computer software list. The software may be used by other parts of the company. The approved computer software list will identify who developed and first used the software. The IT programming unit member of the information systems software committee retains the software folder and the programs in a user-developed software file. The file contains user-developed software found on the approved computer software list and software that is not on the list, but is in the asset management software database.

7   Other users' involvement. If the software will be used as part of a system employed by other users, approval is required by the IS software committee and the heads of the IT programming and computer operations units. To insure there will not be a problem with any integrated operating software or database, a copy of the software folder is sent to the head of the IT programming unit for his/her study. He/she reviews the information with the head of IT computer operations. The programming unit's representative on the committee must confirm that the software meets the firm's information technology standards. Any IT unit head may request a duplicate copy of the software folder. With the approval of the IT programming unit head, the help-desk will support the software.

B   IS-developed software. The IT programming unit of the information systems department may develop software for users or its own needs. User department heads may request the software by a memo to the information systems head. The information systems head may have user management direct the request to the IT programming unit head. The request will be reviewed in light of other requests and the current workload of the available programming staff. If the request is one not requiring a major new system, the information systems head will be notified along with the requesting user department head. A memo or e-mail message will provide what course of action the user manager may take.

1   New software development study. A study to be conducted for the development of new software requires a formal request by approved user management and/or IT unit heads. The request will provide the following information:

❖   When are results of the study to be expected?

❖ What software may be available that can be purchased and used as is or modified for this application?

❖ When will the project be completed and in operation?

After the requested information is returned and studied, the IT programming head summarizes the information in a memo and sends it to the information systems head. The information systems head decides what course of action the IT programming head will take with the project. The reply can be a memo or e-mail.

These procedures are for projects without their own budget—resources are provided from existing budgets. Major system projects, with their required software development, will be provided with their own budgets when annual budgets are granted.

2 **Software maintenance.** Updating current software in use by information system's IT operations or user application operations will require maintenance. A software maintenance request will be sent to the IT programming head and contain the following information:

❖ The completion date needed for the required program changes

❖ Which software programs are modified

❖ What the modifications will contain. Any I/O changes will have attached the current and new I/O layouts

C **Contract programming.** Software development may be contracted for user or IT computer operations. Unless the company has already a blanket vendor contract for software development, competitive bids will be solicited from two or more software contracting vendors. The vendors will be provided with information for contract bid proposals. At a minimum, the request for bid proposals will contain the following information:

❖ Which contact person will be the source for more information and submitting his/her bid proposal?

❖ Will the contract call for maintenance of new programs?

❖ What type of application will be programmed? Examples would be billing, payroll, inventory control, etc.

❖ If maintenance programming is required, in what language is the software written?

❖ What language is the new software to be written in? If the vendor proposes an alternate one, what would be the benefits?

❖ Will the bids requested be for contract hours or a project? For project bids, interested vendors will be provided with the detail information. It is advisable that the project be well defined before requesting project bids.

❖ The due date for bids.

❖ The expected start and finish dates.

❖ What are the skill levels of the people who will be working for the vendor?

❖ What is the dollar amount of the bid?

1 **Hourly contracting.** The programming effort is paid hourly. Enough money should be available to complete the task. Have a contingency reserve set aside. For new program development, running out of money presents a far greater problem than a maintenance task. It's more difficult to finish a partly completed program that someone else has started. The purchase requisition identifies the vendor will be paid for hours worked. Purchasing requisitions identify how the vendor will bill, either lump sum or partial payments. If something other than a monthly check is issued, accounts payable should know.

a **Programming.** The programming can be done in-house or at the vendor's location. The programmers will submit a weekly report of hours worked by day. Each day, the work effort and persons contacted regarding that day's work effort will be recorded. If contact is not related to that day's work effort, why is it being billed? A daily log will be kept of the detail-supporting information for the weekly report. The log may be manually kept and will be the property of the company. It will be submitted weekly to the company's contact person. The vendor (for its own records) may want to make a copy of this log.

b **Company contact person.** The company's software vendor contact person should examine each week's vendor billing information before approving payment. The daily detailed information will be examined weekly. As more time passes, it becomes harder to confirm detailed information. If need be, a contact may be made with the vendor for any questions that may arise. Don't delay this action too long. Vendors' memories are no better than anyone else's.

c **Vendor payment.** Paying the vendor requires a purchase order. The purchase order may be in the form of a blanket purchase order, allowing the purchase order to be paid by accounts payable in installments as approved by the person signing the purchase requisition. The vendor will submit a bill to the company contact person for payment. The bill is confirmed to be correct. Approval is noted, dated, and signed, and then sent to accounts payable. A copy of the bill is made for filing. The dollar amount left that was allotted for the task is noted on the copy before it is filed. If it appears that the task will not be completed before the allotted funds run out, this is reported to the contact person's superior.

2 **Project contracts.** Contract programming by project is for a well-defined programming project with detailed acceptance criteria. No vendor timekeeping is required. The project will have a calendar finish date.

   a **Project tasks.** The tasks within the contracted project are plotted on a Gantt chart. The completion date of each task is reported in writing, dated, and signed by the vendor. It is sent to the information systems project contact person for the project. If it is a user project, the information will be provided to the user vendor contact person. A copy of the Gantt chart is signed and dated for each completed week of the project. The chart represents the work plotted for the work week, Monday through Friday, and is provided to the designated company contact person who receives it by the following Wednesday.

   b **Project contract.** A contract is drawn for the project. It defines in detail what is to be accomplished. The authorized person signs the contract after approval by the firm's legal representative. A purchase requisition with a copy of the contract attached is sent to purchasing. Purchasing sends a purchase order to the vendor who uses the purchase order number for a billing reference. Input and output documents detail the I/O information furnished the vendor. Printed program source and object codes will be provided no later than one week after shown as completed on the Gantt chart. The user provides the test data for detail testing of all conditions that can be expected. Examples of output testing will be provided to the company contact person along with a printed copy of the actual test data used.

   c **Penalty clause.** The contract will contain a penalty clause. The clause states the penalty for each workday the project is late. If the user would benefit from an early completion date, a bonus could be included for each workday it is finished early. The bonus clause would be after all other things are agreed upon. This avoids any padding by the vendor.

d **Bill payment.** An invoice/bill is sent to the company project contact person. The company has 30 days to confirm
that all contract conditions have been met. Any work added
by the company will be paid by issuing a separate purchase
requisition and following the same procedure as the original
project contract. When the project is accepted as complete,
accounts payable is notified by sending them the
invoice/bill with a noted approval, date, and approving
authority signature. The vendor will be paid with one check
for the purchase orders. If there are any unresolved disputes
with the vendor, the firm's legal representative will be contacted for resolution.

Purchased Software

This section covers the purchase and control of software. These are nonpro-
prietary programs. The software's manufacturer is the owner of the source
and object programs. When the operating (object) program and instructions
are packaged for sale, it is for use by one computer. The purchaser has limited claims to the software. Most often the software, registration card, and
instructions are boxed and sealed with shrink-wrap material. To accept a
return without the shrink-wrap, if permitted, the vendor will require a
restocking charge, including the reshrink-wrapping of the box. The program
disks are often in a sealed envelope. The sealed envelope usually contains the
printed warranties and liabilities. Included is the warning that when the seal
is broken, you own the software and you agree to the terms of the license
agreement. This is no longer a returnable product.

The information systems software committee is chaired by the IT asset
manager. Its major task is keeping abreast of new acceptable vendor-provided software. The committee is comprised of the heads of IT units, with the
information technology asset manager as the chairperson. The Purchasing
department may have a representative on the committee.

No less often than a monthly update of any added or deleted software
will be made to the asset management software database. The approved computer software list is updated at the same meeting of the IS software committee meeting. An asset management software database status report is
issued monthly. The report will be made available to committee members
one week before a committee meeting. Minutes of each monthly and special
meeting are kept. Approved copies of the minutes are sent to the committee
members and the head of information systems.

SOFTWARE ASSETS

The information systems software committee members will keep current with software developments in the IT profession and proprietary software development. If there is (IT or user) Beta testing, the status and results will be reported to the members of the committee.

Selected committee members will form a subcommittee to evaluate newly marketed software. Members will read and evaluate published IT reports. Networking with other outside IT people for information can be beneficial, too. This information will be reported to the whole committee. Software that sounds promising will be purchased and tested in a controlled environment. There will be an annual IT budget for this purpose. Results are reported to the whole committee. With the committee's approval, the software is listed on the IS asset management software database if it meets the testing criteria. Beta opportunities can also be considered. There will be a selection procedure, written by a committee member, for buying new software. The procedure is approved by the IS software committee. End-users can also test sample software under consideration not currently available to them through normal IT channels. This testing is limited to sample files or databases and not online with any network operation.

A **Approved software.** Approved software sanctioned by the information systems software committee will be found on the approved computer software list. The software has been used, tested, and approved by the IT programming unit and the information systems software committee. Being on the approved computer software list means it will be available to users or information systems staff. The only question is whether to charge the software to the information systems budget or a user budget. This question will be addressed by corporate policy.

B **Requesting software.** The unit head requesting the software sends a memo or e-mail message to the information technology asset manager or his/her appointed representative. The memo requests the software be installed on an identified computer or computers. This is for software found on the approved computer software list. At times it may be made available from the asset management software database by the IT asset manager. The request will be for software not contained on the approved computer software list.

1 **Other software.** If software is not on the list and is needed, look for it on the asset management software database. If the software is available and approved to be used, it will be installed on the end-user PC.

2 **Special software needs.** There can be a special need for software that is neither on the approved computer software list nor on the asset management software database. The user's manager sends a request memo to the information systems software committee asking that a waiver be granted with a request to purchase the special software. When and if the software is purchased and received, the software information is posted to the asset management software database. The end-user is required to resolve any software problems with the vendor. If the software gains acceptance, it is placed on the approved computer software list and the help-desk will support the software.

C **Unauthorized software.** Unauthorized software should be of concern to the IT asset manager and the IS software committee. Employing unauthorized software can be a very expensive experience for the company. The information systems software committee is responsible for policing all company computers for any unauthorized software whether it is in use or not. Just the software's presence on the hard drive can provide a problem. If the information systems software committee has never screened all the PCs and the task seems overwhelming, contact a few vendors specializing in this. Select one who has worked with the same hardware/software environment. It will not be cheap, but it is cheaper than the alternative. If the firm is small enough, around-the-clock scrutiny over a weekend and an examination of computers may be revealing. The asset management software database should furnish a list of what is authorized on each computer, including laptops. Have all the laptop computers turned in for "upgrading" so they can also be checked.

Once the 100-percent clean sweep is made, perform surprise checks randomly. Each PC and server should be checked no less than once a year. If the task is too large for the committee, hire contract personnel. It can be done during nonworking hours so as not to disturb the daily operation. All unauthorized software is removed, and the asset management software database list is confirmed for accuracy. Any serious violations will be reported to the information technology asset manager. If the problem is serious, the information technology asset manager reports the details to the information systems head.

D **Antivirus procedures.** To start an antivirus procedure, no software will be brought into the firm that does not belong to the firm. Even authorized disks will be checked for viruses before they can be brought into the firm's work area. This includes newly purchased software prior to its release to the users. The antivirus device will contain the latest version of virus protection. Downloading of any Internet information without specially granted permission is absolutely prohibited. If any virus is detected on a computer, the machine will be disconnected from the network. The computer help-desk is notified as soon as possible by telephone. The e-mail service to the problem computer is taken off-line along with the LAN service. The operators will immediately write down all that led up to the problem.

The next step is the recovery process, done by a representative of information systems who works with PCs and their software. If it is a full-time job, it may be called a PC manager, or the PC store manager may have this duty.

E **Approved computer software list.** The approved computer software list contains software that is approved for user acquisition, including approved software operating systems and company-developed software. To discourage the use of any unapproved software, help-desk support will not be provided to any unauthorized computer/user. The list is primarily a screening device for new software acquisitions. Authorized software not on the approved computer software list, but found on the asset management software database, can still run. The asset management software database lists all software that is permitted to be in use and by whom.

Proprietary software can be on the asset management software database (i.e., software developed by members of the firm and owned by the firm). Users who may have a problem with this software will contact the person(s) who developed the software. There will be a list of third-party add-on software the company has purchased and is on the asset management software database. This software has very limited use and is not supported by the help-desk. If help is required, the IT programming unit should be contacted.

F **Software purchasing.** All purchasing of new software will be done by the IT asset manager with a purchase requisition. The requisition will note possible vendors for the software. Software is seldom purchased directly by the user manager. If it is purchased from the manufacturer, it will most likely be an upgrade. User management may acquire this software through its own or information systems' budget.

1 **Unproven software.** When purchasing software, avoid release of version 1.0 of the product. Any release of that kind may have undiscovered bugs. It is safer to wait until the last number replaces the zero. Unless IT programming has been a Beta site for the software, try to avoid brand-new software. This software is not required to be supported by the IT help-desk.

2 **Software stock.** Some software requests can be made from proprietary stock of software. This requires contacting the IT asset manger, who arranges for the installation on the end-user's computer. Purchased software may also be available from the information technology asset manager or the company computer store. The computer store will have a small inventory of purchased software. The head of the company store sends a request to the IT asset manager for any software issuing or restocking.

3 **IT help-desk.** The help-desk supports purchased software as long as it is on the asset management software database. The asset management software database lists all software permitted for use and by whom. This database is the source by which users can be identified for help-desk assistance. Also supported will be user-written software, with or without third-party purchased add-on software if it is on the approved software list. One or more purchased add-on third-party products can be combined with an in-house written program. If the help-desk has any problems with this software, the caller is referred to the IT programming unit.

The IT programming unit is the reference source for third-party-purchased add-on software. This software is not intended as a computer program unto itself. It is to be used within a main program.

Software Copyright Compliance Planning

Software not in compliance with the authorized ownership puts the company in jeopardy of lawsuits by the manufacturer of the software and/or its distribution provider. It is imperative the IS organization has the full support of top management to develop and maintain a policy of software copyright compliance. The plan should be documented and publicized throughout the company. This in itself will provide credibility; the company has a policy in place and will not tolerate any infraction. Employees who knowingly violate the policy will be dealt with accordingly. Repeat offenders can be held liable for costs incurred by their actions and/or be terminated.

The IS software asset manager has full responsibility for enforcing the unwarranted use of copyrighted software used illegally within the company. There are software packages on the market that can assist this process, and vendors who will undertake a continuous or one-time contract.

The total number of software units installed should be no more than what the contract license stipulates. If the number of software units installed is greater than the license allows, consider how many have to be removed or increase the number of purchased units licensed.

9

POLICIES COVERING PCs: MANAGING THE DESKTOP SYSTEM

STAND-ALONE PC POLICIES

Some firms today do not consider PCs as capital assets, while other firms lease this hardware. Leasing reduces the capital asset accounting activity. But because PCs are so inexpensive and accessible, proprietorship rights are not controlled. In actuality this equipment will cost more, produce less, and jeopardize the firm's operation and security if not properly organized and controlled. The IS organization is the most qualified for this function.

Acquisition of PCs

Information systems management sets the standards for PC hardware acquisitions. These cover:

A The lease, purchase, or rental of PC equipment
B The brand of computers acquired
C The brand of peripheral equipment acquired
D Maintenance contracts

Acquisition of Software

Information systems management controls site-licensed software whose charges are based on quantity. The user pays the cost of software.

Departments may purchase their own software if on the list of software that the information systems department supports.

Personal Hardware and Software

No personal hardware or software is allowed. All hardware and software of any kind, including in-house-developed programs, are the firm's sole property. This policy is enforced to reduce problems with equipment, software failure, damage to data files, and the introduction of viruses. To restrict access to the firm's data and/or programs and prevent virus transmission, disks or tapes belonging to the firm are not to be used in personal home computers.

PC Management and User Support

The information systems department is involved in strategic planning for the firm's PC needs. This includes responsibility for hardware, software, maintenance, user-support, and training. The IS department is also responsible for maintaining backup hardware and software, which are available on a loan basis to users and for coordinating and providing PC user training. Training can consist of both formal classes and individual, self-paced instruction.

The degree of involvement varies dependent on the operation requirements of each department. An advisory panel, consisting of management-level staff and line operations personnel, guides information systems management and settles disputes concerning the firm's current and strategic needs.

COMMENT

The firm's management is responsible for providing current policies insuring that PCs provide the best possible service to the firm. PC anarchy has caused the demise of more than one senior executive.

PC COORDINATOR

The PC coordinator's duties and responsibilities will vary from one location to another, depending on needs. The actual title may also vary, but whatever the title, its objective is to ensure that PC policies are enforced.

Responsibilities of the PC Coordinator

Following are responsibilities of the person assigned the position of PC coordinator:

A Process requests for new hardware and software.

B Keep abreast of user hardware and software needs.

C Provide an ongoing hardware and software troubleshooting service for users to handle day-to-day operating problems.

D Provide informal and formal training assistance for PC users.

E Enforce policies regarding PC hardware and software operations.

F Disseminate new hardware and software information.

G Provide backup service for PC hardware and software.

H Provide PC LAN service and/or supervision.

I Maintain a PC electronic bulletin board for users' concerns.

J Maintain a PC store.

K Publish a PC newsletter.

In-house Consulting Service

The PC coordinator acts as an in-house consultant for users of approved PC equipment and software. This equipment can be in desktop, transportable, laptop, or notebook machine form. Assessing present and future needs of these machines is one of the services provided. The consulting service also covers the areas of PC communications and networking. The coordinator is responsible for maintaining a compatible standard for PC and LAN or WAN communications. The coordinator works with user personnel responsible for communications to ensure continuity and compatibility of the PC systems. The PC coordinator's consulting role includes advising end-users on the true capabilities of equipment and helping them to match needs with the proper, cost-effective equipment.

PC access to mainframe databases requires approval by the coordinator before any contact is made with the database administrator and/or data manager. Be careful to reduce the amount of replicated data floating around since it may not be properly labeled regarding age or origin. Database access often requires the owner's permission.

The coordinator maintains a daily log, which is the data source for monthly reports of his/her activities. Depending on cost accounting practices, users may be charged for the time they use. The daily log will record, by user charge code, time spent on the following items (travel time will also be included):

❖ PC hardware troubleshooting

❖ PC software troubleshooting

❖ Informal and formal training assistance

❖ User consulting service

The coordinator's indirect (administrative cost) time is kept in the following categories:

❖ Reading and other education methods used to keep up with current technology

❖ Communication network services

❖ Electronic bulletin board usage and maintenance

❖ Maintaining the PC store

❖ Publishing newsletters and other information

❖ User education and training preparation when not charged to a given department

❖ General administration duties, etc.

PC Training

The coordinator is the training provider for PC and computer workstation users. The coordinator may enlist the services of the IS training unit or the firm's training department to carry out this responsibility. Training may be provided on a group or individual basis. Charges for this service will follow established cost accounting practices. There is no service charge for the loan of text material, the use of self-paced instruction programs, or the loan of instructional hardware.

COMMENT

Using outside training providers is sometimes an efficient way to provide PC training. Use them and release them as required.

The coordinator will maintain an up-to-date library of reading material and self-instruction programs available for users. The latest versions of operating hardware and software manuals will be included. A good support strategy is to ensure that classes provide good reference material along with sheet(s) listing any site-specific variations or tips.

Instructional programs are developed in-house, contracted for with outside developers, and purchased off-the-shelf. Unless developed or purchased for given departments, the cost is applied to the indirect administrative training budget.

The coordinator will require a work area next to or part of the PC store to house his/her office and training development effort. This area will be:

❖ Secured when not in use

❖ Air conditioned and air purified

❖ Equipped with furniture and storage facilities

❖ Soundproof enough in a given part of the area to record voice or other sound

❖ Equipped with a classroom that can double as a studio if no other is provided (This classroom is not required to be in the same area as the computer store facilities.)

A required minimum of capital equipment is needed for a PC training operation. Most of the items will be stationary, but some may be portable and loaned to users. Keep on hand more than one of each item to be loaned. The following PC training equipment is considered the minimum needed:

❖ White board

COMMENT

Many whiteboards can double as a projection screen.

❖ PC video projector

❖ Tabletop lectern

❖ Portable overhead projector

❖ Flip chart (floor model)

❖ Digital or 35mm camera

❖ Camera copystand with lights (If daylight film is used, blue [daylight rendering] photoflood lights should be used to provide the correct color balance.)

❖ VCR and color monitor

❖ Supply items: nonpermanent color markers, overhead transparencies (both write-on and laser printable), spare projection bulbs, flip chart paper, 35mm daylight slide film (film speed of 200 or more), slide trays, and erasers

PC Newsletter

A PC newsletter is a great place to incorporate feedback from the help-desk for systemic problems. If many users are having the same problem, work arounds can be detailed here. This is a great outreach tool for proactive issues, such as pending upgrades. Remember your audience and keep the style conversational; stay away from technical jargon.

The newsletter may be published monthly, but not less than quarterly. It should announce forthcoming training programs, tell who completed which particular programs, announce new hardware or software availability, list hardware and software available for hands-on experience in the computer store, and list contact telephone numbers for PC or network assistance.

An information systems newsletter may be published instead if it incorporates the information needs of the PC users.

The newsletter can be part of the company intranet or printed as hardcopy. If printed as hardcopy, the size of a newsletter should be 8^1/$_2$- by 11-inch: printed on 11- by 17-inch paper and folded into an 8^1/$_2$- by 11-inch document. If this is not possible, stapled 8^1/$_2$- by 11-inch paper will do. Using desktop publishing software to produce the newsletter would be ideal, but high-end word-processing software can also generate a professional looking newsletter. Graphics and photos will enhance its appearance even more. The "slicker" it is, the more likely to be read.

COMMENT

Remember, a late newsletter may not be called a "news letter" by its readers.

PC ACQUISITION PROCEDURES

The PC coordinator is responsible for the inventory control of all PC hardware (desktop, transportable, laptop, and notebook) and software acquisitions. He/she also assists users with any future hardware and software requirements, and should be attuned to PC users' expected needs.

Purchase requisitions for PC hardware, software, and service or consulting contracts are forwarded to the information systems department's PC coordinator who approves the purchase requisitions, then forwards them to the purchasing department. Purchase requisitions are used only for approved budgeted expenditures.

Hardware Acquisition

The procedures for hardware acquisition are:

A **Approved hardware purchases.** Departments with budget approval for hardware expenditures complete a purchase requisition and forward it to the PC coordinator, who checks the capital expense budget listing and confirms the purchase can be approved.

If not on the approved list, the purchase requisition is returned with a memo explaining the problem. If in order, the coordinator dates and signs the purchase requisition and forwards it to the purchasing department.

B **Hardware loans.** Departments requesting a loan of hardware from the PC store send a memo or e-mail to the coordinator with the following information. (In the event of an emergency, a telephone call will do.)

❖ What is to be loaned? Include a checklist of accessories, such as cables and power supplies that must come back with the unit; otherwise, there will be a delay before loaning it again.

❖ Expected length of time for the loan. A firm return date is critical.

❖ Reason for the loan.

❖ The department and person requesting the loan.

❖ Where the equipment will be used.

❖ The person who will be using the equipment.

The person to whom the equipment is released completes an "out card" that shows the date, time, equipment loaned, serial number, and to whom it is loaned. This card is signed by the receiving person and is filed, by date, under the requesting department. When the item is returned, the card is signed and dated by the person returning the item.

The "out card" file is reviewed once per month. Delinquent borrowers are contacted. Cards for returned items are held on file for one year.

If the item is damaged, it is noted on the card, which becomes the source for a damage memo report completed by the coordinator. This memo is sent to the department head of the borrower. Arrangements are made to repair or replace the piece of equipment. The coordinator decides the cost, if any, that will be charged to the borrower's account for the repair or replacement. Ensure borrowers have removed their data and reload the system's standard configuration promptly on its return before shelving it.

C **New hardware acquisition.** The coordinator serves as an information source for future hardware acquisitions by maintaining a published list of "approved" hardware (hardware sanctioned for purchase). The coordinator's role here is enforcing technical standards. Management approves or rejects purchase requests. Allow for inevitable deviations from the standard for valid business reasons. Ensure there are no alternate purchase channels, such as via MRO where PCs and software can be purchased as "repair parts."

If the desired hardware is listed, the user need only provide budgeted funds for procurement.

However, the purchase of unsanctioned hardware requires a request either for a one-time purchase or that the item be placed on the approved list. The procedure for either action is to write an explanatory memo to the coordinator containing the following information:

❖ Item name and vendor's name and address

❖ Cost of the item

❖ Quantity required

❖ Reason special item is required

❖ What happens if item is not approved

❖ Personnel responsible for item's maintenance

❖ Personnel responsible for training and operation support

If required, the coordinator will hold a meeting with the party interested in the new hardware. If alternate approved hardware is not acceptable to the user, and the request is not resolved, the coordinator contacts the head of information systems for disposition of the problem.

The information systems manager informs the requesting party by memo of his/her decision. If the equipment acquisition is still not approved, the user may appeal in writing to the PC advisory panel whose decision is final.

Software Acquisition

Software may be developed in-house or acquired from an outside source. Only consider in-house software development if no commercially available software can be found for less than the in-house cost. Availability of in-house programming personnel is also a consideration. The coordinator, who decides whether the actual programming effort is done in-house or contracted out, makes arrangements for any in-house-developed software. The cost of this effort is charged to the requesting user's department budget.

Software can be purchased for multiple users or a single user. Most software is purchased from vendors for a one-time cost, while some is only available for an annual fee. Also, upgrades are generally available for a single user or multi-users. Purchased off-the-shelf software is available in two forms. One is for the horizontal market, for widespread use across many different kinds of firms. Examples would be word processing or spreadsheet software. The other is for the vertical market, that is, for applications pertaining to given industries. This kind of software may be more flexible, because in some cases the source code is available, making it possible to alter the program to meet the user's own needs.

It is the coordinator's duty to continually seek newer and better software. He/she maintains a published list of approved software, continually updated with equipment newly approved to respond to new needs. Only approved software may be used. In the event that the coordinator does not approve the requested software, the requesting party may appeal in writing to the PC advisory panel, whose decision is final. As part of the coordinator's role as a technical advisor, try to include a budget for training, especially if this software is for several people. It will reduce the number of help-desk calls, raise user satisfaction, and ensure the company's investment returns benefits as quickly as possible.

Software acquisition procedures are as follows:

A **Specially developed software.** A user requiring software that is not available by purchase works with the coordinator to define the needs. The coordinator then submits a memo to the person responsible for PC programming systems and provides enough information so that a project proposal can be developed and the cost estimated. (In some cases, the PC systems programmer and the coordinator may be the same person.) Project proposal information is reviewed with the user requesting the program. If time and money are available, a formal request in writing is issued by the user management.

Program development is handled using the standard procedures for information systems program development. As long as no security problem exists, the new software is made available to other PC users.

B **Purchased software.** The user sends a memo requesting the approved software to the coordinator who reviews the request and, upon approval, sends the software to the requesting party. An internal charge is made to the requesting department's account.

If the software is not in stock, the coordinator will issue a purchase requisition on behalf of the requesting department, which is copied, while another copy will be forwarded to the purchasing unit.

Send a copy of the class schedule along with the software. Since this is from the approved software list, schedule a class. If no local classes are available, see if local junior colleges offer continuing education classes and forward their schedule and registration forms.

It is critical that the PC coordinator maintain software licenses in a fireproof file cabinet, preferably off-site. In case of a disaster, you may be able to use those copies without repurchasing the software (often the manufacturer will even send a "gold" disk if you have adequate documentation). This is a primary company defense in case of a software audit. From the cost side, it is evidence for buying upgrades instead of purchasing new software.

C **Software registration.** All software registration will be handled, completed, and mailed by the coordinator in the company's name.

D **Software library.** Copies of all in-house-developed PC programs and the original licensed software, as well as backup copies of other purchased software, are maintained in a software library. Users with one-of-a-kind software are encouraged to have backup copies here as well. All software will be the most current version in use. Disks out of the shrink-wrap may require bug fixes. The library ensures the latest stable version is provided. The same applies to manuals' errata sheets. The library is part of the computer store and under the control of the PC coordinator.

E **Software demo disks.** Software demo disks will be provided to users requesting them. These can be provided by vendors or developed in-house, and are not charged to the user's account. Preferably these will run on a dedicated PC, as demos may introduce subtle configuration problems and not all software uninstalls cleanly.

COMMENT

The software library may provide an opportunity for potential users to try software before obtaining their own copies. The library also contains proper documentation and user instructions so that software can be tested. The PC coordinator may be called on to demonstrate software or demo programs to potential users.

The PC Store

The PC store is a hardware and software display area. Hours are indicated next to or on the door and listed in the PC/information systems newsletter. It is secured when closed.

The coordinator maintains the PC store for:

❖ Usable hardware displays

❖ Storage of backup hardware for loan to users

❖ PC hardware accessories

❖ Usable software running on company hard drives or floppies

❖ Packaged software

❖ PC supply items

❖ PC furniture

COMMENT

A picture is worth a thousand words and the "real thing" is worth a thousand pictures. The store displays usable items on the "approved list" so that they can be seen and tried. Users are given an opportunity for hands-on experience with sanctioned hardware, software, and accessories. Computer furniture and ergonomic devices are also available. Ideally, when new purchases are made, deliver the demo from the store and set up the new PC in the store. This reduces the likelihood an item will become obsolete in the store. The same rotation holds for emergency spare units. It's a shame when a spare PC becomes obsolete never having seen the light of day.

Communications Acquisition

PC communication systems require some planning, by both the potential user and the coordinator acting as resource person for acquisitions. The coordinator must maintain an information file of LAN (and a lesser degree of WAN) hardware and software needed when considering future acquisitions or upgrading. There are a variety of LAN systems today including wired, wireless, and even one employing power supply lines as the transmitting media. Remote network users (mobile or home offices) utilize modems or the Internet to link with LAN systems.

For modem acquisitions, a user-request memo signed by the user's superior and defining the modem needs is sent to the coordinator. The user is supplied with "approved" modem hardware and software with the required (or a higher) transmission rate and installed by the coordinator.

COMMENT

Fax-modems allow for double duty and convenience. PC network communication acquisitions may require approval of the person responsible for corporate communications. This is especially true with WAN system interfacing or when linking two or more LAN systems. The gateway and modem selection will also require the approval of the organizational communication person. If this is not required, the coordinator will be fully responsible for installing the micro-LAN communication hookup and for providing the users with the required instructions and operation manuals for the online communication systems.

COMMENT

Connectivity over the Internet is replacing information systems host-based systems. The pros, so far, outweigh the cons for this trend. Remote connection to a LAN opens the door to viruses and hackers. Ensure safeguards are in place—a backdoor to loading unauthorized software, etc.

Acquisitions of LAN-based e-mail systems fall under the domain of the coordinator who also is responsible for its maintenance, upgrading, and support.

Database Access Acquisition

PC users requiring access to a mainframe database will consult with the PC manager regarding their needs. The manager reviews the user's needs and contacts the database administrator and the data administrator, if there is one, for user access. Both the database and data administrators' approvals are required for the user to access the information system's database. If another user (in the same work group) owns the database, or part of a network of PCs, the coordinator contacts the data administrator for written approval. If there is none, the coordinator resolves the problem with the user and sends a requesting memo to the database administrator for access.

The coordinator also arranges for new PC users to access the database and provides them with training and an operation manual. Normally, database access front-ends are provided to prevent the uneducated user from "dimming the lights" with poorly designed queries. Including a data dictionary explaining the contents of a field will improve reporting. You cannot use ambiguous field names.

PC OPERATIONS

PC (desktop, transportable, laptop, and notebook) operations utilize recommended manufacturers' standards as outlined in the manufacturers' manuals. These manuals are to be supplemented with those provided by the information systems PC coordinator, which are both purchased and written in-house.

PC Security

Desktop PCs or any stationary PC should be located in a safe environment. The person assigned nonstationary equipment assumes full responsibility for safekeeping both the hardware and the software. Preventing unauthorized access of any PC system should be of utmost concern to all employees.

Physical location.   The room where computers are kept should be locked when not in use. If not possible, seriously consider employing a cable lock to deter any removal of the desktop computer hardware. Keep transportable computers in a safe place at all times, including when the hardware is in transit. All portable computers must be handled as "carry-on luggage" while on public transit. When PCs are being transported for a special event that does not permit them to be carried individually, permission must be requested in writing from the coordinator. Approval is granted in writing, along with the special one-time procedures to be followed for the event.

COMMENT

Because manufacturers' manuals are often written to meet deadlines and need corrections after use, publishers have responded with manuals that are easier to understand.

Today's technology encourages the use of the PC as a user information and learning instrument with the aid of self-paced tutorials or even the "help" key. This technology should not be overlooked by the person responsible for the organization's PCs.

Various operations within the company may have differing degrees of autonomy, but the PC policies, enforced by the coordinator, apply to all PC users.

If a desktop PC is moved to a new permanent location within an area under the jurisdiction of the coordinator, the coordinator is informed in writing within 24 hours of the move. If the new area is not under the jurisdiction of the current coordinator, he/she must approve the move before it takes place and inform the asset manager and the new area's coordinator. The PC coordinator will in turn ensure there is adequate electrical and network connection available in the new location prior to moving the equipment.

Access security.   Stationary PCs with a modem or network and/or hard drives with any restricted information will be required to have one of the following:

❖ A lock

❖ An access security board

❖ An access security board with a lock-slot, so the board can utilize a cable security system

❖ Personal access code software (in the event the PC does not have an available slot for an access security board) or use of a screen-saver password

❖ An access security board with a motion alarm (In the event that a building alarm is available, and the situation warrants, an external connection to the building alarm system should be made. The alarm may be set to notify IS operations, and the firm's own security force, or an outside security service.)

Software and data security.   Software disks are stored in a locked place. Data disks and backup tapes and disks are stored in a PC media safe or other such comparable device if so warranted by the data administrator or coordinator. Where practical, data backups are stored off-site for protection. Encourage users to back up their data directories to the LAN, which is in turn backed up daily and the media stored off-site. Off-site may just be a different building in the same complex.

Daily Operating Procedures

There are standard operating procedures that apply to all PC operations:

A **Turning on the system.** To turn on the system, the operator follows the manufacturer's prescribed procedures. PCs should be rebooted at least once per week for reliable operation. Daily rebooting is recommended for critical systems.

COMMENT

Approved power backup hardware is highly recommended in case of a power failure. If there is no backup, don't use the machines if a power failure is likely.

The operator checks to see that the monitor display and all peripheral equipment are operating properly. If not, consult the operating manual. The operator proceeds when the system is ready.

Check the batteries of portable computers having access to AC power supply. If the batteries require recharging (or to prolong battery life), use the available AC power supply. If the power supplied is outside the U.S., be sure it is compatible with the hardware requirements.

B **Turning off the system.** When turning off the system:
   ❖ Exit from the operating system.
   ❖ Turn off peripherals.
   ❖ Turn off the computer.
   ❖ Remove floppy disks.
   ❖ Turn off the surge protect switch.

❖   Check battery-powered PCs for recharging needs and, when necessary, recharge batteries as soon as possible.

C **Daily operations.** Systems are checked daily by the administrator or user for:

❖   Paper supply in printer. Add paper as needed.

❖   Quality of printing. Replace ribbons or printer cartridges as needed.

❖   Quality of monitor display. Adjust as needed.

❖   Cleanliness of the computer equipment. Cleaning the equipment as needed may be done at the start or end of each workday, and at other times during the day when there is high-volume use.

D **Weekly housekeeping.** The administrator/user vacuums or dusts off the keyboard and wipes clean the monitor glass once a week. Clean high-use diskette heads weekly. If the heads are not often used, a once per month cleaning will suffice.

E **Dust covers.** In areas with a higher than normal amount of airborne dust, dust covers should be used for PCs, keyboards, monitors, and other attached devices when not in use. For very dusty areas, use special keyboard covers that can be employed while using the keyboard. These require periodic replacement; the coordinator/administrator must maintain a supply.

Operation Rules and Procedures

The following rules and procedures apply to the operation of all PCs:

A No food or beverages on or near the hardware or software.

B No smoking near the hardware or software.

C A clean, cool, and dry air working environment is recommended for the computer.

D The computer disks and reading heads must be at least two feet from telephones. Keep other magnetic devices away from the computer, disks, and tapes.

COMMENT

This writer demagnetized some videotapes over some just-purchased software that was hidden under some papers. The new software disks were demagnetized, too.

E   Plug all computers and peripheral equipment into a surge protection unit. Non-computer electric devices should not be plugged into the surge protection outlet or into the same wall plug with the surge protection device. Use only grounded electrical outlets. Plug company-critical equipment into a UPS with a signal to shut down the PC before the UPS batteries die.

F   No illegal copying of software is permitted.

G   No hardware or software may be removed from the firm's premises without the coordinator's written permission for each occasion. Portable computer systems used outside the workplace require a permission letter or ID card signed by the manager to be kept with the system at all times. The permission letter/ID card identifies who has permission to use and carry the authorized equipment and software. It will also contain the serial numbers of the units authorized and identifies the software contained in the system.

H   No personal hardware, software, or disks are allowed on the premises.

I   No hardware or software (including portable equipment) will be loaned to noncompany persons.

J   Floppy disk labels will be written with a permanent marker before they are applied to the disks.

K   Floppy disks will be kept in their disk containers or storage unit when not in use.

Backup Procedures

Backup procedures may vary within the same company. Not all data and software have the same value (although it is better to be safe if not sure). The following procedures are recommended:

A   **New software.** New purchased software is backed up in accordance with the software manufacturer's specifications. If only one copy can be made, the backed-up copy is sent to the coordinator for the software library. After being copied, the new software is tested. If a problem is found, the coordinator is contacted. All copied software disks and tapes will be write-protected.

B   **Hard drive backup procedures.**

1   At the end of each workday, all new data should be backed up onto disks or tape. Some active transactions (such as word processing, billing, etc.) will need to be backed up more often.

2   A backup copy of the hard drive software should be maintained on disk or tape.

> ## COMMENT
>
> A small company in Florida had its PC system stolen along with the AR file, and no backup. It placed an ad in the newspaper promising it would not press charges and offering a reward if the PC was returned undamaged. The company got no response. The U.S. Post Office in Washington backed up its PCs daily. But when the ninth floor of the building burned up, so did its PCs and the backups that were stored in the desks under the PCs.

C **Removable media data.** When data is kept on removable media (floppies, Zip disks, CDs, etc.) and not on a hard drive, the disk is copied for backup. The two copies of the disks are not stored together. It is recommended that the backup copy be write-protected, if applicable.

PC System Crash

In case of a PC system crash, the operator writes down what occurred just prior to the crash and the time of the crash, then calls the coordinator/administrator for assistance. The machine should be left on. Post a sign on the computer stating that the system has crashed and it is not to be used. Portable computers should be taken to the coordinator.

Hardware Problems

For hardware problems, the operator refers to the operating manual. If the problem cannot be corrected, the problem and its effect on the hardware are noted, and the PC manager/administrator is contacted. Post a sign on the (desktop) PC indicating it is not working and is not to be used. If a peripheral device does not work, a sign is placed on the device noting that it is out of order and indicating whether or not the computer is usable without the device.

Software Problems

For software problems, the operator contacts the help-desk. If the help-desk cannot resolve the problem, the operator contacts the coordinator.

Before contacting anyone for assistance, the operator will:

A Write down the details of what happened.

B Make a list of what corrective measures were tried.

C When assistance becomes available, bring the software up on the computer at the place where the problem occurred.

Accessories and Supplies

PC accessories can improve productivity, reduce fatigue, and improve morale. These accessories and supply items are on a "recommended" or "approved list" provided by the coordinator. Listed items will be carried by the computer store; other items not stocked will be listed with their vendors in the store. This information helps when ordering through the Purchasing department. The approved list will be published, updated, and distributed by the coordinator.

COMMENT

If the volume is sufficient, a purchasing agent or unit should be responsible for these items. This not only helps with standardization, but also insures good vendors at competitive prices. The purchasing people are much better at this than the IS people, and they have no problem saying no.

The items can be purchased with the user's department petty cash fund or a budget requisition. Supply items are requisitioned from the unit responsible for office or computer supplies according to standard operating procedure.

Accessories are classified in two groups: ergonomic devices and productivity aids. (The following items are not identified by brand name.)

1 **Ergonomic devices.** PC ergonomic devices are to help the human body interact with the PC system and function with the least amount of fatigue, error, and bodily harm. The following types of ergonomic devices are available on the "recommended list" provided by the PC store:

❖ Keyboard wrist rest

❖ Mouse wrist rest

❖ Foot rest

❖ Ergonomic keyboard

❖ Arm support

❖ Ergonomic adjustable chair

❖ Adjustable workstations for special employees

❖ Radiation and/or glare monitor screen

COMMENT

Remember the requirements of the Americans with Disabilities Act!

---

2 **Productivity aids.** The following, if used properly, have been known to increase productivity:

❖ Tilt 'n turn monitor stand

❖ Copyholder (flex arm, attachable, or standard)

❖ Copyholder light

❖ Diskette storage devices

❖ Cartridge storage devices

❖ Desktop printer stand and/or organizer

❖ PC rollout keyboard system

❖ Keyboard with mouse

❖ Mouse pad

❖ Mouse holder

❖ Keyboard labels for F keys and/or other keys

❖ Wastepaper container and paper shredder

❖ Workstations that include a drawer that can be locked for personal items

❖ Speaker telephone

END-USER COMPUTER COMMITTEE

A committee provides policies and procedures to standardize and provide assistance and training for end-users of computers and ancillary devices. This committee should work with the hardware and software committees, chaired by the information technology asset manager. The hardware and software committee is formed primarily for the standardization and control of hardware and software. The end-user computer committee represents the users and their needs along with an expanded list of office equipment. The committee's duties include being a source of information for users, providing management with user needs, and policing operations to ensure that policies and procedures are being followed.

Committee Organization

The committee is made up of no more than seven or fewer than three enduser unit heads. The purchasing department furnishes a representative to the committee, as will the information systems unit. The chairperson is the information systems representative. If the company has an office manager, he/she should be a member. If the company has a graphics unit, the head of that unit will be on the committee. Most companies have an engineering department with very unique technical needs, and it should be represented on the committee. The size of the committee will vary depending on the size and complexity of the company.

The committee provides policies and procedures to standardize training, and assistance and training for end-users of computers and ancillary devices for the company. The actual name of the committee will not have to comply with the name provided in this manual. The committee will meet once a month and call special meetings as needed. The committee will have notes taken of the meetings. A copy of the approved minutes will be provided to each committee member, the committee's file, the information systems head, the information technology asset manager, the information technology enduser computer technician unit, and the administrative VP.

Secondary Committee(s)

If the company has other sites in different cities, it will have a person, or chairperson, from each site reporting to the corporate committee. If the site is small enough, it will have only one person appointed by the local plant or operations manager. This person does the task for the corporate committee. He/she provides the committee with the location needs and the degree of compliance with the corporate policies and procedures. A copy of the information will also be provided to the local plant or operations manager. If a site is large enough, it will have a committee to resolve local problems and needs. The committee has three to nine members. The site's office manager, graphics unit, purchasing unit, and information systems units will each have a representative on the committee. The local plant or operations manager appoints the committee chairperson.

The committee provides policies and procedures to standardize and provide assistance and training for end-users of computers and peripheral devices at the local level. The actual name of the committee need not be the name provided in this manual. The committee meets once a month and calls special meetings as needed. Notes will be taken of the meetings. A copy of the approved minutes will be provided to each committee member, the committee's file, the local information systems head, the local information technology asset manager, primary company end-users' computer committee, and the local plant or operations manager.

END-USER TECHNICAL SUPPORT

End-user technical support is available in several forms. The information systems organization provides some forms of support. Other end-user support is provided by different vendors. End-user support will be provided in one form or another for stand-alone computers and networked PC systems.

Payment for these services depends on company policies. The payment can come from one central source and/or department budgets. Whichever method is used, a record system will be maintained.

Computer Technician

Computer technician is the title of the IT person in the user support unit who helps with end-user computer and equipment problems. Some organizations use the title of PC manager for this job. In either case, the person in charge of this unit reports to the head of information systems. The end-user contacts this unit when there is no help-desk or the help-desk cannot solve a problem. The problem may be with hardware, software, or a supply item.

Computer technician skill requirements. The computer technician has general knowledge of the users' PC hardware and/or software uses, including supply items. The hardware and software are identified under their respective approved lists. For large, complex organizations there are specialists for lesser-used equipment. Each computer technician will have assigned areas to cover within the company. These areas will have hardware and software similarities. The computer technician is called if the computer operator thinks it has a problem the help-desk cannot walk them through. It could be a problem where the computer technician requested a call to them the next time it happened. The computer technician will more often resolve end user hardware problems than the help-desk, while the help-desk will more often solve the end-user's software operations problems. Help-desk personnel and the computer technicians should get to know each other for their mutual benefit.

It is important that computer technicians have a good understanding of their users' business to recognize a priority call. This helps focus them on critical issues and less on "squeaky wheels." The technician need a patient temperment so they can help users through dumb and embarrassing mistakes without alienating them. Computer technicians are your primary trainers since they can provide a steady stream of tips to users with whom they are constantly in contact. The technicians who run calls must have a quick connection to someone they can refer to for priority resolution (who do I see next?) and for backup in a crisis. This person also is a prime source of feedback to your training and newsletter and should refer troubled users to the trainers.

Computer technician resource requirements.   The computer technician will be provided with a tool kit to cover the kind of hardware he/she will need to resolve problems. This will be carried in an attaché case provided by the company. There will be a minimum of space for spare parts. Supply items that are often used should be stored close to the computer operation. Other items needed may be gotten by someone else, from the source, to save the technician's time. The computer technician will also be provided with a beeper. A mobile phone will be provided to the technician as needed.

Computer technician's responsibilities.   The technician will maintain a daily activity log. The computer technician should perform the following computer tasks at the user's site:

1 Replace faulty computer parts.

2 Perform memory upgrades.

3 Add additional ports to desktop computers.

4 Add an additional I/O device.

5 Check connection cords.

6 Run a virus check and remove any viruses.

7 Check the operation of the modem.

8 Reformat a hard drive.

9 Reload the operating system.

10 Load new software and confirm that it is operational.

11 Install hardware accessories.

12 Perform routine diagnostics.

13 Reboot the system.

14 Remove any unauthorized software from the computer.

15 Disconnect and/or remove unauthorized hardware. The unauthorized hardware device will be turned over to the computer operator's superior.

At times there may be hardware problems requiring the user's computer or attached devices to be taken back to the repair shop. If the time the equipment is away from its operating area becomes a problem, the computer technician will arrange for a loaner to be provided. The loan will be only for the time the user's equipment is not available. If the loaner is the functional equivalent to the old one, then leave it. Expect that loaners that are superior to the old unit to be difficult to get back. Given the time necessary to copy files from the loaner back to the old unit, it may not be worth the fight.

The computer technician's work log. While working, the technician should look for any bootlegged or pirated software. If any is found, record it in the log. If any unauthorized hardware is attached to the desktop computer, record it in the daily log sheet. The superior will acknowledge acceptance of the equipment by signing the computer technician's daily log sheet.

Weekly computer technician's report. The charge time will be portal to portal. The charge time is summarized by user, user's unit, and other duties not charged to a user. Any administration or other nonuser charge time is prorated to service calls. If the company has an interdepartment charge system, the end-user's department is charged for the service time for the maintenance. How these costs are handled will depend on the company's accounting practice.

The computer technician writes a short weekly report to the technical unit's head. The report notes any special hardware or software problems occurring during the week. Any operator problems needing resolution will be recommended. Can the operator problems be remedied with operator training, new operation manuals, or equipment? If the operator problem deals with an ergonomics issue, state what the problem is in the report.

Software Support

There will be software that is not on the current approved computer software list, but is in the asset management software database. PC end-users who employ the software must have it approved for support before a computer technician can help with the problem. Some of the end-users utilizing software will be assigned to a computer technician if the help-desk cannot be of assistance. The end-user is encouraged to contact the IT unit if the help-desk is unable to solve the software problem. The technician will pull the software file folder for the programs and review the documentation before going to the end-user's workplace.

Computer technicians are not expected to solve all the end-user problems they encounter. There will be special hardware and/or software technicians who are not generalists. They will work at the company sites needing their special skills. When the user or help-desk contacts the IT unit for computer support, they will need to provide information to have the proper technician answer the service call.

COMMENT

Consider an outside support contract for critical software that you cannot support. For example, two users needed Pagemaker to build newsletters. It was not feasible to train or hire a support person for them. Instead, arrange an open PO for outside support time.

The asset management software database has the inventory information of legally owned company software. All software on the approved computer software list is on the asset management software database. Not all asset management software database programs will be found on the approved computer software list. Software problems for these programs will not all be resolved by the technician. The kind of software will determine its solution source.

A **End-user computer software.** The software for end-users is found on the approved computer software list. This software is supported by the help-desk and the IT technical support unit.

B **IT computer software.** The software for the IT units is on the approved computer software list. This software is supported by the IT programming unit.

C **IT unit's computer software.** Other IT units using purchased packaged software may call on the IT technical support unit for assistance. If the software was developed by the IT programming unit, it should be contacted for support. This software is in the asset management software database, but seldom found on the approved computer software list.

D **Special computer software.** All software is required to be on the asset management software database. This software can include several types of programs and may be supported by information systems. If the software is not found on the asset management software database, it will not be supported. The question will be asked: How did the user come into possession of the software?

Some special computer software, not on the approved computer software list, but on the asset management software database, can be identified as follows:

1 **End-user software still in use.** End-users can use software no longer available but is still supported. The software may no longer be available on the market or about to be replaced. There is no need to replace the software at present. This software will be supported.

2 **Mainframe computer operations software.** This software is used for mainframe operations and is not available to end-users of PC systems. This software is supported by IT operations programmers. The IT programming unit may help IT computer operations if it developed the program(s).

3 **Software for special applications.** This software is purchased for specially approved application and/or hardware. The software will not be supported. The department that arranged to acquire the software is responsible for obtaining the needed support.

4 **Software testing.** Purchased software for testing for possible future use will not be supported. The person who acquired the program(s) will seek his/her needed support from the vendor.

5 **Turnkey software operations.** Contracts drawn for vendor-developed, turnkey operated systems will be supported by the vendor.

Network Computer Technical Support

Networked PC systems and work group systems are more complex. Their hardware configurations and support needs are more intricate. The network of computers depends on the system server. The network is unique; by itself it can shut down all computing in an enterprise—a single point of failure. The system server computer may have a database. All this requires more support from the information systems' IT units than what the stand-alone PCs require. There will be the need for support from the following IT units:

A **IT technical support unit.** This unit support is available for network or work group operations. The IT technical support unit can store more spare parts for the system at the user site. There should be a more knowledgeable person, such as a lead administrator, of the system operation to resolve some day-to-day operation problems.

The technical support unit provides communications support for a local area network system. If a gateway connection is needed, it will be handled by that technician.

The technical support unit works with the work group's lead administrator for any training needs. If the technical support unit has an IT trainer, this person will provide assistance. If there is no IT training unit, the company training department or a training vendor can be used. The following types of assistance could help with training:

1 Vendor tutorial software

2 Third-party videotapes or CBTs

3 Programmed instruction packages

4 Overhead transparencies

5 Slides

6 Audio instruction procedures

7 Operator instructional manuals

8 Troubleshooting program instructions

9 Lectures and demonstrations

10 Pretests for end-users

B **IT programming support.** The network or work group system developed by IT programming will be supported by them.

C **Database support.** The information systems database unit will be fully involved with any database problems. The database unit representative can restrict access to database file information to prevent files being corrupted. Database support personnel are available to help with any backup and recovery procedures.

Computer Ergonomics Support

If the company has an environmental ergonomics unit, it should be available to provide service to the information systems units. If the service is unavailable, consulting firms are available for this kind of support. Most ergonomic problems do not require a consultant. Someone is selected in the end-user technical support unit and trained. This person will provide support to IT units and end-users of computer devices. College courses and short commercial programs on ergonomics are now available. Books and periodicals are also available.

> ## COMMENT
>
> The Human Factors and Ergomonics Society is a national organization with local chapters. They can be reached at www.hfes.org.

> ## COMMENT
>
> AliMed publishes an excellent ergonomics and occupational health catalog. They can be reached at 800-225-2610 or at www.alimed.com.

Help-desk

The help-desk can be staffed by an information systems unit or be provided by a vendor service. There are advantages to each choice. Staffing hours will depend on the needs of the organization. A centrally staffed help-desk can provide service to more than one company location.

Contracted help-desk service arrangements will require an accurate assessment of the level of help needed by end-users. Determine the costs involved before soliciting bids from vendors. Requests for vendor bid proposals are sent to three or more vendors. The request letter identifies the contact person for the service. Include an expected date for the bid proposal to be submitted.

A key cost driver for contracted help-desk services is the level of service provided. If all that is expected is taking a message and asking a few scripted questions, then just about anyone—anywhere—can take your call. The result is to dispatch a technician. This is synonymous with a simple answering service.

But if help-desk staffers are expected to provide some level of problem resolution during the initial contact, they need the ability to access your data systems for troubleshooting. This may require an onsite office or a dedicated high-speed data line. They must be dedicated to your company's support so anyone answering the phone can be anywhere to take the message.

Security is also a major concern. High-usage items for help-desks are password problems. Since the desk needs access to change these, they may pose a security risk.

Vendor contracting.   After the bid proposals are received, they are compared with each other. Lowest bidders do not always provide the best service. Beware of startup companies without verifiable experience. Calculate the costs for providing the service in-house. This provides a baseline to evaluate the bids.

Write a short-duration flexible contract when beginning a relationship with a new vendor. This provides information to both the vendor and the company about the contents of the final contract. The company's legal representatives review the contract and make recommendations before it is signed.

Budgeting proposal.   Budget proposals for vendor service per call or in-house help-desk operations require a large contingency budget—50 percent or more of the original amount is not unreasonable. A contingency amount should be budgeted even for a flat sum contract. An amount equal to 10 percent to 20 percent should be sufficient.

In-house help-desk.   An in-house help-desk often starts as a pilot project. As the bugs are worked out, it can accommodate more internal customers. Start an in-house help-desk with a lump sum budget. Record the number of contacts by unit and the time spent per contact. This will be helpful for future planning.

There are several ways to operate an in-house help-desk. Which one you use depends on corporate culture, union concerns, etc. The following things should be considered when operating an in-house help-desk:

1 **Operations.** Record conversations to provide an audit trail of the dialogue between the user and the help-desk technician. This reduces and simplifies note-taking by the help-desk staff. Use a voice-mail system to avoid busy signals or no answer when calling the help-desk.

2 **Facility.** The help-desk work area provides rapid access to information needs. It is ergonomically suitable for the task of the help-desk staff. The job is confining and any ergonomic assistance would help reduce the burnout rate for this job. Any change or rotation of duties would also prolong the life of the help-desk technician.

A help-desk is a built-in feedback mechanism for finding out how your systems perform. Use the data!

The help-desk's demeanor is critical. Users' opinion of your department will be greatly shaped by the help-desk; they are the ones users talk to most.

A sophisticated help-desk will save you more expensive staff time if the help-desk personnel are trained and equipped to handle routine system problems.

Maintenance Contracting

All hardware may not be maintained in-house. In some instances, vendor equipment service contracting for some devices might be a better solution. Some peripheral devices are best maintained using vendor contracts. Some leased items include service agreements. Contracts can specify an unlimited number of service calls or charges on a by-call basis. Contracts can provide for spare parts or parts can be charged as installed. Some vendors can offer an array of equipment that they can service. Service can be provided for normal working hours or around the clock.

There can be one or more service vendors. There are firms providing a full-service blanket for most all hardware. Other firms service one or more machines. Consider these options when deciding the service best for the company.

If considering vendors, solicit bids. The bid proposals are reviewed by the IS head or his/her representative and the end-user committee. The optimum vendor is selected and receives the contract. The end-user charges for this service will be determined. There is no problem if company policy dictates how costs are internally handled. If no such policy exists, the end-user committee and information systems management resolve the issue.

Before any maintenance contracts are signed, they are reviewed by the legal representative of the company. Upon approval, they are signed by the authorized management personnel. Purchasing is contacted regarding such contracts. The procedure followed will be the corporate procedure for contracting services.

Sometimes you must outsource repairs for:

❖ Parts availability—They won't sell them to you.

❖ Technical expertise.

❖ Warranty work—usually only good if you will pack it up and deliver back to the factory or a rep. This may not be worthwhile in the case of PCs unless you can afford to remove them from service and send them away.

Equipment with moving parts (like printers) has a higher ongoing maintenance cost than solid-state devices.

Using your asset database, compare the cost of a maintenance contract to the cost of buying several spare devices. Use your spares to replace broken equipment and then send the damaged material out for service on a time and materials basis.

A key component of maintenance contracts is the hours of coverage. Normal working hours coverage is cheapest and 24/7 is very expensive. Keep in mind that this is response time—not maximum resolution time.

10

LOCAL AREA NETWORKS: KEEPING THINGS RUNNING

LAN POLICIES

Computer LANs that are part of information systems can be to some extent autonomous. However, the more the group relies on information systems for assistance, the less autonomy it has. Even with "total" autonomy, a LAN needs to comply with universal standards for hardware and software utilization. It does not have any more autonomy than that found with any stand-alone PC operation.

A Local Area Network system can be a client/server operation employing an information systems server, or an autonomous Local Area Network with its own server system. It can be a closed system or provided with a gateway for external network access. There is no restriction as to the hardware configuration of the group, as long as the equipment is justifiable.

The company is responsible for complying with certain industry practices. Responsibility for assuring that these practices are followed is delegated by management of the corporation to information systems management.

LAN COMPLIANCE PROCEDURES

LAN computer systems can vary in configuration and process within the same corporation. However, the LAN compliance procedures applicable to "common procedures" will be followed by all LANs within the corporation. When operation needs are expanded beyond the common procedures, procedure documentation will conform to the requirements set by information systems.

General Operations

This subsection covers general operations to be followed by the Local Area Network when operating its computer system. Each has a person appointed as the unit's LAN computer coordinator (full- or part-time duty).

A **LAN computer coordinator's responsibilities**

   ❖   Anticipate possible hardware needs.

   ❖   Anticipate new software.

   ❖   Provide information and service for users.

   ❖   Provide for informal and formal training.

   ❖   Oversee operation policies.

   ❖   Be a source for operation documentation.

   ❖   Disseminate new operating information.

   ❖   Provide for needed backup hardware.

   ❖   Be the liaison between the LAN computer operation and corporate information systems.

   ❖   Be a knowledge source for user applications.

   ❖   Perform hardware maintenance.

   ❖   Perform software updates.

   ❖   Perform backup of files and database.

   ❖   Maintain a supply inventory.

   ❖   Be the facilitator for disaster recovery.

   ❖   Be on call for after-hours problems.

   ❖   Maintain computer security procedures.

   ❖   Police system for unauthorized software.

   ❖   Maintain an operation performance problem log.

   ❖   Write a monthly exception report to the unit manager and IS computer operations manager.

B **Workstation operations.** Each workstation is provided with a current operations manual, which may be supplemented by other manuals either vendor-supplied or written in-house. The following standard workstation operating procedures apply to all workstations:

   ❖   Turning on the workstation

❖ Daily housekeeping operations

❖ Weekly housekeeping

❖ Turning off the workstation

C **Operation rules and procedures.** When providing the rules and procedures to be followed by all system users, the LAN computer coordinator explains the rationale behind them.

❖ No food or beverages close to the workstation area.

❖ No smoking near software or hardware.

❖ No telephones near computer disks.

❖ No illegal copying of software.

❖ No personal software allowed.

❖ No personal use of computer system.

❖ No personal disks allowed.

❖ No hardware may be removed from the department.

Operators will inform the Local Area Network computer coordinator of needed ergonomic devices. Those available are:

❖ Keyboard wrist rest

❖ Mouse wrist rest

❖ Foot rest

❖ Ergonomic keyboard

❖ Arm support

❖ Ergonomic adjustable chair

❖ Adjustable workstations for employees with special needs

❖ Radiation and/or glare monitor screen cover

LAN SYSTEMS PROCEDURES

In a Local Area Network client/server operation, information systems computer operations provides the server. The following procedures for this type of LAN computer system operation help insure safety. There could be more than one such LAN computer system within the corporation.

IS Client/Server Support

The IS computer operations help-desk provides support for general computer client/server operations and will be available for Local Area Network users with operation problems. If it cannot handle a problem, it contacts a person who can.

The LAN computer coordinator for the Local Area Network, appointed by the LAN management, addresses particular technical operation concerns from its work area. This person will also be responsible for communicating the group's needs to IS computer operations and/or the systems unit, and has the following responsibilities:

- ❖ Assist the IS trainer with Local Area Network training needs.
- ❖ Provide informal training to computer workstation users.
- ❖ Be a knowledge source for user applications.
- ❖ Be the information systems Local Area Network contact.
- ❖ Maintain a reference library of publications for the Local Area Network.

LAN User Education

The LAN users receive information about and training for the use of its hardware and software. This will be the responsibility of the project management group installing the new system.

After the new system is operational, provisions are made for instructions for subsequent system changes. The Local Area Network computer coordinator assists with this task.

Provisions are made for new employees utilizing the LAN system; suggestions are self-paced learning instruments, such as:

- ❖ Computer tutorials
- ❖ Program learning manuals
- ❖ Audio instruction tapes
- ❖ VCR tapes
- ❖ Operation manuals

The Local Area Network computer coordinator assists with the training of new LAN computer workstation users and is, in addition, responsible for instructing the new user regarding the Local Area Network's utilization of the computer system. The coordinator also informs users of pending operational changes and assists them once the changes are in place.

Workstation Operations

The following are standard procedures for operators of terminals or workstations:

A **Turning on the system.** To turn on the system, the operator follows the operating manual's prescribed procedures. The operator checks that the monitor display and all peripherals are operating properly. If not, the operator consults the manual and proceeds when the system is ready. If the workstation is not working properly, he/she contacts the help-desk whose telephone number should be on the first page of the operating manual.

Before contacting anyone for assistance, the operator will:

❖ Write down the details of what happened.

❖ Make a list of corrective measures tried.

❖ When assistance is available, bring the computer system up to the place where the problem occurred.

B **Turning off the system.** Turn off the system in the following sequence:

1 Exit from the operating system.

2 Turn off peripheral equipment.

3 Turn off the workstation.

4 Remove all floppy disks.

C **Daily operations.** Check hardware daily for:

❖ Quality of the monitor display. Adjust as needed.

❖ Cleanliness of the equipment. Clean the equipment as needed at the start or end of each workday, and at other times of high-volume use.

If the work station has a printer:

❖ Check paper supply in printer. Add paper as needed.

❖ Check quality of printing. Replace ribbons or printer cartridges as needed.

These actions are taken at the start or end of each workday. Some may be necessary more than once a day.

D **Weekly housekeeping.** The administrator/user vacuums or dusts off the keyboard and wipes clean the monitor glass once a week. High-use diskette heads will be cleaned weekly. If the heads are not often used, once per month will suffice.

E **Dust covers.** In areas with a higher than normal amount of airborne dust, dust covers are used for PCs, keyboards, monitors, and other attached devices when not in use. For very dusty areas, use special keyboard covers that can be employed while using the keyboard.

Since these special covers require periodic replacement, a supply should be maintained by the PC coordinator/administrator.

F **Floppy disk backup.** When data is kept on floppy disks and not on a hard disk, copy it for backup. Do not store the two floppy disks, original and backup, together. The backup copy must be write-protected.

Operation Rules

The following rules apply to all persons utilizing the computer system:

❖ No food or beverages on or near the hardware or software.

❖ No smoking near the hardware or software.

❖ The computer and disks must be at least two feet from telephones. Keep magnetic devices away from the computer, disks, and tapes.

❖ No illegal copying of software is permitted.

❖ No hardware or software may be removed from the firm's premises without written permission.

❖ No personal hardware, software, or disks are permitted on the premises.

❖ No down- or uploading of any noncompany software or data is permitted.

Accessories

Accessories are classified into two groups, ergonomic devices and productivity devices, which are to be purchased and coordinated by the Local Area Network computer coordinator. (The following items are not identified by brand name.)

A **Ergonomic devices.** Workstation ergonomic devices help the human body interact with the computer system and function with the least amount of fatigue, error, and bodily harm. The following types are available:

❖ Keyboard wrist rest

❖ Mouse wrist rest

❖ Foot rest

❖ Ergonomic keyboard

❖ Arm support

❖ Ergonomic adjustable chair

❖ Adjustable workstations for employees with special needs

❖ Radiation and/or glare monitor screen cover

COMMENT

Remember the requirements of the Americans with Disabilities Act!

B **Productivity aids.** The following, if used properly, can increase productivity:

❖ Tilt 'n turn monitor stand

❖ Copyholders

❖ Copyholder and light

❖ Diskette storage devices

❖ Desktop print stand and/or organizer

❖ PC rollout keyboard system

❖ Keyboard with mouse

❖ Mouse pad

❖ Mouse holder

❖ Keyboard labels for F keys and/or other keys

❖ Wastepaper container and paper shredder

❖ Workstations that include a drawer for personal items that can be locked

❖ Speaker telephone

Work Group Newsletter

A work group newsletter is a great place to incorporate feedback from the help-desk for systemic problems. If a large number of users are having the same problem, work-arounds can be detailed here. This is a great outreach tool for proactive issues, such as pending upgrades. Remember your audience and keep style conversational and stay away from technical jargon.

The newsletter may be published monthly, but not less than quarterly. It should announce forthcoming training programs, tell who completed what programs, announce new hardware or software availability, list hardware and software available for hands-on experience in the computer store, and list contact telephone numbers for PC or network assistance.

An information systems newsletter may take the place of a separate work group newsletter if it incorporates the information needs of the work group users.

The newsletter can be part of the company intranet or printed as hard-copy. If printed as hardcopy, the size of a newsletter should be $8^1/_2$- by 11-inches: printed on 11- by 17-inch paper and folded into an $8^1/_2$- by 11-inch document. If this is not possible, stapled $8^1/_2$- by 11-inch paper will do. Using desktop publishing software to produce the newsletter would be ideal, but high-end word-processing software can also generate a professional looking newsletter. Graphics and photos will enhance its appearance even more. The "slicker" it is, the more likely it will be read.

11

IT AUDITS: CHECKING YOUR WORK

MANAGEMENT OBJECTIVES AND AUDIT POLICIES

This chapter covers the policies needed to ensure that professional information systems management objectives are maintained. These policies direct management so resources can be properly utilized and monitored. Actions to take, identify, and implement both specific and comprehensive IS organization objectives include the following:

- ❖ Develop IT departmental policies and standards for systems, programming, operations, and users.
- ❖ Ensure prompt and continuous implementation of those policies and standards.
- ❖ Ensure projects are completed on schedule and within budget.
- ❖ Develop a cooperative attitude among IT personnel concerning user's needs.
- ❖ Develop and maintain priorities.
- ❖ Develop and maintain ongoing IS planning.
- ❖ Inform top management of the current and potential benefits of information systems.
- ❖ Maintain optimal budgeting for personnel, hardware, and software.
- ❖ Develop a departmentwide drive for accuracy.

Management Resource Planning

IS management is responsible for the constant monitoring of the performance and output of areas under its direct control. This covers IT systems, software development, and operating systems. End user input should be welcomed. IS management's responsibilities for planning and directing the use of proposed resources, including personnel, hardware, and software, are defined as follows:

❖ Personnel requirements are a major element of resource planning. IT managers are responsible for having the requisite personnel required for current and planned needs. Planned needs will come from the strategic plans developed by the process noted in Chapter 1, *Policies and Plans: Setting the Framework.*

❖ Hardware and software planning is influenced by user justification, selection, and utilization of equipment resources. Requirements for change, replacement, and additions to current hardware and software are determined by the interplay of various factors. Continuous monitoring of hardware and software performance is necessary to determine the most effective course of action.

❖ Network resource planning is required so that different computer systems can interact. The development of technology in this area is constantly changing, requiring the attention of a proactive IS management to remain current.

❖ A database is a volatile resource requiring constant attention to avoid misuse and to provide for the expanding demand for data.

Strategic Planning

IS management uses either the firm's strategic plan as a guide or its own long-range planning, taking into account long-term user needs. Short-range planning must take into consideration long-range strategic plans.

IT management must also be prepared to downsize or expand the information systems areas affected by strategic planning needs. (See section in Chapter 1, "Strategic Planning Process.")

Audit Policies

The information systems operation must satisfy the requirements of both IS audit forms: the management audit and the systems audit. The systems audit is performed by a firm's inside or outside auditors, and is mostly concerned with the system controls and audit trails. A management audit can be a self-evaluation or one performed by an outside audit firm with IS management skills.

COMMENT

An IS operation can pass a systems audit but fail a management audit, in which case the firm pays for more than it gets. Unfortunately, not so many management audits are performed as systems audits or the turnover of IS management personnel would be greater than it is now.

It is common for a CPA firm to run a systems audit of the IS operations when it conducts an audit program. An audit policy should exist ensuring IS is able to have both systems and management audits.

Systems audit requirement policy. An IT operation's controls should minimize undesirable events and also alert system users to potential problems. The system controls should contain an audit trail that is maintained at all times.

Management audit requirements policy. Management audit policy should contain provisions enabling the system to satisfy a systems audit. They should cover the following:

A **Management control.** Comparison of IS costs with the sum budgeted. The amount budgeted must be reasonable for the service provided.

B **Resource allocation.**
   1 Maintenance of priorities in line with needs
   2 Assurance that talent is available for required projects

C **Project management audits.**
   1 Proper project controls in place
   2 Contingency planning in place for unforeseen problems
   3 Project postimplementation audit procedures in place and used

D **Technology audit.**
   1 Verification of the quality of hardware and software
   2 Verification of the staff's technical skills
   3 Verification that application systems have:
     ❖ Proper documentation

❖   Backup procedures

❖   Acceptable programming quality

❖   Standards for maintenance procedures

E   Operations management audit to assure:

1   Proper machine utilization

2   Acceptable recovery and security procedures

3   Acceptable employee skills levels

4   Maintenance of low rerun time

5   Downtime minimums for system

6   Cost-justified operations expenses

The Systems Development Cycle Audit

Correct methodologies must be used so audit standards are met. The following needs to be assured:

A   Preliminary analysis. The investigatory work and analysis required for a proposed system have been done.

B   User service request evaluation. The current system operation, including cost to user, has been assessed. Potential tangible and intangible benefits are detailed and ultimate objectives of requested services assessed.

C   Requirements and objectives. Detailed definitions are assembled and descriptions of requirements and objectives are identified by the users.

D   System design. The design is approached in a standard manner, to satisfy the user's needs.

E   User nomenclature. User terminology is defined at the lowest level of required detail for the project.

F   Manual procedure specifications. The proper level of detail is present in all manual operation specifications that interface with the computer system.

G   Computer programming. Programs are prepared to process data to meet specifications of output and control. Manual inputs and outputs should be compatible with system programs.

H   Documentation. Operations and user manuals are current and easily understood.

I   Implementation

1 Require program testing.

2 Conduct user and operations training.

3 Develop a plan for the conversion with contingency backups.

4 Establish a self-postimplementation plan for final project evaluation.

MANAGEMENT PLANNING

IS planning is becoming more important because of the popularity of strategic planning. The need for joint user and IS operations planning has increased, because the more complex systems become, the more vulnerable they are to obsolescence.

A rapidly changing outside environment increases the need for planning. State and federal regulations can impose program changes, and customer or market demands may require employing new technology. The wise IS manager is attuned to pending changes.

In small IS departments, the IS manager may be responsible for all management planning. Large departments may have a staff assistant or a planning staff unit for most of the work.

Develop Your IS Plan

A **Assign responsibility.** Planning responsibility is a staff-level function. Personnel responsible report to the IS manager and should have the following qualities:

1 A good knowledge of existing and planned applications

2 A good knowledge of IT operations

3 A good knowledge of the firm's operations, requiring ongoing contacts (both formal and informal) with users and users' management

4 Good organizational, budgeting, and cost-accounting skills

5 A good knowledge of currently used software and hardware and an awareness of pending releases by manufacturers and vendors

6 Good technical writing skills

7 Credibility within the firm

B **Prepare a plan context.**

1 Obtain a written record of the past history and success record of the IS department.

2 Maintain an ongoing record of current activities and commitments—how projects fared keeping to time schedules.

3 Know the current constraints of the IS department, such as:

❖ Budgeting status

❖ Status of current hardware and software

❖ Status of IT personnel, including good and bad points

❖ Users' management skill levels

C **Identify organizational goals.** Maintain a list of organizational goals and users' goals. Beware of goal conflicts. Require benchmarks to determine if progress is being made toward achieving goals.

D **Identify organizational goals for IS planning.** Ensure that planning is done and the budget can be justified.

E **Identify planning priorities.** Select first those applications that will help gain IS credibility.

F **Identify resources required:**

❖ Personnel

❖ Hardware

❖ Software

❖ Vendors with credibility

Keep Your IS Plan Current

Because of changing needs and the availability of new technology, periodic updating of IS plans is required. Perform a formal review twice a year. Do not preclude updating in the event of a major change.

Along with the plan status review, perform a risk analysis to review the probability of risk for all planned projects.

COMMENT

Don't undertake too many risky projects at any one time.

RESOURCE MANAGEMENT

This section defines management's responsibilities for directing the use of IS resources, both expense and capital investment items. To properly manage resources, projected requirements are made for personnel, supplies, outside services, purchased software, and hardware.

Inventory of Resources

IS management maintains an ongoing resource inventory. Monitor personnel, software, and hardware with short-term and strategic planning requirements in view. Establish an asset management system for controlling companywide computer hardware and software resources.

A **IS personnel organization.** Maintain an organizational chart of the IS department, containing portraits of management personnel in position boxes.

List the talent available within each unit of the IS department in a personnel inventory. In addition, a personnel profile needs-analysis of each unit is required, making it possible to fill current and projected needs.

COMMENT

An oil company, with its large computer services organization, found this picture-at-a-glance of organizational hierarchy helpful.

B **Software inventory.** Maintain a listing of currently active (in-house developed and purchased) software. The software coordinator will be responsible for making and keeping this list up-to-date.

1 Purchased software information includes:

❖ Dates of purchases

❖ Vendor

❖ Purchase price

❖ Record of user problems

❖ Type of vendor support

❖ Future software needs

2 In-house programmed software information consists of:

❖ Dates programs were written

❖ Revision dates for programs

❖ Author(s) of program(s)

❖ Program reviser (if any)

❖ A record of user problems

❖ Future programming needs

C **Hardware inventory.** A listing of current hardware is maintained and grouped as follows:

1 Mainframe computers

2 Peripheral devices

3 Minicomputers

4 PCs owned by the IS department

5 PCs owned by other users

6 Peripheral devices owned by users

7 Expected future purchases of hardware

Organizational Structure of IS

The organizational structure of information systems is governed by the size and complexity of IT operations. Its distribution, whether centralized or decentralized, also affects its organizational structure.

Standardization is used throughout IS and benefits all information systems, whether centralized, decentralized, or distributed. Its organization is structured so that corresponding user levels can be identified. The three levels, with increasingly detailed procedures, are:

A **Policy level.** This level involves IS and user management working primarily with long-range planning. Policies are refined at this level. Procedures can then be written at lower levels executing the defined policies and agreements. The relationships at this management level are both formal and informal.

B **Supervisory level.** This level makes possible the enforcement of policies by ensuring that proper procedures are developed by IT units. The user supervisory level works with information systems ensuring that user policies are defined in written procedures. Both user and IT supervisors work on a day-to-day basis with the procedures.

Procedures may be altered if both the supervisors and managers agree that policies are still being maintained. The relationships at this management level are both formal and informal.

C **Operation level.** The operations, or working, level relationships of IT personnel and users are both formal and informal. At this level

IT develops the procedures that user operating personnel execute. The process steps are documented, while day-to-day contacts are less formal.

IS SYSTEMS AUDIT

The following are information systems audit procedures ensuring that minimum standards have been established.

Systems and Programming

Systems and programming procedures adequately meet auditing standards when the following have been accomplished:

A The company's application development/acquisition methodology is formalized.

B Written programming standards covering coding techniques, documentation, testing, acceptance, and conversion are satisfactory.

C The segregation of duties into application program development, cataloguing of programs for production, and operating systems programming activities are established.

D Control of program changes is maintained.

E Program documentation library procedures are employed ensuring adherence to systems/programming standards.

F Controls of online programming terminals are maintained.

G Program documentation, including program changes, is complete.

Computer Operations

Computer operations procedures adequately meet auditing standards when the following have been accomplished:

A Compliance with computer operations standards and procedures.

B Reporting mechanisms are used by management to monitor IS operations.

C Equipment maintenance is performed and records of equipment problems are maintained.

D The computer center has proper physical and data security.

E Controls are maintained over information systems hardware, files, databases and production program libraries.

F Proper separation of duties is maintained among input, computer operations, and output.

G A disaster prevention plan is documented, tested and in effect.

H Adequate emergency power supply is in place.

I Recovery procedures and contingency plans are tested and in place.

J Operating systems procedures are in effect.

    1 Duties are separated between production data file maintenance and operating system maintenance.

    2 Documentation of the operating systems is complete.

    3 Controls are in place for changes to the operating system.

    4 Controls are in place for utility programs, primarily those with production data or program file-altering capabilities.

K Data controls are adequate.

    1 Evaluate control points for audit trails.

    2 Compliance exists with written procedures.

    3 Control totals generated at input are reconciled at each turnover point.

    4 There is control of negotiable or sensitive documents generated by the computer.

    5 Compliance exists with data security policies for online terminals.

Teleprocessing and Networks

When teleprocessing or networks are employed, audit procedures ascertain that the following are in compliance:

A A written data security policy is in effect covering all applications employing teleprocessing and/or network systems.

B Data security activities are independent from systems and programming, computer operations, output, and data input.

C Access to operating systems is restricted by user identification and passwords.

D Access codes are properly protected and changed with reasonable frequency.

E Transaction files are maintained for all messages entered by terminal input.

F Unauthorized access attempts are monitored and recorded.

G User manuals adequately describe processing requirements.

H Alternate processing procedures are incorporated into disaster recovery plans.

Database Management

The database management system adequately meets audit standards when the following have been accomplished:

A There is an appointed database administrator.

B Written procedures are employed for maintaining a data dictionary file.

C Transaction logs and procedures effectively allow for recovery of the database.

D Data security measures are employed to prevent unauthorized access of data and/or changes to it.

PCs

Personal computers (PCs) employed outside of the IS operation adequately meet auditing standards when the following have been accomplished:

A There exists a formal institutionwide PC policy and it is followed.

B An assigned individual carries out the function of enforcing PC policies, maintaining an inventory of hardware and software, and assisting users in the use of the system.

C Physical and data security is maintained.

D A disaster recovery plan exists for PC operations.

Work Group Computer Systems

The client/server work group computer systems employed outside of the IT operation adequately meet auditing standards when the following have been accomplished:

A There exists a formal institutionwide work group computer policy and it is followed.

B An assigned individual carries out the function of overseeing client/server work group policies, and assisting users in the use of their system.

C Physical and IS data security is maintained.

D A disaster recovery plan exists and is tested for client/server work group computer operations.

Contracting for Vendor Services

Vendor service contracts adequately meet auditing standards when the following have been accomplished:

A Contracts are approved by the firm's legal authority.

B Vendor(s) fulfill contract requirements.

C Applicable backup and contingency plans are in effect.

D Vendor is financially solid.

E Vendor's staff has confirmed credentials.

Management Postimplementation Reviews

Determine whether the IS management maintains postimplementation reviews and continued reviews of existing systems. Reviews should adequately determine that:

A System designs are consistent with original objectives.

B Computer programs comply with standards.

C Audit trails and controls are satisfactory.

D Program and system testing plans are satisfactory.

E Test results are satisfactory.

F System and program documentation is adequate.

G Program changes are properly reviewed and authorized.

H Program changes are properly author-identified and documented.

I Users are duly informed of changes and provided with revised user operation manuals.

J User training is adequate and timely.

K Source and object programs are in parity with each other.

L User management is satisfied with the system.

IS MANAGEMENT AUDIT

This section provides an overview of the quality of management and supervision desirable for information systems. (The IS management function is no longer foreign to outside auditing firms. To prevent replacement by a facilities management service, IS managers should give particular attention to this section.)

IS Organization

This section covers IS organizational structure and the procedures required to foster an effective management operation.

A Organization

1 The IS and corporate organizational charts should identify:

❖ The organizational structure

❖ IS management reporting directly to senior-level management

❖ Appropriate segregation of duties

2 Key personnel biographical data is recorded and requirements for the positions held are documented.

❖ Qualifications required for the position and credentials of individual holding the position

❖ Staffing-level requirements

❖ Provision for management and technical successions

3 Detailed job descriptions are written for each type of position. The job description represents the actual required work. This information is found and accessible by anyone in a current database file.

4 Adequate continuing management and technical education are in place and monitored.

5 An adequate compensation program is in place for attracting qualified personnel and staff retention.

B Planning

1 An active planning group including members of the user community exists.

2 Minutes are maintained of planning meetings for senior management support.

3 The planning meeting minutes contain:

❖ Dates, times, and personnel in attendance

❖ Status of short- and long-range information systems plans

❖ Current operating standards, including security and backup procedures

❖   The status of IS budgets and the current operating cost

❖   Corrective actions to be taken for any present or future IT deficiencies

❖   Reports or development studies that should be noted

4   Strategic planning:

❖   Documentation of current corporate strategic planning is maintained.

❖   Documentation of IS strategic planning activities is maintained.

❖   Future staffing level requirements by position are maintained and include positions to be created.

❖   Any significant changes affecting the institution's organizational structure, hardware/software configuration, and overall IT goals are documented.

IS Control

IS management requires controls ensuring the operation maintains adequate safeguards at all times.

A   **Management standards and procedure controls**

1   Personnel administration has adequate segregation of duties.

2   Systems development has sufficient audit trails.

3   Computer operations has adequate segregation of duties and limited access to file information. Activities are performed only by authorized personnel.

4   Telecommunications operations has proper access, with assurance that only authorized personnel access the system.

5   Computer-stored information has limited access, only by authorized personnel.

6   Contingency planning procedures are current, tested., and enforced.

7   Disaster recovery procedures are current, published, enforced, and tested. Documentation of test efforts should be available for examination.

B   **Effectiveness of IS reports.** Reports for senior management about IS activities indicate the effectiveness of the IS operation. These reports, also furnished to the IS steering committee, include:

1   Management reports providing current status of software activities

2 Performance and problem reports prepared by user groups

3 Reports of systems utilization and planning prepared by operating managers

4 Internal and external audit reports of IS activities

5 Management audit reports

6 Comparable performance norms available from firms in the same industry

C **Project performance reports.** Ensuring control of projects, performance reports of selected projects are written for management. These reports compare actual performance with project plans. Reasons for any variance are determined and reported.

D **Follow-up documentation.** Keep documentation of management follow-up for the IS control operation. This determines whether or not management took positive action toward correcting the exceptions reported.

IS Financial Analysis

Analyze and compare IS operating costs to that which is considered standard for the same size and type of institution. This is very important when IS has a lump-sum budget.

In analyzing financial statements and IT operating costs one must:

A Consider cost allocation methods used.

B Assure applied cost allocation methods are similar for both lump-sum budgets and user charge-back systems.

C Confirm units of processing are within industrial norms.

D Assure programs are within industrial norms.

E Ensure telecommunication costs of service are competitive.

F Affirm vendor services meet financial requirements:

COMMENT

When users are charged for services, these services can be compared with charges considered normal by outside vendors. Solicit competitive bids for an idea of how costs compare.

1 Obtain the name, location, and Dun & Bradstreet rating of vendor.

2 Determine services are covered by a formal written contract.

3 Determine there is no conflict of interest between any IT employee and vendor.

4 Check vendor invoices against work done ensuring the service was rendered as billed.

COMMENT

Operating costs are a major concern to an IT manager. When top management looks at growing IS costs, members may want to know the service cost if furnished by a vendor or by users performing the same procedures on their own systems.

With decreasing prices and growing capabilities of PCs, more users than ever before are considering having their own systems. This also applies to client/server work group systems.

IS Insurance Coverage

Insurance coverage for information systems is designed with attention to its special needs. The insurance should cover:

❖ Employee fidelity

❖ IT hardware and facilities

❖ Loss resulting from business interruption

❖ Cost of transaction errors or omissions

❖ Extra expense, including backup site expenses

❖ Reprogramming and software expense

❖ Transportation and living expense costs when employees work out of town

❖ Water damage from firefighting

❖ Acts of God

❖ Other probable risks

Public Laws

IS management must comply with a host of public laws. Its main concern is compliance with laws governing employees. These rules are from EEOC, OSHA, or the Wage and Hour Administration. Consult the Human Resource office periodically or when new rulings are issued.

Because of purchased software and off-the-shelf systems, copyright law is now an important consideration. Remember, the company is responsible and liable for the actions of its employees.

COMMENT

A large IS operation in Indiana was cited by the Wage and Hour Administration for not paying overtime to 27 group leaders over a five-year period. The overtime was ordered paid. In another case, the Equal Employment Opportunity Commission would not permit IS management to force a data entry operator to work on Sunday.

COMMENT

Information systems management and audit should not be underrated. A large Midwest company has 15 people in the information systems audit department alone. This is larger than most IS organizations. With company mergers and acquisitions, this demand should increase.

12

SYSTEMS AND OPERATIONS AUDIT

SYSTEMS AND OPERATIONS AUDIT POLICIES

Systems and operations audit policies are more technical than IS management policies. A frequent problem is when no policy is established; technicians then make decisions they are not qualified to make.

Systems Development and Programming

This section covers standards and procedures applicable to the firm's systems development and programming activities. Services purchased from vendors must meet both in-house standards and the business standards the firm requires.

The procedures set forth in this chapter follow recommended standards for policies, determined by industrial norms.

Operations Audit Policies

Operations policies cover teleprocessing, data controls, and all computer operations, including user services. The procedures set forth in the operations sections are governed by industrial norms. When policies affect the audit concerns of operations (data control, user services, and teleprocessing), we strongly recommend that industrial norms be followed.

The size of information systems operations does not alter operations standards. Procedures should guarantee uniformity in all IS operations; this is corporate IS's responsibility.

PCs and work group computer systems must comply with the audit policies. Corporate IS has a dual responsibility: informing users of the policies and ensuring that policies are followed.

PROGRAMMING ACTIVITIES CONTROL

To ensure systems development and programming meet audit norms, procedures set down in this section are presented in more detail than those in other sections. Systems development and programming involvement may range in complexity from purchasing off-the-shelf software systems to developing in-house systems to purchasing turnkey systems.

Standards for Systems Development and Programming

Standards for systems development, programming functions, systems development methodology, and program and system documentation must be adequately defined and followed. There should exist controls for application programs and software changes.

A Develop written standards:
  1 Systems design and development
  2 Software package selection
  3 Application programming
  4 Operating systems programming
  5 Program testing
  6 Systems implementation
  7 Systems and programming documentation
  8 Program change controls
  9 Quality assurance and cataloging
B Application systems design development standards require:
  1 Project feasibility studies
  2 Project cost-benefit analysis
  3 Predetermined progress milestones and follow-up review of progress reports
  4 Documented user approval of proposed systems design
  5 Documented user approval of program tests, user documentation, and user's final acceptance

6 Documented postimplementation studies

C Programming standards require:

1 The use of control totals, programmed audits, and validation checks of input before processing is begun.

2 Audit trails and exception reports of uncommon transactions.

3 Standardized routines and modular coding.

4 Standards for reusable coding practices.

5 Proper involvement of users in major decisions affecting input, logic flow, and output.

6 Test plans, including testing for all conceivable error conditions. Never perform tests with live database files.

7 Completed documentation and user training before systems implementation.

8 CASE tools standards used.

D Documentation standards include:

1 Systems narratives

2 Program narratives

3 Record layout schematics and output formats

4 Database dictionary listings

5 Descriptions of edit checking and programmed controls

6 Current source program documentation

7 User or operator instructions

8 User manuals

9 A chronological listing of program changes

10 Documentation of maintenance changes

11 Prealpha naming conventions

12 Screen display layouts

13 Data element cross-references

14 Index of table field names

E Current user manuals are distributed to all appropriate user departments in the quantity required.

Programming Activities Control

To control programming activities and ensure uniformity and conformity, practice the following guidelines:

A Documents generated for new programs and after-program changes are reviewed, ensuring that documentation contains the following:

   1 Prenumbered program change control forms.

   2 A description of the problem or reasons for change.

   3 Approval of change request by the affected user management.

   4 Name of programmer and date of change.

   5 Signature and date of supervisor who reviewed and approved the actual program change.

   6 Signature and date of program librarian or quality assurance person cataloging the program changes.

   7 Confirmation that a copy of the approval was sent to the audit department.

   8 Any supporting documents, as well as source listings of codes affected by a change and object listings of programs covered by the documentation, are held in the program library.

B All program modifications are reviewed and approved by the user department prior to any implementation.

C Program documentation update must reflect that program changes are being done as soon as practical.

D Changes to the operating system are subject to the same control procedures as application programs.

E Sufficient numbers of persons with training and experience should be available to provide backup for major systems and programming functions.

F Restrict systems programmers' access to application program libraries and documentation to assure security. (These restrictions reduce the possibility of embezzlement by the programmer.)

G Application programmers are denied access to:

   1 Documentation and source listings for the operating system

   2 Production program libraries

   3 Live data files

H Records of temporary program changes using patches or system utilities are maintained and reviewed by supervisory personnel.

I Replace all temporary program changes by properly authorized program changes within a reasonable time.

J The documentation librarian's duties include:

1 Review of documentation during system development ensuring adherence to standards and appropriate authorization of exceptions.

2 Control and safeguard of documentation.

3 Confirmation that revised documentation reflects actual changes.

4 Distribution of documentation to authorized parties.

5 Maintenance of all documentation and standards manuals ensuring they are current.

COMPUTER OPERATIONS

The objective of this section is to provide a base of established industrial norms for computer operations. This section also covers procedures for contingency and recovery planning, applicable to a wide scope of IT operation sizes, along with physical and internal controls.

Computer Room Controls

The computer room environment must be controlled to ensure safe computer operation. The following safeguards are appropriate for a wide range of room sizes:

A Adequate procedures are established ensuring only authorized persons are permitted in the computer room.

B Restrict operation of computer hardware to authorized personnel only.

C Repair of computer hardware is restricted to authorized personnel.

D Computer room facility is adequately protected with:

1 Procedures to minimize the accumulation of paper and other flammables in and around the computer room

2 Heat, smoke, and water detectors

3 Proper portable fire extinguishers

4 A suitable fire control system

5 Waterproof equipment covers

6 Temperature and humidity control equipment

7 Intrusion detection devices

8 Alternate power supply

9 Emergency lighting

E Smoking, eating, and magnets are prohibited in the computer room.

F Adequate on-call personnel are available, and maintenance agreements covering all equipment are up to date.

G Perform preventive maintenance on a regularly scheduled basis.

Computer Operations Management Reporting

IT management needs computer operations reporting for feedback and control. This reporting must be timely and IT management must examine it closely.

Reports include, but are not limited to:

A Detailed hardware problem logs

B Computer-generated reports that include:

    1 Proper program identification

    2 Job processing times

    3 Rerun times

    4 Down times

    5 Operator identification

C Machine utilization and performance reports

D Console logs or automated summaries of such logs that are reviewed for any unusual activity such as reruns, halts, unauthorized use, etc.

Reports must be produced at sufficient intervals to allow proper control and IS management review.

Computer Operation Controls

Computer operation controls govern the personnel running the computer system. Operators should be aware of these procedures that must be enforced.

A Operators are cross-trained, providing backup and reducing dependence on key personnel.

B Operators are prohibited from:

    1 Originating entries for processing

    2 Correcting data exceptions, such as unposted or rejected items

    3 Preparing any general ledger and/or subsidiary ledger entries

    4 Performing any balancing function (reconciliation) other than run-to-run control

5   Running test programs against live or backup files

6   Executing programs from the test library during production runs

7   Copying source or object programs without prior approval

8   Controlling report generation and distribution

C   Operators are denied access to source programs, program listings, and other documentation unnecessary for the processing of their applications.

D   Operators' run instructions must be adequate and current.

E   The computer center must utilize a formal scheduling procedure.

F   Supervisory approval is necessary to add jobs or modify the schedule.

Program/Data Library Controls

The computer program and data library requires its own audit readiness procedures. Site requirements may vary from location to location; therefore, the following are only core duties/procedures required for any library unit:

A   Librarian's responsibilities are prohibited to anyone with conflicting duties.

B   Enforce standard library procedures on all work shifts.

C   Only authorized personnel have library access.

D   Maintain a program and data file for all items under the jurisdiction of the library.

E   Issue data files from the library only on the basis of established run schedules or other evidence of proper authorization.

F   Use external labels to identify tapes and disks.

G   Inventory record of tapes and disks is maintained to identify:

1   Storage location

2   Volume serial number

3   Creation and expiration dates

H   Maintain current copies of the operating system and application programs in the library vault for immediate backup. Maintain a second backup copy of all systems and programs off-site. All fireproof safes must meet ratings for secondary data storage requirements.

I   A machine-readable source program is maintained for each application program listed in the production object library.

J   If backup copies of operating systems, application programs, transaction files, or master files are used, duplicates must be in the library or in the off-site storage location before being used by the IT production operation.

K Periodically test backup operating system and application programs in the library.

L Store magnetic tapes and disk packs in a closed, fire-resistant, and limited-access vault. The fire-resistance ratings must meet code for such items.

M Provide controlled storage areas (on- and off-site) for work group programs, files, and data.

N Provide fireproof controlled storage for blank payroll and accounts payable checks. Keep a beginning and ending control number log.

O Program/data library area contains the following devices:

1 A suitable fire extinguisher system

2 An adequate air conditioning system

3 An adequate fire alarm system

4 An adequate intrusion alarm system

5 A temperature and humidity recording device

DATA CONTROL

The objective of this section is to provide adequate control procedures to maintain accuracy and integrity of data, which includes input, output, and storage of data files and databases.

Input Controls

Inputs to any computer operation must be controlled. These controls will vary depending on need. The procedures are as follows:

A Reference input manuals, including examples (copies) and illustrations (drawings) of source documents, are made available for each data entry operator.

B All data received by the data entry unit is accompanied by prenumbered transmittal batch forms and posted control totals.

C Maintain a log of input received by source.

D Batch control documents received with the input data are retained in an orderly and logical manner for final balancing.

E All transactions, such as item counts, are subject to controls similar to those used for monetary transactions.

F Master file change requests require the following:

1 The request in writing

2 Identification of originating personnel

3 Required approval from the database administrator

G All required procedures must be in place and known by each data entry operator ensuring appropriate processing.

H If the data entry service is not proximate to the sending area, send source documents through a backup procedure.

I To ensure accuracy of critical control fields, verify input by a second data entry operator.

J Require monetary totals and item counts for key-to-disk and key-to-tape systems.

K Retain input transactions for a minimum of 24 hours in the IT computer area.

L Prohibit data entry personnel from originating entries for processing.

M Require supervisory approval for correcting entries that are:

1 Received by, but not charged to, the data center

2 Charged to, but not received by, the data center

N Supervisory personnel regularly review exception and reconciliation items.

COMMENT

Allowing IT-originated entries may be an open invitation to theft.

Output Controls

Output controls cover both printed and microfiche output. The following procedures are to be enforced:

A Review all reports for quality prior to distribution.

B Control procedures must be established ensuring all reports are produced and delivered as scheduled.

C Establish a systematic and orderly plan for pickup and processing of data and the delivery of output data.

   D All distribution procedures should be sufficiently organized and controlled to provide for the delivery of reports to the proper users.

   E Establish procedures for the control of signature stamps.

Database Management Controls

A database administrator, responsible for coordinating and controlling the database, follows established standards and procedures for controlling data records and files used by programmers. The following procedures apply:

   A To maintain security, the database administrator's access to live data, applications source listings, and other application program documentation is appropriately restricted.

   B The data dictionary contains detailed definitions of all data elements.

   C All changes made to the data dictionary require authorization of the database administrator.

   D Required procedures exist assuring the data dictionary remains current and accurate.

   E All procedures covering database recovery exist in the event of hardware or software failure.

   F Transaction log is in place at all times to provide for an audit trail.

   G Report any attempts to violate database security to the IS management from the database administrator in writing.

   H Client/server access controls are in place, and any violation is investigated and reported to the IS management.

DISASTER RECOVERY/CONTINGENCY PLANNING

Disaster recovery audit procedures also contain the contingency planning procedures. Proof that these are in place, combined with periodic testing, ensures proper system functioning.

Disaster Recovery

Effective disaster recovery and contingency plans require maintaining proper on-site and off-site storage facilities.

   A Off-site storage location should contain adequate storage space for:
      1 Source and object production programs
      2 Master files and transaction files to recreate the current master files

3 System and program documentation

4 Operating systems and utility programs

5 Other vital records

B Remote storage facility must contain the proper access control procedures.

C A written emergency plan addresses:

1 Physical security of the computer installation

2 Actions to be taken in specific emergency situations

3 Contingency procedures required to recover from a disaster or computer failure

D A suitable backup procedure can:

1 Provide backup processing for required processing in volume.

2 Provide sufficient processing time necessary to correct the problem.

3 Provide the documentation required so that management can adequately respond to a disaster.

Data Center Contingency Planning

The data center disaster and recovery contingency plans should include:

A Data files and program file backups in place.

B Computer system backup in place.

C A remote storage location for emergency procedures manuals.

D An alternate input and output distribution system with a minimum time required to be operational.

E An online network system ready for a backup if required.

F A complete assignment of duties for reconstruction and off-site processing in the possession of all trusted personnel.

G A complete contingency procedure in place to recover from a disaster or computer failure.

Systems Assurance

The following procedures provide for systems assurance:

A Protect data files, program libraries, and utilities by passwords and other means.

B Change passwords periodically.

C Utility programs with data files or program-altering capabilities are adequately controlled.

D Written procedures covering the acceptance and cataloging of production programs are in place and up-to-date.

E All object code production programs are generated from the most current source code versions.

F Delete all obsolete or unused programs from current production libraries. Move these programs to the off-site storage area. They must be properly labeled and kept for no less than five years before being destroyed.

G Computer center management periodically reviews and updates controls and security relating to data files and program libraries.

H Make proper information available to all concerned about any hardware or software system changes.

I Database management critical records are dumped and stored on a sufficiently frequent basis for needed backup and timely restoration purposes.

J Maintain a procedure providing information relative to the hardware and software configuration of the backup site.

K All outside facilities backup arrangements maintain up-to-date written agreements at all times.

L Client/server operations employing mirrored systems are in agreement. Reconfirm at random intervals.

PC SYSTEMS AND OPERATIONS AUDIT POLICIES

The objective of this section is to establish adequate controls over the use of PCs in an institution. The degree of control necessary depends on the degree of sensitive information handled or the value of processing done by respective PCs.

PC Standards

Standards required for the operational use of PCs, including software and hardware acquisition apply to all PCs used in an organization.

A Standards include:
  1 Use of the output data
  2 Restriction of access to PCs

3 Control of the movement of software and hardware

4 Removal from the institution of any software or hardware

5 Restriction on use of software and hardware to that sanctioned by the organization

6 Restriction on personal use of PCs

7 Modification of hardware or software

8 Piracy of purchased software

9 Backup for all data files

10 Policy that approved games are to be allowed on PCs

11 Restriction of network access to Internet and e-mail to business use only

12 Review of local area networks (LAN) procedures and controls

B Standards covering software and hardware acquisition should include the following:

1 Acquisition will follow standards developed for the institution.

2 Each PC site possesses the required documentation.

3 In-house software development is performed only by sanctioned personnel.

4 Software developed on the firm's time and/or hardware/software is the firm's property.

PC Environment

Environments where PCs are used do not require the same degree of control needed by IS computer operations. However, their users are usually unfamiliar with IS operation requirements and learn those that are applicable. The following are standard environment requirements:

A PC Security

1 Physical security required:

❖ Key locks on hardware

❖ Backup data files secured in approved fireproof files or safes

❖ Access areas restricted

❖ Critical information backed up by IT computer operations

2 Access controls required:

❖ The use of dial-up equipment

❖ Read-only attributes attached to the files

❖ Passwords for access

❖ Encryption of classified data disks

B Housekeeping Environment

1 No foods and liquids on the same desk or table tops containing computer hardware or secondary storage.

2 No telephones or magnetic devices closer than two feet from any data hardware or software.

3 No smoking in the general area of PC operations.

4 Keep the area dust free.

C Power Supply

1 Computer hardware must not share its power outlets with any other devices.

2 Plug all hardware into surge protectors.

3 Areas that may have power supply problems must have UPS (uninterrupted power supply) backup supply units capable of providing power for the full time required to bring down the system.

Inventory Control of Hardware and Software

Maintain an asset management system for all PC hardware and software. Records are kept both by the computer asset manager and also by each user area's highest level of administration. The asset manager is responsible for keeping the various inventory records in balance.

WORK GROUP SYSTEMS AND OPERATIONS AUDIT POLICIES

The objective of this section is to establish adequate controls over the use of the work group and client/server systems in an institution. The degree of control necessary depends on the degree of sensitive information handled or the value of processing done by the respective operations.

Work Group Standards

Standards applicable to all work groups and client/server systems in an organization are required for their operational use and include those for software and hardware acquisition.

A Standards include:

1 Use of the output data

2 Restrictions of access to work stations and terminals

3 Control of the movement of software and hardware

4 Removal from the institution of any software or hardware

5 Restriction on use of software and hardware to that sanctioned by the organization

6 Restriction on personal use of workstations and/or terminals

7 Modification of hardware or software

8 Piracy of purchased software

9 Backup for all data files

10 Backup of server files and programs

11 Policy that games are not to be allowed on the client/server systems

12 Restriction of network access to Internet and e-mail to business use only

B Standards covering software and hardware acquisition include the following:

1 Acquisition follows standards developed for the institution.

2 Each workstation and/or terminal site possesses the required operation documentation.

3 In-house software development is performed only by sanctioned personnel.

4 Software developed on the firm's time and/or hardware/software is the firm's property.

Work Group Environment

Environments of work group or client/server systems will not receive the same degree of control by IT computer operations as information system's own client/server systems. The users of workstations and terminals are not expected to be familiar with IT operation requirements but know those applying to them. The following are standard environment requirements:

A Work Group Security

1 Physical security required:

❖ Key locks on hardware (optional)

❖ Backup data files maintained

❖ Access areas restricted

❖ Critical information backed up by IT computer operations

COMMENT

The CIO/IS head should have a review done of the current systems and operations audit policies and procedures by the firm's outside auditors. If these auditors cannot, have them recommend a source for such a service in writing. The interval between such examinations depends on valid problem discoveries. The more the problems found, the closer the review intervals.

2 Access controls required:

- ❖ Read-only attributes attached to the information systems files and database
- ❖ Passwords for access

B Housekeeping Environment

1 No foods and liquids on the same desk or table tops containing computer hardware or secondary storage media.

2 No telephones or magnetic devices closer than two feet from any hardware or software.

3 No smoking in the general area of PC operations.

4 Keep the area dust-free.

C Power Supply

1 Workstations or terminals do not share power outlets with any other devices.

2 Areas that may have power supply problems require UPS (uninterrupted power supply) units for a limited-time power supply.

Inventory Control of Hardware and Software

Maintain an asset management system for all computer hardware and software. Records are kept by the computer asset manager and also by each user area's highest level of administration. The asset manager is responsible for keeping the various inventory records in balance.

COMMENT

The University of North Carolina found a network server that, although missing for four years, hadn't missed a packet in all that time.

Try as they might, university administrators couldn't find the server. Working with Novell, IT workers tracked it down by meticulously following cable until they literally ran into a wall. Maintenance workers had mistakenly sealed the server behind drywall.—John Rendleman, *InformationWeek*

13

IT HUMAN RESOURCES: KEEPING PEOPLE

IS PERSONNEL POLICIES

Policies governing IS personnel may differ from those in other departments because the nature of IS operations requires some stringency, with peculiar personnel needs. Therefore, we discuss specific IS personnel policies here only to augment corporate personnel policies.

IS Management Objectives

The broad objectives for IS human resources management include the following:

- ❖ Develop IS personnel through training and outside education.
- ❖ Maintain an active recruitment policy.
- ❖ Develop a cooperative attitude among IS personnel concerning users' needs.
- ❖ Develop and maintain an ongoing IS personnel promotion planning system.
- ❖ Maintain a comprehensive and competitive compensation plan for each job position.
- ❖ Maintain ongoing career guidance for employee development.

> ## COMMENT
>
> Computer personnel require special treatment. A *Business Week* article, "Computer People: Yes, They Really Are Different," notes that IT people are motivated more by personal fulfillment and growth than money or job titles. Other research indicates they tend to be more loyal to their profession than to their firm.
>
> The fact that qualified IS personnel are in high demand and job turnover above the norm indicates that retention requires extra effort. Time is required to replace a competent employee, and the replacement cannot be expected to function as well for some time. New personnel may also cost about 15 percent more than current employees; moreover, there may be a project delay.

> ## COMMENT
>
> IT employees *are* different from others, and IS personnel policies and procedures must accommodate these differences for the department to function at the industry norm and to minimize the turnover rate.
>
> Unless the Human Resources department considers a turnover rate of 100 percent per year normal, which an IS operation in Michigan experienced, they must take the particular needs of IS personnel into account.

Recruiting and Selection Policies

Limit recruiting and selection procedures to long-term employment. Don't hire personnel unless they are permanent. Temporary personnel are considered contract workers.

COMMENT

Firms have hired regular personnel for a project, then terminated them when the project was completed to secure "low-priced consulting services." Feeling abused, these unhappy former employees often exposed the firms' unfair employment practices, have committed sabotage before or after leaving, and have sued.

The ideal policy is recruiting and selecting the best people for the job and hiring them on a full-time basis. A wise institution attracts and pays for qualified personnel. The selection process is also a major issue. Better not to fill a position than hire the wrong person.

IS Performance Evaluation Policy

An effective IS performance evaluation system is needed. Evaluations provide both employee and firm with valuable information: Employees are interested in feedback about their performance, and the firm wants to know which employees perform well and which have promotion potential.

Discipline and Termination Policy

Discipline and termination policies fill a special need in information systems. Discipline should not jeopardize any future relations between employees and the firm, but should be fair and acceptable.

Termination of an IT employee requires careful treatment. Procedures must be in place and followed precisely insuring no further trouble from a departing employee.

RECRUITING AND JOB SEARCH

Recruiting and job searches are traditionally performed by the Human Resource department, but most need help recruiting the specific personnel required by information systems. Therefore, the involvement of IT management is crucial.

COMMENT

More than one "fired" information systems employee has attracted negative publicity because of departing misdeeds. Keeping a firm's name out of the headlines requires some special termination procedures.

COMMENT

Even the U.S. government is aware of these special requirements, and uses supplemental job application forms for IS positions.

The growth of IT personnel placement firms shows the need for specialized information systems recruiting. Firms earn their employer-paid fees by delivering the IT personnel needed for the job. However, use care in choosing a placement firm. One human resource manager thought a candidate with ten years of IT experience qualified for a systems analyst position. When the IT manager interviewed the candidate, he discovered the candidate had been a data entry supervisor for almost all of the ten years. Better IT personnel placement firms screen out such candidates.

Methods of Recruiting

To obtain experienced personnel, the following procedures for recruiting IT candidates have been very successful when augmented with traditional forms:

A   Pay a bonus to present employees for recruiting and hiring qualified personnel. The benefits of this are:

1   Proven personnel usually recommend qualified persons like themselves.

> ## COMMENT
>
> Find a good firm and work with it. Be careful it does not place your "better" people with other firms. If it does, find another recruiting firm fast. Have the firm work with IT management, not the Human Resource department.

2   The cost for the Human Resources department to find job candidates or to pay a recruiting firm's fee is more than the bonus paid to an employee (which should be no less than $1,000).

3   Current personnel have a vested interest in finding the right person for the job. Employees can know what is needed better than Human Resources or the recruiting firm.

B   Consult the person leaving, who knows the job better than anyone else, and can help define job requirements.

C   Take the time to locate a quality recruiting firm.

D   When a candidate is found, send his/her job application to the Human Resources department to confirm the credentials and work experience. Computer operations applicants, by the nature of their job, will also require a retail credit check.

E   Avoid nepotism at all costs. Because of the controls needed for an IS operation, hiring relatives causes nothing but problems. Relatives tend not to abide by the same rules as nonrelatives. They tend to cover up more errors and have higher rates of orchestrated thefts.

College Recruiting

College is an excellent source for entry-level IT employees, but some special effort is required to recruit the correct candidates. Graduating students can have formal training in the IT area, but a degree in computer science won't guarantee a person is qualified for entry-level IT positions. Many know coding but lack business knowledge or expertise in the particular languages used by the recruiting firm. Some of the better students may have worked as student help-desk persons. They've experienced contact with student users and can be more familiar with IT problems.

Two-year technical school programs usually focus on applied industrial needs with only a limited number of liberal arts courses. Two-year graduates

COMMENT

One noted Midwest university Computer Science department did not offer any COBOL courses. Unless a company was willing to change to PASCAL, retraining was necessary if those computer science graduates were hired.

Some university teachers leave a lot to be desired. They have little, if any, background in applications programming and applications they use are mostly math oriented. Other schools or universities have teaching staffs with industrial experience so students graduate ready to fit into the industrial environment.

COMMENT

An intern from a well-known university, who was smart but obnoxious, was not hired by the company where he served his internship. The IT manager contacted every other division in the company insuring this intern was not hired. A candidate must mesh with the corporate culture and, more important, with the firm's IS culture. One misfit on an IT project is worse than having one less person to do the work.

often cannot be placed directly into salaried positions. Here the wage and hour regulations are very restrictive. Confirm these regulations with Human Resources prior to hiring a job candidate from one of these programs.

No matter what level of school recruiting, make an effort to learn something about the faculty and the programs offered. When a school offers the necessary training, inform its placement office of the company's needs. Ordinarily, the school will try to place the better students first. The school may even use the company's guidelines to assist with the planning of future programs.

One program proven successful for many firms is the internship. With interns the company gets to know the prospective candidate. The student not only has to perform, but also "fit in." If hired by the firm, they will already know the IT operation and corporate culture.

Environmental Influences

In employee recruitment, consider the environmental factors. The IT working environments of a programmer, a data entry operator, and a systems analyst are all different. Recruit prospective employees to fit in with the working climate. Current economic conditions and the nature of the labor market affect recruiting. Recruiting becomes difficult when the economy is overheated.

COMMENT

There is a current trend to import programming talent with or without green cards. One Ohio consulting firm hired a foreign graduate student at the firm's expense, and with much effort, helped the programmer get a green card. Within a week of receiving his green card, the programmer quit and started his own competing consulting company.

Employees are poor candidates for management and systems analysis positions when they have little or no loyalty to the firm and local community. As to IT needs, the best way to utilize imported programming talent is to use employment firms that have talent for hire. Using these firms has worked out well, and given potential employees a chance to "earn their salt."

Other factors influencing recruiting are governmental regulations, both federal and state equal employment opportunity (EEO) legislation. Human Resource offices are acquainted with EEO laws and should be used as a reference regarding these regulations.

COMMENT

IT members should know they were hired because of their skills, not because of EEOC requirements. One does not need government regulations to hire qualified women, the handicapped, or minorities; it just good business sense.

SELECTION OF IS PERSONNEL

Use the same criteria for hiring IT personnel whether from inside or outside the firm. Base the decision to promote or transfer a person to the information systems department on the person's qualifications. If the outside and inside talents are equal, the inside person may be a better choice since this encourages greater firm loyalty. Promotion or transfer of poorly qualified personnel based on company politics can create problems for IS management.

A Diagnostic Approach to Selection

IS management has to choose personnel from a list of candidates who best meet the selection criteria, while considering current environmental conditions. The size and complexity of the IT operations, its status within the firm, and technological volatility will all affect selection and attraction of the right personnel.

A second circumstance affecting the decision for IT is the current labor market. If there are many applicants, the selection decision can be complicated. If there is only one applicant, selection is relatively easy, but there is also a danger this person is unqualified. It is better to continue recruiting than select the wrong candidate. If the person is qualified, do not hesitate, because he or she may be hired by someone else.

Selection Criteria

For a selection procedure to succeed, the personal characteristics required for effective job performance should be specified by the prospective employee's immediate supervisor. Selection techniques can be suggested and used by the experts in a firm's Human Resources department to uncover these defined characteristics. Selection criteria are summarized under the following categories: education, experience, personal characteristics, and future growth potential. They reflect characteristics of present employees who are happy and successful in the same position.

A selection is made by rating the different candidates on specified criteria, weighted according to past proven results that can be verified by bona fide documentation. Candidates are ranked by these scores. The following are part of the selection procedure:

A **IS application form.** A separate application form (either in place of or in addition to the general company application form) is used to glean information required for filling an IS position. It is developed by the IS management, and requested technical information is approved by the IT supervisors. Before use, the form is sent to the Human Resources department to insure illegal questions are not included.

B **Formal education.** Educational criteria must be validated against job performance. The amount and type of education correlating with job effectiveness are determined for use in the selection procedure. Formal education can indicate ability, skills, and the applicant's level of accomplishment. Beware of the wage and hour rules regarding what constitutes a salaried position, which does not qualify for overtime pay. Contact the Human Resource people to insure that a given position warrants the salaried status. IS management should examine:

1 An official transcript sent by the school. Evaluate courses and grades.

COMMENT

Computer World publishes an annual salary survey that is one of the best. How competitive is the firm within its industry and national location by job type?

Government regulations often influence selection. One data entry operator was hired, then terminated, because the person's religious beliefs prohibited working on Sunday. When the terminated employee filed for unemployment compensation, the government brought an EEO suit against the firm. The person was reinstated with back pay. To avoid this problem, the Human Resources department should be asked to help when anything unusual arises in the candidate selection process.

2   The school's catalog describing the relevant courses.

3   The kind of hardware and software used by the school.

4   Applied or theoretical orientation of the school's IT teaching staff.

C   **Experience.** Another criterion for selecting IT personnel is experience. First choice should be a person formerly successful in the same type of job. The more experience the better, to a certain point. Someone who has only programmed for ten years would be unsuitable for a lead systems analyst position. The nature of the applicant's experience should be considered. A person working on multiple projects in a demanding environment for four years is usually a better selection than someone doing only payroll maintenance programming for ten years. If the new position requires only maintenance programming skills, the latter would be the wiser selection. Ways to confirm experience are:

1   Have more than one interviewer talk with the candidate. Use interviewers with opposing technical views so the candidate is forced to be honest.

2   Have the candidate bring samples of written documentation. Confirm the originality of his/her work.

3   Check the candidate's references; contact former co-workers and employers. A phone call to each produces better results than a written request.

TESTING FOR IS PERSONNEL

The Human Resources department should administer tests that measure skill levels, aptitude, and personality. Because of EEOC laws, tests are required to be job related and validated, i.e., that job performance correlates with the test results. There are "tests in print" measuring programming or data entry aptitude. Manual dexterity tests can be used for data entry positions. For systems analysts, analyze the desired criteria by more than one test.

Don't limit testing to entry-level personnel. A person who has been a programmer for five years could have been a poor programmer for five years. Well-organized firms recognize this. One source of tests is the book *Tests in Print*.

Test Selection

Whichever test is selected, pretest it with current employees first. Scores correlating with the known performance records of employees can establish confidence in the tests. No one choice will be 100 percent dependable, but using

> ## COMMENT
>
> For example, a COBOL teacher with two years' teaching experience and six years' industrial experience applied for a job as a COBOL programmer with a national company in St. Louis. She took a programming aptitude test and passed. But not all experienced programmers can, and their work may reflect this.

validated tests is one of the best objective methods for selecting the best person for the job. Some tests are not skill tests but measure what might be expected after a person is trained. Save time and money by training the right person, not just someone who knows the right buzzwords.

EMPLOYMENT INTERVIEW

Employment interviews begin after candidates have passed the preliminary screening and testing. There are three general types: structured, semistructured, and unstructured. All three involve interaction between two or more parties: the applicant and one or more representatives of the potential employer. Don't limit the process to only one method.

The Structured Interview

The structured interview is best for people with little or no interview experience. It is suitable, with little training, for peer or working supervisors. A list of questions is prepared in advance. Questions can be divided between the interviewers or repeated using different versions. This is an effective tool to determine the candidate's truthfulness and knowledge of information technology. Questions should be forced choice (i.e., yes or no), so the interviewer need only indicate the applicant's response on a printed form. This approach is very restricted but provides an opportunity to analyze an individual's technical skills.

The Semistructured Interview

In a semistructured interview, only major questions are prepared in advance. Conducting this interview requires greater skill and preparation than the structured interview. It allows more flexibility than the structured approach.

A skillful interviewer can probe freely into areas that merit further detail. This approach combines enough structure to insure important information is collected. This allows for comparison with other applications and facilitates the exchange of information in a freer manner than the strictly structured interview.

The Unstructured Interview

The unstructured interview is best left to experienced interviewers. There may be a prepared list of topics but the interviewer retains the freedom to adapt to the individual candidates. The unstructured interview's reliability may be questioned, but it does provide the manager with subjective information. This interview's results can be compared with others given to the same candidate(s) in the same fashion.

Interview Review

When an interview is concluded, each interviewer puts his/her objective analysis of the applicant into writing. This information is forwarded to the manager making the hiring decision. If the decision is close, the manager may call a meeting of all interviewers to discuss the merits of the applicant(s).

The analysis tends to be subjective with multiple interviewers. Each level, from peer to senior management, has its own analysis of the applicant. All peer interviewers will not only want to have someone competent, but someone who fits into the work group. Senior management may look for different traits that meet the current to future needs.

PERFORMANCE REVIEW

While most firms have performance review procedures, information systems may require additional reviews because performance is a function of ability as well as skill and effort. For example, a programmer who works late, comes in on weekends, and exerts great effort receives a good performance review and a raise. However, one highly skilled person who exerts less effort could possibly replace this same programmer and ten more like him/her.

This creates a major problem in reviewing the performance of programmers and systems analysts. The systems analyst may be one of the most difficult to rate on performance. On the other hand, evaluating data entry operators presents few problems. The output less the error rate is considered the performance. IT performance determination is vulnerable to subjectivity, depending on the specific position in question.

Computer Operations Performance Review

The operations area is less complex and more objective in analyzing a person's performance. In addition to the standard evaluation procedures, the following are also recommended:

A **Data entry.** The data entry operator's performance is ordinarily measured by the volume of data input, less the error rate. However, don't judge all data entry operators alike. The kind of source documents an operator processes affects performance. Handwritten documents that have to be coded or words requiring abbreviations slow the input rate and increase the error rate. The standard measure of keystrokes-per-minute is not a fair method of measurement and comparison.

One efficient method is to employ a tool from the industrial engineer's domain, MTM (Motion Time Measurement). This method analyzes the source document and the human effort required in capturing the data into computer digital form; it therefore determines a realistic standard. Some systems and procedures analysts have been trained in this technology. If no one in IS has this skill, contact the industrial engineering department. If there is no industrial engineering unit in house, get an outside source from a technical service agency.

B **Computer operations.** The computer operator's performance is best judged by the efficiency of running the computer operation. The control logs and system monitoring software allow evaluation of performance. In addition, the appearance of the computer center area provides some idea of housekeeping skills. Surprise visits by management on the night and weekend shifts also provide information. That operators never know when to expect a visit helps increase efficiency.

The evaluation of operations personnel tends to be subjective. Personalities become a factor when evaluating personnel such as the computer operator, data librarian, or the data output and distribution operators. Because these evaluations could become subjective, two or more supervisors should evaluate each employee. If the operation is large enough, rotation of supervisors and/or personnel (for cross-training as well as employee evaluation) should be considered.

Programmer's Performance Review

Program productivity is not easily measured, resulting in subjective performance reviews. Productivity of programmers rises when they know they are being observed. (This increased production is called the "Hawthorn effect.") Programming productivity can be affected by:

❖ Program design changes originated by the customer

- ❖ Kind of language used
- ❖ The detail level of the documentation
- ❖ Quality of the information furnished for the program(s)
- ❖ The soundness of the test data
- ❖ The working environment
- ❖ The amount of supervision required

The above, which may affect the programmer's productivity, must be considered when reviewing performance. Avoid assessments based on lines of code per given time period or pages of documentation per month. Performance reviews may be enhanced by the following:

A **Peer review.** Have IT peers anonymously rank each other's performance. Include programmers, systems analysts, and computer operations personnel.

B **Time by program function.** A function is an action or activity, usually at the lowest definable level of structured programming.

- ❖ A function has fewer than 55 coding statements.
- ❖ A function has one entry point and one exit point. The time taken to complete a function is a better gauge of productivity than the time taken to write a specific number of lines of code. The number of functions completed in given time intervals provides information about the programming skill level of the person coding, along with their error rate.

Systems Analyst's Performance Review

Systems analysts are difficult people to review objectively. Often, the person's body language and personality can affect the appraisal. Another problem is that it takes so long to see the results of a systems analyst's efforts that appraisals may be distorted.

The number of procedures added to the firm's performance review process for systems analysts is limited. The following considerations may help:

A Have programmers provide an anonymous appraisal ranking of each systems analyst. A preprinted form is used to collect evaluations and any remarks.

B Have user managers appraise system analysts who worked on terminated projects. A preprinted form for this purpose is used to collect evaluations and any remarks.

C Use peer evaluation. Use preprinted forms to collect evaluations and any remarks.

D Evaluate their project performance. How did he/she complete measurable task unit completion times compared to the estimated times? The project manager should provide a project evaluation of each member during and at the termination of each project. A preprinted evaluation form is used for the in-process and final evaluations.

E Examine the status of the project after termination by the projects coordinator. Systems project manager or leaders will have no better evidence for their evaluation.

EMPLOYEE TERMINATION

To protect the company, information systems managers use special termination procedures. Departing IS employees have many opportunities for destructive activities.

Employees leaving on good terms will have an exit interview. If no provision for this exists, information systems or information technology management conducts the interview. A preprinted exit form, approved by the CIO or IS head, is used to have a structured exit interview. The Human Resource manager should examine the form for approval, to limit any company liability.

Termination Procedure

Employees terminated for any reason require the following additional IS termination procedures:

A Notify the employee away from the work area.

B Remove the employee's password from the system before the notice is given.

C Have the employee turn in his/her IS identification and any keys or magnetic cards.

D Escort the employee outside the building. If the employee needs transportation to get home, provide it.

E Collect and box the employee's personal items. These may be picked up in the lobby or sent to the terminated employee's home address within two days. Require a confirmation of delivery receipt.

Exit Interview

After giving notice, all employees should be interviewed by someone other than their own supervisor as soon as possible. This interview is to learn why the employee quit. The preprinted IS exit form provides for a structured exit interview. Data collected from departing employees may indicate an undesirable situation exists and may give management an opportunity to correct it in the future.

If the exit interview reveals the departing employee is upset, the CIO/IS head is notified immediately to review the information. The CIO/IS manager determines if the termination procedure, on page 321, should be enacted to prevent possible retaliation against the firm by the departing employee.

EMPLOYEE DEVELOPMENT

IS employees are uniquely attuned to the need to keep up with ever-changing technology. Earning a promotion requires even more effort. The better employees, if not provided educational opportunities by the firm, will pay for it themselves. They will also be less loyal because of it. They will depart at the first advantageous opportunity, leaving the firm with lesser quality employees. This education and training is necessary for IT employees and has to be provided beyond that for the rest of the firm.

IS Skills Inventory

A skills inventory is maintained for each employee of the information systems operation. It should be kept as current as any other file and should consist of the following:

A Person's name and ID number

B Date the person started with IS

C Starting salary and title

D Formal education received

E Other training received

F Certifications received

G Current job title

H Current supervisor

I Start date of the current position

J Current salary and benefits

K The promotion potential of the employee:

    1 Ready for a promotion.

    2 Will be ready with more training.

    3 Will be ready with more experience.

4 Will be ready with more training and experience.

5 Is not ready and may never be ready.

6 Will never be ready.

L Foreign languages spoken

M Future education plans

N Future training plans

O Hobbies or interests that could benefit the firm

P Next goal/promotion objective within the firm

Q Status when hired by information systems:

1 If transfer employee:

❖ Date started with firm

❖ Title and department of last position before joining IS

2 Previous employer:

❖ Name of firm

❖ Position held

❖ How long position held

❖ Why he/she left former firm

3 Student

4 Graduated from formal education

The skills inventory file is online, with very limited access, since a person accessing the file will be able to generate a hardcopy of selected employees' records.

Replacement Order

The replacement or promotability order is depicted on an organizational chart as an inverted tree with the head or CIO of the IS organization at the top. As a systems chart, it is large enough to show the overall interrelated job positions.

Below each position's box and connected to it is another box listing the three most likely candidates for the position ranked in order of promotability. With each name is the person's title, length of time in the current position, and the code found in the skills inventory, which represents his/her promotability status.

Before this chart is produced, the IS organization must have a well-defined organizational chart with positions properly titled. For security reasons this needs to be a manual chart, produced and kept up-to-date by the IS head or a delegated employee.

Continuing Education and Training

The IS operation has its own person coordinating the education and training pursuits of IS personnel. It is recommended the same person also maintain the skills inventory, since the two responsibilities are clearly related. The person writes a yearly report, before each budget request time, reporting the success of the continuing education and training program.

This person maintains records of the effectiveness of different programs. The person should be both an advisor to and an information source for those seeking education or training information. An inventory of forms is maintained for employees applying for monies for education or training, and for expense reports. Reimbursements to employees are permitted for:

- ❖ Seminars
- ❖ Vendor courses
- ❖ College tuition (for job-related or degree requirement)
- ❖ IT subscriptions to publications not currently available at the firm
- ❖ Professional dues
- ❖ Attending professional events

> ## COMMENT
>
> Some firms curve the tuition reimbursement to grades received; others pay a given percentage, from one-half to full tuition expense. Those curving the reimbursement to the grade pay 100 percent for a B, and books and mileage for an A. When George was with General Electric, the training was on company time if directly applicable to your job. If not, courses still could be taken, with half the time at company expense. Other education or training was on the employee's own time.

EMPLOYEE COMMUNICATIONS

There are many avenues for employee communications: e-mail, fax, memos, newsletters, rumor boards, telephone, voice mail, information meetings, and work meetings. (The newsletter is covered in a section in Chapter 9, "PC

Newsletter." Meetings are covered in Chapter 5, "Project Management.") More than one method should be used to communicate important employee information.

E-Mail, Faxes, and Memos

E-mail, faxes, and memos should be brief and to the point. Avoid personal comments and local color. Where possible, the e-mail, fax, or memo should be written so that, to save time, no reply is needed: "If no response is provided, so and so will be permitted, not permitted, or admitted by you."

Rumor Board

Address rumors immediately. One way is by use of the "Rumor Board."

A A person concerned about a rumor writes it on a slip of paper and places it in a locked box attached to the department bulletin board.

B Management reads the slip of paper and places a response on the bulletin board.

This same idea may be used on a computer network or e-mail, which speeds up the whole process.

IS Telephone Communications

Speak normally and clearly. Answer the telephone by the name listed: by person ("Sam Jones speaking") or by department or unit ("mailroom").

Speak at a normal speed. If you are providing information that the other person is recording, ask if a pencil is handy. When reading a list of numbers, go slowly and read the numbers in groups. For example, with the number 2379446193, repeat it as 23-79-44-61 and 93. On the telephone it is OK to break the ice with informal conversation. In fact, it is better to mix business and informal conversation.

IT EMPLOYEE COMPENSATION

IT pay is high compared with some others but can be low for several reasons. One reason might be the IS head is not making enough himself/herself, and will not have a subordinate making more. Another reason is that some industries pay more than others do, so people change to industries paying more.

Pay is not the major concern for IT people. Depending on which survey one reads, the importance of salary varies. Some place it about fifth in what an IT person looks for in a job. Pay in one firm may be high for the industry, but company benefits may be meager.

Determining IT Pay

There is a universal procedure for performing wage surveys. A consultant in IT wage studies is retained. This avoids internal conflicts known to occur with IT salary surveys. Consultants render unbiased reports. They have the credibility to support their findings. Also have the consultant collect data on cost-of-benefits packages.

Before calling the consultant, have all job descriptions well defined and titled properly. This saves time and money. Do not provide any current salary or benefit information. The consultants should provide the firm with comparable salaries for all jobs within the IS organization. The organizational structure and staffing levels are needed to assist with the IT management salaries. The consultant should be familiar with the hardware complexity and total staff working within IS. When the study is completed, it is then safe to reveal the internal pay and benefit scale of IS. Another reason for not providing the information at the start is to convince top management that the information didn't influence the consultants' end results. This information will help the consultants rectify any major pay difference in any of the job positions.

The next step is determining what percentile level is agreeable to top management. To be competitive, the pay scale should not be any lower than the upper third for the geographic region. This is recommended in IT supplemental personnel policies, and is a top management decision. It may not be resolved until after planning for the next budget year. If funds are available, problem areas may require attention now.

IT Benefits Package

The consultant's report provides the benefit amounts paid by other firms. The IT supplemental personnel policies recommended amount is for the average benefits, spousal and family, to be within the upper third of the region. This is a top management decision. Benefits may be more of a problem than salary, because benefit programs are geared to the company as a whole.

One solution is outsourcing the IS operation to implement an attractive salary and compensation package. Another approach is for the company to implement a cafeteria-style benefits program. The information systems unit could easily have the larger dollar amount needed without any problems. The other solution would be to raise the salaries even more so that the two together would be what is needed.

The ultimate solution is having a cafeteria plan. It provides an equal amount of money for each employee at the same job level. Employees select what's best for them:

❖ Life insurance
❖ Medical plan with options for dental and optical
❖ Company-matching 401k plan
❖ Stock purchase options
❖ Subsidized child care
❖ Profit sharing
❖ Paid membership in clubs or organizations
❖ Extra vacation days
❖ Tuition reimbursement
❖ Paid book and publication subscriptions

IT EMPLOYEE BURNOUT

No employee should suffer from burnout. Any supervisor responsible for pressure and time demands resulting in an employee's experiencing burnout is subject to a reprimand. The details for the reprimand are placed in the supervisor's folder. This will also include project managers or leaders.

Company Assistance

The management of information systems will do whatever is needed for the employee's recovery. The company pays for any medical and therapy assistance. Information systems will also arrange for the company employee to have a week's vacation to recuperate. This will not be counted as employee vacation. Non-IS company employees will be granted the same privilege at IS expense. At the signs of impending burnout, management may help prevent it.

The following are suggestions to combat the problem:

❖ Encourage the person to take a seminar someplace that will reduce the strain and include a weekend "on the house" for some fun time. He/she may include his/her family in this weekend. No contact between company and employee will be allowed during this time.
❖ Periodically rotate IT tasks.
❖ Allow for telecommuting and more flexible work hours.
❖ Limit overtime.

❖ Limit on-call demands.

❖ Reassign workloads.

❖ Encourage feedback.

❖ Schedule social group activities for meeting project milestones.

Signs of Burnout

IS management should be aware of any signs of impending burnout. Symptoms of burnout are:

❖ Extreme dissatisfaction with their work

❖ Notice of heavy drinking during lunch or after work

❖ Reduced productivity

❖ Panic attacks

❖ Use of drugs

❖ Marital problems

❖ Problems working with co-workers

❖ Persistent eating, sleeping, and fatigue disorders

❖ Noticeable signs of depression

IT EMPLOYEE PRODUCTIVITY

The first consideration of worker productivity is what management does about it.

The buck stops at the manager's desk. The United States has some of the world's best and worst management. An MBA doesn't guarantee a person has management and leadership skills required for IT management. IT productivity requires management and leadership skills.

IT Management Productivity

There are several indicators of good management: low employee turnover and absenteeism, no employee sabotage, good productivity, and a reliable employee suggestion system. The signs may look good but must be confirmed. Some ways to confirm this in information systems are:

❖ Projects are finished when planned.

❖ Completed projects are finished within budget.

❖ End-users have faith in information system reports.

❖ Most IT job promotions are filled from within the company.

IT managers must actively work outside their offices. Do not depend on memos and the telephone to understand IT productivity. The following suggestions can help management actively promote IT production:

❖ Encourage participatory management.

❖ Ask what can be done about problems, and listen.

❖ Set realistic norms and goals.

❖ Utilize real quality circles.

❖ Employ time management.

❖ Delegate and follow up.

❖ Learn when to say no.

❖ Set deadlines.

❖ Finish what is started.

❖ Do difficult jobs during the more productive time of day.

❖ Make a daily timetable.

❖ Do the unpleasant things first.

❖ Realize employee behavior may be due to weak supervisors.

❖ Management requires feedback to gauge productivity results. One way is the question and suggestion box. Also praise managers who deliver results. Inform them if they are meeting your goals as the project moves along, not a month later.

IT Employee Productivity

It is more difficult measuring IT personnel's productivity than production jobs. Areas hard to monitor are systems and programming. Programmers are too often measured on how hard and long they work, and how many lines of code they write. The ignored programmer is often the one who could do the same program in much less time with half the lines of code and no test data errors. He/she will not get the credit or raise but will leave the firm.

To discover programmer productivity, survey other programmers about how they would rank their colleague's skills. Do this at employee review time. The feedback could be informative. Other ways to get feedback are:

❖ End-users speak well of the help-desk and other IT assistance by programs and systems.

❖ Utilize work simplification studies for programmers and systems people.

❖ Compare performance with other projects and tasks.

❖ Have all projects' work effort ranked regarding each member's contribution to the project's completion.

❖ Have a programming contest. Identify your best programmers. This may also confirm management's suspicions.

❖ What course grades are received?

❖ Notice who is the most helpful and who people go to for help.

❖ Review how systems conversions are made. Are the end-users satisfied with the assistance, training, help-desk response, and the presence of project members during and after the conversion?

REMOVING PROBLEM IT EMPLOYEES

There will be times when an employee has to be removed from his/her job. The person may also be a problem with other IT or end-user employees; therefore, the only solution is removal. This may be required from time to time. This procedure must be in place before it's needed.

Firing Problem IT Employees

Firing an employee for reasons other than stealing, sabotage, or physically assaulting a co-worker requires some documentation. The following should be practiced before terminating an employee:

❖ Provide honest feedback on areas requiring improvement and document the information.

❖ Don't expect things to improve—report incidents when they occur, and document the time and date of what was said.

❖ Present the information during evaluations, and have the employee sign that he/she has received the information.

❖ Be very clear about standards governing the person's responsibility.

❖ Prepare for the termination quietly. Have all his/her computer access cut off at a given time. Have him/her return anything that he/she may have removed from the company site.

❖ Inform the individual that he/she is a good employee but not suited for his/her job.

❖ Provide any assistance in planning his/her next career move. Consider using outplacement professionals for assistance with the transition process.

❖ Inform him/her that his/her personal items will be packed that night and sent to his/her home. Any company property (e.g., books or training material) must be returned.

❖ Have the employee escorted to his/her car. If he/she does not have a car, call a cab and have the company pay for it.

❖ Let the employee know he/she can feel free to use the company as a reference.

IT MANAGEMENT COMPETENCIES

It is not enough having technical knowledge, skills, and experience to be successful in an IT management position. As technology becomes integrated with every aspect of a business, the business community expects solutions from IT management. Technology solutions reduce complex business processes, cut costs, and manage independent work activities. General management skills rather than traditional technical management skill set help make an effective IT manager.

Seven Key Competencies

IT management is much more than implementing, supporting, and maintaining systems. It is working closely with business line management and end-users to best understand their needs and requirements. It is working as a member of a cross-functional team designing new systems. Change does not happen when a new system is implemented and new policies are established. IT management needs to influence behavior change to support the new system. Once the IT function focused on knowing how to use machines; now it's focused on how people use information.

There are seven key competencies that are needed for the successful IT manager.

A Business knowledge. This involves having an overall knowledge of how business works, including understanding policies, practices, and trends affecting the industry and the organization. It also includes identifying current and future competitors and the strategies and tactics making them successful. The IT manager should be able to discuss IT issues in the context of finance, sales, marketing, logistics, and distribution to evaluate the best business technology solutions. With this knowledge the IT manager becomes a better business partner, aware of the issues, priorities, and concerns of their internal customers. IT management moves from a functional focus to a big picture focus.

With the big picture view, the IT manager enables the company to best benefit from technology as a business resource. Today e-commerce alone is changing how organizations do business. An example is the emergence of Amazon.com, which is challenging the methods of other booksellers such as Borders and Barnes & Noble.

B **Communication.** For the IT manager to be a true business partner in the organization, he/she will need to communicate his/her knowledge and perspective related to technology and the business. This message has to be communicated with the audience perspective in mind. Not all business partners are literate in IT terminology; therefore, choose words wisely to communicate effectively. A skilled communicator expresses his/her thoughts clearly, concisely, and in a manner appropriate to the audience.

Organize communications so the main point of the message is clear. Messages that are too wordy, have grammatical or usage errors, or are disorganized are ineffective and present a poor image of the IT function.

Knowing when to communicate is as important as knowing how to communicate. When in doubt about communicating an issue, inform the appropriate parties. Very rarely are internal customers complaining that an issue has been overcommunicated.

C **Customer-focused.** The first step in providing excellent customer service is knowing the customers, their needs, and their expectations. This information should be received firsthand from the customer, not what the IT manager believes the customer needs are. Customer contact involves regular communications to keep up to date on changing needs and expectations. Once customer information is gathered, decisions should be made with the customer perspective in mind.

IT management must be committed to providing exceptional customer service. IT management's role is to identify and remove any barriers to providing top-notch service. Some of these barriers include excessive paperwork, acceptance of the status quo, or front-line workers lacking decision-making authority. The IT manager also seeks feedback from the customer. The IT manager has to handle criticism, complaints and special requests. This is all part of improving customer service.

Some organizations have established "Service Level Agreements" with their internal customers. These agreements specify and measure the services IT provides to its internal customers. These are often established with a team of IT professionals and representatives from the business units to benchmark current service levels and to negotiate future needs and service levels.

D **Interpersonal skills.** At all levels inside and outside the organization, interpersonal skills are critical in building effective teams and in meeting organizational goals and productivity levels. Interpersonal skills involve treating people fairly and with respect, being approachable, showing a personal interest in others, being positive in all interactions, using diplomacy and tact in volatile situations, and developing a more accepting view of others' strengths and weaknesses.

The IT function is sometimes seen as being more interested in technology than people. To overcome this stereotype, it is important that IT management is visible in the organization and increases contact with those outside their own department.

E **Project management.** A project is often defined as a problem with a defined schedule for a solution. Project management is different from general management, which involves managing repetitive activities. Project management involves defining, planning, and meeting project objectives. These objectives include performance levels, time commitments, and cost issues.

Effective project management skills rely on the ability to organize resources and activities. Problem-solving skills are as important as organizational skills. Use problem-solving skills to simplify complex processes and identify opportunities for synergy and integration. A strong knowledge of the business and organizational culture helps identify the best solution when problem solving.

Because project management skills involve coordinating people, excellent interpersonal and communication skills are key. Many projects use team members from different functions in the organization, which means the project manager has no direct authorization over these individuals. Strong communication and interpersonal skills are helpful in dealing with issues that may occur because of this situation.

F **Strategic outlook.** With technology constantly changing, strategic thinking is paramount in any IT organization. A strategic outlook requires anticipating future trends and consequences and envisioning credible possibilities for the future success of the organization. The person with a strategic outlook displays curiosity, flexibility, and breadth of knowledge and interests. The person must have critical, conceptual, creative, and intuitive thinking skills. The higher his/her role in the organization, the more strategically focused the individual must become.

G **Team builder.** Much of the work in the IT arena involves teams. Teams are established when implementing new financial software, developing a Web site, or identifying business requirements for a new marketing system.

A team builder establishes a common cause and shared mindset among team members. This person also creates a strong sense of morale and team spirit that supports open dialogue and open lines of communication between team members. The skilled team builder knows the best teams comprise a variety of skills and abilities, and brings out the best from each team member. The effective team builder recognizes that success or failure of the project depends on each team member fulfilling his/her role.

Methods for Developing Competencies

Once key competencies are identified, the IT organization begins assessing the skill level of its current and future management population. Skill assessments, supervisor and peer observations, and feedback from customers are effective skill assessment tools. Once skill levels are assessed, establish a development plan. Few individuals fully demonstrate the above-mentioned skills, but people can develop these skills if properly trained. Just as technical skills can be learned and practiced, so can the competencies listed above. Here are several methods to develop the skills discussed earlier.

A **Job rotation.** Job rotation ranges from a complete job change temporarily to acting as a project manager for a small assignment. It can include filling an IT position or performing general management responsibilities temporarily.

B **Memberships.** Use associations to gain and share information about products, best practices, and the newest developments in technology. Associations exist at the national, regional, and local level for those in the IT industry from CIO to IT professional. Below is information on four IT trade associations:

❖ Society for Information Management
Chicago
Phone: (312) 527-6734
Fax: (312) 245-1081
Web site: www.simnet.org

❖ Association of Information Technology Professionals
Park Ridge, IL
Phone: (847) 8124
Fax: (800) 224-9371
Web site: www.aitp.org

❖ The Conference Board and the Information Management Center
New York
Telephone: (212) 339-0403
Fax: (212) 980-7014
Web site: www.conference-board.org

❖ The Information Management Forum
Atlanta
Telephone: (770) 455-0070
Fax: (770) 455-0082
Web site: www.infomgmtforum.com

C **Mentoring.** A mentor helps a junior person identify areas for improvement, develops an action plan, provides feedback, and holds the person accountable for improving his/her performance and skill level. Mentors also seek out opportunities for the mentored to attend or make presentations at upper management meetings they would not normally attend. These events provide an excellent opportunity for upper management to notice the mentored. Mentoring is an effective tool, especially helpful in learning to navigate a company's culture and politics.

The mentor also gains from the relationship. The mentor develops his/her management skill, and is often credited for the mentored's success.

Some mentoring programs are formal, including policies, training for mentors, and a defined process for matching mentor and mentored. Less formal programs rely on the mentor and mentored making their own contact.

D **Reading.** There are many IT magazines and books, but to understand general business issues and strategic thinking skills, use other books and publications. Check *Forbes, Fortune, Wall Street Journal, Harvard Business Review, Wired, Fast Company,* and *Strategy and Leadership,* a publication of the Strategic Leadership Forum.

E **Training.** Use both internal organizational training programs and outside sources. Large organizations have complete curriculums for developing the competencies discussed earlier. Colleges and universities across the country have executive education programs focusing on management skills.

Some include the University of Pennsylvania's Wharton School, Stanford Continuing Education Executive Programs, and University of Michigan Business School. Other training sources include the American Management Association and the Center for Creative Leadership.

IS TELECOMMUTING POLICY

Telecommuting is a growing IT alternative to the traditional office-bound work practice. Telecommuting benefits both the employee and the employer. Improperly implemented, however, due to poor policies and procedures, it can be disastrous. Require a formalized policy to develop program procedures. If a program already exists, examine it carefully to determine if appropriate modifications are required. If none, then the firm's policy may be adapted. If modifications are required, add them as "riders" applied to existing policies.

Before a policy is adopted, establish the telecommuting definitions. The policy can apply to any forms of telecommuting. The definition and taxonomy are the following:

❖ Telecommuting is providing telecommunications hardware and software to an employee working out of the house. Most often this work is done from, but not limited to, an employee's home.

❖ A full-time telecommuter is an employee whose work is performed off-site. At times, the employee will have to be away from his/her place of work. This can be for staff meetings, seminars, etc. If this is not possible for the employed telecommuter, other arrangements will be required. The definition of *full-time* is that 100 percent of the work effort is done 100 percent of the time as a telecommuter. The employee is not required to be a full-time employee, and the hours of work can be defined, not defined or flex time. (See "IT Flex Time Policy.")

❖ A part-time telecommuter works part time at his/her company site and the rest of the time as a telecommuter. This can be a part-time or full-time position. It can even be a job-shared arrangement (see "IT Job Sharing Policy") or flex time (see "IT Flex Time Policy").

❖ Extended workday telecommuters are employees extending their full-time workday. This can be for days normally off, and include after-hours telecommuting. Limit this form of telecommuting to salaried personnel.

There could be problems with hourly workers' time records and overtime problems, but none with salaried personnel. Provide Human Resource management with policies and procedures for telecommuting IT employees. The Human Resource manager will approve the policy in writing. The Human Resources department can assist the development of the program and can provide formal follow-up feedback as to the program's success.

COMMENT

Telecommuting has gained popularity over the last few years. There will soon be over 10 million telecommuters in the United States. Information technology is a natural for this work arrangement. With the shortage of available IT personnel, this can be an attractive option attracting new employees. With the advent of TV cable modem, the speed of telecommunications has far exceeded the telephone line modem for Web site and e-mail. access Some of the documented benefits have been:

❖ Marked employee productivity

❖ Greater job satisfaction

❖ Less job turnover

❖ Lower absenteeism

❖ Lower company work-site expense due to:

— Annual office floor space cost

— Reduced employee parking requirements

— Reduced janitorial service costs

— Less need for utilities

Some handicapped workers would prefer to work at home. Others could work from remote sites, greater distance, or even out of the country. Employees could benefit from the following:

❖ Lower day care costs

❖ Lower transportation costs

❖ Less travel time and fighting traffic

❖ Less time spent getting ready for work

❖ Reduced eating-out costs

❖ Reduced wardrobe investment

❖ Less need for a second car

❖ More flexible lifestyle

❖ Can have the radio on

Test the feasibility with a pilot test program, limited to a given area of information systems. When the program has been in operation for six or more months with success, proceed with a more permanent operation plan. Both programs will require budget requests.

Contract service personnel can provide telecommuting services. The arrangement would be on a test basis before signing a formal final contract. All contracts require the corporate legal advisor's approval before any commitment in writing. This service is permitted worldwide.

Set up a budgeted account for this operation's expense and capital expenditures. The budgeted expenditures are classified as the following:

A Capital expense
- ❖ PC system and software
- ❖ Office furniture
- ❖ Power backup, UPS and/or generator

B Telecommuter operational expense
- ❖ Utilities allowance
- ❖ Hardware maintenance contract
- ❖ Help-desk contract/service
- ❖ Computer and office supplies
- ❖ Replacement parts
- ❖ Software updates

C Administrative expense
- ❖ Off-site insurance
- ❖ Training remote workers
- ❖ Employee off-site insurance

D Off-site supervisory expense

IT JOB-SHARING POLICY

Job sharing can benefit both parties. Two different skill levels, not necessarily equal, can fill one full-time position. They may share the same IT talent or not, but could share the same office facilities. It does not require each have half of the job. Divide this position as flex-time responsibilities or even telecommuting. Flexibility can attract higher skilled talent than more traditional routes for IT specialties. Fill the position with salaried employees.

Pay for job-shared positions will not require equal pay for equal time. The employee benefits package may not be the same for both parities. The cafeteria benefit plan provides for a more resolvable distribution of benefits. Paid vacation time as part of the benefit program should resolve the vacation question. Some preagreement about taking unpaid vacation time may be in order for this arrangement.

This policy attracts better talent to the IT opportunities with the firm. It assures a backup is available. It is better to lose a half person specialty than a whole, if that position is the only one IT has. This provides for safer backup than that talent being vested in one person. Depending on the responsibility, the job sharing may be done by related people, as long as one of the people, upon giving notice of leaving the firm, would not affect the other member, too.

IT FLEX-TIME POLICY

Flex time has been tried successfully. This is when the IT staff has open windows of time to arrive or leave work provided an eight-hour day is completed. This also applies to telecommuting and job-sharing positions. The job may be hourly or salaried depending on the position.

There will be core time when all employees are required to be present: for meetings, training, etc. This will be no less than a three-hour window. Core time is at the discretion of the CIO/IS head. The flex-time window will be no more than four hours on each side of the core time. Anyone abusing this will be placed back on standard work hours the IS operation maintains.

14

IT TRAINING:
BUILDING THE TEAM

IT TRAINING POLICIES

Information technology training begins with the orientation of new personnel and continues to help employees meet changing technology skill requirements. Computer personnel realize their skills can quickly become obsolete. This is one of the reasons they move on to jobs providing opportunities to learn new skills.

An IT training policy provides the opportunity for ongoing education and training of IS employees and information systems users. An IT department functions effectively only if its personnel and users are properly trained.

Conduct an evaluation after each training course or program is completed. A second evaluation follows three to six months after.

MANAGING IT TRAINING

Traditionally, training responsibility has come under the jurisdiction of computer operations managers. IT training is not limited to information systems personnel, but extends to all system users; therefore, the training head for IT should control the training function and report to the head of IS.

The scope of IT training covers areas from new employee orientation to retraining current employees in new technologies. Employees should be able

COMMENT

IT training costs exceed ten billion dollars a year in the United States, but in fact, direct training expense is normally far less than the cost of the employee's time during the training.

to draw on a host of training opportunities, because no one single device serves all needs.

Keeping Records of Training

Each IS employee file contains education and training information, including training the employee brings to the department and recommendations for future training. All additional training received is posted to a file that is part of the IS skill inventory. (See the section "Employee Development" in Chapter 13 for more procedure information.) Starting a file is simple; keeping it up-to-date is a more challenging task. Don't neglect this.

IS employee-training files contain the following information.

A **Education and training before joining the IS department.**
  1 Degrees received, courses taken, dates, and grades
  2 Dates of noncredit courses taken
  3 Type of work-related material read
  4 Dates of certifications received
  5 Listing of professional memberships and any offices held
  6 The hardware type and software used if the employee owns a personal computer

B **Future education and training benefiting the employee.** Establish the training needs of each employee. This information can justify a training program and give the people on record first choice. Priority is as follows:
  1 Training or education that helps develop personnel for current positions:
    ❖ Areas of weakness
    ❖ Areas that require training to stay current with new technology
  2 Training or education needed for promotion

C New education or training received

1   Upon completion of training not provided in-house, each employee forwards to the IT department a memo containing the following to be included in the employee's file:

❖   What training was received

❖   Who provided the training

❖   What grade was received, if any

❖   When the training was received

2   Upon completion of in-house programs, the overseer of IT training programs forwards the necessary information for inclusion in the training record files. For non-IS people, a memo will be sent to each supervisor listing which of their employees have completed the training and indicating the following:

❖   What training was received

❖   When the training was conducted

❖   Personnel who are to receive credit for completing the program

Employee Recognition

When an employee completes an in-house course, his/her supervisor should present a certificate for course completion. Certificate forms are available from most office supply firms and should be completed and signed by the head of training and also the IS manager.

Education Information Booklet

The IT education unit provides an "education information booklet" to all new IS employees as part of an orientation package. Revised editions are distributed to all current IS employees. It should contain the following information:

A   IS outside education policy and procedures. Outline the type of support the firm provides for outside education and training, and the procedures required to apply for sanctioned education outside the firm.

B   Scheduled courses offered by the training unit. Detail the courses offered, including dates and times, requirements for admission, and procedure for enrolling in courses and/or programs.

C   A list of self-paced training packages available. This list is available from the IS training unit and includes videotapes, self-teaching texts, and PC self-instruction programs.

D **Publications available.** A list of books and journals should be available in the IT training department and/or computer store.

Non-IS Employee Training

The need for IT training is not limited to the IS department. Make companywide training available to all computer users. This not only provides needed training, but helps to create goodwill between IS and the rest of the firm. The charge-back for these services depends on corporate cost accounting procedures.

Request for training may be initiated by a user or an IS project leader. A user's request should be in the form of a memo from the user's management, directed to the IT trainer. If a project leader desires the service, make it part of the formal project effort.

Furnish a list of users completing each course to the employee's supervisor(s) by a memo from the head of the IT training unit. All persons completing the program receive certificates of completion forwarded to the employee's supervisor for presentation.

Outsourced Training

Because not all information systems departments have resources available for in-house IT training, it's common to use outsourcing firms for professional IT training at the firm's location. See Chapter 15, *Vendors: Getting the Goods,* for more information.

Recordkeeping of outsourcing personnel training is still done by the IS department for IS personnel. User training is provided by a person delegated by the head of IS. Costs will be paid from the IS training budget. User training can be charged back to the user's budget and prorated if need be. This is all dependent on the internal accounting practice of the company.

Training evaluation is performed by a person from the IS department at the end of the course or program. Payment may be governed by the results of the evaluation. If so, inform accounts payable of this procedure before the outside firm bills for the service. The follow-up three- to six-month evaluation, also performed by the IT training department, is particularly important to alter future training if needed. The evaluation is also an effective way to judge the provider of the outsourced training.

Annual Reporting

The IT training unit should submit an annual report of activities, including cost.

> ## COMMENT
>
> Cost justification (relating dollars to return on investment) of training dollars spent can be a problem because most of the returns are intangible. Any input from user management can help. However, intangible items contribute to the company's bottom line and should be listed in the annual report. There is a worldwide fast-food chain known for its training programs and even more for its success story.

Time required to produce instruction packages is often more than anticipated. Preparation time rule of thumb for a lecture presentation with simple overheads can be as much as 15 hours for each lecture hour. Producing a 30-minute video presentation can take up to 200 hours. General planning, setup, reporting, and equipment repair will consume time. All these hours are reported. Treat each new program as a project with individual cost of materials and time cost reported. Compute time cost as hourly cost plus benefits.

> ## COMMENT
>
> Be aware that training and education evaluations can be subjective. People tend to give higher appraisals when they are entertained.

Both students' and trainers' time is a cost factor. With new technology, training and preparation time can be reduced. Therefore, the training department should house an array of software and hardware tools to be effective. Drop ineffective resources. Include plans for the coming year, as well as current year results, in the annual report. The report should also contain activities of the training unit for the year. The following items are reported:

❖ The number and size of classes conducted.
❖ The number of self-study programs completed.

❖ The number and purpose of new programs developed.

❖ The total number of people served by the training unit.

❖ A list of participant evaluation comments with any supervisor's comments or memo information.

NEW EMPLOYEE ORIENTATION

First impressions are lasting, and in time, those employees reacting negatively may depart for another firm. To create a positive, lasting impression during the employee's first few days, the IT department follows two simple procedures. First, designate a mentor. Second, give the employee a welcome education package.

COMMENT

A insurance company in Ohio thinks so highly of this training that they developed and carefully follow a detailed procedure for new employee indoctrination and education.

IS Orientation Package

This package is a compilation of useful information for the new IS employee. It should contain the following information:

A **Organization description.** At a minimum, the organization description includes an explanation of each unit function and identifies those in charge. An organizational chart is useful for large departments.

Include a short chronological history of the information systems operation. This provides the new employee with information about promotion tracks, areas of vested interest, and fast-track employees. Note IS's position within the organization.

B **Equipment and facilities.** List all the hardware in use and its locations. Identify personnel authorized to use the equipment.

A facilities map should include the locations of the restrooms, dining areas, and restricted facility areas.

C **Telephone numbers.** Provide an up-to-date telephone directory of the firm. Include a supplementary list of numbers for frequently called IT units, personnel, and services.

D **E-mail listing.** Indicate the proper way to address e-mail to other employees.

E **Mail.** Note when and how the employee will receive his/her mail. This covers both interoffice and outside mail (U.S. Postal Service, UPS, FedEx, etc.).

F **Forms.** Include a listing of all important forms required by IT personnel, providing the name and number of each form, its source and destination(s), purpose, and any other special information.

Include samples used by the new employee's unit. The needs of computer operators are not the same as systems analysts, so packages for new employees may contain different forms.

G **Schedules.** Include schedules of operations in the procedure package. These can be daily, weekly, or monthly. For daily schedules include begin and end times of normal activities, such as breaks and lunch hours.

The weekly, monthly, and annual schedules contain paydays, holidays, vacation scheduling, and meetings. Some IT departments publish monthly listings of employees' birthdays.

H **Glossary and practices.** This section contains a list of common terms and acronyms used by IS and the firm. Note practices that are extremely important or different from the industry norm.

I **Unit procedures.** This section contains a listing of all IT procedures and where they are explained. Use a check-off list for each type of IT procedure. Check off and date as new employees read the material.

COMMENT

A firm in Michigan, for its own reasons, does not run a slash through the character zero. They place the slash through the alpha character O. There were problems because a new programmer was unaware of this practice. Emphasize unusual department practices to minimize difficulties.

J   **IS project descriptions.** New programmers, systems analysts, and other staff personnel should be provided a list of current and pending IS projects. Note a short description of the objective, as well as target dates, along with the project managers' names.

Mentor Assignment

Sometimes IS orientation requires a "personal touch." The new employee is assigned a mentor, someone to give a permanent positive impression of the firm. The selected mentor should be personable, someone who the new employee feels comfortable about asking questions concerning procedures. The mentor must also be patient. Often a simple question answered calmly by a mentor is critical for a new employee. The mentor should not be condescending, which only makes the new IS employee nervous and doubtful about his/her future.

Remember that first impressions are lasting. A new IS employee joins the department with high hopes, and a mentor's positive attitude can become infectious, reinforcing these high expectations.

EMPLOYEE TRAINING

This section does not attempt to address the detailed, day-to-day procedures of running a training unit, which are up to the head of training. IT managers should have a grasp of what to expect.

Determining Training Needs and Objectives

The first step is determining given objectives. Next, make an instructional assessment of each person involved in the learning project. What does each need to learn? All IT training or educational projects should contain this information in their "training project" documentation.

Determine the kind of learning to be accomplished. There are three basic classifications of learning, each requiring different training instruments. They are:

A   **Cognitive domain.** Cognitive learning requires intellectual activity of some sort, such as making judgments, synthesizing information, applying learned information, interpreting information, and recalling information. This is the most common form of learning in IT training.

B   **Psychomotor domain.** Psychomotor learning requires muscle coordination and includes hearing and eye movement. Traditionally this has been associated with IT keyboard data entry, but with the advent of PCs the need for these skills has expanded.

C   **Affective domain.** Affective learning involves values and attitudes. It includes changing undesirable attitudes and may be required in training users with values or attitudes affecting productivity or the success of projects and operations.

Select the training instrument after determining instructional needs. At the same time, develop evaluation criteria determining when the learning objective has been met. This evaluation may be an exam—written answers to questions, performance of a task or procedure, or execution of a response to a given condition.

Exams can be written confirming that the desirable learning level has been met. This is criterion-referenced testing. People who master a test at the level required by the learning criteria pass. If a whole group does not meet the criteria, the learning project has failed. This is a better evaluation than a subjective evaluation by employees upon completing training.

Types of IT Training

Training can be provided in a formal manner for groups or informally for individuals. Formal IT training can be divided into two types: instructor-based and self-paced. Instructor-based training includes seminars, classroom workshops, and one-on-one instruction.

One-on-one instruction may be the best training, but is the most expensive. Classroom instruction is less expensive, but the cost of the students' time must also be considered. Sending employees away for vendor class instruction can be expensive if employees are out-of-town overnight.

There can be problems with classroom workshops and seminars. All personnel involved may not have time off at the same time. More than one group may have to be scheduled at a time, and even then there can be scheduling conflicts.

For these reasons, self-paced instruction has gained popularity in information technology. The training is available to fit schedules and people can work at their own pace.

Self-paced instruction is not only reading manuals and other vendor-furnished materials. It includes PCs, audiocassettes, and video. Use PC tutorials with software in the form of CDs, floppy and Zip disks.

When selecting a training approach, the trainer ensures it's appropriate for the learning domain needed. Test the hardware and/or software before any commitment to buy or lease.

For informal education/training of both user and IT personnel, have reading material available. Computer journals and magazines are a good source of up-to-date information. The average systems analyst should spend at least seven to eight hours a week just reading. IS management personnel have been known to do even more.

PRESENTATION METHODOLOGIES

Successful training presentations require a capable presenter, supported with instructional tools and a proper learning environment. It is management's responsibility to supply these. The instructor has the final responsibility for the learning presentation. Preparation can average 15 hours for each hour of delivery. The more frequent the presentation, the more preparation can be justified. A good 30-minute sound slide production can take 200 or more hours to produce. Thanks to TV, today's students recognize quality media productions. The presentation can run from a few minutes to an extended program of many hours.

There are several good publications covering industrial instruction and presentations, with some of the better ones free. One recommended is *Presentations*, published monthly by Bill Communications Human Performance Group, 50 South Ninth St., Minneapolis, MN 55402. National organizations, including Toastmasters International and industrial training groups, help people develop presentation skills. Reference material for both organizations and publications is available in the public library.

One of the best, if not the best, training facility in the world is McDonald's® Hamburger University in the Chicago area. McDonald's would not be successful today without its training program. Not only is training conducted using top-of-the-line technology, but it is also cost-justified and administered by qualified management. This training is not limited to Hamburger University but incorporated at every level of McDonald's operations.

Presentation Room

Conduct the presentation in a room adequate for presenting instructional materials. It should be large enough to comfortably house learners without distractions, with enough light for note taking. The temperature should be between 68 and 72 degrees.

Rooms can be rented off-site, if need be, when adequate rooms are unavailable or to get the people away from work distractions. The instructor should be familiar with the room before he/she commits to using it.

Conveniences enhancing the presentation are:

❖ Lights controllable by the presenter
❖ Power outlets in locations needed

- ❖ A whiteboard for writing or projection
- ❖ A lectern
- ❖ Restrooms close by
- ❖ Place for learners to hang their coats
- ❖ Tables with comfortable chairs
- ❖ A ceiling-mounted screen that can be tilted to be perpendicular to a projector

Presentation Devices

The trainer selection of presentation aids is limited only by his/her budget. Operation of training devices may be augmented by the vendor and by demonstrations. The company's own training department may also help. Before using any new device, the trainer should be familiar enough with its operation to concentrate on the presentation, not the device.

Consider both audience size and composition before preparing a media presentation. Time allotted will determine the amount of information presented and consumed. The location, importance of the presentation, and time limits all influence the choice of presentation materials.

- ❖ The importance of the presentation determines the cost, time, and effort expended. Will the presentation require several types of visuals and can the cost be justified?
- ❖ The purpose of the presentation determines which visual materials are employed. If mainly to inform, PowerPoint presentation software may best be chosen. If explaining complicated information, such as new procedures, systems, concepts, or numerical information, chart and graph overheads might be employed so the presenter faces the audience.
- ❖ Consider audience education level and corporate status when making the visuals.
- ❖ Do not assume the audience's technical knowledge. If possible, do some research. Better to understate technical complication than overstate it.
- ❖ Remember, whatever visuals are used in a presentation are to enhance what is said, not replace or detract from it.

Effective visuals are designed for simplicity, clarity, and visibility. The following suggestions should be helpful when constructing these aids:

- ❖ Proofread before presenting. Look for misspellings and information errors. Have someone else verify the materials for you. Set the presentation aside for a day or two, then give it a final look.

❖ If there is too much information to fit on the visuals, make handouts.

❖ Never have more than six to eight words per line on the screen.

❖ Use only key words or phrases in the visual. This gives the presenter something to say.

❖ Never read the visual information for the audience.

❖ Add colored backgrounds and colored lettering for impact.

❖ Do not show lots of numbers. Information is better visualized by employing graphs or charts.

❖ Do not overuse computer-generated clip art.

❖ Remember KISS: Keep It Simple and Short. Show each visual briefly, less than a minute. Don't overload it with information.

A **Flip charts.** Flip charts endure because they are simple to use, quick to prepare, and inexpensive. They are bulky to carry, but many conference rooms still have them. There are portable versions easier to carry in their cases. Smaller ones may be used for up to fifteen or twenty people; larger ones are good for groups of thirty or more. Following are recommendations that can improve the presentation when using this instrument:

1 The easel

❖ Consider using more than one easel.

❖ When using more than one, position each so it can be seen by everyone.

❖ Make sure the easel is tall enough so that all can see the bottom of the pads.

❖ Use sturdy easels with a lip to hold different colored marking pens.

2 Easel pads

❖ Not all pads have the same spaced mounting. Make sure all easels and pad holes match up.

❖ Use perforated pads because it is easier to remove pages from them.

❖ Writing on white pad paper shows up more clearly than on colored paper.

❖ Using lined pads makes writing before an audience neater.

❖ If more than one easel is used, try different lightly colored pads. They may help the delivery.

❖ Use paper heavy enough that the audience cannot see pages under the one being used or shown.

3 Marking pens

❖ Use wide felt-tip, watercolor markers. Permanent markers bleed through the paper and cannot be used on the whiteboards.

❖ Multicolored markers add variety to the presentation.

❖ Have a systematic method for employing colors, such as using green for page headings and items needing attention, and black for other items.

❖ When not using the pen, place it on the easel lip.

❖ When the pen starts to squeak, it is running out of ink. Discard it.

❖ Have a good supply of colored pens.

❖ Avoid using light red pens as red is difficult to read from a distance. Also, about 12 percent of men are color blind, and the most common color they have a problem with is red.

4 **Prepared pages.** There are advantages to preparing flip charts in advance. For one, the printing will be neater and more legible. Class time will not be wasted writing. In addition, notes can be prewritten in pencil, unseen by the audience until the presenter goes over them with a felt-tip pen. If some pages are prepared in advance, a second easel is recommended for writing during the presentation. The following are suggested to enhance the prepared pages presentation:

❖ Have a computer printer produce flip charts in color. If your firm does not own a printer for the size needed, find a graphics firm or large copy shop that does.

❖ When traveling, place the rolled-up charts in a large cardboard mailing tube.

❖ Insert blank pages between thin pages so the audience cannot read what comes next.

❖ If using a large number of prepared pages use extra easels.

5 **The use of flip charts.** First visualize, then write an outline (on $8^1/2$- by 11-inch lined paper) of the presentation. After the outline is complete, highlight key points to be printed on the flip charts. The outline and any other notes can later be penciled on the edges of the flip chart pages. Do this after the pages have been lettered.

If there is only one easel available, place blank pages between the lettered ones for writing on. Notes can still be written on these blank pages. The following are suggestions which should help improve the presentation:

- ❖ Print the block letters one to one-and-a-half inches high.
- ❖ Use wide felt-tip markers.
- ❖ Use the colors in some consistent fashion.
- ❖ Limit the number of lines of information to ten if the audience is small, and to eight if the group is large (over 25 feet away).
- ❖ Write key points in a shortened form. Abbreviations and acronyms are okay.
- ❖ When writing during the presentation, pencil in the words beforehand.
- ❖ Allow 20 to 30 seconds after writing before flipping the page. Give audience members time for any note taking and thinking.
- ❖ Never stand in front of the easel after you have just completed writing.
- ❖ Minimize loss of audience eye contact except when writing.
- ❖ Practice your presentation a few days before in the designated room. If presentations are new to you and/or if this is a presentation important for your career, practice it a week in advance in the designated room and have it videotaped. You do not need anyone to run the camcorder. Just put it on a tripod.

B **Overhead projectors.** Overhead projectors have been popular for presentations for some time. Low price makes them attractive; laser and inkjet printers can produce appealing color overheads.

Today's computer technology makes this device even more popular. One projector allows computer output to be projected through an LCD overhead panel.

There have been other improvements to the old design. Portable compact overhead projectors are available, although they cannot employ the LCD overhead panel. Automatic transparency feeders are also available. The continuous roll-feeding device provides a source of blank film to write on, freeing the presenter from standing next to the projector.

Additional information and advice about this device follows:

1 Overhead projector concerns:

❖ Always have a spare bulb.

❖ Make sure the screen is usable.

❖ Lower room light level to enhance the projected image, but keep it high enough so people can take notes.

❖ Have heavy-duty extension cords available when needed.

2 Ways to produce transparencies:

❖ Color inkjet printers

❖ Laser printer

❖ Copy machine

❖ Heat transfer

❖ Write-on

❖ Continuous roll transparencies

3 Resources for transparency material:

❖ PowerPoint software

❖ Digital cameras

❖ Clip art

❖ Scanners to input slides or photographs and hardcopy to a PC for producing overhead transparency output

4 Markers

❖ Overhead color projection pens

❖ Permanent color markers

❖ Extra markers or pens

5 Using the overhead projector

❖ Write on the whiteboard with erasable projection pens. This allows the presenter to add to what is projected on the board.

❖ Look at the audience while reading.

❖ The size of the printing should be large enough to read when it is lying at your feet while you are standing.

❖ Allow twenty to thirty seconds at the end of each overhead for note taking.

❖ Do not crowd the overhead with copy.

❖ Use color pens and transparencies to enhance the presentation.

❖ Face the audience while operating the computer keyboard and/or overhead projector.

❖ Never leave the light or screen for any length of time without a transparency in the projector.

❖ Use graphics to enhance a presentation. Computer presentation software is available with alternatives to the use of a bullet chart. (You are reading a bullet chart now.)

❖ Using transparency overlays adds impact to the overhead presentation. Overlays allow the presenter to build and reveal concepts, focusing the audience's attention on the evolving subject. As an example, a bullet chart can be built by superimposing lines of information, adding one bulleted line or section at a time, from succeeding layers of transparencies. In this instance, the pages are hinged so they will be in the proper position when overlaid and projected onto the screen.

❖ Carrying the transparencies can become a problem, as static electricity can stick them together. A simple solution is placing them in transparency frames, which makes handling easier. Using a frame blocks out any unwanted light from around the edge during the projection. In addition, the edge of the frame provides space for presentation notes.

6 **LCD overhead projector.** This device is used either stand-alone or with an overhead projector and allows PC-generated information to be presented on the screen. With the proper hardware and software tools, it can greatly enhance the overhead presentation. The same presentation considerations apply to this as to the overhead projection method.

COMMENT

PowerPoint from Microsoft is probably the most popular program for creating slide presentations to be used with an LCD overhead projector. Microsoft can be reached at www.microsoft.com.

Visual information can be imported from other sources. Digital still cameras can photograph artwork which can be inputted to the system for display on the screen. Live photos, in color, can be taken of subjects or even of people in the audience and projected on the screen during the presentation.

7 Digital program presentations. With the availability of digital video cameras, even motion pictures can be inputted, along with digital stills on CDs, to the PC and displayed on the screen. If seriously considering digital video, look into digital projectors. It simplifies the hardware requirements for projecting still and moving images. If using this type of presentation material often, consider a multimedia PC system.

Digital CD PC programs can be developed for a group screen presention or a self-paced PC learning package. Depending on the need, it can be a supporting instruction tool or a self-contained stand-alone package.

These software program applications are commonly referred to as "digital CD-slide show programs," even though they may contain "film clips." The orchestrated visuals, sound, transitions and titles result in professional outputs. The DVD is the newest technology for final digital outputs that training units can now afford to utilize.

COMMENT

There are software packages available for all levels of expertise. Adobe Premiere, Ulead Video Studio, and Videoware are some of the many available. Your available supporting hardware and time to learn the skills needed to put programs together should dictate how professional your software should be.

8 Slide projectors. The 35mm slide projector is used today. It provides better quality presentations than digital images for large groups. Slide projectors with sound added make for excellent, large-scale multimedia presentations.

For small groups, the easy-to-carry Caramate in its self-contained box can be placed at the end of a conference table and the slides projected on the wall, on a pull-down screen or rear-projected onto its own 12- by 12-foot screen. With its self-contained sound tape system, it is an excellent teaching instrument, well suited to a self-paced learning program.

Photographs of subjects and copy material can be made with a 35mm camera. Use a 35mm single-lens reflex camera with a micro lens, with a Kodak gray scale card for correct light meter readings. It is also recommended that Kodak 35mm Ektachrome daylight slide film be used, since this film can also be used for electronic flash or daylight. For correct light color balance, use 250-watt blue light bulbs available from a commercial photo store.

Use a photocopy stand to copy a lot of material. Place the gray scale card over the flat copy work, then take a reading for the exposure. If the item is not flat, place it on the background and focus. Remove the item, replace it with a gray scale card, then take a light meter reading. Return the item to its proper position and take the picture with a manual exposure.

Both the Kodak slide projector and the Caramate unit will use Kodak's 80- and 120-slide trays. Any one slide should not be shown for more than 30 seconds. Therefore, a presentation with only one tray will be limited to less than an hour. For both units (Kodak and Caramate), a cassette tape is used for the sound. With a stereo tape system, one track is used for the sound and the other track for slide changing marks. Slide sound productions require some justification as it can take over a month's time to produce a quality half-hour program.

C Other devices

1 Sound presentation is useful, for example, in walking a person through a set of instructions for a particular procedure. The person can hear the instructions and, with hands and eyes free, take notes or perform the indicated actions.

2 Video (digital and analog) productions are even more involved than slide sound or CD productions. Video can be used by any presenter for limited applications, but any major effort should be left to people with the skill and editing equipment needed.

   Showing VCR tapes for information and instruction is an increasingly available way of presenting programs. Some computer vendors have training videos. There are also videos for all kinds of PC instruction. If you can, preview before you buy.

3 The computer can deliver a program via floppy disk, CD, or network that can be available for a group to view at its convenience or for a single-person tutorial. The program can employ text, graphics, stills, motion pictures, simulations, or interactive learning.

15

VENDORS: GETTING THE GOODS

VENDOR POLICIES

The size of information systems operations and the uneven demand for IS services influence the type and amount of outside services required. In addition, available funds must be balanced with need: The two are seldom in accord. Outside service vendors can be management consultants, application service providers, Web hosting providers, and outsourcing and contract personnel.

The best policy for dealing with outside vendors is exercising good business practices based on sound moral and ethical codes. Depending on its dealings with vendors, the firm can lose or gain respect from other vendors, employees, and the industry at large.

Vendor Selection

How does one select a firm that will actually deliver what is wanted, when it is wanted, and at the agreed price? The two major participants in this scenario are the firm providing the service and the firm purchasing the service.

Vendor service contracts should be signed based on the optimal solution for the IS department, not just on price. To avoid any form of possible collusion, there must not be any family or close personal relationships between a vendor and personnel with selection authority in a firm.

All agreements between a firm and the vendor must be in writing. The contract agent of each organization is the person signing; or else a designated person is specified in the agreement. Both parties signing must have the authority to represent their respective firms. Each contract should have a cancellation and a performance clause included.

COMMENT

Unfortunately, there are charlatans only in business to make a fast buck and some firms that overrate their services. Steering the company through the minefield of vendor incompetence is only half the challenge; the other is understanding one's own firm. An unrealistic internal cultural assessment can spell disaster for any undertaking even when employing the most competent service organization.

COMMENT

Be careful not to develop enemies when acting as head of an information systems organization. Information systems personnel are mobile; their paths cross in unexpected ways. Interaction with a past co-worker may be required in job searches. Attempt to steer clear of problem situations, but, in business as in marriage, many discoveries are made after the contract is signed.

Outside Services

The computer field is too complex to master all of its facets, let alone the technology necessary to deal effectively with outside services. For this reason, services of the firm's purchasing unit and/or legal staff might be requested. If the firm is too small to have in-house experts, rely on an outside service for this expertise.

The purchasing department provides information about vendors with which the company deals. For instance, it is advisable to know, when possible, if a vendor will still be in business next year. Part of the Purchasing department's responsibility is knowing the financial status and reputation of vendors as well as the quality of their merchandise. This is information an IS department head should have before beginning negotiations.

The Legal department reviews any contract with a vendor before large sums of the firm's capital are committed. There are a growing number of attorneys with this type of expertise who may be of assistance. The firm's attorneys should include a penalty clause in the event the vendor does not perform according to the agreement.

Most firms have a procedure to confirm upon receipt that an item meets purchase order requirements and to start the payment process for the invoice or bill received. This is usually not the case when purchasing outside services. Therefore, the IS manager must contact the Accounts Payable department before the bill arrives to insure only services stipulated in the contract are paid. In addition, a delay of payment can be used to force an obstinate vendor to be cooperative in meeting contract obligations.

IT Outsourcing Policies

IT outsourcing is not the same as out-tasking. Out-tasking is traditional supplemental staffing for peak activity periods, while outsourcing is identified as a noncore function or one that is not directly involved with the major money-making areas of the firm.

The area for the outsourcing operation(s) is budgeted annually. Vendor contracts that expire within the next budget year require a new contract proposal one month before the cut-off for budget considerations. If the current vendor's performance or new proposal is unsatisfactory, an RFP (Request for Proposal) is sent to no fewer than two other vendors.

COMMENT

To assist in the refinement of policy and strategy for outsourcing acquisition, The Outsourcing Institute may be contacted at (516) 681-0066 or at its Web site at www.outsourcing.com.

IS management must have a clear set of long-term goals and objectives for outsourcing efforts. Outsourcing should be used:

❖ For operations difficult to manage and staff

❖   To supply talent/resources unavailable in the organization

❖   To reduce internal operation costs

❖   To free resources for other efforts

❖   To bring improvements and benefits on board faster

CONSULTING SERVICE CONTRACTING

Consulting services are often justified because in-house skills are unavailable, extra manpower is required, or the firm is seeking an unbiased, objective opinion. Consulting firms have a variety of talented personnel with special skills who justifiably may not be employed in an IS operation. Because work is usually divided into projects and accomplished at that level, these specialists are valuable for specific undertakings. Many of these personnel are well-paid, ambitious individuals who enjoy the variety of challenging assignments that only a consulting firm offers.

Projects and conversions can require more manpower than normally available. Hiring extra people for such undertakings, then terminating them after completion of a task creates morale problems. Because consultants are temporary, they are ideal for these situations.

Outside consultants can be totally objective because they are not embroiled in the organization's political struggles. Therefore, they should be able to render excellent professional judgments. Unfortunately, whoever hired the consultant may sometimes have influenced the selection of a "cooperative" consultant, thereby losing objectivity.

Kinds of Consulting Organizations

Consulting firms provide a wide array of skills. Some are part of an accounting firm while others are separate entities; the services provided can and do vary widely.

Some firms are computer-related. Feasibility studies and/or total systems design and implementation may be specialties. They may also provide specialized skills in the areas of database systems, communication networks, IS audits, and related functions. Use these consultants on a temporary basis for a specific project or to troubleshoot a given problem.

Other firms may provide software development services and programming talent. These services require a great range of skills from coding to systems analysis and have a wide range of prices. There must be assurance that skill levels are commensurate with costs and that promises are kept. Some firms have been known to promise more than they deliver.

Accounting firms offering IS consulting services are expensive because of their interest in high-revenue contracts. Their area of expertise tends to center on financial and accounting systems. If there is a need for assistance in this area, contact a firm's own CPA first.

In the final analysis, the area of the country and metropolitan density determine what is available. A good source of information is other local IS management who required such services. There is nothing wrong with trying out a new firm; however, test performance with small "safe" projects before entrusting a major undertaking and a critical completion date. Include a time contingency when establishing due dates. The time needed will vary based on proven skills of the consultant and the importance of the finish date.

COMMENT

The wise IS manager uses caution when hiring because consulting can be an avenue for gaining instant professional status with very little money or education. In one case, a student who failed a systems analysis course and dropped out of college later became a computer systems analysis consultant with a record of failures. No official board certifies or regulates computer consultants, and no codification of standard skills and procedures exists.

Consultant Relationship Procedures

Consultants can be a valuable asset if a proper relationship is present. They can be effectively employed or acquired for all the wrong reasons. Therefore, it is imperative that proper conditions are maintained maximizing the benefits a consultant provides while minimizing the cost. There are several procedures to follow when acquiring the services of an outside consultant.

A   Have defined goals. The more nebulous the goal, the more time and money are spent on the project. Since consultants charge hourly, the more defined the goal, the less cost in time and money. The area should be well defined to narrow the scope of the project. In addition, do not acquire a consultant for any of the wrong reasons, such as:

1   To let the consultant be the bearer of bad news for projects in trouble.

2   To have the consultant as a political ally, the outside "expert" with credibility to justify decisions already made. This is an expensive practice.

3   Being impressed with the out-of-town expert. There sometimes seems to be a correlation among price, the distance traveled, and perception of the expert's skills. Management may be unduly impressed with a consultant's title, especially one who travels from afar and has "Ph.D." after his/her name.

    Consultants often come up with solutions gleaned from present employees. There is really nothing wrong with this because a good consultant explores all possible solutions. It does, however, irritate competent in-house personnel.

4   To be a surrogate. A weak project manager may require a consultant to make decisions. However, a consultant serves at the staff level and should never take online responsibility. If this is needed, a "facilities management" service should be contracted. It is the less expensive route to take and creates fewer problems.

B   **Define specifications and scope.** This gives the consultant a clear understanding of what to do and what to avoid. Make very clear what is expected as far as specifications and have this confirmed in writing.

Any wasted effort will be included in the bill even if the firm does not get what it wanted.

Because of the high turnover in the computer field, personnel may be here today and gone tomorrow. This also applies to new small consulting firms.

C   **Required documentation.** The documentation left behind after the completion of a project may be the only source of reference when the job is finished. Proper documentation must also be provided for the consultant insuring the consultant knows what is expected. Documentation is expensive and is all too often debased to save time or money. Saving in this way will create more expenses later. When defining documentation requirements, make sure the consultant's and firm's standards are indistinguishable using the firm's format.

D   **Monitoring the consultant's progress.** Agree to a monitoring procedure for the consultant in writing before signing a contract. Obtain feedback on the status of the consultant's work at predetermined time intervals by defining efforts in the smallest measurable units and relating them to percentages of the total. As progress is reported, the cumulated percent of progress completed can be compared to the cumulated dollars spent. These two values should be in accord to assure dollars budgeted will not be depleted before the project is completed. The effectiveness, or lack thereof, of the consultant's performance should not be a surprise at the end. A visual monitor could be a Gantt chart comparing the percent of units completed to the percent of funds billed by the consultant to date.

Consultants are self-directed persons; they must be to survive in the profession. However, they may be sidetracked by extending their scope or may misinterpret directions received from more than one source. As with any newly employed personnel, consultants should not be left alone for long periods of time. Nor should there be any misunderstanding as to the status of an in-process project. This should be well-documented in clear and understandably written, dated, and signed reports.

CONTRACT PERSONNEL

There may be reasons for using additional manpower for a project or for conversion to a new system. In these cases, use talented temporary personnel, not consultants, working in-house. These individuals vary in skills and include data entry personnel, clerks, trainers, coders, programmers, and systems analysts. Length of stay varies depending on when they are needed for a project. These people will be paid through the accounts payable system like any other outside service.

This talent can be obtained in a number of ways. Although consultants might provide some of these services, they can be an expensive choice.

Some vendors may also provide systems and/or programming services. Smaller firms tend to make this choice when acquiring a new computer system. Even mainframe vendors may have personnel available at an hourly rate that may also be negotiable depending on the competitive climate.

Justifying Contract Personnel

Many reasons for acquiring contract personnel are the same as for contracting a consultant. However, contract personnel are less expensive than consultants, and there may be other benefits to the company. Consider the following when deciding to go with this arrangement:

A **Contract personnel staffing.** Other than being paid through the accounts payable unit, contract personnel are treated like the firm's own personnel. They should be assigned work like regular employees, with the understanding there is no long-range commitment. Assignments can run from a few hours to an almost ongoing basis. Some years ago contract workers were thought of as semi-skilled at best. Today they are found at the technical or management level.

B **Adjunct status.** Employees on a contract basis are "adjunct" to the project. Their connection is to the project or task, not the firm. A set sum of money is budgeted for a project with a given number of billable hours. To avoid the assumption of ongoing employment status, inform contract personnel of the given number of hours budgeted for the project. If their work is monitored, poor performance can be detected early and an inadequate person replaced by someone else more competent before the money runs out.

C **Monitoring performance.** When a contract person is finished with a project, his/her performance level should be established and recorded. If the same person is used in the future, that performance level can be used to compute a reasonably accurate schedule. It is a good practice to try out personnel on small tasks before making long-range commitments.

D **Specialization availability.** For a one-time effort, it is often cheaper to hire a contract person than incurring the expense of in-house training (even assuming that in-house personnel are available to concentrate their energies on acquiring a new skill). A specialist who constantly uses a talent, continually honing it, can perform at a higher skill level than anyone trained in-house for just one project.

E **Maintaining employer reputation.** When large projects or parallel operations occur without contract personnel, the question arises as to what will happen to surplus personnel after the demand is over. Whether or not job security doubts are justified, employees will begin to notice other job opportunities. The most valuable are the candidates who can most easily find opportunities elsewhere. This can leave the firm with less qualified employees to run the operation after conversion.

Because employers compete in a market for skilled talents, it is best not to earn the reputation of hiring, then firing skilled personnel. As the firm compares job candidates when hiring, people seeking employment compare the merits of different firms. One of the major reasons for job candidates not accepting a firm's offer is its unstable employment profile. This is one reason it is a good practice to contract skilled workers when demands fluctuate.

On the other hand, there are some valid reasons for not contracting personnel. One involves the learning curve, the time needed to master the job or learn about a firm. This is not so much of a problem with lower-level jobs.

Another reason is that part-timers are less loyal. While this is a valid concern, many contract workers are comfortable with temporary employment and commit to the task at hand.

The more professional the responsibility, the greater the loyalty of the person to the profession than to the firm. This may account, in part, for the turnover of skilled personnel who feel their firms are not giving them opportunities to gain professional maturity.

Also, contract people might make work for themselves to extend their employment, another reason for monitoring their work effort.

Contract Personnel Source Procedures

Vendors may be a good, but not the only, source for obtaining contract personnel. Often the hardware vendor does not have the staff or the price is too high.

Use the Yellow Pages when looking for contract personnel. If an area has limited resources, the local library can provide the Yellow Pages from cities in the general area. These services may be listed under more than one category. Check "computer services" or "information systems contracting firms." Computer service firms usually limit the available talent to programming and computer systems personnel.

Data entry firms may have a wide selection of data entry or clerical personnel available. For training needs, look under "training" or "education services" and see what computer service firms offer.

There are also self-employed and third-party-employed contracting personnel. Their skills and dependability vary widely. Be careful when using a new firm without an established track record. There have been reported cases of contract programmers planting "time bombs" in their programs to insure they are fairly paid. Delay of payment to confirm all goes well might also be a problem because many new firms are undercapitalized. Dealing with such firms is the same as sailing uncharted waters: It may yield surprises.

Think carefully before hiring any contract personnel. When there are delays finding temporary people, managers tend to lower their standards. Therefore, time is required to prove the worth of contract people on the job. More caution is necessary than for regular personnel because contract people are not loyal to the firm and can create havoc when working with a firm's regular employees in established departments.

With all this in mind, the following procedures for contract acquisition should be followed:

A **Referral contacts.** Try to find a contracting service firm through contacts with other firms. Referrals are the best way to find proven personnel contractors. Maintain memberships in IS professional organizations to provide these contacts.

B **Yellow Pages.** If referrals do not provide satisfactory results, the Yellow Pages are always a last resort. Check your area's first. If there are not more than three or four contracting services listed, check the local library for out-of-town telephone books. Be sure to contact no fewer than three or four firms for comparison.

C **Competency verification.** When the selection has been narrowed down to no fewer than three vendors, verify past performance. Ask each vendor for three or more customer references to be contacted by telephone and of whom you can ask the following questions:

1 Would you seek the firm's services in the future?

2 Did the vendor complete the project in the agreed time?

3 Was the cost of the service within the bounds expected?

4 Did the talent offered come up to expectations?

5 Did the vendor leave behind sufficient documentation?

6 Did the vendor's employee get along with your firm's users and IS people?

7 Were the contract employees available after the project for clearing up any problems?

8 Did the contract employees follow your standards for procedures and documentation?

D **Purchasing department's role.** After selecting possible contract candidates, contact the Purchasing department, which should be involved with the request for bids. Many lack experience here; however, they have the resources to help avoid selecting the wrong firm. Purchasing should, as a minimum, do the following:

1 Confirm the Dun & Bradstreet ratings of each firm selected.

2 Have the firms checked out as to their business status in their community.

3 Submit the requests for bids.

4 Establish contacts with the bidding firms.

5 Play their usual role in purchasing. They are trained to say no to vendors.

6 Submit in writing the status and ranking of firms asked for bids.

7 Assist in drawing up the contract. Depending on its nature it would be wise to have Purchasing ask the Legal department to review anything that is to be signed, before legally committing the firm.

E **Reviewing bid offers.** All bid offers should be reviewed with the help of the Legal and Purchasing departments. After approval, inform all parties in writing as soon as possible. Include those not getting an offer; they may be needed in the future.

F **Contract outline.** The contract should contain no less than the following:

1 The start and finish dates.

2 The names of people assigned to the project. A copy of each person's resume should be included if not previously received.

3 Number of hours that will be expected for each person assigned to the project.

4 The ground rules:

- ❖ Contract employees' office space
- ❖ Tools that will be made available
- ❖ Vendor contact person
- ❖ Contact person for contract employees
- ❖ What procedure is required to remove a contract person from a project
- ❖ The hours of the day they are expected to be present
- ❖ How they will be paid
- ❖ What penalty fees will be charged for being late with a project
- ❖ What rewards will be allowed for completing the project early
- ❖ What constitutes a completed job

IS OPERATION SERVICES

Information systems may need expertise best provided by outside operation services. These can be hardware, technical, or management skills and can be provided online or in batch mode.

Hardware/Software Needs

Outside computer services may be appropriate when an application is too large or too specialized for in-house IS operation. A service bureau or ASP is an economical alternative if the application is not performed frequently enough to justify a hardware purchase. If on-site I/O is preferred, a time-sharing service is a reasonably priced alternative. For one-of-a-kind or seldom-used complex applications, time-sharing is appropriate.

There are also turnkey services available that can be designed for specific applications. These provide the hardware and operating systems software, along with the applications software. In either case, the company is billed for hardware, running time, and any special software rentals.

The company can supplement its computer services through the use of full-service bureaus, public databases, and backup system services.

A **Service bureaus and application service providers (ASPs).**
Service bureaus solve a number of problems by providing data entry services, various computer services, or machine-time rental. Full-service bureaus provide a wide range of services tailored to the specific needs of a customer. These range from providing a turnkey operation at the customer's site to performing functions part of a systems operation at the service bureau's location. Subscription service bureaus and ASPs provide opportunities to share a computer application system with other subscribers. The reports produced can be specialized, but the programs and the basic system are the same.

This shared computer application system has very specialized applications and is often used for a specific system or procedure. Reasons for considering this service are twofold. First, the specialized service has a higher level of expertise than an in-house computer operation. Second, the cost is substantially lower than performing the same procedure in-house. Billing or providing mailing labels is a sample of what may be offered.

Following are some major reasons for seeking assistance from a service bureau or ASP:

❖ To add capacity to an overtaxed in-house computer system

❖ To reduce in-house computer demands by farming out some computer applications during peak load periods

❖ To convert a mass of hardcopy data to a captured computer form, or convert one kind of computer data file to another

❖ To provide a reliable source of computer hardware backup

❖ To assist with parallel testing of a new system before the actual acquisition of the new hardware

The procedure for acquiring the services of service bureau firms is fairly simple. Most firms have a price list for services. However, the business is very competitive, and should your company require anything other than normal procedures, you should receive several bids.

Following is the procedure in seeking the services of an IS service bureau or ASP:

1 Seek someone in the IS profession able to provide referrals.

2 If unable to locate three or more firms by referrals, use the local Yellow Pages. If these provide fewer than three firms, consult the local library for out-of-town phone books.

3 Confirm competency by asking for current customer referrals, and ask those customers the following questions:

❖ Would they recommend the service firm to others?

❖ Did the service firm complete their work as promised?

❖ Did the cost of the services match the agreed-upon cost?

❖ What kind of relations did their employees have with the firm?

❖ What is the best thing about their service?

❖ What is the worst thing about their service?

4 Contact the Purchasing department after selecting two or more firms. It should:

❖ Confirm the Dun & Bradstreet ratings of each firm.

❖ Have the firms checked out as to the business status in their community.

❖ Have the firms submit requests for bids.

❖ Establish a contact person to deal directly with the bidding firms.

❖ Have the contractors submit bids in writing.

5 Review received bids and issue a purchase requisition to the Purchasing department for the company selected. Notify the chosen firm. Also, notify the firms not selected, explain why, and thank them.

6 Set up a payment method and notify Accounts Payable about forthcoming billings. Approve invoices prior to payment.

B **Public databases.** Public database services are less expensive than having this same service provided in-house. Neither public database nor time-sharing systems are commonly provided in-house because performing these services is beyond the financial limits of most firms.

Public database information systems are available to the general public, and the types of customers utilizing these services range from large firms to single persons working in home offices. The service may be thought of as a dial-up computerized reference library.

The basic hardware required is a terminal or a PC and a modem. The faster the modem, the better, but check local phone lines to confirm they can transmit the information at the desired speed. If printed output is required, find software to quickly download information to save line time. Printers will not run at the speed of modem transmission rates. Check the possibility of dialing into the public database service by using a local phone number or over the Internet. This saves money.

There are four major types of vendors of public database services:

1 Commercial services containing one or more databases. The Dow-Jones and *The New York Times* are two examples.

2 Commercial services offering access to numerous databases produced by other firms or publishers but that may also contain vendor-produced databases. The information provided can range from scientific to business and financial. The hourly access rate usually varies from one database to another within the same vendor's service. Dialog, Lexus, Nexus, and VU/TEXT are some firms providing such services.

3 Government and nonprofit organizations. ERIC is a nonprofit public database service providing an educational research database. The federal government offers several services, including the National Library of Medicine with online medical data.

4 The Internet, which provides for a host of worldwide accessible databases.

C **Backup system services.** If one of today's interactive online computer systems goes down, severe problems can occur. A large, multi-site IS operation can provide its own backup. A UPS (uninterrupted power supply) is required, insuring that service is accessible in the advent of a power failure.

However, small companies often cannot afford to own backup hardware. Luckily, backup services are available to be used only in the event that a system fails or if the backup system needs to be tested. It is not a service that provides extra computer power for peak load periods. This service is an expensive off-site backup with a monthly standby fee plus additional utilization charges. The switch-over can be performed so that no interruption in service is detected by online users.

Outsource Management

Traditionally facilities management services have been contracted to replace the management of IS computer operations. Today, outsourcing is often used instead. Contract outsourcing services for a wide range of IS operations include:

- ❖ Help-desk services
- ❖ Maintenance
- ❖ Training
- ❖ Programming
- ❖ Systems analysis

- ❖ Database operations
- ❖ Network operations
- ❖ Website operations
- ❖ IS computer operations
- ❖ End-user computing

COMMENT

One large, well-known corporation contracted all of its IS responsibilities. Accounting-oriented people developed a multimillion-dollar manufacturing system that turned into a multimillion-dollar disaster. Make sure the outsourcing organization has the skills needed for the area in question. Also, beware of the bait-and-switch routine. Some well-known consulting accounting firms have been known to pull this. Remember the saying, "caveat emptor"—"buyer beware."

Facilities management/outsourcing of computer operations does not provide new hardware or software; it utilizes what is in place. This does not mean that an existing operation will not be changed at a later date. Existing operating personnel may be replaced with more competent people if necessary. Personnel may be terminated if there is an overstaffing problem.

Facilities management/outsourcing of computer operations might be considered for the following reasons:

1   To reduce operating cost through better management. Outside management with no internal loyalties may be needed to make necessary staffing changes.

2   To start up an operation. Once a professional facilities management service starts up an operation, the department can be turned over to internal operations management. The outside service can stay on temporarily to ensure everything is up and running, while permanent personnel have a chance to develop skills necessary to run the department.

3 To avoid unionization or break a union shop. Using an outside management service or outsourcing converts the facilities to a nonunion operation without going through a difficult decertification process.

4 To provide services where no in-house talent is available.

There are some problems with using a facilities management/outsourcing service operation: The operating responsibility shifts away from the firm's own controlled management, and the outside management may not understand the firm's peculiar needs.

There is also a morale issue involved when acquiring a facilities management/outsourcing service. Information systems personnel may resent reporting to an "outsider." This can be a greater problem when there is an expected reduction in the workforce. The problem could escalate to sabotage.

SELECTION PROCESS

Selecting vendors for outside services and hardware requires the application of stringent evaluation procedures. Note that off-the-shelf software selection does not require this same procedure. Evaluate this software before making vendor selection. In this case, the item selected determines the vendor.

COMMENT

In the final analysis, computer operations has to do the job asked of it—and do it while being price-competitive. Often a facilities management arrangement provides the fastest route for accomplishing these goals.

Request for Proposal

When IS management is ready to receive vendor proposals, a formal request for proposal (RFP) letter will be sent to all possible candidates. The RFP defines the format of the proposal, insuring that a responding vendor can be evaluated and compared with others.

Such a request for service is different from that for hardware. (Service RFPs include outsource RFPs.)

A **Proposal for specific hardware/system.** This request approach specifies the hardware or hardware configuration. The item is clearly identified, and the RFP basically asks for a price quotation. The RFP can be open-ended, allowing the vendor to offer newer or different technology for a given price.

B   **Proposal for system operation.** This request approach defines the desired system and asks the vendor to translate the performance objective into a hardware configuration. The system operation requirements must be well-defined, including:

❖   System design defining documentation

❖   Security required

❖   Types of user access

❖   I/O volume

❖   Network requirements

❖   Method of system installation

❖   Evaluation criteria/benchmarks for measurement

❖   Vendor maintenance, training, and operation support

❖   Reliability level required

❖   System expandability

❖   Current and future database requirements

❖   Computational and process time requirements

❖   Off-line data-storage requirements

❖   Hardcopy output requirements

❖   Price/budget constraints

❖   Current installations running with proposed system

❖   Current users of vendor's systems

❖   IS contact person

❖   Vendor contact person

C   **Proposal for outsourcing/service.** This request for proposal is for an ongoing service contract with a given time limit. Either party not wanting to renew gives written notice to the other party three months before the end of the contract. Renegotiate before this three-month period.

The service is billed monthly at a flat rate or prorated by volume. A method for recording service provided and cost should be in place. No invoice should be paid until this information is confirmed.

A detailed description of the service to be provided is required for the RFP. Any terms not used by the information technology industry will be identified in the RFP. The following items should be considered:

- ❖ System operation documentation
- ❖ Security required
- ❖ Service volume
- ❖ Reliability level required
- ❖ Performance evaluation criteria
- ❖ Service volume expandability
- ❖ Hours and days of service
- ❖ Facilities required by vendor
- ❖ Identification of vendor's employees
- ❖ IS contact person
- ❖ Vendor contact person
- ❖ Clients of vendor's service
- ❖ Contacts for confirming vendor's credibility
- ❖ Length of time vendor has been performing this service
- ❖ Principal owners/officers of vendor's firm

D **Proposal for one-time service.** This request for proposal is for a one-time service contract. This can be for a project that runs over a given time or an operational task. The service is billed monthly or upon completion. Benchmarks are required ensuring that service billed was rendered. The invoice should not be paid until this is confirmed.

A detailed description of the service to be provided is required for the RFP. Any terms not used by the IT industry will be identified in the RFP. The following items should be considered:

- ❖ System operation documentation
- ❖ Security required
- ❖ Service volume
- ❖ Reliability level required
- ❖ Performance evaluation criteria
- ❖ Service expendability
- ❖ Hours and days of service
- ❖ Facilities required by vendor
- ❖ Identification of vendor's employees by task
- ❖ One-page resume for each consulting employee
- ❖ Amount of time to be spent on tasks by each employee

❖ IS contact person

❖ Vendor contact person

❖ Former clients of vendor's service

❖ Contacts for confirming vendor's credibility

❖ Length of time vendor has been performing this kind of service

❖ Principal owners/officers of vendor's firm

Evaluating Vendor Proposals

Analyze all proposals received. The elements to be compared should be in the same sequence on each proposal. Give copies to each evaluator, with a date and time selected to meet and discuss them.

Vendors who provide clear and complete information asked for in the RFP and meet preliminary evaluation standards are selected for more detailed analysis. Those that do not will be removed from further consideration.

Vendors' proposals should address the specification elements noted in the RFP. Clear statements should be made by the vendor about the items addressed, including:

A Hardware

❖ Hardware configuration

❖ Size of primary memory

❖ Execution time

❖ Cache memory

❖ Transfer rates

❖ Disk capacity and access time

❖ Maximum I/O channels

❖ Brand and model numbers

❖ Functional descriptions

❖ Performance measurements

❖ Mean time between failures

❖ Maintenance provisions

❖ Parts availability

❖ Backup system options

❖ UPS provisions

❖ Operation manuals quality

❖ Published evaluation information

❖ Benchmark by actual workload samples

B Software. This covers contract programming, custom software service, source code of available software, and off-the-shelf software.

❖ Documentation clarity and completeness

❖ Program maintenance or updates availability

❖ Customer support available

❖ Software guaranteed virus-free

❖ Customer training resources available

- ❖ Next expected release
- ❖ Compatible operating systems
- ❖ Language software was written in
- ❖ Amount of primary memory required
- ❖ Best operation at determined level of primary memory
- ❖ Published evaluation information
- ❖ Benchmark by actual workload samples

C **Service/outsourcing.** Base evaluation of service or outsourcing on the reputation of the chosen firm. Its past and current service quality should be investigated carefully.

COMMENT

It is a common practice for some firms to showcase their best people to get the contract signed, and afterward send in their third string. Even worse, you are charged for the first-rate talent.

This practice is not limited to unknown firms. Some of the "better" nationally known firms do it, too.

Some things that can assist in the selection of a service firm are:

- ❖ Confirm credentials.
- ❖ Make certain names of specific people and the amount of time they will spend on the project are in the contract.
- ❖ Ask for former and current customer references.

D **Contact with vendor's customers.** Make a final evaluation before signing any contract. Make telephone calls to a vendor's customers with a similar operation. Ask if they would recommend the vendor's product or service. If they do, set up a site visit.

Visit the operation and observe anything reflecting the vendor's accomplishment. Since most people are reluctant to offer negative information, ask the following:

1 Would you use the same vendor again? If so, why? What has been the major problem with the vendor? Do you know other users of

the vendor's product? Are they generally happy? If so, why? Who are the other users? What are their names and telephone numbers?

2   How long does it take for a vendor's response? Are the people who respond knowledgeable and friendly? Has the vendor ever lied? Has the vendor had the resources to resolve your problem(s)?

3   Does the hardware/software satisfy your needs? Follow up with questions about how long they have had the system and how often it has gone down. Ask about its expandability and upgrading possibilities.

4   Do the users like the system or service? Ask to talk to users and confirm this. Ask users their likes and dislikes about the system or service and why.

5   Ask how long it took to put the hardware/software into operation. Did they receive adequate training? Are the operator's manuals easy to understand and follow?

6   Is the operation or service provided better than what they could do themselves, and why? Is the service worth the cost?

7   Were there any unexpected or hidden costs? What was the nature of these costs? Were the costs reasonable? Was the vendor confronted? If so, what was the reaction?

8   Were the vendor's employees easy to work with? Did their salesperson follow up after the sale? Does the vendor exhibit a genuine interest in the success of the service or product?

9   If you were starting all over, what would you do differently?

Vendor Selection

Final selection is based on more than one factor. To make the process more objective, set up a weighted matrix to compare vendors by selection factors, with the weight of any one factor a percentage of the whole. An example may be seen in Exhibit 15–1. The nature of the item being requested by an RFP determines the factors and their weights. Determine the factors and prepare the matrix parameters before the request for proposal is mailed out to avoid a subjectively weighted matrix.

In the sample presented in Exhibit 15–1, a consultant is being chosen to install a client/server database. Exhibit 15–2 presents selection factors for a firm manufacturing secondary storage devices. Note each chart contains different weighted factors, chosen for the particular need.

EXHIBIT 15–1. Vendor Selection Matrix 1

Date 11/28/2001
Consultant to Install a Client/Server Database

Factor	Weight	Vendor A	Vendor B	Vendor C
How long in business	.1			
Quality of staff	.4			
Track record	.4			
D and B rating	.1			

EXHIBIT 15–2. Vendor Selection Matrix 2

Date 11/28/2001
Manufacture Secondary Storage Devices

Factor	Weight	Vendor A	Vendor B	Vendor C
How long in business	.2			
Sales personnel	.2			
Track record	.4			
D and B rating	.2			

Compilation of the weighted factors is best done using the Delphi method. Have seven or nine people familiar with the proposal needs independently list those factors and their corresponding weights each considers important for the vendor to possess. Send the lists to a person not involved with the selection to compile. This person makes a list of all the factors and returns this new list to the participants. They will once again go through these factors, choosing and weighting their choices. Again, the papers are sent to the person not involved with the selection who groups together the factors (together with their weights) most prevalent. He/she discards those assigned low-weight values or mentioned only once. The possible combinations are then placed on one sheet of paper and copies are distributed to all contributors for reselection. This process is repeated until a general consensus is reached.

Vendors passing the preliminary selection process are rated from one to ten by the same seven- or nine-person panel or by a new panel. An example of this rating system is shown in Exhibit 15–3. Each rating (from one to ten) is then multiplied by its weighted factor to get a vendor rating value. These values are then totaled by vendor. The one with the highest total is rated first, as shown in Exhibit 15–4.

The vendor rated number one is chosen to receive the contract and will then submit, usually, a standard contract, which of course will be in his/her favor. The vendor's representative will be invited to discuss this offered contract in the information systems head's office.

COMMENT

At this meeting the IS head could be drinking coffee out of the vendor's competitor's cup. This, believe it or not, has helped negotiate a more favorable contract. If not a coffee cup, some other sign of a competitor's presence can give the same message.

Contract terms will be negotiated by the vendor's representative and IS management. Training, documentation, conversion, performance, and acceptance are all included in the bargaining process. Some items in general to consider are:

❖ Delivery or start dates
❖ Finish or completion dates

EXHIBIT 15–3. Vendor Selection Matrix 3

Date 11/28/2001
Manufacture Secondary Storage Devices

Factor	Weight	Vendor A	Vendor B	Vendor C
How long in business	.2	10	5	1
Sales personnel	.2	3	5	9
Track record	.4	2	6	8
D and B rating	.2	8	9	7

EXHIBIT 15–4. Vendor Selection Matrix 4

Date 11/28/2001
Manufacture Secondary Storage Devices

Factor	Weight	Vendor A	Vendor B	Vendor C
How long in business	.2	10 * .2 = 2.0	5 * .2 = 1.0	1 * .2 = 0.2
Sales personnel	.2	3 * .2 = 0.6	5 * .2 = 1.0	9 * .2 = 1.8
Track record	.4	2 * .4 = 0.8	6 * .4 = 2.4	8 * .4 = 3.2
D and B rating	.2	8 * .2 = 1.6	9 * .2 = 1.8	7 * .2 = 1.7
Vendor Total Rating		5.0	6.2	6.9
Vendor Ranking		3	2	1

- ❖ Vendor vs. customer responsibilities
- ❖ Pricing methods for purchase, lease, or rent
- ❖ How and when vendor will bill
- ❖ Removing vendor's disclaimers
- ❖ Provisions for equipment, software, and personnel backup
- ❖ Emergency and preventive maintenance
- ❖ Provision for detailed specifications for hardware, software, or service performance
- ❖ Contract for outsourcing on a job-by-job basis
- ❖ Realistic launch dates for implementations
- ❖ Using only one vendor at a time to avoid conflict in the working environment
- ❖ Avoiding long-term contracts with new or unproven vendors

Any contract includes performance clauses and penalties for nonperformance or late delivery times. After negotiation, the final contract is examined by the company's legal representative before it is signed.

16

MOBILE DEVICES:
WIRED FOR SUCCESS

MOBILE DEVICE POLICY AND SCOPE

Mobile device policy formalizes standards for how Personal Digital Assistants (PDAs), wearable computers, single and two-way pagers, browser-enabled mobile phones, and related portable devices are used and managed within the organization. This policy applies whether the mobile devices are used on or off company property and mandates the endorsement and support by the CEO/head of the organization.

This policy covers all mobile devices not traditionally considered computers, but that store and/or collect information that is in some way connected to the organization. It covers all data and information from the input of raw data to the disposition of output documents and/or data. All raw source material and stored data is company property and may be used only for company-approved activities. Examples of covered items include customer lists, company directories, schedule information, etc.

Operation Policy

Information systems is responsible for maintaining and enforcing a companywide operation program for all mobile devices. The head of information systems assigns the responsibility to an IT unit to coordinate usage of mobile devices. An end-user committee is formed, containing no more than seven or fewer than three end-users. Include a Purchasing department representative on the committee. A representative of the IT unit chairs the committee. The committee follows management's policy and defines it for companywide policies and procedures.

All user unit heads will comply fully with the policies. There will be enforcement procedures in place. Each unit head is provided with a policy and procedures manual, which includes a recommended equipment list. Refer to the approved equipment list for all acquisitions. In cases of mobile needs not on the approved list, a request memo is sent to the committee chairperson. The committee may grant a waiver.

Personally owned mobile devices and other equipment of any kind are not allowed on company property without special permission from the policy committee.

MOBILE DEVICE INVENTORY

The information systems unit head assigns the mobile device inventory responsibility to the IT manager. If there is no inventory or equipment tracking system in place, the IT asset manager will establish one.

Tagging Mobile Devices

Devise a coding method before the tagging of equipment begins. Tag devices upon receipt with a sequential numbering system. The numbering of mobile devices employs a two-character preface, followed by a space and a sequential number. The two-character preface identifies the type of mobile device being tagged.

After the inventory system is in place, an agent of the asset manager tags upon receipt of new devices. The device and packing slip is compared with a copy of the purchase order confirming that what was received was ordered. Supply items received are checked with the packing slip and a copy of the purchase order. If the purchase is by a blanket purchase order, the quantity received each time is added to the total received to date and the quantity compared with the original blanket-ordered quantity.

Use a bar-coded tag along with a visually identified number posted on the tag. New mobile devices received will have tags made and attached to the item. After the tag is secured to the device, it is used as its identification number during inventory checks, and when the device is moved to a new location, repaired, or disposed of.

Mobile Device Inventory System

A computer inventory system is maintained for each type of mobile device. The following file record information will be maintained for each mobile device:

- Tag number, prefix, and sequential number
- Date of purchase
- Original cost
- Manufacturer's code number
- Vendor from which the device was obtained
- Purchase, lease, or free-trial code identification
- Last date of preventive maintenance
- Last date of repair service
- Last date of warranty service
- Maintenance code

Provide a telephone number for end-users needing maintenance. This number can be an IT service unit's number doing preventive or repair maintenance, or the vendor's number.

Annual reports are run by type of equipment, department assigned, department total, and grand total by type of equipment. Amount of usage is also reported when such records can be provided. When equipment is acquired, moved, or disposed of, the information will be used to update the information database files.

MOBILE DEVICE MAINTENANCE

The information systems unit head assigns the mobile device maintenance support to the IT service unit. The IT service unit head compares maintenance service with vendor and in-house service for quality and cost. The service may be a form of hybrid mix of vendors and in-house service. The maintenance service should be reviewed annually because of changing technology, availability of in-house vendor service personnel, and the needs of the company.

In-house Maintenance Control

The IT service unit performing in-house maintenance will perform whatever mobile device repairs and preventive maintenance they can. Cost and in-house availability is a determining factor regarding who performs what service. A service telephone number is available for people needing service. This may be called the *service desk*. The service desk assists the end-user by telephone about a device problem. If the problem cannot be resolved by telephone, the service desk informs the caller he/she will be called back. The service desk person then contacts an in-house service person or the vendor with the service contract.

The service desk has vendor warranty or repair service information. The end-user is informed when he/she may expect the service person to arrive.

In smaller operations, the help-desk and the service desk may be combined into the same job. These smaller operations may also have the IT PC services unit people perform some of the mobile equipment maintenance. There is also the value of having well-trained power users. It broadens the scope of their job and provides for a level of care not requiring a skilled technician's attention. The extra training is well worth the investment. With this, smaller operations may not require a full-time help-desk.

Service Budgeting

Budgeting for in-house maintenance control and the service desk comes from the IT service unit's lump-sum budget. Although the item purchased may come from a department's budget, the IT service support cost may or may not be charged to the department. This charge will depend on the company's accounting policy.

All service maintenance done by the IT service unit is reported on a daily service log. The completed work log sheets are turned in daily to the IT service unit's head. The log report contains the following information:

- ❖ Service person's name
- ❖ Machine number serviced
- ❖ Time spent on the service call
- ❖ Type of call: service, preventive maintenance, or operator problem
- ❖ Any replacement parts used

Departments purchasing their own mobile devices with their own budget require funds to obtain their own maintenance service. The departments have to request funds for this maintenance service in their budgets. Some leased items may come with a provided service agreement.

All service performed by the in-house IT service unit or vendor is reported by the IT service unit. The IT service people provide their daily report to the IT service unit head. The service desk records the vendor service. The vendor code number and device number are reported. The vendor's service document is turned over to the help-desk. Each day the service report is given to the unit head along with the vendor's service document—a copy is made for the IT unit head and the original copy is sent to the department head. A request for vendor service may come in one of the following forms:

- ❖ Time and parts
- ❖ Blanket maintenance contract
- ❖ Warranty service call

Maintenance Service Report

Vendor maintenance is reported by the device types that each vendor has a contract to repair. The kind of vendor maintenance service reported is shown as warranty, preventive, or service maintenance. Time and replacement parts service charges are listed.

The monthly maintenance service reports will list the devices and locations that were serviced. The report provides the following information:

❖ What type of device was serviced

❖ Who performed the service

❖ The estimated cost for the service

❖ The kind of in-house service performed

❖ The kind of vendor service performed

❖ What kind of service was performed

❖ What kind of service was performed on the device the last time it received a service call

❖ When the last service call date was and what the current service call date is

❖ A total monthly expense by device type and a monthly grand total—there will be a year-to-date cost by device type and a year-to-date grand total

A second report (IT and Vendor Maintenance Cost Report) is printed with information by vendor and the IT service unit. The report will list who provided what service to which devices. The report lists the subtotal cost for the month. Year-to-date costs are listed by the service provider and a grand total year-to-date sum is given.

Vendor Maintenance Contracting

The IT unit head, the asset manager, and a purchasing department representative will work together to solicit vendor contract bids. The same purchasing department representative should be used from year to year. It would be beneficial if the same purchasing agent is also responsible for mobile supplies and computer supplies.

After IT has identified which items they cannot do or service because they lack the required people, a list is composed of the devices requiring vendor's maintenance bids. A form letter is used listing all the items for which bids are requested. Vendors can provide an offer for any one item, any number, or the entire lot of items listed.

The list of vendors to contact can come from the IT service unit's head, the IT asset manager, and the purchasing department's representative. It is the purchasing department representative's responsibility to check each vendor before they are sent the letter. The purchasing agent can use information his/her department may already have. Contacts with other firms' purchasing departments may be a source of information along with the firm's D&B rating.

When composing the request for bids letter, provide as much information as possible. A vendor company contact person is provided in the letter. Any site visits are arranged through the company's contact person. The letter furnishes the name and telephone number of the contact person, and the last day the bids will be received. The following information will be furnished in the vendor letter or attachment to the letter:

❖ A list of unit types that the bid calls for servicing

❖ The number of units for each unit type

❖ The age and condition of each device

❖ Units that are under current warranties, and when those warranties expire

If a particular vendor's bid is selected, would they be willing to provide a help-desk telephone number? This allows for company employees to contact them for information or a service call. Will there be a charge for this service if it is available?

Vendor selection is based on several variables. Each variable is weighted before the request for bid letters are dispatched. Vendor analysis is based on this matrix. See Chapter 15, *Vendors: Getting the Goods,* for information about setting up a weighted matrix. Short-term contracts may be considered for yet unproven vendors. Before any contract is signed, contact the firm's legal representative, who has the last word before the firm's authorized representative signs it.

OPERATION OF MOBILE DEVICES

Mobile devices cover a wide range of applications and complexities. The total investment in mobile devices can be difficult to track and is not known in most companies. More important, the data kept on mobile devices is difficult to track and control.

Meanwhile, most mobile devices operate without a central sense of direction. Without the orchestration and guidance of information systems, their costs continue to grow while their efficiency diminishes. A major part of con-

COMMENT

According to an *Information Week* Redefining Business study of 600 IT execs on the adoption of wireless technology, more than 40 percent of respondents had planned to purchase handheld computers and other wireless technology in 2000.

trolling mobile devices is the procedures set forth by an IT unit of information systems.

Information systems is responsible for maintaining and enforcing a companywide software application policy for all mobile devices. The acceptable application software list is maintained in the asset management software database, and is updated monthly by the information systems software committee. Installation of unauthorized application software is not permitted. Help-desk support is not provided for unauthorized application software.

Personal Data Assistants (PDAs)

A PDA is a small hand-held computer used to write notes, track appointments, contacts, and otherwise keep your life in order. Early PDAs required data to be input using a keypad with keys the size of Chiclets, but more recent models (e.g., the Palm Pilot or Palm PC) use a combination of pen-based input and character recognition software to accept user input. Many can also be used to send and receive e-mail and browse the Internet. Information in the PDA can be synchronized with data in a PC-based application such as Microsoft Outlook.

Information systems is responsible for maintaining and enforcing a companywide synchronization policy for all mobile devices. A standard synchronization package should be selected that supports all the different PDAs in use at the company. The applications and data to be synchronized must also be determined. It is desirable to use synchronization software that can be administered from a single server to control what is being transferred to and from the PDA. Other items to consider include:

> **Filtering of data**—Information systems must determine what subset of data records is to be synchronized with the PDA. Filter setting can protect sensitive data that should not be synchronized and can be used to save time by transferring only data that is actually needed.

COMMENT

The popularity of PDAs can prove a headache for corporate IS departments. Palm and Windows CE have long targeted enterprise customers, touting the benefits of employees connecting remotely to corporate databases of information via their hand-held computers. According to Ken Dulaney, vice president at Gartner Group, the influx of new products, designs, and technologies will add 10 percent in technical support costs.

Field mapping—This is used to map fields from the PC application to the PDA application. Information systems must create standards for which data fields can be synchronized and where they map between the PC and the PDA.

Conflict resolution—Data kept on both a PC and a PDA have conflicts when data is changed in one or both places. Establish policies to resolve these conflicts.

Control at the server—Some synchronization products allow settings to be controlled at a central server. This also makes it possible to synchronize over the LAN without being connected to a PC.

The use of PDAs makes good backup procedures even more critical, as there are more opportunities for data to be changed inadvertently. Verified backups before the first synchronization are very important.

PDA users are notified that the data on the PDA is valuable and sensitive company information, and must be protected. All PDAs should be password-enabled to prevent unauthorized access to the data if the PDA is lost or stolen.

WAP-enabled Cellular Phones

A WAP-enabled cellular phone allows users to access the Internet using their cellular phones. Information systems is responsible for maintaining and enforcing a companywide usage policy for all cellular phones. Usage should be monitored periodically to insure that the phones are used for business-related purposes.

COMMENT

Intellisync from Puma Technology synchronizes data from all Windows-powered Pocket PCs, hand-held PCs, and Palm devices with a broad number of PC-based PIM, contact management, and groupware applications using advanced features like conflict resolution, filtering, and field mapping. Intellisync supports Microsoft Outlook 97/98/2000, Microsoft Schedule+ 7.0/7.0a/7.5, Lotus Notes 4.5/4.6, Lotus Organizer 2.12/97/GS/4.1/5.0, Novell GroupWise 5.2/5.5, Symantec ACT! 3.08/4.0/4.01/4.02, GoldMine 3.2/4.0, Meeting Maker 5.0.3/5.5, and other PC-based PIMs.

Cellular phone users are notified that the data on the cellular phone is valuable and sensitive company information, and must be protected. All cellular phones should be password-enabled (if possible) to prevent unauthorized access to the data if the cellular phone is lost or stolen.

COMMENT

The market research firm Strategy Analytics predicts that as many as 525 million WAP-enabled devices will ship in the U.S. and Western Europe by 2003.

Wearable Computers

A wearable computer is a computer used by users who must be mobile. The system is normally worn on a belt, with optional peripherals including a wrist-mounted touch-screen display, voice-enabled headset, and a head-mounted monitor. Information systems is responsible for maintaining and enforcing a companywide usage policy for all wearable computers.

Wearable computer users are notified that the data on the wearable computer is valuable and sensitive company information, and must be protected.

All wearable computers should be password-enabled to prevent unauthorized access to the data if the wearable computer is lost or stolen.

Information systems is responsible for setting up processes for backing up data on all wearable computers. Procedures include standards for use of docking stations, connections to the LAN, and backing up data to a server. A directory on a server that is regularly backed up is created for storing data and applications from the wearable computer. Instructions for backing up data and applications are created by information systems and provided to all users of wearable computers.

COMMENT

IBM's Almaden Research Center is working on Personal Area Network (PAN) technology, which uses the natural electrical conductivity of the human body to transmit electronic data. In the future, a user of PAN technology will be able to transfer information via touch rather than issuing typed commands or pressing buttons. For example, your computer might recognize you as you if you simply touch the keyboard. This capability could yield significant benefits in the area of access control and data privacy.

Power Users

A power user is a person using a particular device on a regular basis (usually daily), who becomes very knowledgeable about its operation. This person usually enjoys sharing information about using the device with others in the organization. Ask power users if they could be contacted if a new user needs assistance. If they agree, their names should be listed as power users with the instructions given to new users.

A power user should be able to operate and perform minor device adjustments. He/she knows how to replenish its expendable stock items, and perform standard housekeeping and preventive maintenance procedures. A power user is able to be walked through some of the malfunctions by the service desk or a maintenance person over the telephone. At the service desk will be a power user's location book with the power user's name, telephone number, and location listed. A second listing will be by location with the power user's name and telephone number listed. This is used to contact another power user who is close by for assistance when the nearer power user is not available.

Mobile Device Operations Procedures

These are the operating procedures furnished to all device users. The operator procedure manuals are furnished by the IT service unit or the systems and procedures unit. The manuals will provide operator instructions, minor maintenance instruction, backup procedures, and procedures for troubleshooting. Minor preventive maintenance procedures are provided.

The procedure manuals contain any manufacturer's furnished material helpful to clarify the device's operation. The illustrations used by the manufacturer could be beneficial to the operator. Close-up and wide-view photographs would be helpful if included in the operator procedure manuals.

A prototype manual is developed and tested before it enters service. Use an unskilled person for the test. This should be done with more than one subject. Avoid the brightest person in the area and any experienced operator for debugging the procedure manual.

Supply Requisitions

Use the standard supply requisitions that the firm has in place. If the form is outdated or there is no form, one will be designed by the IT systems and procedures unit.

A central supply location is placed to limit the travel time involved. This prevents unnecessary travel for the person seeking supplies. The supply center could also function as supply distribution location for the end-user computer operations supplies. Supplies that are not too large can be delivered by interoffice mail. A requisition system is employed to obtain supplies. The unit head approves the requisition after all the items are listed with their respective quantities. A line is drawn across the lines not used by the person before signing the requisition. Depending on company accounting practice, supplies are charged to the unit receiving them or from a lump-sum company budget. Spot-checks on usages for units that employ a lump-sum budget are recommended. The loss on supply items can be costly to a company. The supply area is locked when unattended. Supplies stored in operating units are locked at the end of the day or locked at all times if the area is not easily visible.

Service Desk Assistance

Help-desks, along with service desks, cannot solve all user problems. It requires other assistance to service the user's special needs. Some operations, such as mobile phones, are better off with vendor-supplied service. Vendor help and service desks for special systems can provide much better service than an in-house service. If the company is willing to provide an in-house service desk and support it, there are still vendor services providing better assistance. They will do it better, and the equipment will be up and running faster.

The asset manager publishes an approved mobile device acquisition list for new mobile device purchases. This covers what is in-house, currently operating, and found on the mobile device inventory property list, but not on the approved mobile device acquisition list. The mobile device inventory property list is company property, identified and tagged. The approved mobile device acquisition list is a list of items that the IT service unit can repair or for which the service desk has a vendor contact. The service desk also has the mobile device inventory property list and the source of service for each item. Some items were company property before the service desk assistance program was established.

Some devices either have a long life span and never need to be replaced, or are no longer manufactured—they can be replaced only with used equipment. The help-desk will have a special number to call to have the item serviced. In cases of this kind, it is best to have a power user trained to do most of the repairs and preventive maintenance. Contact the vendor service person only if the problem is beyond the scope of a power user or one is unavailable. Some of the items may not use the English measuring system and may require special tools to repair the equipment, or the manufacturer may be the only one making the tool.

The service desk does not have to be covered at the company site any more than the help-desk. This is why many vendor help-desks are not found at company sites. This may be more difficult when having the vendor provide full-service desk coverage. If coverage is needed past normal working hours, service desk personnel can be on call at their homes for specific time periods. This can also apply to help-desk personnel. These two jobs can be combined into one in smaller firms. There would be one number to call in the event of a problem. There is also the possibility that the problem may be related to both the help-desk and the service desk. The help- and service desk person should be able to have at home the current information he/she has at work. Have it installed in a notebook computer.

USER AND IT SUPPORT TRAINING

The provision for training covers a wide area of needs. The technology skill levels required for each mobile device will be multilevel. Vendor-contracted mobile device service will not require so many levels of skills as an in-house service program. The service desk has the skill level available for each device listed in the mobile device inventory property list. Depending on the nature of the problem, a skill level is determined to resolve the problem. The item listed will have posted to it the persons who can perform a given level of skill. A person with a higher level of skill can perform a lower level of skill task, but a lower-level skilled person should not perform a higher-level skill task. The training certifies a level at which the service person can perform a task.

The training provided is for certain skill levels. This training is for vendor- and company-serviced equipment.

User Training

The user should learn the basic operation of the device to produce the desired results: the more complex, the more to learn. Changing batteries would be considered a task level expected of a user. Loading applications into a PDA is much more complex, but still a user's job. Provide user training in more than one form:

A **New user training.** When a new mobile device is to be used by users, conduct the training in class. The vendor or a power user conducts the classes. The vendor provides handouts. The company instructor provides any additional handouts needed. A video or slide presentation is helpful along with any hands-on training.

Compile a list of the people attending the meeting. Anyone missing the class is notified they should attend the next class offered. If the classes are over, they take the individual training provided to new employees later.

B **New employee training.** Anyone missing class will take the self-paced individual training. New employees having no experience with the device receive self-paced individual training. They are credited with receiving the instruction for the new device. Part of the instruction is provided to the user as on-the-job training (OJT) instruction.

Power User Training

The power user training is given for all users desiring recognition as power users. Training can be from more than one source. The IT service unit holds classes for power users or OJT instruction for devices they maintain. The power users receive manuals from the IT service unit.

Vendor training programs are provided at the company site or the vendor's place of instruction. The vendors provide manuals. The IT unit provides power user procedure manuals. Some sort of certificate is provided by the vendor showing the person is now a certified power user for the given mobile device.

The power user should be able to provide OJT to new device users. They should be able to operate the device, make adjustments to its operation, and perform some light preventive maintenance. They are the key contact persons in the area for users, service desk, vendor service people, and the IT service personnel.

IT Service Unit Training

Each IT service person has a list of devices that they service for their own records, along with the service desk and the IT unit head. Training comes from one of the following sources:

❖ OJT

❖ A self-paced learning program provided by the vendor

❖ Attending vendor's classes

❖ Passing a qualifying exam for the equipment

❖ Taking a correspondence course from the vendor or a private correspondence program

Service Desk Training

Effective service desk people are often individuals with some IT service experience. Their training can come from the areas where the IT service person receives his/her training—as a power user and from operator training. It helps a new service desk operator to work with an experienced worker, which is a form of OJT learning. On days when the workload is light, they may try manning the service desk.

Service desk personnel are expected to work overtime and be on call at their homes. The unit has one or two laptop computers that service people can take home with them when on call. They are expected to have no less knowledge than a power user about each device and a general knowledge about vendor-maintained devices. They should have enough knowledge to assist a user and communicate with a service person working for the company or vendor. They should be able to assign service people effectively. They can reduce maintenance costs with the proper assignments and the ability to walk users through problems.

MOBILE DEVICE ACQUISITION PROCEDURES

Budgeting can come from a corporate lump-sum budget or department budgets or both.

Budgeting Procedures

Each department submits its expected needs for the following year's budget. This is based on the last year's budget plus inflation, replacement of old equipment, and new needs. It is supported by the utilization of the current equipment and forecasted usage for the next budget year.

Budgets will be needed for supplies and replacement of current equipment. Departments with their own hardware for one-of-a-kind use will require a budget for maintaining the equipment.

The information systems IT service unit needs a budget for its operation. The unit needs a budget for capital expenses benefiting the whole company plus a replacement parts budget. Also, a vendor service budget is required.

Requisition Procedures

Budgeted items can have a requisition issued. The requisition goes to the IT asset manager to confirm it meets standards or requires a standards waiver.

The requisition is approved and sent on to the budgeting department so it can adjust the records. It's then sent on to the Purchasing department.

Purchasing Procedures

Purchasing receives the approved purchase requisition. If needed, they will take care of the competitive bids for the item. After the purchase order is sent to the vendor, a copy is sent to receiving and accounts payable.

Receiving Procedures

The agent for the asset manager or a special order item representative inspects the item for approval. After it is approved, a receiving notice is sent to accounts payable.

The asset manager's agent affixes a tag to the device and records the information. The information is sent to the asset manager.

17

THE INTERNET

PURPOSE OF THE INTERNET AND E-MAIL POLICY

Internet and e-mail policy formalizes standards for how the company connects to the outside world though the Internet and e-mail. While the Internet provides access to a wealth of valuable information and facilitates communication, it also opens the potential for others to access the company's valuable proprietary information. Internet access and e-mail are valuable and costly corporate resources and must be used only for company business. Irresponsible use reduces their availability for critical business operations, compromises corporate security and network integrity, and leaves the company open to potentially damaging litigation. This policy mandates the endorsement and support by the CEO/head of the organization.

Scope

The Internet and e-mail policy covers all types of connections to the outside world through the Internet. The types of connections include:

❖ Individual computer using a POTS (plain old telephone service) connection through a modem

❖ Work group server using a dedicated dial-up POTS connection through a modem

❖ Work group server using an ISDN, DSL, T1, or cable modem connection

The policy also covers all activities performed while using the Internet, including but not limited to browsing (viewing Web pages), using e-mail, Instant Messaging, and transferring files using FTP (file transfer protocol).

Policy Objectives

This policy provides guidelines ensuring the secure, proper, and reliable use of the Internet. Policy objectives should be flexible enough to cover new methods of Internet connectivity as they become available.

The company's Internet and e-mail usage policy are part of the new employee orientation process. Any new or existing employees sign an acknowledgment that they have received a copy of this policy. The Internet and e-mail usage policy also appears in the employee handbook. An online message appearing when the user logs onto e-mail or the Internet is helpful to remind employees of this policy. The company should offer training sessions on Internet and e-mail usage.

COMMENT

An analysis of a survey of more than 9,000 MSNBC.com readers found one in five men and one in eight women admitted using their work computers as their primary lifeline to access sexually explicit material online. Other studies have revealed that 70 percent of e-porn traffic occurs between 9 A.M. and 5 P.M. on weekdays.

METHODS OF INTERNET ACCESS

There are several methods to connect to the Internet from an individual workstation. Each individual workstation might have its own connection to an Internet service provider (ISP), or be connected through the work group or corporate LAN. The connection itself can be on-demand or continuously connected to the Internet. Each method has its own set of advantages and disadvantages.

Individual Access

The technically simplest method to connect to the Internet is for each individual PC to connect directly to an ISP using a modem and a POTS line. The user's PC connects to the local ISP using dial-up networking (if using Microsoft Windows) and uses a browser to view content on the World Wide Web.

The IT technical support unit develops the procedure for connecting to the Internet through individual PCs. The procedure will be distributed to users requiring individual Internet access. The IT technical-support unit also determines the browser software used and may need to install the browser on the user's PC if not preinstalled.

An advantage of this method is there is less direct exposure of the LAN to the outside world if any existing LAN connection is unplugged. Another is the user's PC is exposed for only the time he or she is connected. This gives hackers less opportunity to gain access to the user's PC. Personal firewall software should be used as a form of protection while connected to the Internet.

A disadvantage of individual connections to the Internet is the lack of centralized monitoring or control. Usage standards cannot easily be enforced, and virus protection is left up to the user. Speed is severely limited when using a modem and POTS line. Any time you have a connection to the Internet, the machine with which you connect and any subsequent machine behind it are subject to unauthorized access.

When using the Internet via an individual connection, the following procedures must be followed:

❖   Personal firewall software must be installed and active.

❖   Any LAN connections must be unplugged.

❖   Virus-scanning software must be installed and active.

COMMENT

Examples of personal firewall software include ZoneAlarm and WinProxy. ZoneAlarm from Zone Labs costs less than $20; see their Web site at www.zonelabs.com for the latest information. WinProxy 3.0 from Ositis is a personal firewall and proxy product. They can be reached at www.winproxy.com.

Corporate/Networked Internet Access

In most cases employees have access to the Internet and e-mail from their workstations through the corporate or work group LAN. The LAN is connected to the Internet through a router and/or proxy server; this acts as a firewall to protect the LAN from unauthorized access. The user's PC uses a browser to view content on the World Wide Web.

The IT technical support unit develops the procedure for connecting to the Internet through the corporate or work group LAN. The procedure is distributed to users requiring Internet access. The IT technical support unit also determines the browser software used and may need to install the browser on the user's PC if not preinstalled.

An advantage of this method is Internet usage can be centrally monitored and controlled. Also, a centralized firewall (either software or hardware) is used to protect the LAN from unauthorized access. Virus software is centrally installed and kept up-to-date.

A disadvantage of Internet access through the corporate or work group LAN is there is a single point of failure protecting the LAN from the outside world. The connection is normally up 24/7, which gives hackers more opportunity to test your protection. Any time you have a connection to the Internet, the machine with which you connect and any subsequent machine behind it are subject to unauthorized access.

When using the Internet via the corporate or work group LAN, the following procedures must be followed:

❖ Firewall software or hardware is installed at the point of connection to the Internet.

❖ Virus-scanning software is installed. All downloaded files and e-mails are scanned for viruses.

❖ The IT technical support unit generates a weekly report. The report shows the most frequently visited Web sites and total time connected to the Internet for each user.

COMMENT

Losses related to Distributed Denial of Services (DDOS) attacks in early 2000 that shut down several popular Web sites could easily come to more than $1.2 billion, according to a report from the Yankee Group.

INTERNET SECURITY POLICY

The information systems unit head assigns the responsibility for Internet security to the IT manager. Internet security policies are critical for protecting corporate systems while connected to the Internet. The IT unit responsible for the corporate Internet connection develops and enforces security procedures protecting corporate systems while connected to the Internet.

A connection to the Internet not only connects a computer to systems all over the world, but also with all computers it may be connected to over a LAN. The Internet was not designed to be very secure, as open access for research purposes was a major consideration. Other factors making an Internet connection a possible security problem include:

❖ **Vulnerable TCP/IP services**—A number of the TCP/IP services are not secure and can be compromised by knowledgeable intruders; services used in the local area networking environment for improving network management are especially vulnerable.

❖ **Ease of spying and spoofing**—The majority of Internet traffic is unencrypted; e-mail, passwords, and file transfers can be monitored and captured using readily available software. Intruders can then reuse passwords to break into systems.

❖ **Lack of policy**—Many sites are configured unintentionally for wide-open Internet access without regard for the potential for abuse from the Internet; many sites permit more TCP/IP services than they require for their operations and do not attempt to limit access to information about their computers that could prove valuable to intruders.

❖ **Complexity of configuration**—Host security access controls are often complex to configure and monitor; controls that are accidentally misconfigured often result in unauthorized access.

Firewall Usage

A firewall is a system providing security to a network. A firewall includes a number of items such as policy, network arrangement, and technical controls and procedures. The firewall protects the network from probing by unauthorized users and allows only authorized access to the system.

Management first defines the type and level of security desired for the Internet connection for the protection of company information resources. Issues to consider include:

❖ Dial-in policy

❖ SLIP and PPP connections

❖ Which Internet services the organization plans to use (Telnet, FTP, etc.)

❖ Assumptions about security versus usability (When does a service become too risky to use?)

❖ Access to internal resources from the Internet

❖ Restriction of access to approved sites only or restrict only certain sites

❖ Use of chat programs such as mIRC and ICQ

❖ Use of streaming audio and video

There are two types of access control—explicit denial or explicit approval. Explicit approval restricts access to approved sites only and denies all other services by default. This is the more secure method, but more difficult to implement and maintain. Explicit denial restricts only certain sites and is easier on users, but new services that become available may expose the network to security problems.

The firewall installed should have the following features:

❖ The firewall should be able to support a "deny all services except those specifically permitted" design policy, even if not the policy used.

❖ The firewall should support the company's security policy, not impose one.

❖ The firewall should be flexible; it should be able to accommodate new services and needs if the security policy of the organization changes.

❖ The firewall contains advanced authentication measures or contains the hooks for installing advanced authentication measures.

❖ The firewall employs filtering techniques to permit or deny services to specified host systems as needed.

❖ The IP filtering language should be flexible, user-friendly to program, and should filter on as many attributes as possible, including source and destination IP address, protocol type, source and destination TCP/UDP port, user, and inbound and outbound interface.

❖ The firewall uses proxy services for Internet services such as FTP and Telnet, so advanced authentication measures can be employed and centralized at the firewall. If services such as NNTP, http, or gopher are required, the firewall contains the corresponding proxy services.

❖ The firewall contains the ability to centralize SMTP access, to reduce direct SMTP connections between site and remote systems. This results in centralized handling of site e-mail.

❖ The firewall accommodates public access to the site, so public information servers can be protected by the firewall but segregated from site systems not requiring the public access.

❖ The firewall should contain the ability to concentrate and filter dial-in access.

❖ The firewall contains mechanisms for logging traffic and suspicious activity and contains mechanisms for log reduction so logs are readable and understandable. Mechanisms for alerting someone when suspicious activity occurs are also important.

❖ If the firewall requires an operating system such as Unix, a secured version of the operating system is part of the firewall, with other security tools as necessary ensuring firewall host integrity. The operating system should have all patches installed.

❖ The firewall is developed so its strength and correctness is verifiable. It should be simple in design so that it can be understood and maintained.

❖ The firewall and any corresponding operating system are updated with patches and other bug fixes in a timely manner.

INTERNET USE POLICY

The company encourages the use of the Internet and e-mail to make business and communication more effective. However, Internet service and e-mail are valuable, costly corporate resources and their purpose is to facilitate company business. Irresponsible use reduces their availability for critical business operations, compromises corporate security and network integrity and leaves the company open to potentially damaging litigation.

COMMENT

A problem for employers is an influx of Web sites that pay end-users to surf, search and send e-mail. These sites entice employees to use their Internet connections at work to earn a little extra cash on the clock. This is in contrast to most employees' slow connection at home. A survey of at-work Internet usage by Nielen/NetRatings found that the 7,000 employees in the survey spent an average of 67 minutes at iWon.com during a one-month period.

Tracking Internet Usage

The company tracks all Internet transactions by employees. The purpose is simply to enable the company to manage its Internet and e-mail resources in a cost-effective and efficient manner and to plan more efficiently for future technology expansion. Please note that the company does not currently intend to examine the content of communications over the Internet, whether in e-mail, chat, or any other medium. The intention is to monitor the existence of the traffic being generated, much like a telephone bill tracks the calls made, the numbers called, the time of the calls, but not the content. In this manner the company will be aware of how its resources are being used, where they are needed, where new capacity is required, and other infrastructure management issues. Additionally, because of the vulnerability to litigation over inappropriate conduct in the workplace environment, it is the company's responsibility to ensure company resources don't support inappropriate activities.

Internet and E-mail Usage Guidelines

To ensure all employees understand their responsibilities, the following guidelines are established for using company e-mail and Internet access. Any improper use of the Internet or e-mail jeopardizes the company's legal standing and will not be tolerated.

A **Acceptable uses of company e-mail and Internet access.** The company provides Internet and e-mail access for business usage. Every staff member has the responsibility to maintain and enhance the company's public image and to use company e-mail and access to the Internet in a manner that reflects well on the company. The company recognizes there will be occasional personal use on lunch breaks and during nonworking hours (with the approval of management), but this shall not be excessive or unreasonable.

B **Unacceptable uses of company e-mail and Internet access.** The company e-mail and Internet access may not be used for transmitting, retrieving, or storage of any communications of a discriminatory or harassing nature or materials that are obscene or "X-rated." Harassment of any kind is prohibited. No messages with derogatory or inflammatory remarks about an individual's race, age, disability, religion, national origin, physical attributes, or sexual preference shall be transmitted. No excessively abusive, profane, or offensive language is to be transmitted through the company's e-mail or Internet system.

Electronic media also may not be used for any purpose that is illegal, against company policy, or contrary to the company's best interests. Solicitation of noncompany business, or any use of the company e-mail or Internet for personal gain, is prohibited.

C **Communications.** Each employee is responsible for the content of all text, audio, or images that he/she places or sends over the company's e-mail and Internet system. No e-mail or other electronic communications may be sent hiding the identity of the sender or representing the sender as someone else or someone from another company. All messages communicated on the company's e-mail and Internet system should contain the employee's name.

Any messages or information sent by an employee to another individual outside the company via an electronic network (e.g., bulletin board, online service, or Internet) are statements that reflect on the company. While some users include personal "disclaimers" in electronic messages, there is still a connection to the company, and the statements may legally be tied to the company. Therefore, the company requires all communications sent by employees via the company's e-mail and Internet system comply with all company policies and do not disclose any confidential or proprietary company information.

D **Software.** To prevent computer viruses being transmitted through the company's e-mail and Internet system, there is no downloading of any unauthorized software. All software downloaded is registered to the company. Employees contact IS if they have any questions.

E **Copyright issues.** Employees on the company's e-mail and Internet system may not transmit copyrighted materials belonging to entities other than the company. Note that nonadherence to this policy puts the company in serious legal jeopardy, opening up the company to significant lawsuits and public embarrassment. All employees obtaining access to other companies' or individuals' materials must respect all copyrights and may not copy, retrieve, modify, or forward copyrighted materials, except with permission. Failure to observe copyright or license agreements may result in disciplinary action including termination. If an employee has questions about any legal issues, he/she speaks with their manager or IS before proceeding.

F **Security.** The company routinely monitors usage patterns in its e-mail and Internet communications. Reasons for monitoring are many, including cost analysis, security, bandwidth allocation, and the general management of the company's gateway to the Internet. All messages created, sent, or retrieved over the company's e-mail and the Internet are the property of the company and should be considered public information.

Notwithstanding previous comments regarding the company's current intention not to monitor content, the company reserves the right to access and monitor the content of all messages and files on the company's e-mail and Internet system any time in the future with or without notice. Employees should not assume electronic communications are totally private and should transmit highly confidential data in other ways. E-mail messages regarding sensitive matters should warn that such communications are not intended to be secure or confidential. This is good business sense.

G **Violations.** Any employee who abuses the privilege of company-facilitated access to e-mail or the Internet can be subject to corrective action including termination. If necessary, the company reserves the right to advise appropriate legal officials of any illegal violations.

COMMENT

One source of Internet usage monitoring software is Sequel Technology. Their product supports all major Internet platforms. The software reports usage, volume, and protocol information, as well as cost allocation. They can be reached at www.sequeltech.com.

E-mail Etiquette

As e-mail has replaced paper-based communication but has also become a substitute for having a conversation, the proper use of e-mail etiquette has become increasingly important. Communication received in an e-mail does not easily convey the mood and emotions of the communicator. Most messages come across harsher than intended. The following are useful guidelines for communicating by e-mail.

A **Be brief.** E-mail messages should be concise and to the point. It is helpful to think of your e-mail as a telephone conversation, except you are typing instead of speaking. You should also make your main point as quickly as possible. Many software programs used for reading e-mail allow for a preview mode, where only the first few sentences are displayed. Many people receive hundreds of e-mails a day and use this preview mode to determine which e-mails they will read completely.

COMMENT

Thank you for sending me a copy of your book—I'll waste no time reading it. —Moses Hadas (1900–1966), book reviewer.

B **Use the subject line wisely.** An accurate subject line is helpful for determining which e-mails merit closer attention by those who receive mountains of e-mail, but be careful not to earn a reputation for overhyping your message in the subject line; your really important messages may not get read.

C **Use grammar and punctuation correctly.** Poor grammar and punctuation reflect poorly on the sender. Don't overuse exclamation points (sometimes called "bangs") in an attempt to emphasize the importance of your message. If something is important, it should be reflected in your text, not in your punctuation.

D **Use special formatting sparingly.** Avoid the use of fancy formatting. What looks great using your e-mail client software may look like gibberish to the recipient. Stick to commonly available fonts, and realize that the spacing as displayed by the recipient may be different from that in which the message was sent, especially when displaying columnar data.

E **Abbreviations.** Abbreviation use is rampant with e-mail. In the quest to save keystrokes, users have traded clarity for confusion (unless you understand the abbreviations). Avoid using abbreviations that you would not normally use in a paper-based communication. Some of the more common abbreviations follow.

This:	*Means this:*
BCNU	be seeing you
BTW	by the way
FAQ	frequently asked questions

FWIW	for what it's worth
FYI	for your information
HTH	hope this helps
IMHO	in my humble opinion
LOL	laughing out loud or lots of luck
OBO	or best offer
ROTFL	rolling on the floor laughing
RTFM	read the funny manual
TNSTAAFL	there's no such thing as a free lunch
TTFN	ta ta for now
TTYL	talk to you later
<G>	grinning
<J>	joking
<L>	laughing
<S>	smiling

F **Smilies or emoticons.** Smilies or emoticons (emotional icons) are used to compensate for the inability of written communication to express the emotions, facial expressions, and gestures seen in a verbal or face-to-face communication. Emoticons can be useful in avoiding misunderstandings of the writer's intentions. Most emoticons are designed to resemble what a person's face would look like if rotated 90 degrees counterclockwise. The most commonly used emoticon is the smiley face :) or :-), which resembles a person smiling. Following are some more examples:

This:	*Means this:*
: (or :-(	unhappy
;-)	light sarcasm
;->	heavy sarcasm
:-|	indifference
:-/ or :-\	undecided
:-0	surprise
:-p	tongue sticking out
:-S	loss of words

Emoticons are typically found at the end of sentences and usually refer back to the prior statement. Use them sparingly, as their meanings are not universal.

G **Salutations.** Each situation will be different, but in general, use what you would in a business letter. Some form of salutation should be included in every e-mail as a common courtesy.

H **Signatures.** Do not rely on your e-mail address to inform the recipient who sent the e-mail. You should sign your e-mail just as you would a business letter. Include your full name, title, company name, and telephone number. You may want to also include your e-mail address, because it can sometimes be difficult to locate your e-mail address within the e-mail. Avoid using quotes or images at the end of your e-mail.

I **Printing e-mail.** Avoid printing a paper copy of e-mails received unless absolutely necessary. Most e-mail systems allow you to create folders for storing old e-mails if you need to save a copy.

COMMENT

According to an American Management Association survey published in *The Wall Street Journal,* 27 percent of major corporations surveyed in 1999 monitored employee e-mail; 84 percent of those told employees that their e-mail was being monitored.

J **Privacy.** Remember, e-mails are not private. The company reserves the right to monitor e-mail content ensuring that the e-mail system is used for appropriate purposes. Also, no security is 100-percent hacker-proof; someone outside the company may intercept and read your e-mail. Routing of e-mail is not without errors; someone other than the intended recipient may receive your e-mail. Do not send anything by e-mail that you would not place on the company bulletin board.

K **Other.** Remember, all recipients may not read your e-mail immediately. While your e-mail usually arrives quickly, this is not always the case. E-mail is not designed for immediacy (that's why you have a telephone); it's designed for convenience. Do not use e-mail to schedule a meeting the same day or for anything requiring an immediate response.

COMMENT

The consequences of e-mail content were highlighted in the Microsoft anti-trust trial, where the government used e-mails written by Microsoft executives to undermine their credibility. Statements made by executives in e-mails contradicted their public statements.

Avoid using e-mail to deliver bad news. You cannot answer questions when a person reads the e-mail.

If you receive an e-mail causing you to have a strong negative reaction, avoid responding immediately by e-mail. Use the telephone to clear up any possible misunderstanding.

Using all capital letters in an e-mail is the equivalent of SHOUTING.

When replying to an e-mail, either leave the old message as part of the new one or clearly reference your response. Do not assume the reader knows exactly what you're talking about.

Instant Messaging

Instant Messaging is one of the most popular and most interactive services on the Internet. Using an Instant Messaging program such as ICQ or mIRC, you can chat instantly with anyone anywhere in the world. Many companies find instant messaging to be a useful tool for communicating with co-workers and customers. If you are on the phone, a message can be sent that pops up instantly on your screen. But the capability to interrupt concentration—such as a ringing telephone—makes Instant Messaging very disruptive in the office. Many Instant Messaging programs won't work through a firewall and can be difficult to monitor. The use of external servers to distribute the mes-

COMMENT

According to Media Metrix, over 29 million home users and about 7 million business users use Instant Messaging.

sages can present a security issue. Information systems is responsible for developing policies and procedures for using Instant Messaging programs.

Internet Training

Training for connecting to the Internet and for using the e-mail system is provided by the information system's IT training unit. If the site does not have an IT training unit, training material is made available by the local training unit. If unavailable, the company information systems organization provides the training material.

Internet connection and e-mail system usage training is available as individualized training. The material is loaned to the user, then returned to the unit providing the material. The training provided will be in one of the following forms:

A **Tutorial.** The user will learn via a tutorial. The user—at his/her own pace and as time is available—learns how to connect to the Internet and use the e-mail system. The user is provided with a learning guide with step-by-step instructions that assumes basic knowledge of the computer's operating system. After the user has completed all items in the learning guide, he/she returns the tutorial to the training unit.

B **On-the-job training.** The on-the-job training (OJT) is provided by an experienced Internet user. The OJT instructor has a learning guide provided by the information systems organization. The IS organization provides the user with a copy of the learning guide via the instructor.

The OJT instructor follows the learning guide when working with the student. They proceed as time and the student's learning skills permit. A skill test is provided with the learning guide to ensure the student's mastery of the material.

ACCEPTABLE USE AGREEMENT

An acceptable use agreement is put in place ensuring all employees understand and agree to the company's Internet usage policies. The employee's immediate supervisor reviews the policy with the employee insuring the employee understands the seriousness of the policy.

Sample Acceptable Use Agreement

Following is a sample e-mail and Internet user agreement that is signed by all existing employees and by all new employees at orientation. The employee receives a copy, and another copy is placed in the employee's personnel file.

E-MAIL/INTERNET USER AGREEMENT

Employee Agreement:

I have received a copy of XYZ Company's E-Mail and Internet Acceptable Use Policy #_____, dated _____. I recognize and understand that the company's e-mail and Internet systems are to be used for conducting the company's business only. I understand that use of this equipment for private purposes is strictly prohibited.

As part of the XYZ organization and use of XYZ's gateway to the Internet and e-mail system, I understand that this Acceptable Use Policy applies to me. I have read the aforementioned document and agree to follow all policies and procedures that are set forth herein. I further agree to abide by the standards set in the document for the duration of my employment with XYZ Company. I understand that e-mail and Internet usage may be monitored by the company to ensure compliance with the Acceptable Use Policy.

I am aware that violations of this Acceptable Use Policy may subject me to disciplinary action, up to and including discharge from employment. I further understand that my communications on the Internet and e-mail reflect XYZ Company worldwide to our competitors, consumers, customers, and suppliers. Furthermore, I understand that this document can be amended at any time.

_____   _____
Employee's Signature   Date

_____
Employee's Printed Name

_____
Manager's Signature

USE OF APPLICATION SERVICE PROVIDERS

Application Service Provider (ASP) policy formalizes standards for how ASPs are used and managed within the organization. With the increasing shortage of skilled workers to operate systems in-house, more companies turn to ASPs to manage and maintain their system infrastructure. It is critical that the information systems group manage the selection and use of ASPs ensuring the company receives the value the ASP was hired to provide. This policy mandates the endorsement and support by the CEO/head of the organization.

Definition

An ASP is a supplier who makes applications available on a subscription basis. The ASP model works similarly to the time-sharing systems used in the 1960s and 1970s. ASPs typically provide access to the following types of applications:

❖ Supply chain management
❖ Accounting
❖ E-purchasing
❖ Human resources
❖ Recruiting
❖ E-mail
❖ Document and workflow management
❖ Customer relationship management
❖ Group scheduling
❖ Help-desk
❖ Secure collaboration communities

An ASP combines service offerings traditionally not offered by one company. The four primary ingredients are the following:

1 **Packaged software applications.** Licenses to products developed by ISVs are sold for a sizable upfront fee or on a per-use basis.

2 **Data centers and connectivity.** Data-center services are offered by hosting companies (e.g., Level3), hardware companies (e.g., IBM), and telecom providers (e.g., MCI/UUNet). Telecom and business Internet service providers (ISPs) provide connectivity.

3 **Application monitoring and ongoing support.** Firms such as AmQUEST, Digex, and Data Return typically offer application monitoring. Ongoing support is typically offered at the first level by firms such as Support Technologies. SIs or ISVs typically provide second-level support.

4 **Systems implementation and integration.** Systems integrators (SIs) or the service arms of ISVs traditionally offer these services.

The ASP is used to provide access to a single application or can be used to replace the entire user desktop.

COMMENT

Over one-third of information technology and development managers at large corporations expected to rent applications from application service providers in 2000, according to a study conducted by Evans Marketing Services (EMS).

Application Outsourcing Policies

Corporate and IS management must have a clear set of long-term goals and objectives for the outsourcing of applications. ASPs should be used:

❖ For operations difficult to manage and staff. ASPs can reduce head-count needs.

❖ To avoid hardware and software obsolescence.

❖ To improve focus on core competencies. Most companies do not include IT as part of their core competency.

❖ To supply talent and/or resources unavailable in the organization.

❖ To reduce internal operation costs.

❖ To make applications available to a mobile, distributed workforce.

❖ For their ability to scale rapidly.

❖ To make IT cost more predictable.

❖ For turnkey solutions. The role of general technology contractor shifts from the company to the ASP.

❖ To free resources for other efforts.

❖ To bring systems up and running faster. ASPs can generally deliver software to a customer more rapidly than in-house resources or an external software developer can.

The areas for which an ASP is used are budgeted annually. ASP contracts that expire within the next budget year require a new contract proposal three months before the cutoff for budget consideration. If the current ASP's performance or new proposal is not satisfactory, an RFP will be sent to no fewer than two other vendors.

ASP VENDOR SELECTION PROCESS

Selecting a vendor to provide application services requires the use of stringent evaluation procedures. Not only must the applications themselves be evaluated, but hosting facilities, bandwidth, and support capabilities must also be carefully considered. The relative newness of the ASP market and the volatility of the stock market upon which they rely for funding make the selection of the right ASP extremely important. Betting your organization's technology infrastructure on a company that may experience a sharp drop in its stock price may cause you trouble. If its stock price drops, the company may not have the money to invest in research and development, which may impact your ability to service your customers.

In addition to technical considerations, constantly reevaluate with whom you do business. Have a companywide agreement on the criteria for choosing a technology vendor. Get involved in a professional network of CTOs that you can talk to on a regular basis about technology providers' performance. Bet your infrastructure on a combination of established and newer companies. The best dot-com companies, and the ones most likely to stay in business, are those that have formed a technology and business alliance with an established company such as IBM, Microsoft, or Oracle. These more established companies have done their own evaluation of technology providers and found them credible partners. A small sample of ASPs are listed below:

ASP	Product	Web Site
eALITY	eALITY eXPress	www.eality.com
eOnline Inc.	SAP R/3	www.eonlineinc.com
Great Plains Software	eEnterprise	www.greatplains.com/hosting
Smart Online, Inc.	Small business software	www.smartonline.com
TeleComputing	Microsoft BackOffice	www.telecomputing.net
USIS	Health medical applications	www.usishealth.com

ASP Request for Proposal

When IS management is ready to receive vendor proposals, a formal request for proposal (RFP) letter is sent to all possible candidates. The RFP defines the format of the proposal ensuring that a responding vendor can be evaluated and compared easily with others. The RFP should cover the following items:

❖ Type of applications to be outsourced
❖ Minimum performance requirements and evaluation criteria

- ❖ Reliability level required
- ❖ Level of integration with other systems required
- ❖ Any required reporting capabilities
- ❖ Service volume expandability
- ❖ Vendor contact person
- ❖ IS contact person
- ❖ Vendor maintenance, training, and operation support
- ❖ Current users of the ASP's systems

This request for proposal is for an ongoing service contract, with a given time limit. The service is billed monthly at a flat rate or prorated by transaction or user volume.

All items in the contract with the ASP are negotiable. A three- to five-year contract is typical. Standard support is usually 12/5 (twelve hours a day, five days a week) with 24/7 support available at an additional cost. Systems with a small number of users are typically placed on a shared server with other customers of the ASP. Dedicated servers are available for an additional cost. The base fee per user normally covers the infrastructure at the ASP (but not the cost to connect) and any software licenses required. A fixed amount of hard-disk storage space is usually included, with 100 MB per user typical. Carefully evaluate what your users need and try to ensure as much as possible is covered in the standard agreement. As with any major purchase, add-ons can significantly add to the cost of the service.

The method by which you will connect to the ASP is also an important consideration. A dedicated frame relay connection to the ASP is the most secure and reliable, but usually more expensive than connecting over the Internet. A connection over the Internet can be much less reliable, as overall Internet traffic can impact your performance. Using a dedicated frame connection, a good rule of thumb is 10 users for a 64K line, twenty users on a 128K line, and fifty to sixty users on a full T1 connection. For the same connection over the Internet, about one-half to two-thirds as many users can be supported as on the frame connection. For each vendor selected to receive a copy of the RFP, assign an internal IS person the task of being the liaison between that vendor and the company. That person's job is to manage the communication between the vendor and the company and to encourage the vendor to provide its best response to the RFP. Encourage the vendor to put the maximum effort into its response, especially if the vendor suspects that another vendor may have an advantage. Even if another vendor is selected, any attractive items in the losing vendors' proposals can be used as negotiating points with the vendor ultimately selected.

Evaluating ASP Vendors' Proposals

All proposals received are analyzed using a predetermined set of criteria. The elements compared should be in the same sequence on each proposal. Copies are given to each evaluator, and a date and time are selected to meet and discuss them.

Vendors providing clear and complete information requested in the RFP and meeting preliminary evaluation standards are selected for more detailed analysis. Those who do not will be removed from further consideration.

The vendors' proposals should address the specification elements noted in the RFP. Clear statements should be made by the vendor to address the following items:

❖ Credentials of the firm

❖ Former and current customer references

❖ Documentation clarity and completeness

❖ User-training and implementation resources available

❖ Process to ensure data security and availability

❖ Reliability of service

❖ Scalability of service

❖ Availability of support

❖ Quality of support (credentials of staff, average length of service, etc.)

❖ Security of connection

❖ Physical security of the data center

❖ Next expected release of the software

❖ Types of reports issued detailing application access and usage statistics

❖ Management of the software upgrade process

❖ Dedicated or shared server

❖ Storage space available per user and cost

❖ Backup and redundancy resources available

❖ Customization options available, if any

Current and former customers are contacted to discuss their experiences with the vendor. The following questions are helpful for obtaining useful information:

1 Would you use the same vendor again? If so, why? What has been the major problem with the vendor? Do you know other users of the vendor's product? Are they generally happy? If so, why? Who are the other users? What are their names and telephone numbers?

2   How long does it take for the vendor to respond to problems? Are the people who respond knowledgeable and friendly? Has the vendor ever lied? Has the vendor had the resources to resolve your problem(s)?

3   Does the application satisfy your needs? Follow up with questions about how long they have had the system and how often it has gone down. Ask about its expendability and upgrading possibilities.

4   Do the users like the service? Ask to talk to users and confirm this. Ask users what they liked and disliked about the service and why.

5   Ask how long it took to put the application into operation. Did they receive adequate training? Are the user manuals easy to understand and follow?

6   Is the service provided better than they could do themselves, and why? Is the service worth the cost?

7   Were there any unexpected or hidden costs? What was the nature of these costs? Were the costs reasonable? Was the vendor confronted about this? If so, what was the reaction?

8   Were the vendor's employees easy to work with? Did their salesperson follow up after the sale was made? Does the vendor seem to have a genuine interest in the success of the service?

9   If you were starting all over, what would you do differently?

COMMENT

A recent report from Deloitte Consulting estimates the entire United States market for ASPs, Web hosting, and application outsourcing at close to $10 billion. It is projected to grow to more than $50 billion by 2003.

ASP VENDOR MANAGEMENT

Managing a long-term ASP project is not an easy task. Some of the reasons for difficulty include:

❖   Pricing and service levels established at the beginning of the contract do not contain meaningful methods for measurement and improvement of service.

❖ Expectations and assumptions of both parties change over time. Most contracts cannot anticipate changes in technology, personnel, business processes, etc.

❖ Cultural differences between the two companies can cause misunderstandings and mistrust.

❖ Differences in the goals and objectives of the two companies can cause problems.

❖ Lack of management oversight may cause priorities to become out of sync with the reasons for entering into the contract in the first place.

Service Level Agreement

Information services and affected business units must work together to determine the service level requirements for the applications that are outsourced to the ASP. These service levels are determined at the outset of the agreement, and used to measure and monitor the supplier's performance. The service levels are written in a contract called a Service Level Agreement (SLA). The SLA defines the consequences for failing to meet one or more service levels.

The SLA should include the following sections:

❖ A precise definition of key terms.

❖ Specific service levels for all key categories (system availability, help-desk responsiveness, security administration, change management, etc.).

❖ Frequency of service level measurement (usually monthly).

❖ Weighting by importance of key service levels.

❖ Calculation of credits for missing service levels.

❖ Calculation of credits for frequency of missing service levels. Increased frequency of missed service levels might increase the service credit by some predetermined factor. The performance factors specified in the SLA not only provide an objective measure of the vendor's performance, but can serve as a basis for termination of the service if threshold service levels cannot be met. Other "non-key" performance levels can be specified to add to the case for termination if warranted.

Typical credit for failure to meet routine service levels ranges from 5 to 15 percent, with penalties for severe service failures reaching 20 to 25 percent. *Force majeure* clauses excuse a party's failure to perform if the failure resulted from an act of nature such as an earthquake or other natural disaster beyond the party's control. The ASP vendor will attempt to include as much as possible in this category; define it as narrowly as possible. Under no circumstances should a *force majeure* absolve the vendor completely from its responsibilities.

The SLA might also include provisions for rewarding the vendor for extra value-added services provided. Make sure these services will really add value before agreeing to payment.

Negotiating and designing an SLA is difficult and time consuming, but a fair and comprehensive SLA is critical for a successful ASP relationship. During the negotiation, both parties learn a lot about how their future partner approaches various aspects of their relationship.

18

END-USER IT DEVELOPMENT

END-USER IT DEVELOPMENT POLICY

End-user IS development policy focuses on autonomous individual and work group operations. However, this autonomy does not allow disregarding normal industry development practices. End-users who manage their own IT resources are expected to follow the policies and procedures as recorded in this instrument.

End-user development has a liaison relationship with corporate IS if no other relationship is defined, which provides information and guidelines used to develop its systems. These guidelines are established to avoid corporate lawsuits and public embarrassment on the part of end-user system development.

COMMENT

Every day more tools become available for end-users to develop their own custom applications. Tools from Microsoft are especially popular; FrontPage allows users to create their own Web pages; Access is used to create database applications; and even Word can interface with backend systems using Smart Tags to create custom applications.

End-user management is fully responsible for any employees not abiding by the information and guidelines provided by corporate information systems. Repercussions resulting from noncompliance will be dealt with accordingly. The procedures offered here apply only to information and guidelines for end-user IS development.

END-USER IS PROJECT DEVELOPMENT

End-user IS project development focuses on individual and work group operations. These activities can cover the following:

❖ Analyze end-user requirements.

❖ Analyze end-user workflows.

❖ Evaluate turnkey systems.

❖ Develop user applications from available software packages.

❖ Write user application programs using sanctioned software.

❖ Conduct feasibility studies.

❖ Conduct procedure analysis.

❖ Perform end-user systems design.

❖ Implement end-user systems.

Project development will include the following phases of project methodology:

❖ Identify a problem.

❖ Define the scope of the problem.

❖ Conduct a feasibility study.

❖ Assess the results of the feasibility study.

❖ Conduct a procedure analysis.

❖ Analyze the procedure.

❖ Select or develop the solution.

❖ Implement the solution.

❖ Evaluate the results.

❖ Document the operation for further implementation.

End-user IS Project Team

The concept of a project team has long been used by corporate IS which has involved users in a largely secondary role, if any. The end-user IS project team does not require corporate IS, but, depending on need, may request corporate IS systems' assistance. The relationship of corporate IS and end-user project efforts depends more on their individual cultures than on technology.

The end-user IS project team is mostly representative of a single area of the company which, whether it be a division, department, or section, has user management with a vested interest in the project. This interest is more than budgetary. The project team members are mostly from this same area of the company.

The team is formed to resolve problems identified within its own area. End-user management appoints a project leader, who is informed about the scope of the problem, and requests a feasibility study.

The project leader conducts a feasibility study on his/her own. If assistance is required, it may be drawn from the area being studied. After the feasibility study results are assessed and accepted by user management, the project undertaking starts. The selection of the end-user IS project team is up to the project leader. All members of the project team, including the leader, continue the duties of their primary jobs.

The job profile of the team members varies with the needs of the project. The following are possible team member titles and the respective skills required:

A Project leader

1 Maturity. The person must be recognized for his/her maturity in handling political situations.

2 Administrator. The person must be able to routinely perform day-to-day part-time administrative activities, such as reporting, requisitioning, memo writing, etc. This includes the ability to set and follow schedules, meet deadlines, and handle resources and any budgets. A proactive administrator is more desirable than a reactive administrator.

3 IT skills. The project leader must have the technical skill to gain the respect of the user staff and management.

4 Company knowledge. The person should know the formal organization chart, but more important must understand the informal organization to help the project progress smoothly.

5 Delegator. The person must delegate and recognize that when a project team member is successful, that member gets all the credit. When the member fails, the project leader shares this failure.

6 Communicator. The project leader keeps the project team, management, and others with vested interests in the project well informed. This includes informal day-to-day oral communication, written communication, formal presentations, teaching, and chairing meetings.

7 Innovator. The project leader is not limited to traditional solutions. He/she must be innovative and encourage others to be the same.

8 Leader. The project team must be able to lead through the most trying times. The leader must be able to work under pressure, remain calm, keep the project objective in focus, and still be sensitive to the team and others.

9 Maintain two jobs. The leader still has the responsibility of another job. The other position may be related to the users' IS operation or not.

B Project team members. These people must possess skills needed for the project to be successful. They are available part-time for the duration of the project, but still retain their other primary responsibilities. The people could have the following project titles:

❖ Programmer (Visual Basic, SASS, etc.)

❖ Project librarian

❖ Project secretary

❖ Forms designer

❖ Data entry operator

❖ Corporate IS personnel on loan

These personnel can be loaned for the user project for given time limits. They can act as consultants and/or project workers. They have talents normally not found in an end-user operation.

❖ Systems analysts

❖ Systems and procedure analysts

❖ Analyst programmers

❖ Forms designers

❖ Database designers

❖ Senior programmers

❖ Network specialists

End-user IS Project Formulation

After people have been selected by the project leader and approved by management, they meet to formalize and plan the project. The leader assigns tasks and develops a schedule with the team.

To complete an end-user project requires various skills and knowledge. At times the project may require the assistance of the corporate IS systems department which may be free or charged back to the user's budget. Tasks involved can be to:

- ❖ Utilize project management software packages.
- ❖ Perform feasibility studies.
- ❖ Document data flows and procedures.
- ❖ Design data collection tools.
- ❖ Conduct analysis interviews.
- ❖ Perform observations of current operations.
- ❖ Perform statistical analyses.
- ❖ Perform cost-benefit analyses.
- ❖ Design software application programs.
- ❖ Conduct software package evaluations.
- ❖ Write application programs.
- ❖ Design operator-supporting materials.
- ❖ Sell users on the merits of alternative systems.
- ❖ Train users for the operation of systems.

The project planning and formalizing effort will:

- ❖ Determine the project scope and tasks.
- ❖ Confirm the team has the skills needed.
- ❖ Confirm that members have time for their duties.
- ❖ Determine what kind of assistance is needed from corporate IS and how much.
- ❖ Finalize planning tasks.
- ❖ Reassess member talent and required time available.
- ❖ Assign specific project tasks.
- ❖ Assign vendor contact person.

SYSTEM DOCUMENTATION

It is essential to understand the current system employed in the user's area before a new system can be devised to replace it. The current system must be completely documented.

This documentation requires the analyst to make personal contact with user operational personnel, giving him/her an opportunity to develop a rapport and establish a relationship based on trust with the current operators of the system. This is necessary to insure positive attitudes toward the pending new system. In addition, the higher the level of cooperation, the better the data collected will be.

Current system documentation activities should include the following:

- ❖ Define documentation scope.
- ❖ Study current published procedure.
- ❖ Study actual process.
- ❖ Document actual procedure.
- ❖ Confirm documentation.
- ❖ Redefine scope.
- ❖ Complete documentation of analysis.

Current System Documentation

Before any effort is expended on the development of an end-user system, a thorough understanding of the current system and a required needs analysis are prerequisites. This study helps avoid repeating the mistakes of the past.

- ❖ **Define documentation scope.** The boundaries of any proposed system are defined before any effort is spent to delineate the scope of the operational activities utilized by the end-user information system.

  The scope of an end-user information system seldom extends beyond the boundaries of any one department or area of operation. Information collected for the defined area of scope may reveal what is expected is not possible. The scope of the study often shifts, expands, or even contracts from its original definition.

  It is important to identify key employees involved in the analysis. It is also important to reveal the critical operations and their priorities. Interpersonal, political, and microculture elements can alter the project scope. Deal with these carefully because the project requires the collaboration of all involved people to be successful.

- ❖ **Study current published procedures.** The formal, published procedures are studied before examining the actual procedures to provide information about those originally developed. Later, when studying the actual procedures, investigate deviations.

  Read existing documentation with a general overview. This includes looking at organizational charts, annual reports, mission statements, former budgets, and the policies and procedures manual.

As the study becomes more involved, more specific aspects of the current operation are examined, including such items as any former procedure analyses, cost studies, systems planning information, current forms and personnel staffing reports. The person doing this study will want to have his/her own file, so some documents will need to be copied.

❖ **Study actual process.** To understand the actual current process, follow the actual procedure through from beginning to end. This investigation also covers the unstructured processes of the area under study. When a change from the prescribed procedure is discovered, note the reason for it. If there is no formal documentation of these processes, the analyst doing the study has to record these findings in the project report and complete the needed documentation.

❖ **Document actual procedure.** The collected information is documented in the form of flowcharts, forms, and written information. The actual procedure information is collected in the form of worker interviews, observations, work sampling, and questionnaires.

❖ **Confirm documentation.** The analyst verifies the flowcharted procedures; while doing so he/she notes any problems because of user management preferences, worker attitudes and the department's culture. The political and social environments as well as worker personalities are critical to the development of the end-user system.

❖ **Redefine scope.** After collecting all the data, redefine the scope of the project if necessary. This information is then presented to the highest level of management within the department or division, i.e., the person responsible for the project approval and budget. This person has the final responsibility for the scope, which can change during the course of the project.

❖ **Complete documentation of analysis.** Completing the documentation and assembling it for the feasibility study shortens the project delivery date.

Information Collecting Techniques

Information is collected when a system is reengineered or created. The proposed operation may be a simple, short procedure or a complex end-user system application. But, whatever the end project, information is required for its design.

Members of the project team or IS personnel are responsible for gathering this information. There are techniques available making it possible to obtain the most current information needed to design an end-user system.

A **Document review.** Collect printed materials utilized to operate a manual or computer system. Analyze them to provide as much information as possible about the operation: cost, job requirements, and detailed process information. The documents are grouped by type:

1 General documents

- ❖ Organization charts
- ❖ Annual reports
- ❖ Department budgets
- ❖ Policy manual
- ❖ Job descriptions

2 Procedure operations

- ❖ Procedural manuals
- ❖ Process flowcharts
- ❖ Former procedure studies
- ❖ Work measurement studies
- ❖ Work sampling studies
- ❖ Internal and external forms

B **Current computer system**

- ❖ System flowcharts
- ❖ Dataflow diagrams
- ❖ Document flowcharts
- ❖ Data dictionary
- ❖ Programming flowcharts
- ❖ Monitor displays
- ❖ Operation logs
- ❖ Operation manuals

C **Operational personnel interviews.** Conduct interviews in the same manner as presented in Chapter 3, sections "Information Gathering Interviews" and "Document the Interviews."

D **Work sampling studies.** Work sampling is covered in Chapter 3.

E **Current operating costs.** Collect cost information for the operating department including cost per measurable unit of output. Break down cost information as follows:

1 **Direct labor cost.** This includes direct labor for the operating department, including per-unit cost (the cost of processing one unit through the operation). Examples would be the cost per purchase order processed, or the cost to complete a customer order. Costs will also note employee benefit expense.

2 **Indirect labor cost.** This includes management, training, support, and corporate prorated indirect cost. Compute the cost for the operating department. Compute per-unit indirect labor cost.

3 **Direct material cost.** This is the direct material cost per unit processed.

4 **Indirect material cost.** This the cost of supply items:
   ❖ Paper clips
   ❖ Paper
   ❖ Printer toner and ribbons
   ❖ Expensed work aids
   ❖ Expensed computer software
   ❖ Computer disks
   ❖ Other general expensed office items

   Indirect material cost is reported as the total cost and also prorated to show the per-unit cost of output.

5 **Space cost.** This is the standard charge per square foot for the department's office space and utilities. This is reported as the total cost and also as the prorated per-unit cost of output.

6 **Capital depreciation cost.** This is the annual capital depreciation cost to the department and the prorated per-unit cost of output.

7 **Other costs.** This includes all costs not already covered. (Examples are employee bonding costs, software and hardware leased, etc.) This is reported as the total unit cost and also as the prorated per-unit cost of output.

F **Data dictionary.** If there is an existing computer system in place, the data dictionary is brought up-to-date.

END-USER IS FEASIBILITY STUDY

The end-user IS feasibility study is conducted to determine the feasibility of proceeding with the innovation considered for the end-user work group or stand-alone computer system. The information collected by the end-user project team is a major input to this analysis.

To justify a new end-user system, it must satisfy three feasibility requirements:

A **Economic feasibility.** Economic feasibility analysis determines if the solution meets measurements of cost effectiveness. This is justified on the basis of cost/benefit analyses.

B **Technical feasibility.** Technical feasibility analysis determines if the solution is technically practical: Is the technology available and can the end-user and the facilities accommodate the solution?

C **Operational feasibility.** Operational feasibility analysis determines if the solution meets end-user requirements: Does the solution fit into the end-user operational environment and meet the requirements of an acceptable time schedule? It also ascertains if human factor requirements will be met for the users, and if it fits into the social work scene.

End-user Feasibility Study File

When starting the feasibility study, a feasibility file folder is labeled with the title of the study and will accumulate the following:

❖ An accumulated table of contents
❖ All memos related to the study
❖ E-mail documentation
❖ Vendor correspondence
❖ Vendor literature
❖ Accumulated costs data for the feasibility study
❖ A log listing the calendar days and hours worked on the feasibility study
❖ Documentation of all meetings
❖ A telephone log regarding all phone calls made and attempted
❖ A copy of the final report

Feasibility Study Report Requirements

Format the feasibility study report in the following manner:

❖ Cover page, containing project title, author, and date
❖ Overview of the request
❖ Rationale for initiating the information systems project, or for changing an existing system
❖ The body of the final report providing the details of the project

❖ Exhibits

❖ Summary, containing recommendations, estimated costs, estimated calendar time needed, and estimated man-hours of all persons involved in the project

Economic Feasibility Analysis

The economic feasibility analysis determines if the solution can be justified on the basis of cost and benefits studied separately—if possible, by two different people—then compared. The decision is affected by this cost-benefit analysis that looks at the payback calculations.

A **Cost identification.** Costs are classified as:

1 **Development costs.** There are one-time costs incurred while the system is being developed. Personnel time, including fringe benefits, is stated in dollars. Development costs can contain:

❖ Personnel costs

❖ Hardware purchased

❖ Software development or purchase

❖ Document preparation

❖ Site preparation

❖ Furniture and fixtures

❖ End-user training costs

2 **Operating costs.** Operating costs are ongoing costs incurred while the system is in operation.

❖ Operation personnel costs, plus benefits

❖ Lease of hardware and software

❖ Consumable supplies

❖ Communication expense

❖ Ongoing hardware and software upgrades and maintenance

❖ Ongoing training

3 **Variable costs.** These are costs based on production volume and include costs for such items as:

❖ Supplies based on the workload

❖ Telephone and WAN line charges

❖ Utilities used

❖ Maintenance costs

❖ Overtime costs

4 Intangible costs. Intangible costs are those not easily converted into a dollar value. These come in many forms; some examples are:

❖ Customer dissatisfaction

❖ Time lost for learning new system

❖ Learning errors incurred

❖ Duties expanded due to creeping enlargement of scope

B Benefit identification. Benefits for end-user information systems come in various forms and must be totaled for a complete cost/benefit analysis. They can be classified as:

1 Tangible benefits

❖ Personnel dollars saved

❖ Intangible benefits

❖ Morale improvement

COMMENT

There is often a misconception about computing personnel dollars saved. One might think if a new software package saves each company secretary one hour a week of work, then the forty secretaries the company has will provide a savings equal to one secretary. Wrong!

The company will most likely keep all forty secretaries and the cost will still be the same; therefore, no direct savings. However, if the secretaries are paid for overtime work, and overtime can be reduced, this can be credited as a savings.

2 Cost-displacement benefits. Cost-displacement benefits occur when the end-user information system provides for more efficient task performance. This, in effect, makes the end-user more productive by saving time or money.

An example is the use of a spreadsheet software package in the Cost Accounting department. If enough of these cost-displacement benefits assist the department, one or more cost accountants could be eliminated. Or, if a person left the department, he/she would not have to be replaced.

3   **Value-added benefits.** These benefits occur when the end-user increases his/her effectiveness. Value-added benefits are long-term results based on short-term operation costs. One example is when operation cost remains the same but customer billing is increased. Cost of new technology subtracted from benefits over time can produce a dollar savings. This technology also attracts new business because of the organization's enhanced status. Value-added benefits are often realized with professional and managerial personnel. A good example is the laptop computers (short-term cost) used by attorneys in courtrooms (long-term results: elimination of time to transcribe notes, among others).

Value-added benefits can be obtained by:

❖   Providing more time for reviewing designs, proposals, or alternatives

❖   Reducing the calendar time needed for designs, analysis, research, or planning

❖   Reducing effort required for administrative duties

❖   Permitting more opportunities for professional collaboration among colleagues in workgroup efforts

C   **Cost/benefit analysis.** After the total costs and benefits are computed and verified, begin the cost-benefit analysis. Utilize one or more of the many techniques available to do this.

Because of the short life spans of hardware and software, don't use lengthy payback periods. A timeframe of three to five years is still reasonable. Whichever cost-benefit technique is employed, the analysis should be unbiased. The payback time should not be extended simply to justify the need, because maintenance costs can grow exponentially.

1   **Payback analysis.** Payback analysis or cost/benefit comparison helps determine the time it will take for the proposed system to pay off the cost of developing and installing the new system. To compute the number of years necessary to recover costs:

❖   Compute dollar total of expected benefits.

❖   Compute dollar total of expected operation costs.

❖   Subtract expected operating costs from expected dollar benefits.

❖   Divide total development costs by average net annual expected benefit.

This gives the number of years or payback period expected to recover this cost. The expected recovery cost is a one-time cost for the system development.

2 **Operational benefits.** This is the estimated cost savings accrued during routine administrative operations of the proposed system.

3 **Time-valued payback.** Time-valued payback is the discount rate found in a present value table, which represents anticipated interest earning, inflation depreciation, etc., over a given time. An up-to-date present value table is essential to find the factor needed to determine the time-valued payback. The longer the payback, the less the return on investment because the dollar's buying power becomes deflated because of interest revenue lost.

4 **Net present value.** Knowing the net present value allows the analyst to compute the time value of money and compare different investment opportunities that may have different costs, discount rates, and benefits.

Determine the costs and benefits for each given year of the system's life span. The yearly adjusted costs and benefits are compared to the current dollar value of the investment. Compare these figures with the adjusted costs and benefits to arrive at a final new present value, which can be positive or negative. A positive net present value indicates that the return exceeds the comparison rate, while a negative indicates that the proposed project return is less than the value of a comparative investment. A zero net present value indicates that either investment would yield the same.

Technical Feasibility

The technical feasibility of the proposed solution is the practicality of its adapting to the technology available. The technology can seldom, if ever, be altered for the sole convenience of the solution. This study must address all five of the following items:

A **Availability of technology.** Information technology expands at a rapid rate. Many technical obstacles existing a few years ago have now been overcome. If a technology problem does exist, shelve the proposal for a while until the technology is further developed.

The technology needed to make a proposed innovation feasible may be waiting in the wings of the current stage production. By working with an informal information network and developing a good vendor relationship, a member of the end-user project may discover this knowledge. This is one of the reasons some organizations use to justify becoming a Beta site.

Both hardware and software are upgraded frequently, bringing new technology to the market daily. The project leader should follow these developments closely.

B   **Practicality.** The hardware and software technology needed to implement the proposed project may be available, but it must also be practical. Many questions must be asked:

- ❖   Is it affordable?
- ❖   Will the vendor be in business next year?
- ❖   Can the item be modified?
- ❖   Has the item been proven over time?
- ❖   What is its track record with users?
- ❖   Is the source code available?
- ❖   What about vendor support and documentation?

C   **Availability of technical skills.** The necessary end-user talent must also be available. If there is no in-house talent, the training cost and/or time required may or may not be justifiable. Outside assistance may or may not be practical.

D   **Project delivery schedule.** The project delivery schedule must be practical. When working back from a required finish date, the start date might have already passed. Or the vendor's promised delivery date might be too late to utilize the technology when needed.

E   **Obsolescence problem.** It is important to make certain, if possible, that the proposed process performs as desired. Deliverable technology can become obsolete before the system is installed or too soon after installation. If so, the payback time might not be completed because of this obsolescence.

Hardware manufacturers no longer stock replacement parts because of shortening product life cycles. Some supply items might also no longer be available.

Operational Feasibility

Operational feasibility analysis determines if end-user IS requirements are feasible. These operational concerns cover the end-user's individual and group process and political needs. The proposed system or innovation needs to satisfy these requirements.

A **Is the problem worth correcting?** Will the new innovation be worth the effort for correcting the problem?

COMMENT

A large Midwest teaching hospital installed an online laboratory information system. One of the supposed benefits was having the billing information downloaded to the business computer, thereby reducing billing time and data entry cost. However, laboratory technicians and medical doctors were entering the data. This resulted in a higher error rate than before, as well as lost time for key personnel.

B **What is the users' attitude?** The management is sold the new system and approves its creation, but the users are the ones operating it. Because the new end-user system affects their daily work efforts and relationships and their traditional ways of working, gaining users' acceptance can become a challenge.

Introducing new technology or a new system can create outright resistance, hostility, and even worker sabotage. This may be because it lowers a worker's importance within a group, diminishing the power and status that the former job provided. End-user work groups may lose their power, status, and credibility within the company.

This attitude can destroy a new system. The problem can be noticed during the interviewing phase of the systems analysis. Blind work group questionnaires are also informative. Once attitudes surface, make plans to alter them. Some suggestions are:

- ❖ Have user management show strong visible support.
- ❖ Provide end-user education.
- ❖ Encourage end-user design involvement.
- ❖ Reevaluate worker job descriptions, presenting more opportunities.
- ❖ Provide new worker status symbols.
- ❖ Upgrade job titles.
- ❖ Present the total picture to workers.

❖ Inform them of their new job responsibilities and the increased status, as well as value to the company, that the jobs will give them.

❖ Improve worker environment.

❖ Have an open house to show off the new system.

❖ Provide news coverage about the workers and their new system in the company newspaper.

To be effective, it is recommended that two or more of these suggestions be followed.

C **What is the political environment?** A stable political environment provides a better opportunity base for end-user IS development than one in transition or volatile. One major advantage of end-user IS development over corporate IS development is end-user developers have a far better understanding of user political problems.

If there are political problems between departments, having two independent end-user IS operations may make more sense than a corporate-sponsored integrated system involving both. Corporate IS should stay clear of warring departments.

D **Are there end-user skill problems?** There can be end-user skill level problems. Senior management personnel cannot always be expected to have keyboard skills. Workers who traditionally operated at lower-level clerical positions can be intimidated by a computer system. The terminology, the mystique, and the lack of skills can present a challenge to any group of workers.

Meet this challenge by providing hands-on opportunity for all personnel to play with the computer. They can begin by playing simple games. There is far less apprehension when a user can beat the computer in a game.

The next step is presenting a slowly paced training program, beginning in formal classes and proceeding to self-paced program learning, with tutorials last. A trainer should be available to work closely with these people. Some may not master the skills needed as fast as desired, but a skills handicap is like a physical handicap in that provisions must be made to circumvent it. Once these people master the needed skills, they generally become dedicated employees.

END-USER PROCEDURE ANALYSIS

After the feasibility study has been completed, end-user management must make a decision. The choices are:

❖   Abandon the project.

❖   Proceed with the installation (less complex undertakings or prototypes).

❖   Proceed with procedure analysis and systems design.

This section is concerned with the third possible decision: end-user procedure analysis. When designing a new system, the proposed output should
be the same as the old system or better, incorporating features that the current system does not provide. To deliver the desired new system, the elements
of the current system must be analyzed in detail.

Simple projects that do not have involved elements do not require a procedure analysis to begin. More complex projects, however, will utilize a prototype operation to expedite the process and correct any systems problems
during the shakedown operation.

Detail Process Documentation

The process is studied in detail from the input point to the finalization of the
process within the scope of the project. For a current manual operation a
detailed Procedure Flowchart is drawn of the process elements. See the
"Procedure Flowchart" section on page 40 in Chapter 2 for the process. For a
current computer operation, a dataflow diagram is drawn down to the lowest
detail level to show the process elements. See the "Dataflow Diagrams" section on page 42 for the process.

Drawn flowcharts are examined by the employees performing each task
to confirm their authenticity and are examined by all operational people
involved. Data information held in files should also be confirmed.

Procedure Data Analysis

The procedure data analysis covers current user opinions, operating costs,
operations, and the actual procedures that drive the present system. While
the end-user's opinions may be subjective, other collected data is objective
and correct but might not be totally representative.

Take care to insure that enough information is available when analyzing
the collected data.

A Value of current operation. Address the effective points of the
current operation. How well does it actually perform?

❖   Does it satisfy current end-user management?

❖   Are the costs within reason?

❖   How well does it meet output needs?

COMMENT

For one particular system, the data collected noted a weekly volume of 720 units processed. So the new system was designed to handle 750 units per week. After the system was operational, it was discovered that of the average 720 units processed in a week, 303 had to be processed on Mondays. The system could handle only 125 a day (750/5 days). The information collected was correct, but was not all the information needed.

B **Cause of problems**
- ❖ What are the causes of the problems?
- ❖ Can the problems be corrected in a new system?

C **Achievability of project goals**
- ❖ Will the proposed technology achieve the goals?
- ❖ Can goals be reached within the cost estimated?

D **Enhancement opportunities.** How can the proposed system best add benefits to the present operation? These benefits will often be items that are not considered by current end-users and their management. In fact, enhancements may be a byproduct of the proposed technology.

Recording Analysis Information

The information collected is recorded and placed in the project folder for future reference. A copy is given to each project member and the project-sponsoring management.

It will be documented in the following format:

A **Title page.** This contains the project name, date, and project team members with their project and normal work titles.

B **Summary introduction.** This is a one-page introduction and project summary report. It should note the end-user IS project objectives.

C **Body of report.** This will contain the detailed information collected and the analyzed results. Unfamiliar terms will be defined.

D Appendices

- ❖ Sample of forms collected
- ❖ Vendor literature
- ❖ Flowcharts
- ❖ Sample of any questionnaires used
- ❖ Sample of any work sampling forms used

If the report reveals any major items of concern, an information meeting is held with end-user management and all members of the project team. The project leader delivers an oral presentation covering the report and any concerns.

In preparing for the meeting, the project leader should:

- ❖ Obtain a room.
- ❖ Send meeting notices, choosing the time based on management availability.
- ❖ Prepare a presentation outline.
- ❖ Prepare visual aids. (See "Presentation Devices" in Chapter 14 on page 351.)
- ❖ Rehearse the presentation in the room provided.
- ❖ Confirm that all invited management will attend.

After the meeting, resolve the issues discussed. Send out memos to this effect. If required, schedule a follow-up meeting.

END-USER IS DESIGN

After the detailed analysis is completed and no problems remain, the end-user IS project team may start the design phase. The designers do not have total freedom for synthesizing an optimal design. One or more factors beyond their control may influence the final design:

- ❖ Inflexibility of off-the-shelf software
- ❖ No source code available for purchased software
- ❖ Corporate policy constants
- ❖ End-user political problems
- ❖ Corporate IS's end-user policy
- ❖ Budget reduction for proposed system

The design process begins after identifying the design scope and constants. One of the major design constraints is the software driving the proposed system. The required software will come in one of the following forms:

❖ Off-the-shelf software

❖ Purchased software, object code only

❖ Purchased software, object and source code

❖ Program(s) to be written

Know this information before the end-user IS design starts. The design tasks follow a given sequence as indicated.

Design Phase

Begin the design process with a general design overview. The general design evolves through successive iterations into a detail design level suitable for being turned into computer program instructions and/or manual procedure operations.

A **General logical system design.** The general logical design concentrates on content components and the data-handling operation of the system without regard to hardware or software needs. The logical concept is first drawn at the context level of a dataflow diagram. (See "Dataflow Diagram" on page 42 in Chapter 2.)

B **General physical system design.** This next step includes the instruments needed to perform the tasks. Dataflow diagram, level zero, is utilized. Hardware, software, and people needs of the evolving system come into consideration at this level.

C **Detail operation design.** This next level uses level one of the dataflow diagram. It defines which procedures will be followed by end-user operational personnel and which program modules will be required.

D **Program design level.** Construct the monitor screen displays at this level. Format output documents. Use the same illustrations as required for the Input-Output Prototype. (See the "Types of Prototyping Methods" section in Chapter 3 on page 80.)

This prototype does not have an operating program. The program design level also has no coded programs but has the detailed information needed to write them. At this level the monitor screen displays and output forms can receive final approval or be altered so that the next step, program implementation, can be started.

E **System programming.** Complete the programming tasks at this level. This can consist of a written program or a purchased program with the source coding provided. Do whatever customizing is necessary and possible with off-the-shelf software. All program documentation is completed and placed in a program project folder.

Human Factor Considerations

Much has been written about human factor problems in end-user application systems. These problems are valid and occur when the system designers do not take human needs into consideration. One major concern is that all people do not have the same size, weight, or environmental requirements.

A **Workstation ergonomics.** Adding a keyboard to the standard desk height, which is higher than a typing table, can cause problems. To be ergonomically correct (most comfortable for a user) the keyboard should rest on an adjustable tabletop. The tabletop should be movable to place the keyboard keys from about 25 to 32 inches from the floor.

The chair is the most important item of furniture at the workstation. The chair seat should adjust from about 15 to 21 inches from the floor. The backrest should also adjust both up and down, and back and forward. The seat width and depth should be available in more than one size. Four or more casters support the chair.

The monitor has an adjustable support so that the viewing screen can be set horizontal to the eye height. The light display should be adjustable for both output and contrast.

The desk or workstation provides enough top space to spread out items needed to work and store them. There is a lockable area for personal items.

B **Office area.** The general office area is clean and neat. There are sufficient electric outlets because computer outlets are not shared with other electrical items. Power surge protectors and a UPS may be considered, too.

Lighting is important when working all day at a workstation. The ambient light is a fluorescent or indirect tungsten bulb. Window light can be a problem if the light does not come from the north. To reduce glare, windows not facing north should be to the left or right of the user at a monitor screen.

With laser and inkjet printers, office noise is less of a problem today than previously. Use drapes and other noise-control devices to reduce or mask noise if it is present.

C **Monitor screen display.** It is still more difficult to read a monitor screen than a newspaper, and laptop computers are even worse. Better and bigger monitors reducing some of the problems are appearing on the market.

However, screen glare and reflection from current monitors results in discomfort and eyestrain. There is also a tendency for screens to be clearer in the middle than at the margins. Screen image sharpness leaves something to be desired. Contrast can be adjusted and a selection of three or four colored monitor screen covers may provide a solution for this.

D **Keyboard.** There are increasing numbers of different keyboards appearing on the market. There are also a number using ergonomic-related design. More laptop keyboards provide for wrist rests and have built-in pointing devices.

E **Screen output display.** Screens, as well as input documents and output hardcopy, require ergonomic considerations. People in the U.S. still read from left to right and top to bottom, whether it be hardcopy or screen displays.

When designing the screen display, keep the following in mind:

❖ Avoid red and black combinations because of the number of colorblind people who cannot see red as a distinct color.

❖ Know the users and their needs.

❖ Keep instructions for use simple.

❖ Optimize operations, using touch-screen menus, pointers, etc.

❖ Keep screen commands simple.

❖ Be consistent with all systems.

❖ Place most often used items on the screen at the top left side.

Project Completion and Acceptance

After the design effort has been completed, the project should be wrapped up with the following:

A **Documentation.** The design and operation documentation is completed. The operator's instruction manual is completed and tested by a random selection of no less than 20 percent of the operating personnel. The documentation of the detail system design and programming are accurate and complete, presenting no problems with maintenance later.

B **Training.** Training is provided to all operations personnel. Independent learning instructions are provided to new employees.

Provisions are in place for independent learning of later modifications to the system.

C **End-user management presentation.** The completed end-user IS design is presented to end-user management for final acceptance and support before implementation.

D **End-user operations presentation.** This is a presentation for all end-users. Encourage end-user management to be present to give its support to the new system.

1 **Introduction.** The senior end-user manager makes the introduction, explaining why the project was started. He/she makes it clear that end-user management wanted and supported the project and its objective from the beginning.

2 **General overview of the system.** The project leader introduces all the project team members. He/she gives a general overview of the system and its benefits.

The following will be stressed during the presentation:

❖ It is the end-users' system.

❖ There was a need for it.

❖ It will be better for all concerned if everyone provides 100 percent support for the implementation and operation of the system.

❖ There can be problems expected with any new system, but the project team will be there to help. Users should not be afraid to ask questions or ask for help. There is a need also to learn the operation manual.

3 **Close of the presentation.** Just before the meeting ends, open it to questions.

EXTERNAL END-USER ASSISTANCE

External assistance can be available either from within or outside the company. Depending on corporate policy, the corporate IS organization can freely provide this service or it can be charged back to the requesting department. If not charged back and the corporate IS organization is capable of giving assistance in the timeframe needed, utilize its services. If there is a charge, obtain a cost estimate.

If the corporate IS department is unable to supply the needed service, cannot within an acceptable timeframe, or does not have the expertise required, issue outside service bids. If the IS service is billable and available, outside bids should be issued to determine the least expensive source.

The service from an outside source can be consulting or contract services. See Chapter 15, *Vendors: Getting the Goods,* for policies and procedures.

Software Vendors

With the growth of end-user IS software, vendors are encouraged to market vertical software produced for a restricted market of common users. An example would be Solomon Software of Findlay, Ohio, which produces and markets accounting software limited to accounting end-users. Vertical market software is found for the following areas (among others):

- Accounting
- Human resource management
- Car body repair shops
- Manufacturing
- Purchasing
- Engineering
- Construction

- Billing
- Scheduling
- Publications
- Drafting
- Statistical analysis
- Photography

Another kind of software for general end-user applications is horizontal software. Horizontal software are applications used widely throughout companies. The three common types are word processing, spreadsheet, and database applications. This software has a supplemental use by many company end-users, but often has a primary use within some departments. Examples would be word processing for the administrative staff and spreadsheets for the cost-estimating department.

Demand for off-the-shelf software increases as more PCs are used. More vendors develop end-user software and provide services, such as both free and billable help-desk assistance, for their customers.

One of the best sources of vertical software vendors is professional publications where many ads target end-user applications. Horizontal software ads appear primarily in computer literature; however, they also appear in publications ranging from the daily *Wall Street Journal* to the weekly *US News and World Report.*

Vendor Assistance

Because end-user computing is found in a variety of user areas, assistance for such end-users is often beyond the resources of the corporate IS department. However, it can be found in the vendor market.

A **Full-service consulting vendors.** These are nationwide firms providing a wide array of consulting services for the end-user IS project.

B **Specialty end-user vendors.** These are consultants or service providers with the skills for given areas of end-user applications.

C **Contract vendors.** These vendors provide services across such different end-user applications as:

- ❖ Contract programming
- ❖ Networking
- ❖ Database
- ❖ Client/server

D **Turnkey vendors.** These vendors provide the total system package, which may contain the following:

- ❖ Hardware
- ❖ All the software
- ❖ Network system
- ❖ Database system
- ❖ Training
- ❖ Operational manuals
- ❖ Help-desk

E **Outsourcing vendors.** These vendors install and/or operate end-user IS operations. These vendors are more involved in the operation than turnkey package vendors because they also operate the system.

F **Application service providers.** These vendors provide standardized software such as accounting packages, CRM software, etc., hosted at their location and accessed over the Internet or a dedicated connection.

Finding vendors is easier because of the growth of this industry. Local vendors advertise in the Yellow Pages, while national vendors advertise in national publications. Local vendors are a good source for a single-site operation; national firms are better for multiple-site operations.

National professional consulting societies and members of national professional societies are both sources for finding vendors. Another source is published directories of consultants. The local library may also be helpful.

Vendor Contacting

One way to contact a vendor is with a request for information letter (RFI). This gives the vendor an opportunity to analyze the client's needs and match them with what he/she offers. The RFI provides the following information:

❖ The nature of the end-user IS application

❖ The time window within which it is to be developed

❖ The current resources available to the end-user

❖ The expected goal of the project

❖ The company contact person's name, phone number, and e-mail address

If the end-user has firmed up plans and is seeking a vendor for a given service, a request for proposal (RFP) is sent to vendors. This is a detailed document specifying the needed services, which might be a consulting service to provide contract services. See Chapter 15, *Vendors: Getting the Goods,* for more information.

END-USER IS IMPLEMENTATION

Implementation is the start-up of the end-user IS system. This is scheduled at a lull (or slow) time in the end-user's cycle of operation. Present the new system to the end-users in a positive light.

The process is like launching a newly constructed ship; it will either float or sink. A lot depends on the attitude of the end-users, which profoundly affects the success of the system.

COMMENT

The author worked on one project where the end-users wanted the system to work at all costs. It had to be shut down because of design problems. The users did not want to give up their system. They were upset and wanted to keep on trying.

Types of Implementations

The implementation can be carried out in any one of four ways, each having pros and cons.

A **Parallel implementation.** This is a popular and safe way of implementing a new system, definitely recommended for critical applications. It is safe because the old system is not unplugged until the new system has proven itself. Both the new and the old are operated in parallel. A learning curve is allowed for end-users to be brought up to the needed skill level before the conversion is made.

Parallel implementation also costs more than the other types. Extra people need to be recruited, trained, used, then let go. In this situation, extra contract workers are the best solution.

However, implementation during lull time reduces the number of contract workers needed and, in some cases, the entire process might be handled using only overtime.

B **Phased implementation.** Phased implementation occurs when the new system is placed into operation in phases. This reduces the load carried by the end-users. There is less to learn at one time, and the new system can be pulled back if needed. This transition can proceed at the rate best suited to the situation.

However, not all end-user systems lend themselves to this type of conversion; it can also prolong conversion over a longer time period.

C **Pilot/prototype implementation.** This form involves choosing a developmental site that offers the best chance of success with the new system. Then, if the system works, it can be implemented at other sites. Using a single site first is a safer procedure. The effort to train the end-user operations people is extensive. In this situation, the workers are screened to obtain those attributes needed for a successful conversion. The pilot/prototype is refined until operating at the desired level of efficiency.

However, success at a pilot/prototype development site in Salt Lake City does not guarantee the same success in New York City. People, local culture, and operations are not always the same. Sometimes the process to convert all other sites at once takes more resources than available.

D **Direct cut-over implementation.** This type requires that operations be cut over to the new system at the same time the old system is terminated. Some applications can be handled only in this manner. It

COMMENT

There was a company in Michigan that attempted a direct cut-over implementation that did not work too well. The system was such a failure that a correct inventory could not even be provided for the firm's bankruptcy auction.

is a fast way of starting a new end-user IS system, and less costly than the other methods of conversion, especially parallel implementation.

Any failure made public, however, can be a disaster. While provisions to return to the old system are in place, the credibility of the new system can be undermined.

Implementation Requirements

A combination of factors and attitudes is required for the implementation to be successful. Some factors are recognized as important long before the conversion is executed, but they are most effective if all work in concert from the very beginning.

They are:

A Systems design. The quality of the final product has all the earmarks of excellence. The project team, the end-users, and management are elated about the delivery system; their attitudes alone will impact the success of the conversion.

The performance and reliability level of the system satisfies the users' requirements. The users look forward to using the new system, because it will do something for them.

B User involvement. End-users are very much a part of the new system because of their involvement in the analysis and design. Their input is recognized as important to the success of the implementation and operation of the new system. It is this esprit de corps that supplies the momentum essential to the undertaking; the end-users believe their system will not fail.

C User-management commitment. Management commitment provides the resources needed for the end-user project team. However, resources alone will not guarantee success. Management must demonstrate its eagerness for the success of the project. It must set the tone for the workers.

D Resources/value. Resources committed to the project reflect the value of the project to the company. Cost-benefit analysis can confirm this value and the resources committed. There should be a direct correlation between the two: the greater the value, the more resources can be committed.

Implementation Success Factors

There are universal factors that affect the success of a project, including end-user IS projects:

A **Project size.** Project size directly affects the level of risk. The larger the project, the more calendar time required. The longer the calendar time, the more the opportunity for requirements to change. The more requirements change, the less likely the implemented system will succeed because the need is no longer the same.

The larger the project size, the more members required for the project team. The more members on the project team, the greater the communication problems. The greater the communication problems, the more the opportunities for project errors and project delays.

It is better to have several smaller projects than one large one. The efficiency rates and success rates are much higher for smaller projects.

B **Complexity risk.** The more complex the project, the greater the risk for implementation. There are just too many interdependent things that can go wrong.

Dividing a complex project into smaller ones seldom is possible. The success of this type of project would be enhanced by using a pilot/prototype implementation.

C **Technology risk.** The newer and more complex the technology, the greater the risks. The first release of a given software package usually has more bugs than the third release.

A pilot/prototype is a good candidate for implementation. Indeed, the direct cut-over implementation of a risky project has been called a kamikaze implementation.

Implementation Follow-up

All end-user IS implementations are required to have a follow-up evaluation to answer a number of questions:

❖ Is the system operating as planned?

❖ Are the end-users happy with the system?

❖ What parts of the system are not working?

❖ Was the system oversold?

❖ Was the cost-benefit analysis correct?

❖ What else needs to be done?

The list can continue. No one point in time is the best time to begin implementation follow-up. Data is collected as an ongoing process. Different problems happen at different time intervals and new corrective actions create new items to evaluate.

Reports of the follow-up findings are given monthly until the operation is fine-tuned. Later, as the system becomes obsolete, the entire analysis and design process begins again.

End-user IS evaluation should include the following:

A **Evaluation items.** The items to be evaluated come from end-user management, the project leader, project members, and corporate IS systems. The basic questions may address the evaluation of the total system and its parts.

B **Evaluation criteria.** The criteria used are provided by the same people who established the evaluation items. The criteria must be objective. Industry norms may assist in the criteria selection.

C **Evaluation instruments.** Evaluation instruments are items such as turnaround time, benchmark comparisons, errors per unit of process, ratio of customer complaints, worker overtime, etc.

D **Evaluation data.** Collect data from the following sources: the help-desk, system performance logs, operator questionnaires, error logs, customer complaints recorded, etc.

E **Analyze collected data.** Analyze the data using past performance information and industry standards.

F **Design corrective action.** Corrective action will be designed and documented. The documentation is sent, with a cover memo, to the end-user manager. On receipt of this document, end-user management, the project leader, other project members involved, and any outside persons who were involved will meet to design corrective action for resolution of any problems. The end-user manager has to approve any designated corrective action.

G **Carry out the corrective action.** The corrective action is executed. At a given predetermined date, unless there is an emergency, the process is evaluated again.

19

END-USER IT COMPUTER OPERATIONS

END-USER POLICIES

End-user IS policies cover end-user IS work groups and end-user stand-alone PCs autonomous from the corporate systems. However, autonomy does not allow end-user operations to disregard normal industry operation practices. They must follow the policies and procedures as recorded in this instrument. They have a liaison relationship with corporate IS if no other relation is defined. Corporate IS provides information and guidelines used to operate end-user information systems. These guidelines are established to avoid corporate lawsuits and any public embarrassment.

End-user management is fully responsible for any employees who do not abide by the information and guidelines provided by corporate information systems. Any repercussions resulting from noncompliance will be dealt with accordingly. The procedures offered here apply only to information and guidelines for end-user computer operations.

End-user Computer Work Groups

"End-user" computer work groups as part of information systems can be somewhat autonomous. However, the more the group relies on information systems for assistance, the less autonomy it has. Even with "total" autonomy, it needs to comply with universal standards for hardware and software utilization.

An end-user work group system can be a client/server operation employing an information systems server, or an autonomous work group with its own end-user server system. It can be a closed system or provided with a gateway for external network access. The hardware configuration of the end-user work group is not restricted as long as the equipment is justified by end-user management.

The company is responsible for complying with certain industry practices. Responsibility for assuring these practices are followed by the end-user work group is delegated by end-user management.

End-user PC Policies

Information systems controls site-licensed software. The user pays the cost of software with charges based on quantity.

Departments may purchase their own software. However, if not on the list of software the information systems department supports, they cannot expect user support for that particular choice.

Personal Hardware and Software

No personal hardware or software is allowed. All hardware and software, including in-house-developed programs, is the sole property of the firm. This policy is enforced to reduce problems with equipment, software failure, damage to data files, and the introduction of viruses. To restrict access to the firm's data and/or programs and prevent virus transmission, disks or tapes belonging to the firm are not to be used in personal home computers.

Backup Hardware and Software

End-user IS is responsible for maintaining backup hardware and software. Arrangements with the corporate computer store are made by end-user management for the availability of hardware backup as needed, on a loan basis, to end-users.

End-user Training

The information systems department is responsible for coordinating and providing PC training for end-users. This consists of both formal classes and individual, self-paced instruction.

END-USER WORK GROUP OPERATIONS

End-user work group computer systems can vary in configuration and process from one area to another within the same corporation. However, the end-user work group operations procedures applicable to "common procedures" are to be followed by all groups in the corporation. When operation needs expand beyond the common procedures, procedure documentation conforms to the requirements set by information systems.

General Operations

This subsection covers general operations followed by the end-user work group when operating the computer system. Each group has a person appointed as the unit's computer coordinator (full- or part-time duty).

A   Computer coordinator's responsibilities

❖   Anticipate possible hardware needs.

❖   Anticipate new software needs.

❖   Provide information and service for users.

❖   Provide for informal and formal training.

❖   Oversee operation policies.

❖   Be a source for operation documentation.

❖   Disseminate new operating information.

❖   Be the liaison between the end-user work group computer operation and corporate information systems.

❖   Be a knowledge source for user applications.

❖   Perform hardware maintenance.

❖   Perform software updates.

❖   Perform backup of files and database.

❖   Maintain a supply inventory.

❖   Be the facilitator for disaster recovery.

❖   Be on call for after-hours problems.

❖   Maintain computer security procedures.

❖   Police system for unauthorized software.

❖   Maintain an operation performance problem log.

❖   Write a monthly exception report to the end-user unit manager.

B   End-user workstation operations. Each workstation is provided with a current operations manual. Other manuals supplied by vendors or written in-house may supplement this manual.

There are standard workstation operating procedures applicable to all workstations:

- ❖ Turning on the workstation
- ❖ Daily housekeeping operations
- ❖ Weekly housekeeping
- ❖ Turning off the workstation

C **End-user operation rules and procedures.** When providing rules and procedures to be followed by all end-users, the computer coordinator explains the rationale behind them.

- ❖ No food or beverages close to the workstation area.
- ❖ No smoking near software or hardware.
- ❖ No telephones near computer disks.
- ❖ No illegal copying of software.
- ❖ No personal software allowed.
- ❖ No personal use of a computer company.
- ❖ No personal disks allowed.
- ❖ No hardware may be removed from the department.

End-user operators should inform the coordinator of any need for ergonomic devices. The devices available include:

- ❖ Keyboard wrist rest
- ❖ Mouse wrist rest
- ❖ Foot rest
- ❖ Ergonomic keyboard
- ❖ Arm support
- ❖ Ergonomic adjustable chair
- ❖ Adjustable workstations for employees with special needs
- ❖ Radiation and/or glare monitor screen cover
- ❖ Special telephone needs

COMMENT

Remember the requirements of the Americans with Disabilities Act!

CLIENT/SERVER PROCEDURES

In an end-user work group client/server operation, information systems computer operations provides the server. The following procedures for this end-user work group computer system operation help insure the safety of the IS computer operation. There could be more than one end-user work group computer system within the corporation.

IS Client/Server Support

The IS computer operations help-desk provides support for general computer client/server operations. It is available for end-user work group users with operation problems. If a problem cannot be handled by help-desk employees, they contact someone who can help.

The end-user work group's particular technical operation concerns are addressed by a person from its end-user work area. This person is appointed by the work group management and will be identified as the computer coordinator. This person is also responsible for communicating the work group needs to IS computer operations and/or the systems unit.

The coordinator's responsibilities are to:

❖ Assist the IS trainer with end-user work group training needs.

❖ Provide informal training to computer workstation users.

❖ Be a knowledge source for user applications.

❖ Be the information systems' end-user work group contact.

❖ Maintain a reference library of publications for the end-user work group.

End-user Work Group Education

The end-user work group receives information about and training for using its hardware and software. This is the responsibility of the IS project management group installing the new system.

After it is operational, provisions must be made for instructions for subsequent system changes. The coordinator assists with this task.

Provisions are made for new employees utilizing the end-user work group system. There are self-paced learning instruments, such as:

❖ Computer tutorials
❖ Program learning manuals

- ❖ Audio instruction tapes
- ❖ VCR tapes
- ❖ Operation manuals

The coordinator assists with the training of new end-user work group computer workstation users and is responsible for instructing the new end-user regarding the work group's utilization of the computer system. The coordinator also informs end-users of pending operational changes and assists them once changes are in place.

Workstation Operations

There are standard operating procedures for operators of terminals or workstations:

A **Turning on the system.** To turn on the system, the operator follows the operating manual procedures checking to see that the monitor display and all peripherals are operating properly. If not, the operator consults the manual and proceeds when the system is ready. If the workstation is not working, contact the help-desk. Put its telephone number on the first page of the manual.

Before contacting anyone for assistance, the operator will:

- ❖ Write down the details of what happened.
- ❖ Make a list of what corrective measures were tried.
- ❖ When assistance is available, bring the computer system up to the place where the problem occurred.

B **Turning off the system.** Turn off the system in the following sequence:

1 Exit from the operating system.
2 Turn off peripheral equipment.
3 Turn off the workstation.
4 Remove all floppy disks.

C **Daily operations.** Check hardware daily for:

1 Quality of the monitor display. Adjust as needed.
2 Cleanliness of the equipment. Clean the equipment as needed at the start or end of each workday, and at other times when there is high-volume use.

If the workstation has a printer, do the following:

1 Check paper supply in printer. Add paper as needed.

2 Check quality of printing. Replace ribbons or printer cartridges as needed.

D **Weekly housekeeping.** The end-user administrator/user vacuums or dusts off the keyboard and wipes clean the monitor glass once a week. Clean high-use diskette heads weekly. If the heads are not often used, a once-per-month cleaning will suffice.

E **Dust covers.** In areas with a higher than normal amount of airborne dust, use dust covers for PCs, keyboards, monitors, and other attached devices when not in use. For very dusty areas, use special keyboard covers that can be employed while using the keyboard. These require periodic replacement; therefore, the coordinator should maintain a supply.

F **Floppy disk backup.** When data is kept on floppy disks, copy the floppy disk. Do not store the two floppy disks, original and backup, together. The backup copy must be write-protected.

Operation Rules

The following rules apply to all persons utilizing the end-user work group computer system:

❖ No food or beverage on or near the hardware or software.

❖ No smoking near the hardware or software.

❖ The computer and disks are at least two feet from telephones. Keep other magnetic devices away from the computer, disks, and tapes.

❖ No illegal copying of software.

❖ No hardware or software may be removed from the firm's premises without written permission.

❖ No personal hardware, software, or disk is permitted.

❖ No down- or uploading of any noncompany software or data will be permitted.

Workstation Accessories

Accessories are classified into two groups: ergonomic devices and productivity aids. The devices are to be purchased by the end-user work group department. The coordinator is responsible for coordinating this effort. (The following items are not identified by brand name.)

A **Ergonomic devices.** Workstation ergonomic devices help the human body interact with the computer system and function with the least amount of fatigue, error, and bodily harm. The following types are available:

- ❖ Keyboard wrist rest
- ❖ Mouse wrist rest
- ❖ Foot rest
- ❖ Ergonomic keyboard
- ❖ Arm support
- ❖ Ergonomic adjustable chair
- ❖ Adjustable workstations for special employees
- ❖ Radiation and/or glare monitor screen cover

COMMENT

Remember the requirements of the Americans with Disabilities Act!

B **Productivity aids.** The following, if used properly, have been known to increase end-user productivity:

- ❖ Tilt 'n turn monitor stand
- ❖ Copyholders
- ❖ Copyholder and light
- ❖ Diskette storage devices
- ❖ Desktop print stand and/or organizer
- ❖ PC roll-out keyboard system
- ❖ Keyboard cover
- ❖ Mouse pad
- ❖ Mouse holder
- ❖ Keyboard labels for F keys and/or other keys
- ❖ Wastepaper container and paper shredder
- ❖ Workstations that include a drawer for personal items that can be locked
- ❖ Speaker telephone

END-USER PC COORDINATOR

The end-user PC coordinator's duties and responsibilities vary from one location to another, depending on needs. The actual title of coordinator may also vary, but whatever the title, this person ensures that PC policies are enforced.

Responsibilities of the PC Coordinator

Following are the responsibilities of the person assigned to the coordinator position:

- ❖ Process requests for new hardware and software.
- ❖ Keep abreast of end-user hardware and software needs.
- ❖ Provide an ongoing hardware and software troubleshooting service for end-users to handle day-to-day operating problems.
- ❖ Provide informal and formal training assistance for PC users.
- ❖ Enforce policies regarding PC hardware and software operations.
- ❖ Disseminate new hardware/software information.
- ❖ Provide backup service for PC hardware and software.
- ❖ Provide PC LAN service and/or supervision.
- ❖ Maintain a PC electronic bulletin board for end-users' concerns.

In-house Consulting Service

The coordinator acts as in-house consultant for end-users of sanctioned PC equipment and software. The PCs can be desktop, transportable, laptop, or notebook machines. Assessing present and future needs of these machines is one of the services provided. The consulting service also covers the areas of PC communications and networking. The coordinator is responsible for maintaining a compatible standard for PC and LAN or WAN communications. He/she also works with personnel responsible for communications to ensure continuity and compatibility of the PC systems. The PC coordinator's consulting role includes advising end-users on the true capabilities of equipment and helping them match business needs to the proper, cost-effective equipment.

PC access to mainframe databases requires approval by the coordinator before any contact with the database administrator and/or data manager. Be careful to reduce the amount of replicated data not properly labeled as to age or origin. Database access often requires the owner's permission.

The coordinator maintains a daily log that is the data source for monthly reports of his/her activities. The daily log records time spent on the following items (travel time will also be also included):

❖ PC hardware troubleshooting

❖ PC software troubleshooting

❖ Informal and formal training assistance

❖ User consulting service

The coordinator's indirect (administrative cost) time is kept in the following categories:

❖ Reading and other education methods used to keep up with current technology

❖ Communication network services

❖ Electronic bulletin board usage and maintenance

❖ User education and training preparation when not charged to a given department

❖ General administration duties, etc.

PC Training

The coordinator is the training provider for end-user PC and computer workstation users and may enlist the services of the IS training unit or the firm's training department in carrying out this responsibility. Training is provided on a group or individual basis. Charges for this service will follow established cost-accounting practices. There is no service charge for the loan of text material, the use of self-paced instruction programs, or the loan of instructional hardware.

COMMENT

Outside training providers are sometimes an efficient way to provide PC training. Use them and release them as required.

The coordinator maintains an up-to-date library of reading material and self-instruction programs available. Include the latest versions of operating hardware and software manuals.

Instructional programs are developed in-house, contracted for with outside developers, and purchased off-the-shelf. Unless developed or purchased for given departments, the cost is applied to the indirect administrative training budget.

The coordinator requires a work area to house his/her office and training development effort. The whole area will be:

❖ Secured when not in use

❖ Air conditioned and air purified

❖ Equipped with furniture and storage facilities

❖ Equipped with a classroom that can double as a meeting room

A required minimum of capital equipment is needed for a PC training operation. Most items are stationary, but some are portable and loaned to users. Have on hand more than one of each item to be loaned. The following PC training equipment is considered the minimum needed:

❖ Whiteboard (Many whiteboards can double as a projection screen.)

❖ Table-top lectern

❖ Portable overhead projector

❖ Flip chart (floor model)

❖ 35mm slide projector

❖ 35mm camera with flash attachment

❖ Camera copy stand with lights (If daylight film is used, blue daylight-rendering photo flood lights should be used to provide the correct color balance.)

❖ VCR and color monitor

❖ Supply items: nonpermanent color markers, overhead transparencies (both write-on and laser printable), spare projection bulbs, flip chart paper, 35mm daylight slide film (film speed of 200 or more), slide trays, and erasers

PC ACQUISITION

The coordinator is responsible for the inventory control of all PC hardware (desktop, transportable, laptop, and notebook) and software acquisitions, and should be attuned to PC users' expected needs. He/she also assists users with any future hardware and software requirements.

Purchase requisitions for PC hardware, software, and service or consulting contracts are forwarded to the coordinator who approves the purchase requisitions and forwards them to the end-user manager, who in turn approves them and forwards them to the Purchasing department. Use purchase requisitions only for approved budgeted expenditures.

Hardware Acquisition

The procedures for hardware acquisition are as follows:

A **Approved hardware purchases.** Departments with budget approval for hardware expenditures complete a purchase requisition and forward it to the coordinator who checks the capital expense budget listing and confirms the purchase can be approved.

If the purchase is not on the approved list, the requisition is returned with a memo explaining why. If in order, the coordinator dates and signs the purchase requisition and forwards it to the end-user manager for his/her approval. It is then forwarded to the Purchasing department.

B **Hardware loans.** End-users requesting a loan of hardware from the coordinator provide the following information:

❖ What is to be loaned? Include a checklist of accessories, such as cables and power supplies that must be returned with the unit. Otherwise there will be a delay in loaning it again.

❖ Expected length of time for the loan. A firm return date is critical.

❖ Reason for the loan.

❖ The department and person requesting the loan.

❖ Where the equipment will be used.

❖ The person who will be using the equipment.

When the equipment is released, an "out card" with the date, time, equipment loaned, serial number, and to whom it is loaned is completed and signed by the person receiving the equipment. The card is filed, by date, until the item is returned when it will again be signed and dated by the person returning the item.

The "out card" file is reviewed once per month. Contact delinquent borrowers about returning the equipment. Cards for returned items are held on file for one year.

If the item is damaged, it is noted on the card, and the card becomes the source for a damage memo report to be completed by the coordinator. This memo is sent to the end-user department head of the borrower. Arrangements are made to repair or replace the piece of equipment at a cost to be decided by the coordinator. That amount is reported to the end-user head. Ensure they have removed their data, and reload the system's standard configuration promptly on its return before shelving it.

C **New hardware acquisition.** The coordinator serves as an information source for future hardware acquisitions and maintains a published list of "approved" hardware, i.e., sanctioned for purchase. If the desired hardware is listed, the user need only provide budgeted funds to acquire the equipment.

The purchase of hardware not sanctioned requires a request either for a one-time purchase or for the item to be placed on the approved list. For either action, write a memo to the coordinator explaining the special request and containing the following information:

❖   Item's name, and vendor's name and address

❖   Cost of the item

❖   Quantity required

❖   Reason special item is required

❖   What happens if item is not approved

❖   Personnel responsible for item's maintenance

❖   Personnel responsible for training and operation support

If required, a meeting is held with the party interested in the new hardware and the coordinator. If an alternate piece of approved hardware is not acceptable to the user, and the request is not resolved, the coordinator contacts the head of information systems for resolution of the problem.

The information systems manager will inform the requesting party by memo of his/her decision. If the equipment acquisition is still not approved, the user may appeal in writing to the PC advisory panel whose decision is final.

Software Acquisition

Software may be developed in-house or acquired from an outside source. In-house software development is pursued only if no commercially available software is available for less than the in-house cost. Also consider the availability of in-house programming end-user personnel. Arrangements for any in-house-developed software are made by the coordinator. The actual programming effort is done in-house by end-user personnel or the corporate IS programming unit, or contracted out by the coordinator. The cost requires the end-user head's approval because it is charged to that department's budget.

Software can be purchased for multiple users or a single user. Most software is purchased from vendors, with some only available for an annual fee. Also, upgrades are generally available for a single user or multiple users. Purchased off-the-shelf software is available in two forms: one is for the horizontal market, for widespread use by many different kinds of firms (word processing or spreadsheet software); the other is for the vertical market, for applications pertaining to given industries. This kind may be more flexible because sometimes the source program is available. This makes it possible to alter the program to meet the user's own needs.

The coordinator maintains a published list of approved PC software to be continually updated with newly approved equipment. It is the duty of the coordinator to continually seek and respond to needs for newer and better software. Only approved software may be used. In the event that the coordinator will not approve requested software, the requesting party may appeal in writing to the corporate PC advisory panel whose decision is final.

Software acquisition procedures are as follows:

A **Specially developed software.** When a user requires software not available by purchase, the coordinator works with the user to define the needs and assigns the project to an end-user programmer. If one is unavailable, the coordinator submits a memo to the person responsible for corporate PC programming systems and provides enough information so a project proposal can be developed.

Review project proposal information with the user requesting the program. If time and money are available, a formal request in writing is issued by the end-user management.

Program development is handled using the same standard procedures as for information systems program development. As long as no security problem exists, the new software is made available to other PC users.

B **Purchased software.** The user sends a memo to the coordinator requesting the approved software. The coordinator reviews the request and, if in order, sends the software to the party requesting it. If need be, an internal charge is made to the requesting department's account.

If the software is not in stock, the coordinator issues a purchase requisition on behalf of the requesting department and sends it to the end-user head for approval.

Since this software is from the approved list, hold a training class. Send a copy of the class schedule along with the software. If no local classes are available, see if local junior colleges offer continuing education classes and pass on the schedule and registration forms.

It is critical that the PC coordinator maintain software licenses in a fireproof file cabinet, preferably off-site. In the event of a disaster, you may be able to use copies of software without repurchasing the software (often the manufacturer will even send a "gold" disk if you have adequate documentation). This is a primary company defense in case of a software audit. From the cost side, it is evidence for buying upgrades instead of purchasing new software.

C **Software registration.** All software registration is completed and mailed by the coordinator in the company's name.

D **Software library.** Copies of all in-house-developed PC programs and the original licensed software, as well as backup copies of other purchased software, are maintained in the end-user software library under the control of the coordinator. Encourage users with one-of-a-kind software to have backup copies housed here as well. All library software is the most current version in use.

E **Software demo disks.** Software demo disks are provided to users requesting them and will not be charged to the user's account. They can be provided by vendors or developed in-house.

COMMENT

The software library provides an opportunity for potential users to try software before obtaining their own. The library contains proper documentation and user instructions to test software. The coordinator may be called on to demonstrate software or demo programs to potential users.

Communications Acquisition

PC communication systems require some planning on the part of the potential user and the coordinator. The coordinator acts as a resource person for PC communications acquisitions; this requires the maintenance of an information file of LAN (and to a lesser degree, of WAN) hardware and software to be used when considering future acquisitions or upgrading. There are a variety of LAN systems today, including wired or wireless. There is even one that employs power supply lines as the transmitting media. Remote network users (working from mobile or home offices) utilize modems to link with LAN systems.

For modem acquisitions a user-request memo signed by the user's superior and defining the modem needs is sent to the coordinator. The user is supplied with an "approved" modem with the required (or a higher) transmission rate. The appropriate hardware and software are supplied and installed by the coordinator.

COMMENT

Fax–modems allow for double duty and convenience.

PC network communication acquisitions may require approval of the person responsible for corporate communications. This is true with WAN system interfacing or when linking two or more LAN systems. The gateway and modem selection also requires the approval of the organizational communication person. If not, the coordinator is fully responsible for installing the micro-LAN communication hookup. Users are provided with the required instructions and operation manuals for the online communication systems by the coordinator.

LAN-based e-mail has started to replace information systems host-based systems. Some major reasons for this move are: lower prices, availability of Windows support of LAN-based e-mail, and emerging mail-enabled applications.

Acquisitions of LAN-based e-mail systems, as well as their maintenance, upgrading, and support, are the ongoing responsibility of the coordinator.

Database Access Acquisition

PC users requiring access to a mainframe database consult the coordinator who then contacts the IS PC manager regarding their needs. The manager reviews these and contacts the database administrator for user access. If the organization has a data administrator, this person is also informed of the user's needs. Both administrators' approvals are required for the user to access the information systems database. If the database is another user's (in the same end-user work group), or part of a network of PCs, the coordinator contacts the data administrator for written approval. If there is none, the coordinator resolves the problem and sends a requesting memo to the database administrator for access.

The coordinator makes arrangements for new PC users to access the database and provides training and an operation manual.

PC OPERATIONS

PC (desktop, transportable, laptop, and notebook) operations utilize recommended manufacturers' standards as outlined in the manufacturers' manuals supplemented by those provided by the information systems PC manager. The supplemented manuals are both purchased and written in-house if unavailable from outside sources.

> ## COMMENT
>
> Because manufacturers' manuals are often written to meet deadlines and need correction after use, publishers have responded with some that are easier to understand.
>
> Today's technology encourages the use of the PC as a user information and learning instrument with the aid of self-paced tutorials or even the "help" key. This technology should not be overlooked by the person responsible for the organization's PCs.
>
> Various operations within the company may have differing degrees of autonomy, but the PC policies, enforced by the coordinator, apply to all PC users.

Today's technology encourages the use of the PC as a user information and learning instrument with the aid of self-paced tutorials or even the "help" key. The person responsible for the organization's PCs should not overlook this technology.

Various PC operations within the company may have differing degrees of autonomy, but the appropriate policies, enforced by the coordinator, apply to all PC users.

PC Security

Desktop or any stationary PCs are located in a safe environment. The person assigned a nonstationary PC assumes full responsibility for the safekeeping of both the hardware and the software. Preventing unauthorized access of any PC system is of utmost concern to all employees. The following items address the PC security issue:

A **Physical location.** The room where the computers are kept is locked when not in use. If not possible, seriously consider employing a cable lock to deter any removal of the desktop computer hardware. Any transportable computers are kept in a safe place at all times, including the time the hardware is in transit. All portable computers must be handled as "carry-on luggage" while in public transit. When PCs are being transported for a special event and cannot be carried individually, permission must be requested in writing from the coordinator. Approval is granted in writing, along with the special one-time procedures to be followed for the event.

If a desktop PC is moved to a new permanent location within an area under the jurisdiction of the coordinator, he/she will be informed in writing within 24 hours of the move. In the event that the new location is not under the jurisdiction of the current coordinator, he/she must approve the move before it takes place and then inform both the asset manager and the new area's coordinator of the move.

B   **Access security.** Stationary PCs with a modem or network and/or hard drives with any restricted information are required to have one of the following:

❖   A lock

❖   An access security board

❖   An access security board with a lock-slot, so the board can utilize a cable security system

❖   Personal access code software in the event the PC does not have an available slot for an access security board

❖   An access security board with a motion alarm (In the event that a building alarm is available, and the situation warrants, an external connection to the building alarm system should be made. The alarm may be set to notify IS operations, and the firm's own security force, or an outside security service.)

C   **Software and data security.** Software disks are stored in a locked place. Data disks and backup tapes and disks are stored in a PC media safe or other such comparable device if so warranted by the data administrator or coordinator.

Daily Operating Procedures

There are standard operating procedures that apply to all PC operations:

A   **Turning on the system.** To turn on the system, the operator follows the manufacturer's procedures.

COMMENT

Approved power backup hardware is recommended in the event of a power failure. If no such device is connected to the system, take care not to use the machines when a power failure is likely.

The operator checks to see that the monitor display and all peripherals are operating properly and, if not, consults the operating manual. He/she then proceeds when the system is ready.

Portable computers having access to AC power supply are checked for battery status. If they require recharging (or to prolong battery life), use the available AC power supply. If the user is outside of the U.S., be sure the power supply is compatible with your hardware requirements.

B **Turning off the system.** When turning off the system:

❖ Exit from the operating system.

❖ Turn off peripheral equipment.

❖ Turn off the computer.

❖ Remove floppy disks.

❖ Turn off the surge protect switch.

❖ Check battery-powered PCs for recharging needs, and when necessary, recharge batteries as soon as possible.

C **Daily operations.** Systems are checked daily (by the administrator/user) for:

❖ Paper supply in printer. Add paper as needed.

❖ Quality of printing. Replace ribbons or printer cartridges as needed.

❖ Quality of monitor display. Adjust as needed.

❖ Cleanliness of the computer equipment. Cleaning the equipment as needed may be done at the start or end of each workday, and at other times during the day when there is high-volume use.

D **Weekly housekeeping.** The administrator/user vacuums or dusts off the keyboard and wipes clean the monitor glass once a week. Clean high-use diskette heads weekly. If the heads are not often used, a once per month cleaning will suffice.

E **Dust covers.** In areas with a higher than normal amount of airborne dust, dust covers should be used for PCs, keyboards, monitors, and other attached devices when not in use. For very dusty areas, use special keyboard covers that can be employed while using the keyboard. These require periodic replacement; therefore, a supply should be maintained by the coordinator/key operator.

Operation Rules and Procedures

The following rules and procedures apply to the operation of all PCs:

A No food or beverage on or near the hardware or software.

B No smoking near the hardware or software.

C A clean, cool, and dry air working environment is recommended for the computer.

D The computer disks and reading heads are at least two feet from telephones. Keep other magnetic devices away from the computer, disks, and tapes.

E Plug all computers and peripherals into a surge protection unit. Don't plug noncomputer electric devices into the surge protection outlet or into the same wall plug with the surge protection device. Use only grounded electrical outlets.

F No illegal copying of software.

G No hardware or software may be removed from the firm's premises without written permission, for each occasion, from the coordinator. Portable computer systems used away from the workplace require a permission letter or ID card signed by the coordinator to be kept with the system at all times. The permission letter/ID card identifies who has permission to use and carry the authorized equipment and software. It will also contain the serial numbers of the units authorized and identifies the software contained in the system.

H No personal hardware, software, or disk is allowed.

I No hardware or software (including portable equipment) will be loaned to noncompany persons.

J Floppy disk labels will be marked with a permanent marker before they are applied to the disks.

K Floppy disks are kept in their disk containers or storage unit when not in use.

Backup Procedures

Backup procedures may vary depending on the area of use within the company. Not all data and software have the same value (although it is better to be safe if not sure). The following backup procedures are recommended:

A **New software.** New purchased software is backed up in accordance with the software manufacturer's specifications. If only one copy can be made, the backed-up copy is sent to the coordinator for the software library. After being copied, the new software is tested. Contact the coordinator if a problem is found. All copied software disks and tapes will be write-protected.

B **Hard drive backup procedures.** The following is recommended for hard drive backup procedures:

   1 At the end of each workday, all new data should be backed up onto disks or tape. Some active transactions (such as word processing, billing, etc.) will need to be backed up more often.

   2 A backup copy of the hard drive software is maintained on disk or tape.

C **Removable media data.** When data is kept on removable media (floppies, Zip disks, CDs, etc.) and not on a hard drive, copy the disk for backup. Do not store the two copies of the disks together. It is recommended that the backup copy be write-protected if applicable.

PC System Crash

In the event of a PC system crash, the operator turns off the power, records what occurred just prior to the crash, as well as the time, and contacts the coordinator or administrator for assistance. Post a sign on the computer stating that the system has crashed and the equipment is not to be used. Portable computers should be taken to the coordinator.

Hardware Problems

For hardware problems, the operator refers to the operating manual. If the problem cannot be corrected, the problem and its effect on the hardware are noted, and the coordinator or administrator is contacted. Place a sign on the (desktop) PC indicating it is not working and not to be used. If a peripheral does not work, place a sign on the device noting it is out of order and indicating whether or not the computer is usable.

Software Problems

For software problems, the operator contacts the help-desk. If the help-desk cannot resolve the problem, the operator contacts the coordinator.

Before contacting anyone for assistance, however, the operator will:

❖ Write down the details of what happened.

❖ Make a list of what corrective measures were tried.

❖ When assistance becomes available, bring the software up on the computer at the place where the problem occurred.

Accessories and Supplies

PC accessories can improve productivity, reduce fatigue, and improve morale. These accessories and supply items are on a "recommended or approved list" provided by the coordinator and carried by the corporate computer store. Other items not stocked will be listed, with their vendors, by the computer store. This information helps when ordering through the Purchasing department. The approved list of items is published, updated, and distributed by the coordinator.

The items are purchased from the user's department petty cash fund or with a budget requisition. Accessories are classified as production aids or ergonomic devices. Supply items are requisitioned from the unit responsible for office or computer supplies. The standard operating procedure for requisitioning office supplies or computer supplies is followed.

Accessories come in two groups: ergonomic devices and productivity aids. (The following items are not identified by brand name.)

A **Ergonomic devices.** PC ergonomic devices help the human body interact with the PC system and function with the least amount of fatigue, error, and bodily harm. The following types are available on the "recommended list" provided by the PC store:

❖ Keyboard wrist rest

❖ Mouse wrist rest

❖ Foot rest

❖ Ergonomic keyboard

❖ Arm support

❖ Ergonomic adjustable chair

❖ Adjustable workstations for employees with special needs

❖ Radiation and/or glare monitor screen

COMMENT

Remember the requirements of the Americans with Disabilities Act!

B **Productivity aids.** The following, if used properly, have been known to increase productivity:

❖ Tilt 'n turn monitor stand

❖ Copy holders (flex arm, attachable or standard)

❖ Copy holder light

❖ Diskette storage devices

❖ Cartridge storage devices

❖ Desktop print stand and/or organizer

❖ PC roll-out keyboard system

❖ Keyboard cover

❖ Mouse pad

❖ Mouse holder

❖ Keyboard labels for F keys and/or other keys

❖ Wastepaper container and paper shredder

❖ Workstations that include a drawer that can be locked for personal items

❖ Speaker telephone

END-USER ASSET MANAGEMENT

Developing, installing, and operating an asset management system is complex. The development and installation is handled as an end-user asset management project, and the installation provides a well-documented, operating end-user asset management system.

COMMENT

The corporate computer asset manager should contact the Software Publishers Association at 1730 M St. NW, Suite 700, Washington, D.C. 20036-4510, or call (800) 388-7478 for current PC and client/server information. A copy of the Association's latest newsletter is available on the Internet at www.spa.org, and antipiracy information is available through its home page. Software Publishers Association can provide information, courses, and membership opportunities. Have both the project manager and corporate computer asset manager attend a Software Publishers Association seminar.

A project leader is appointed who, in addition to having the qualities and skills of a good project leader, is familiar with end-user PC hardware and software, and understands software licenses and copyrights.

Developing the Asset Management Plan

The project leader and the corporate computer asset manager develop the asset management plan, with the approval of the end-user head. The plan should contain the following:

A **Asset management project team.** An asset management project team is formed, the size to be determined by the end-user head.

B **Preplanning survey.** The project team develops a hardware and software asset management plan. Before the plan is completed, a survey is conducted as to current:

❖ Internal hardware controls

❖ Internal software controls

❖ Acquisition procedures for hardware and software

❖ PC data and software protection

❖ Software license compliance

❖ Unauthorized PC hardware

This information defines the current status used as a control. It also provides information on how the asset management system can be installed with a minimum of conflict and effort.

C **Asset management plan.** The plan utilizes the information from the preplanning survey to:

❖ Define components of the proposed asset management system.

❖ Draft a project timetable.

❖ Plan the selection of standard software.

❖ Plan for the communication and implementation.

❖ Plan for the needed controls.

❖ Select a user test area for the system.

❖ Determine project and operation costs.

Plan Implementation

The implementation of the plan is a major part of the asset management project. Following are its major areas:

❖ Selecting and obtaining delivery of software

❖ Installing the software

❖ Testing the software

❖ Training operational personnel

❖ Setting up the help-desk

❖ Preparing for a system audit

❖ Asset tagging the hardware and making an inventory of the software

❖ Establishing proof of purchase

❖ Taking corrective actions

❖ Developing a continual audit program

❖ Putting in place an operating hardware/software acquisition system

❖ Maintaining a PC users' education program

❖ Installing and maintaining a disaster recovery system

❖ Providing a network security and virus-protection system

Implementation and Operation

The implementation starts in a prototype area, preferably one offering the best opportunity to debug the system. After a particular area is operational, the system can be implemented in additional areas. Following are steps to be followed to implement and operate the new asset management system:

A **Inventory of hardware.** Take the inventory in the shortest calendar time possible. After each unit has been inventoried, an update procedure—augmented by random inventory spot-checks—should be established to maintain a current inventory.

Tag each hardware item with a scannable inventory tag placed on the equipment in the same location for each type of hardware.

Each new acquisition of hardware must be tagged before the system is operational. The cost, department, and employee-assigned ownership of the hardware is input to the PC inventory system.

B **Physical inventory of software.** Take the inventory of PC software at the same time as the hardware inventory or later. This depends on the system software selected. The software on each PC and file server is identified and logged in. Unauthorized software is purged and recorded in order to identify to what degree, for each area and user, software violations have occurred.

This software data, by each PC (desktop, laptop, and notebook system) and person responsible for that computer, is input to the PC inventory system. Cost, department, and employee-assigned ownership information relating to new PC software added later will also be input to the system.

C **PC inventory system.** The PC inventory system is used by departments and employees within departments to maintain an ongoing PC hardware and software inventory. The system will generate a physical inventory report by department after the first and each of the subsequent inventories. The report is also run at the end of each fiscal year and upon demand by the software coordinator. A copy of the department report is sent to the department head and to the software coordinator. It lists the following:

❖ The department name

❖ The date the physical inventory was taken

❖ The name, total quantity, and total cost of each software type

❖ The total cost of the department's software inventory

❖ The number of each kind of software removed

A detailed listing of each employee and his/her assigned PCs is also produced. A copy of this Department Users Report is sent to the coordinator and the department head, and is available for the software coordinator, if requested. It contains the department name and the date of the inventory. This report also lists the following by each employee:

❖ Hardware assigned

❖ Software on each computer after inventory

❖ Unauthorized software removed, by computer

❖ Total cost of hardware

❖ Total cost of software

❖ Total cost of both hardware and software

A Department Hardware Inventory Report is run after the Department Users Report for each department. A copy is sent to the department head, to the coordinator, and to the corporate computer asset manager. It lists:

❖ The department name

❖ The date the report was run

❖ The hardware type, quantity, and total cost of each type

❖ The total cost of the department's hardware inventory

A Total Hardware/Software Asset Report is run, listing the hardware/software assets by department. There are four columns across each page: department name, number of PCs, total original investment for hardware/software, and average age of department PCs. The bottom line indicates totals of the same information for the whole company. This report is run at the end of the fiscal year and upon demand. It is sent to the head of information systems, the controller, and the corporate computer asset manager.

20

PERIPHERAL AND NON-PC SYSTEMS

CORPORATE POSITION

The information systems unit provides central computer operations for the firm along with the responsibilities for LAN, WAN, and voice corporate communications. The control and standardization responsibility of end-user stand-alone and work group PCs is also the responsibility of information systems. The remaining natural area left that would be an inherent extension of the information systems unit's responsibility would be corporate peripheral service devices. The importance of policy concerning peripheral and non-PC systems mandates the endorsement and support of top management of the organization.

Peripheral service devices are information-processing apparatuses used by the company to conduct day-to-day business office operations. Traditionally, these devices are used in office areas and other company areas requiring information processing for customer service or products. Having these devices standardized and controlled by information systems reduces their total cost of operation and improves the overall service to the company. This may be accomplished at a local operating firm or at multiple sites a company may have.

Scope

The devices can be stand-alone, used in work groups, or systems that cross work group boundaries. The scope of this area of information systems corporate responsibility can cover, but is not limited to, the following company-owned, rented, leased, or loaned peripheral service devices:

- ❖ Fax machines
- ❖ Copy machines
- ❖ Offset lithography
- ❖ Micrographic systems
- ❖ Wireless networks
- ❖ Digital audio–visual equipment
- ❖ Multimedia PC systems
- ❖ Nonlinear video editing systems
- ❖ Digital photo editing systems
- ❖ Video duplication machines
- ❖ Compressed speech computer systems
- ❖ In-house video communications systems
- ❖ Library CD information systems
- ❖ Other related devices

Policy Objectives

Policy objectives are standardization, data logging, controlling, and inventorying these devices. The objective is to also optimize the utilization of these devices. This responsibility includes the maintenance, the provision for procedural operating instructions, operator training, and equipment placement for optimum utilization. Supplies are purchased at the best cost for company-wide control and standards utilization. Purchasing works in concert with the information systems to obtain uniform products and supplies at the best price.

INVENTORY OF PERIPHERAL SUPPORT EQUIPMENT

The information systems unit head assigns the peripheral support systems inventory responsibility to the IT manager. If there is no inventory or equipment system in place, the IT asset manager establishes one.

Tagging Peripheral Support Equipment

Devise a coding method before tagging equipment. Tag computer hardware upon receipt by a sequential numbering system. Peripheral support systems will employ a different form of coding. Use a two-number prefix followed by a space and a sequential number on the tag.

The prefix number identifies the type of peripheral support equipment. After the inventory system is in place, an agent of the asset manager does the tagging upon receipt. The equipment and packing slip is compared with a copy of the purchase order confirming that what was received was ordered. Supply items received will be checked with the packing slip and a copy of the purchase order. If the purchase is by a blanket purchase order, the quantity received each time is added to the total received to date and the quantity compared with the original blanket-ordered quantity. Use either a bar-coded tag, along with visually identified numbers posted on the tag, or a line scanner to insure the correct identification number is read. New hardware items received have tags made and attached to the item. After the tag is secured to the equipment, it is used as its identification number (during inventory checks, when it is moved to a new location, repaired, or disposed).

Peripheral Support Equipment Inventory

A computer inventory system will be maintained for each type of peripheral support equipment. The following file record information will be maintained for each unit of hardware:

❖ Tag number, prefix, and sequential number

❖ Date of purchase

❖ Original cost

❖ Manufacturer's code number

❖ Vendor purchased or leased from

❖ Purchase, lease, or free-trial code identification

❖ Last date of preventive maintenance service

❖ Last date of maintenance service

❖ Last date of warranty service

❖ Maintenance code

A telephone number is provided for the organization doing the maintenance. This number can be the IT service unit's telephone number doing the preventive or repair maintenance. Each vendor can perform warranty service, preventive maintenance, or repair service.

Annual reports are run by type of equipment, department assigned, department total, and grand total by type of equipment. The usage will also be reported when such records can be provided. When equipment is acquired, moved, or disposed of, the information is used to update the information database files.

MAINTENANCE OF PERIPHERAL SUPPORT EQUIPMENT

The information systems unit head assigns the peripheral equipment maintenance support to the IT service unit. The IT service unit head compares maintenance service with vendor and in-house service for quality and cost. The service may be in the form of a hybrid mix of vendors and in-house service. The maintenance service is reviewed annually because of the changing technology, availability of in-house and vendor service personnel, and the company's needs.

In-house Maintenance Control

The IT service unit performing in-house maintenance performs whatever peripheral equipment repairs and preventive maintenance possible. Cost and in-house availability are determining factors as to who performs what service. A service telephone number is available for people needing service.

Call this the service desk. The service desk assists the person with a problem by telephone. If the problem cannot be resolved by telephone, the service desk asks the caller to place an out-of-order sign on the machine. The help-desk informs the caller they will be called back. The service desk then contacts an in-house service person or the vendor with the service contract.

The vendor is contacted for a warranty or repair service call. The service desk has that information. The person contacting the service desk is informed when the service person is expected to arrive, and asked to write the information on the out-of-order sign posted on the inoperative machine. In smaller operations, the help-desk and the service desk are combined into the same job. These smaller operations may also have the IT PC services unit people perform some of the peripheral support equipment maintenance. This is the value of having well-trained power users. It broadens the scope of their job, and provides for a level of care not requiring a skilled technician's attention. The extra training is well worth the investment. With this, smaller operations may not require a full-time help-desk.

Service Budgeting

Budgeting for in-house maintenance control and the service desk comes from the IT service unit's lump-sum budget. Although the item purchased may come from a department's budget, the IT service support cost may or may not be charged to the department. This charge depends on the company's accounting policy. All service maintenance done by the IT service unit is reported on a daily service log. The completed work log sheets are turned in daily to the IT service unit's head. The log report contains the following information:

❖ Service person's name

❖ Machine number serviced

❖ Time spent on the service call

❖ Type of call: service, preventive maintenance, or operator problem

❖ Any replacement parts that were used

Departments purchasing their own equipment with their own budget require funds to obtain their own maintenance service. The departments request funds for this maintenance service in their budgets. Some leased items may come with a provided service agreement. All service performed by the in-house IT service unit or vendor is reported by the IT service unit. The IT service people provide their daily report to the IT service unit head. Vendor service is recorded by the service desk. The vendor code number and machine number are reported. The vendor's service document is turned over to the help-desk. Each day the service report is given to the unit head along with the vendor's service document—a copy is made for the IT unit head and the original copy sent to the department head. A request for vendor service may come in one of the following forms:

❖ Time and parts

❖ Blanket maintenance contract

❖ Warranty service call

Maintenance Service Report

Vendor maintenance is reported by each contracted machine type. Vendor maintenance service reported is shown as warranty, preventive, or service maintenance. List time and replacement parts service charges.

The monthly maintenance service reports lists the machines and locations serviced. The report provides the following information:

❖ What type of equipment was serviced

❖ Who performed the service

❖ The estimated cost for the service

❖ The kind of in-house service performed

❖ The kind of vendor service performed

❖ What kind of service performed

What kind of service was performed on the machine the last time it received a service call? When was the last service call date and what was the current service call date?

There is a total monthly expense by machine type and a monthly grand total. There is a year-to-date cost by machine type, and a year-to-date grand total.

A second report (IT and Vendor Maintenance Cost Report) is printed with information by vendor and the IT service unit. The report lists who serviced which machines. The report lists the subtotal cost for the month. Year-to-date costs are listed by the service provider and a grand total year-to-date sum.

Vendor Maintenance Contracting

The IT unit's head, the asset manager, and a Purchasing department's representative work together to solicit vendor contract bids. Use the same Purchasing department's representative from year to year. It's helpful if the same purchasing agent is also responsible for peripheral supplies and computer supplies.

After IT has identified which items they cannot do or will not be able to service because of lacking the required people, a list is composed of the equipment requiring vendor's maintenance bids. A form letter is used listing all items up for bid. Vendors can bid on any one item, any number, or the entire lot of items listed.

The list of vendors solicited can come from the IT service unit's head, the IT asset manager, and the Purchasing department's representative. It is the Purchasing department representative's responsibility to check each vendor before it is sent the letter. The purchasing agent can use information his/her department already has. Contacts with other firm's purchasing departments are a source of information along with the firm's D and B rating. When composing the request for bids letter, provide as much information as can be given. A vendor company contact person is provided in the letter. Any site visits are arranged through the company's contact person. The letter furnishes the name and telephone number of the contact person, and the last day bids will be received. The following information is furnished in the vendor letter or attachment to the letter:

❖ A list of unit types the bid calls for servicing

❖ The number of units for each unit type

❖ The age and condition of each

❖ Units under current warranties, and when their warranties expire

If a particular vendor's bid is selected, would they be willing to provide a help-desk telephone number? This allows for company employees to contact them for information or a service call. Will there be a charge for this service if available?

Vendor selection is based on several variables. Each variable is weighted before sending the request for bid letters. Vendor analysis is based on a matrix. See the section "Vendor Selection" in Chapter 15 for information about setting up a weighted matrix. Short-term contracts may be considered for yet unproven vendors. Before signing any contract, contact the firm's legal representative, who has the last word before the firm's authorized representative signs it.

Outsourcing Legal Ramifications

Outsourcing different applications from companies has provided mixed results, some good, some bad.

The IRS has defined rules to classify a person as an employee. IRC 530 of the Revenue Act of 1978 provides relief from some consequences of misclassification of employees as independent contractors. There are twenty guidelines presented in Rev. Rule 87-41, along with other IRS data. Some of the key guidelines of Rev. Rule 87-41 are:

A **Working on the employer's premises,** especially when the work could be done elsewhere. This is indicative of an employer/employee relationship.

B **Method of payment.** Payment by the hour, week, or month generally is indicative of an employer/employee relationship. Payment by the job generally indicates that the person is an independent contractor. A lump sum may be computed by the number of hours required to do a job at a certain rate per hour.

C **Furnishing tools and/or materials.** An independent contractor ordinarily furnishes his/her own tools and materials.

D **Working for more than one firm.** The service provider's ability to work for more than one service recipient at the same time is indicative of an independent contractor.

E **Service available to the general public.** That a service provider makes his/her services available to the general public is indicative of an independent contractor. A business telephone listing is supportive of this guideline.

F **Business investment.** The investment by a service provider in facilities is a factor tending to indicate an independent contractor. The investment must be significant and essential. The investment must be essential to the contractor. The investment by the service provider in facilities adequate to perform the services contracted for indicates the status of an independent contractor.

There may be other legal ramifications with labor unions and the contract. Here, a good labor relations attorney is a wise investment. If programming outsourcing results are used in classified software development for the government, it could be a major problem. Outsourcing to parts of the world using prison labor can also be problem. Outsourcing to discharge employees over the age of 40 years also could spell trouble with the EEOC.

PERIPHERAL OPERATION PROCEDURES

Peripherals cover a wide range of applications and complexities. Most companies do not always know the total investment. Meanwhile, most peripherals operate without a central sense of direction. Without the orchestration and guidance of information systems, costs will grow while efficiency diminishes. A major part of controlling this operation are the peripheral operation procedures set forth by an IT unit of information systems.

Posted Device Operations

Less complex operating peripheral devices require only a simple set of posted operation instructions. If possible, the operating instructions are placed on or near the device. Lettering size should be bold enough to be seen and read in a minute or less.

The operator instructions should refer to a separate document of troubleshooting instructions. At the end of the troubleshooting instructions a contact person—not the operator—should be identified if there is a problem with the machine. This could be the area administrator or a person known to be a heavy user of the equipment. If none of these are listed or are unavailable, post the service desk phone number.

Support Operator Responsibility

This is a person responsible for turning on the machine in the morning and turning it off before closing for the day. His/her name is posted as the support operator to be contacted if the machine needs attention or operator assistance. When turning on the machine in the morning, check its running condition and that it is supplied with its needed usable material. The support operator is able to operate and perform minor machine adjustments. He/she will know how to replenish its expendable stock items, and perform standard housekeeping and preventive maintenance procedures. The support operator is able to be walked through some of the malfunctions by the service desk or a maintenance person by telephone. At the service desk is a support operator's location book with the support operator's name, telephone number, and location listed. A second listing is by location with the support operator's name and telephone number listed. This is used to contact another support operator who is close by the unit for assistance when a unit's support operator is unavailable.

Machine Operator Procedures

These are the operating procedures furnished to support operators and stand-alone peripheral machine operators. The operator procedure manuals are furnished by the IT service unit or the systems and procedures unit. The manuals provide operator instructions, minor maintenance instruction, and procedures for troubleshooting. Minor preventive maintenance procedures are provided. The procedure manuals contain any manufacturers' furnished material helpful to clarify the machine's operation. Illustrations used by the manufacturer could be beneficial to the operator. Close-up and wide-view photographs are helpful if included in the operator procedure manuals. A prototype manual is developed and tested before being placed into service. Use an unskilled person for the test. Do this with more than one subject. Avoid the brightest person in the area and any experienced operator for debugging the procedure manual.

Supply Requisitions

Use the firm's standard supply requisitions form. If the form is outdated or there is none, the IT systems and procedures unit will design one.

Place a central supply location to limit the travel time involved. This prevents unnecessary travel by the person seeking supplies. The supply center could also function as supply distribution location for the end-user computer operations supplies. Supplies small enough can be delivered by interoffice mail. Other items that are too large for interoffice mail will require a daily run to deliver the items.

Employ a requisition system to obtain supplies. Requisitions are approved by the administrator or unit head after all the items are listed with their respective quantities. A line will by drawn across the lines not used by the person before signing the requisition. Depending on company accounting practice, supplies will be charged to the unit receiving them or from a lump-sum company budget. Spot-check usage employing a lump-sum budget. The loss on supply items can be costly. The supply area is locked when unattended. Supplies stored in operating units are locked at the end of the day or locked at all times if the area is out of view.

Service Desk Assistance

Help-desks, along with service desks, cannot solve all user problems. It requires other assistance to cover the user's special needs. Some operations, such as turnkey systems, are better off with vendor-supplied service. Vendor help- and service desks for special systems can provide better service than in-house service. If the company is willing to provide for an in-house service desk and support it, there are still vendor services that can provide better assistance. They do it better, and the equipment will be up and running faster.

The asset manager publishes an approved peripheral acquisition list for new peripheral purchases. This covers what is in-house, currently operating and found on the peripheral inventory property list, but not on the approved peripheral acquisition list. Peripheral inventory property list is company property, identified and tagged. The approved peripheral acquisition list is a list of items the IT service unit can repair or for which the service desk has a vendor contact. The service desk also has the peripheral inventory property list and the source of service for each item. Some items were company property before the service desk assistance program was established.

Some items either have long life spans and never need to be replaced or the item is no longer manufactured—it can be replaced only with used equipment. The help-desk has a special number to call to have the item serviced. In these cases, have the power user trained to do most of the repairs and preventive maintenance. Contact the vendor service person only if the problem is beyond the scope of the power user or one is unavailable. Some items may not use the English measuring system and may require special tools to repair the equipment, or the manufacturer may be the only one that makes the tool.

The service desk does not have to be covered at the company site any more than the help-desk. This is why so many vendor help-desks are not found at company sites. This may be more difficult than having the vendor provide full-service desk coverage. If coverage is needed past normal working hours, service desk personnel can be on call at home for specific time periods. This can also apply to help-desk personnel. These two jobs are combined into one in smaller firms. There is one number to call in case of a problem. There is also the possibility the problem may be related to both the help-desk and the service desk. The help- and service desk person should have at home the current information that he/she has at work. Install it in a notebook computer.

OPERATOR AND SERVICE TECHNICIAN TRAINING

The provision for training covers a wide area of needs. The technology skill levels required for each service item will be one or more levels. Vendor-contracted peripheral service will not require so many levels as an in-house service program. The service desk has the levels of skill available for each item in the peripheral inventory property list. Depending on the problem, a skill level is determined to resolve it. The item listed has posted to it the persons who can perform a given level of skill. A person with a higher level of skill can perform a lower level of skill task. But a lower-level skilled person should not perform a higher-level skill task. The training will certify a level at which the service person can perform a task.

The training provided is for certain skill levels. This training is for vendor- and company-serviced equipment.

Operator Training

The operator should learn the basic operation of the device to produce the desired results. The more complex the device, the more to learn. The job of putting paper into a copy machine is considered a task level not expected of an operator. Video editing is more complex, but also an operator's job.

Operator training is provided in more than one form:

A **New device operator training.** When a new peripheral device is introduced, conduct the training in class. The vendor or the administrator conducts the classes. The vendor provides handouts. The company instructor provides any additional handouts needed. Have a video or slide presentation along with any hands-on training.

Compile a list of the people attending the meeting. Notify anyone missing the class that he/she should attend the next class offered. If the classes are over, have the person who missed the class take the individual training provided to new employees later.

B **New employee training.** Anyone missing class takes the self-paced individual training. New employees with no experience with the equipment receive the self-paced individual training. They are credited with receiving the instruction for the new equipment. Part of the instruction is provided by the operator as OJT instruction.

Support Operator Training

Support operator training is given for all devices in his/her job area that need the attention of a support operator. Training can be from more than one source. The IT service unit holds classes for support operators or OJT instruction for their devices. Support operators receive operator manuals from the IT service unit.

Vendor training programs are provided at the company site or at the vendor's place of instruction. The vendors provide manuals. The IT unit also provides operator's procedure manuals. A certificate will be provided by the vendor showing the person is now a certified support operator for the given machine. The support operator should provide OJT to new device operators. They are able to clean the machine, make adjustments to its operation, and perform some light preventive maintenance. They are the key contact persons in the area for operators, service desk, vendor service people, and the IT service personnel.

IT Service Unit Training

Each IT service person has a list of equipment he/she services for his/her own records, along with the service desk and the IT unit head.

Training will come from one of the following sources:

- ❖ OJT
- ❖ A self-paced learning program provided by the vendor
- ❖ Attending vendor's classes
- ❖ Passing a qualifying exam for the equipment
- ❖ Taking a correspondence course from the vendor or a private correspondence course

Service Desk Training

Effective service desk people are often individuals with some experience as IT service persons. Their training can come from the same areas the IT service person receives his/her training—as the support operator and from operator training. Have new service desk operators work with experienced workers, which is a form of OJT learning. On days when the workload is light, have them try their skills at manning the service desk.

Service desk personnel are expected to work overtime and be on call at their homes. The unit has one or two laptop computers that service people can take home when on call.

They are expected to have no less knowledge than a support operator about each device and a general knowledge about vendor-maintained devices. They should have enough knowledge to assist an operator and communicate with a service person working for the company or vendor. They are able to assign service people to be used most effectively and best serve the company's needs. They can reduce maintenance costs with the proper assignments and the ability to walk operators through problems.

PERIPHERAL DEVICES AND SUPPLY ACQUISITION PROCEDURES

Budgeting can come from a corporate lump-sum budget, department budgets, or both.

Budgeting Procedures

Each department submits its expected needs for the following year's budget. This is based on last year's budget plus any inflation, replacement of old equipment, and new needs. It is supported by the utilization of the current equipment and forecasted usage for the next budget year. Budgets are needed for the department's use of supplies and replacement of current equipment. Departments with their own hardware for their one-of-a-kind use require a budget. The information systems IT service unit needs a budget for its operation. They need a budget for capital expenses that benefit the whole company plus a replacement parts budget. Also, a vendor service budget is required.

Requisition Procedures

Budgeted items have a requisition issued. The requisition goes to the IT asset manager who confirms it meets standards or requires a standards waiver.

The requisition is approved and sent to the budget department to adjust their records, then sent on to the Purchasing department.

Purchasing Procedures

Purchasing receives the approved purchase requisition. If needed, they take care of the competitive bids for the item. After the purchase order is sent to the vendor, a copy is sent to the Receiving department and Accounts Payable.

Receiving Procedures

The agent for the asset manager or a special order item representative inspects the item. After it is approved, a receiving notice is sent to Accounts Payable.

The asset manager's agent affixes a tag to the machine and records the information. The information is sent to the asset manager.

GLOSSARY OF IT TERMS

ABORT To cancel, or terminate, a program, command, or operation while in process.

ACCESS To retrieve data or program instructions from "secondary storage" (hard disk, floppy disk, or tape) or another online computer device.

ACCESS CODE An identification code or password used to gain access to a computer system.

ADDRESS A unique identifier associated with a station, line, path, or unit. Addresses of main memory are for instructions or data locations. LAN addresses are assigned for each device on line. Random access storage requires an address locator to find the actual location address of the record sought. For example, finding John Smith's record in storage would require matching "John Smith" to the address location that holds the record. Tape devices have no address locations. A tape drive would have to read the name element of each record until it located the one for John Smith.

AFTERMARKET The market for peripherals or software created by the sale of large numbers of a specific brand of computer. For example, sales of the IBM 400 computer have created a market for software or hardware peripherals developed by companies other than IBM.

ALGORITHM A specific set of mathematical and logical procedures that a computer can follow to solve a problem.

ALPHANUMERIC CHARACTERS Character letters (A to Z), numbers (0 to 9), punctuation, and special symbols.

AMERICAN NATIONAL STANDARDS INSTITUTE (ANSI) Organization devoted to the voluntary development of standards. It has worked with the computer industry to develop standards for languages such as FORTRAN and COBOL.

ANALOG A continuously varying electrical signal with an infinite number of amplitudes.

ANSI SCREEN CONTROL A set of standards developed by ANSI to control the information display of computer monitor screens.

API (Application Program Interface) A method of allowing an application to interact directly with certain functions of an operating system or another application.

APL (A Programming Language) A high-level language used for programming scientific or mathematical applications.

APPLICATION A term referring to a software program that accomplishes a certain task.

APPLICATION LAYER The layer of the OSI model concerned with application programs such as electronic mail, database manager, and file server software.

APPROVED LIST A list of computer software and/or hardware for which the IS department provides user support.

ARCHITECTURE A system's architecture is described by the type of components, interfaces, and protocols it uses and how these elements fit together.

ARCHIVAL BACKUP A procedure to backup or copy files in secondary storage onto another secondary storage device.

ARPANET A wide area network developed by the Defense Advanced Research

Projects Agency that primarily connects universities and government agencies on the Internet.

ASCII (American Standard Code for Information Interchange) A standard for encoding characters (including the upper- and lowercase alphabet, numerals, punctuation, and control characters) using seven bits. The standard set is 128 characters; IBM expanded this to 256 by adding an eighth bit to each existing character. This expanded set provides graphic, mathematical, scientific, financial, and foreign language characters.

ASP (Application Service Provider) An ASP deploys, hosts, and manages access to a packaged application to multiple parties from a centrally managed facility. The applications are delivered over networks on a subscription basis. This delivery model speeds implementation, minimizes the expenses and risks incurred across the application life cycle, and overcomes the chronic shortage of qualified technical personnel available in-house.

ASSEMBLER Software that transforms an assembly language source code program into machine language. One assembler instruction code produces one machine language instruction.

ASSEMBLY LANGUAGE A lower-level programming language in which one statement is written for each machine language step.

ASYNCHRONOUS COMMUNICATIONS SERVER A device on a LAN that provides the capability for network workstations to access ASCII applications via switched communications lines.

AUDIT TRAIL A means of locating the origin of specific data that appears on final reports.

BACKGROUND PROCESS On a multitasking operating system, an operation that runs in the background while a second operation runs in the foreground.

BACKUP A copy of a file, directory, or volume placed on a separate storage device for the purpose of retrieval in case the original is accidentally erased, damaged, or destroyed.

BAR CODE A printed pattern of vertical lines used to represent alphanumerical codes in a scannable reading form.

BATCH PROCESSING Grouped transactions into a single batch for processing.

BENCHMARK A standard measurement used to test the performance of hardware or software.

BETA TESTING Using and testing software not yet put on the market by the vendor.

BIT A binary digit; must be either a zero (on) or a one (off). The smallest possible unit of information in a digital system.

BIT ORDER The order of transmission of a serial system. Typically, the least significant bit (LSB) is sent first.

BORDER RULE Heavy rules at the top or bottom of or completely around a printed form.

BOTTLENECK A factor restricting the flow of data through a system. When a bottleneck exists, performance is limited.

BRIDGE A device used to connect LANs by forwarding packets across connections at the media access control sublayer of the data link layer of the OSI model.

BROADBAND A transmission system in which signals are encoded and modulated into different frequencies allowing for transmission of more than one input signal over the same line simultaneously.

BROADCAST A LAN data transmission scheme in which data packets are heard by all stations on the network, but are only received by the intended station.

BROWNOUT A period with low voltage electric power because of increased demands.

BUFFER A memory device holding information temporarily to compensate for differences in speed between computer components.

BUG A programming error causing a program or a computer system not to perform as expected.

BUNDLED SOFTWARE Software that is included with a hardware system as part of the total price.

BUS A common connection. Networks broadcasting to all stations, such as Ethernet broadcasting to ARCnet, are considered bus networks.

BUS (PC) The connectors on a PC motherboard into which expansion boards are plugged.

BYTE Eight continuous bits representing one character in memory.

BURSTER Machine used to separate continuous forms into single-part forms or sets.

CACHE To read data into a memory buffer so the information is available whenever needed and does not have to be read from the disk again.

CACHE BUFFER An area in RAM used for caching.

CAD/CAM Computer-aided design/computer-aided manufacturing.

CALENDAR TIME The actual duration of a project, from the date it starts to the date it is completed. This includes both work and nonwork days.

CAMERA-READY COPY Any material ready to be photographed for reproduction without further change. May be typewritten copy, reproduction proofs, art work, or previously printed material.

CD A compact optical disk with over six hundred and fifty million characters of storage.

CD READ/WRITE DRIVE A CD read- and write-only-once device employing compact optical disks.

CD/ROM DRIVE A read-only optical storage device employing compact optical disks.

CLIENT A computer that accesses the resources of a server. See "client/server."

CLIENT/SERVER A network system design in which a processor or computer designated as a server, such as a file server or database server, provides services to clients' workstations or PCs.

CLIP ART A collection of graphic images available for use with desktop publishing.

COAXIAL CABLE A commonly used cable type that is relatively insensitive to noise interferences, consisting of one or two insulating layers and two conductors. A central conductor wire is surrounded by the first layer of insulation. An outer shielding conductor is laid over the first layer of insulation. Usually the cable is then covered with a second layer of insulation.

COLLATING Gathering sheets or computer records in proper preidentified order.

COLOR CODING Use of different colored stock, tinting, or printed marks on individual parts of a set to aid in identification and distribution.

COLUMN HEAD A heading that identifies a series of entries to be made in columnar sequence below.

COMMUNICATIONS PROTOCOL A list of parameters and standards governing communications between computers employing telecommunications.

COMPILER A program that reads high-level program coding statements (source code) and translates the statements into machine executable instructions (object code).

COMPOSITION Typographic material that has been set and/or assembled. Also, the process of preparing this material for printing.

COMPUTER STORE An IT support unit of information systems providing company employees with the opportunity to view and try out approved hardware and software.

COMPUTER SYSTEM A complete computer installation with all the required peripherals needed for elements to work with each other as one system.

CONCENTRATOR A 10 BASE-T hub. A multiport repeater for Ethernet/802.3 used over unshielded twisted-pair cable.

CONSOLE A computer display terminal consisting of a monitor and keyboard.

COPY PROTECTION The inclusion in a program of hidden instructions intended to prevent unauthorized copying of software.

CORRUPTED FILE A file containing scrambled and unrecoverable data.

COST-BENEFIT ANALYSIS A projection of the costs incurred in and benefits derived from installing hardware, software, or a proposed system.

CPM (Critical-Path Method) A process used in project management for the planning and timing of tasks relying on the identification of a critical path. The time needed for the series of tasks along the critical path determines the total project completion time.

CRC (Cyclical Redundancy Check) This ensures the validity of received data.

CUSTOM FORM Form manufactured to unique order specifications by a vendor.

CUT FORMS Forms delivered as individual sheets, not bound or padded.

DAT (Digital audio tape) Popular tape backup format.

DATA Units of information stored on some type of magnetic media that can be called into a computer program for use.

DATA COMMUNICATIONS The transfer of information from one computer to another.

DATA DICTIONARY A list of data elements used in database management programs. Each data element contains information about its use, its size, its characteristics, who can use it, who can alter it, who can remove it, and who can only view it.

DATA ELEMENT A field containing an element of information used in records found in database management systems. Examples would be FICA number, name, part number, etc.

DATA INDEPENDENCE Data stored in such a way that users can gain access to it in a database system without knowing where the data is actually located.

DATA MANAGER A person responsible for the management of all corporate data. The database manager may report directly or indirectly to this person.

DATA PROCESSING The preparing, storing, or manipulation of information within a computer system.

DATA RECORD A complete addressable unit of related data elements expressed in identified data fields used in files and database systems.

DATA REDUNDANCY The same data stored in more than one location.

DATABASE An organized collection of information, in random access secondary storage, made up of related data records. There can be more than one database in a computer system.

DATABASE MANAGEMENT PROGRAM A data application program providing for the retrieval, modification, deletion, or insertion of data elements. Database systems tend to reduce "data redundancy."

DATABASE MANAGEMENT SYSTEM (DBMS) The operating software system that provides for the access and storage of data.

DATABASE MANAGER The person responsible for managing the corporate IS database. This person reports to the head of corporate information systems, but can report to the corporate data manager, too.

DATABASE SERVER The back-end processor that manages the database and fulfills database requests in a client/server system.

DATAFLOW DIAGRAMS A method of showing dataflows all on one page. It starts at the lowest detail level, which is the system level. Corresponding process parts are all shown in more detail, each on its own page. Dataflow diagrams have their own flowcharting symbols.

DDOS (Distributed denial of service) Denial-of-service attacks are attacks whereby a hacker floods a network server with data in an attempt to crash the system. A distributed denial-of-service attack uses multiple computers all attacking at the same time.

DEBUGGING The procedure of locating and correcting program errors.

DECISION TREE A graphic representation of all possible conditions or processing alternatives and end results. It resembles the branches of a tree growing out from the main trunk.

DECOLLATOR Machine used to separate continuous forms into individual piles or to remove interleaved carbon(s).

DEDICATED FILE SERVER A file server that cannot be operated as a user's server workstation. See "file server."

DE FACTO STANDARD A standard based on broad usage and support.

DEFAULT A value or option that is chosen automatically when no other value is specified.

DEMODULATION The process of recovering information impressed on a carrier signal by modulation.

DESKTOP PUBLISHING The use of a PC to generate camera-ready copy for printing. Requires the use of one of the available desktop publishing software programs.

DINGBAT Stock symbol, such as a star, triangle, dot, or arrow, usually used for visual emphasis.

DIRECTORY An index to the files stored on a disk that can be displayed on the monitor.

DISK CHANNEL All components, including the disk(s), that connect a disk drive or drives to a file server. This includes the host adapter or disk controller and cables.

DISK CONTROLLER A hardware device associated with a disk drive that controls how data is written to and retrieved from the disk.

DISK DRIVE The unit in a computer that reads and writes information to and from disks.

DISK DUPLEXING A method of safeguarding data whereby the data is copied simultaneously to two hard disks on separate channels. If one channel fails, the data on the other channel remains unharmed. When data is duplexed, read requests are sent to whichever disk in the pair can respond faster, decreasing the file server's response time.

DISK MIRRORING A method of safeguarding data whereby the same data is copied to two hard disks on the same channel. If one of the disks fails, the data on the other disk is safe. Because the two disks are on the same channel, mirroring provides only limited data protection; a failure anywhere along the channel could shut down both disks and data would be lost. See also "disk duplexing."

DISTRIBUTED PROCESSING SYSTEM A computer system designed for multiple users with fully functional computer access.

DO/WHILE LOOP A loop control structure that carries out its functions as long as an external condition is satisfied in a program.

DOCUMENTATION The instructions and references providing users with the necessary information to use computer programs and systems or alter them at a later date.

DOCUMENT FLOWCHART A flowchart constructed all on one page showing the flow of documents used in a given system. It shows the documents traveling from left to right across a page from one user to another. Each user is in its own vertical column.

DOMAIN NAME SERVICE HIJACKING A hack in which inquiries seeking one domain are routed to another domain without the user's knowledge. Such attacks on the Internet's control structures could make packets of information undeliverable, quickly snarling traffic on the network.

DOT-MATRIX PRINTER An impact printer that causes the ends of pins in the form of characters, numbers, etc., to strike against a ribbon for printing text.

DOWNLOADING The reception and storage of data from one computer to another, often via data communications.

DSL (Digital Subscriber Line) DSL is a modem technology that transforms ordinary phone lines (also known as "twisted copper pairs") into high-speed digital lines for ultra-fast Internet access.

DUMP Transferring the contents of computer main memory to a printer or a secondary storage device.

DVD (Digital Video Disk) A high-density compact disk for storing large amounts of data, especially high-resolution audio–visual material.

ELECTRONIC MAIL (E-MAIL) A network service enabling users to send and receive messages via computer from anywhere in the world.

EMULATOR A computer program that makes a programmable device imitate another computer, producing the same results.

ENCRYPTION The scrambling of information for transmission over public communication systems. The receiver requires the same technology key to unscramble the coded information.

END-USER A person who benefits directly or indirectly from a computer system.

ERGONOMICS The science of designing hardware, tools, and the working environment taking into account human factors so as to enable people to interact more comfortably and more productively.

ERROR MESSAGE A display on a computer screen or hard-copy stating a computer program is unable to perform as programmed.

EXPERT SYSTEM A computer program containing the knowledge used by an expert in a given area that assists nonexperts when they attempt to perform duties in that same area.

FACSIMILE The exact reproduction of a letter, document, or signature. Sometimes abbreviated as "fax."

FAULT TOLERANCE Resistance to system failure or data loss.

FAX The transmission and reception of documents between two locations via telecommunications.

FAX SERVER A network device or service providing a LAN workstation access to incoming or outgoing faxes across the LAN.

FEASIBILITY STUDY A study to determine the possibility of undertaking a systems project.

FILE A name given to a collection of information stored in a secondary storage medium, such as a tape or disk.

FILE ALLOCATION TABLE A table on a disk recording the disk location of all the file parts.

FILE SERVER A computer providing network stations with controlled access to shareable resources. The network operating system is loaded on the file server and most shareable devices, such as disk subsystems and printers, are attached to it. The file server controls system security. It also monitors station-to-station communications. A dedicated file server can be used online as a file server while it is on the network. A nondedicated file server can be used simultaneously as a file server and a workstation.

FILE SHARING The ability for multiple users to share files. Concurrent file sharing is controlled by application software, the workstation operating system, and/or the file server/database server operating system.

FLOPPY DISK A removable secondary storage medium using a magnetically sensitive, flexible or firm disk enclosed in a plastic envelope or case.

FLOWCHART Analysis tool consisting of a diagrammatic representation of a system process or abstract relationship, normally made up of labeled blocks or keyed symbols connected by lines.

FORM A preprinted document available as flat or continuous.

FORMAT The size, style, type page, margins, printing requirements, etc., of a printed piece.

FORMS DESIGN The art or science of devising a form to efficiently fill a given function or systems need; includes selection of materials, construction, and layout.

FRONT-END PROCESSOR A specialized computer that relieves the main CPU, taking over line control, message handling, code conversion, and error control.

GANTT CHART A project scheduling tool using graphic representations to show start, elapsed, and completion times of each task within a given project. It can also show the planned scheduled (S) time and the actual completed (C) time. The Gantt chart indicates the status of a given project at any point. A Gantt chart employing dollars can also illustrate money budgeting for given tasks vs. money spent. Gantt chart monitor screen displays are available with some project management software. This allows for online reference of the status of projects that can be networked. Gantt charts can also be drawn on various size sheets of paper. The $8^1/2$- by 11-inch size is inserted in binders for project progress recording. Larger size sheets of paper can be used for displaying Gantt charts in the project team work areas.

GATEWAY A device providing routing and protocol conversion among physically dissimilar networks and/or computers.

GIGABYTE (GB, G-BYTE) A unit of measure of memory or disk storage capacity; two to the thirtieth power (1,073,741,824 bytes).

HACKER A technically knowledgeable computer enthusiast who enjoys programming but is not usually employed as a programmer.

HANDSHAKE A predetermined exchange between two computer systems in order to establish communication.

HARDCOPY Printed output from a computer system or typewriter.

HARDWARE Electronic components, computers, and peripherals that make up a computer system.

HOST ADAPTER An adapter card that attaches a device to a computer's expansion bus.

IBM TOKEN RING IBM's version of the 802.5 token-passing ring network.

INFORMAL UNIT ORGANIZATION The unofficial unit organization structure and culture. It also identifies the undercurrent of power within the unit.

INFORMATION SYSTEMS The department within a company that is responsible for computer information systems processing and the storage of all centralized data.

INFORMATION TECHNOLOGY The different techniques required to perform the task of information systems processing. The technology units within the information systems organization are required to be orchestrated by the information systems head.

IN-HOUSE Denotes that the task is done within the company.

INPUT DEVICE Peripheral hardware that inputs data into a computer system.

INTELLIGENT WORKSTATION A terminal containing PC processing capability that runs independently or in conjunction with a host computer.

INTERFACE A shared boundary between two systems, such as between data communications (terminating) equipment and data terminal equipment (DTE). Also a boundary between adjacent layers of the ISO model.

INTERNAL IT AUDITOR A person representing the company with internal information technology auditing. He/she follows the guidelines provided by the CPA firm's auditors. They are concerned with computer systems audit trails and the security of the hardware, software, and data.

INTERNET The largest network in the world. Successor to ARPANET, the Internet includes other large internetworks. The Internet uses the TCP/IP protocol suite and connects universities, government agencies, businesses, and individuals around the world.

INTERNETWORK Two or more networks connected by bridges and/or routers; a network of networks.

ISP (Internet Service Provider) An ISP is used as your local connection to the Internet. It provide other companies or individuals with access to, or presence on, the Internet.

JAZ DRIVES Jaz drives employ secondary storage cartridges that hold one or more gigabytes.

JUSTIFY In composition, to space out lines so each is a designated length.

LAN (Local Area Network) Typically, denotes a short-distance, high-speed network.

LASER PRINTER A high-resolution printer that uses electrostatic reproduction technology, like electrostatic copy machines, to fuse text or graphic images onto plain paper.

LEASED LINE A full-time link between two or more locations leased from a local or interexchange carrier.

LIBRARY A collection of programs and data files for a computer system's off line storage.

LOCAL AREA NETWORK (LAN) The linkage of computers within a limited area so users can exchange information and share peripherals. This linkage can be wired or wireless.

LSB (Least Significant Bit) The bit with the least binary weight in a character.

MAINFRAME A large computer, generally with high-level and multiprocessing power and the capacity to support many users at once.

MARGIN The blank area along any edge of a sheet that must be kept free of printing due to production considerations.

MEGABYTE (MG, M-BYTE) A unit of measure for memory or disk storage capacity; two to the twentieth power (1,048,576 bytes).

MILESTONES Used with Gantt, CPM, and PERT charting to show when measurable units of task(s) have been completed. With Gantt charts, the actual milestones can be drawn on the charts.

MINICOMPUTER A multiple-user computer, generally with more power than a personal computer yet not so large as a mainframe.

MODELING An analytical process based on mathematical network behavior formulas called models used to predict the performance of product designs.

MODEM A device converting digital signals to analog and analog signals to digital between computers via telephone transmission.

MODULAR PROGRAMMING A style of programming requiring that program functions be broken into modules. It is a form of program segmentation and is the correct way to code procedural programs. This is also a good way to write reusable code. Quick BASIC and Visual BASIC programming require this type of program coding.

MONITOR Screen for viewing computer output. It is also called a CRT.

MULTIPLEXER An electronic device combining several signals into one to save transmission cost. Time division multiplexing (TDM) and frequency division multiplexing (FDM) are used in various aspects of LAN data communications.

NETWORK A series of points connected by communications channels. Public networks can be used by anyone; private networks are closed to outsiders.

NETWORK ADMINISTRATOR A local area network manager who is responsible for maintaining a network.

NETWORK INTERFACE CARD (NIC) A circuit board installed in each network station allowing communications with other stations.

NONDEDICATED FILE SERVER A file server that also functions as a workstation.

OBJECT CODE The machine-readable instructions created by a computer or assembler from source code.

OBJECT-ORIENTED PROGRAMMING A type of programming in which the data types and the allowed functions for a data type are defined by the programmer.

OFFSET An adaptation of stone lithography whereby the design is drawn or photographically reproduced on a thin, flexible metal plate or other medium from which the design is transferred.

ONE-TIME CARBON Carbon paper designed to be used within a form for just one writing or printing and then discarded.

ONLINE DEVICE A peripheral device externally attached to a computer.

PACKET A basic message unit grouped for transmission through a public network such as ITU-TSS X.25. A packet usually includes routing information, data, and sometimes error-detection information.

PARALLEL PORT A printer interface allowing data to be transmitted a byte at a time, with eight bits moving in parallel.

PASSWORD A security identification used to authorize users of a computer system or given program.

PC (Personal Computer) Smaller computers employing microprocessor chip technology. These can be identified as palm type, mini-notebooks, notebooks, laptops, transportable, desktop, workstations and microcomputers.

PC COORDINATOR An end-user person responsible for the coordination and operation of an end-user PC operation. The person can have full- or part-time responsibility for this duty, and can be hourly or salaried, union or nonunion.

PC MANAGER A person responsible for managing and providing support to and training for users of PCs. This person reports to IS management. Since this position is almost always a full-time responsibility, it is advisable it be filled by a salaried worker.

PDA (Personal Data Assistant) A small hand-held computer used to write

notes, track appointments, and otherwise organize your life. Early PDAs required data to be input using a keypad with keys the size of Chiclets, but more recent models (e.g., the Palm Pilot) use a combination of pen-based input and character-recognition software to accept user input. Many can also be used to send and receive e-mail and browse the Internet.

PEER-TO-PEER A network design in which each computer shares and uses devices on an equal basis.

PERIPHERAL A physical device (such as a printer or disk subsystem) that is externally attached to a workstation or directly attached to the network.

PERT (Programmed Evaluation Review Technique) A planning and control tool for defining and controlling the tasks necessary to complete a given project. The PERT chart and CPM charts are one and the same. The only difference is the manner in which task time is computed. The CPM chart uses only one expected time. With the PERT system, the time required for each task is computed as follows: The longest expected time, the shortest expected time, and four times the expected time are totaled and divided by six. This gives the expected time needed.

POTS Plain old telephone service.

PRINT SERVER A device and/or program for managing shared printers. Print service is often provided by the file server, but can also be provided from a separate LAN microcomputer or other device.

PROGRAM RUN BOOK Operating instructions for the benefit of those who run a given program, including any restart procedures in case of program failure. Most often used by mainframe computer operators, but can also be provided for minicomputer operators and PC users.

PROJECT SLIPPAGE Occurs when a project's critical path milestone finish date is not met. The critical path of a PERT or CPM chart determines the project completion time. See "CPM." Projects that are not using PERT or CPM technology can have project slippage, too. It is first recognized when it becomes obvious that the project finish date will be later than planned.

PROTOCOL A formal set of rules setting the format and control of data exchange between two devices or processes.

QUICK BASIC An improved form of BASIC that is available from Microsoft. It has been available as part of its Windows software. The programming must be written in a modular form.

RECOMMENDED LIST A list of software that the IS department recommends and for which it provides user support. The list can also contain recommended IT hardware for users.

RECORD LOCKING A data-protection scheme preventing different users from performing simultaneous writes to the same record in a shared file, thus preventing overlapping disk writes and ensuring record integrity.

REDIRECTOR Device in a workstation that sends data to the network or keeps it in the workstation for local use, as appropriate.

REPEATER A device used to extend cabling distances by regenerating signals.

REUSABLE CODE Code that is written in a structured modular format allowing it to be used at a later time with no (or minor) changes for other programming efforts.

RING TOPOLOGY A close loop in which data passes in one direction from station to station on the LAN. Each workstation on the ring acts as a repeater, passing data on to the next workstation.

ROM Read-only memory that is found on CDs and permanent microcomputer main memory.

ROUTER Hardware and software routing data between similar or dissimilar networks at the network layer of the OSI model.

SCANNER A PC input device that copies documents into computer memory.

SCHEMA Schema and sub-schema are the tools used to define the structure of a database.

SECONDARY STORAGE Any place where computer data or program instructions are stored, other than main memory (RAM or ROM).

SERIAL PORT A port allowing data to be transmitted one bit at a time.

SERVER A network device providing services to client stations. Servers include file servers, disk servers, and print servers. See "client/server."

SHIELDED TWISTED-PAIR CABLE Twisted-pair wire surrounded by a foil or mesh shield to reduce susceptibility to outside interference and noise during network transmission.

SIMULATION A technique for evaluating the performance of a network before downloading it. Simulation employs timers and sequences as opposed to mathematical models to reproduce network behavior.

SITE LICENSING Procedure in which software is licensed to be used only at a particular location.

SIZE SNOWBALL EFFECT The larger the project size and/or the longer the required project calendar time, the more likely that additional time and effort will be needed to complete the project. As more time and effort are required, these snowball, which in turn extends the finish date and increases the final cost. The user's needs change over time. The longer a project takes, the more the user can justify changes to the final product, and the number of changes will snowball. In addition, these changes that are required for a useable product also take even more time to install, which can justifiably require more changes.

SOURCE CODE Written program code before the program has been compiled into machine instructions.

SPAGHETTI CODE The name given to the first method of computer program coding. Program steps were written without any formal structure and meandered through the program. Tracing these program steps was like following a string of spaghetti in a bowl. Contrasted to "structured programming."

STAR TOPOLOGY A LAN topology in which each workstation connects to a central device.

STAR-WIRED TOPOLOGY A ring network (such as a token-passing ring) cabled through centralized hubs or connection devices to create a physical star topology. Using this, individual stations and whole sections of the network can be removed or added easily.

STATISTICAL MULTIPLEXER A multiplexer that allocates time on the channel to active inputs only. It greatly increases line capacity.

STRUCTURED PROGRAM-MING A standard requiring programs to be written in modular forms without the use of GO TO statements.

SURGE PROTECTOR An electrical device that prevents high-voltage surges from reaching the computer system.

SYNCHRONOUS TRANSMIS-SION Transmission of data during which the components of the network are all controlled by a single timing source.

TERMINAL A keyboard and display screen through which users can access a host computer.

TERMINAL EMULATION Software enabling a personal computer to communicate with a host computer by transmitting in the form used by the host's terminals.

THIRD-PARTY VENDOR A firm marketing hardware for manufacturers.

TOKEN BUS A network using a logical token-passing network. A service can only transmit data on the network if it is on the token.

TOKEN-PASSING RING A LAN design in which each station is connected to an upstream station and a downstream station. An electronic signal, called the token, is passed from station to station around the ring. A station may not send a transmission to another station unless it has possession of a free token. Since only one token is allowed on the network, only

one station may broadcast at a time.

TURNKEY SYSTEM A system in which the vendor takes full responsibility for complete system design and provides the required hardware, software, operations manual and user training.

TWISTED-PAIR CABLE Wiring used by local telephone systems.

UPS (Uninterrupted Power Source) A device providing electric backup power to a computer system or other devices when the normal electric power fails. This occurs so quickly that the operation of devices that depend on electricity is not interrupted.

USER-FRIENDLY A computer system easy for persons with no computer experience to use, causing little or no frustration or upset.

VISUAL BASIC A more advanced form of programming than Quick BASIC, available from Microsoft. Program operation is screen-driven, which makes the program user-friendly. As with Quick BASIC, it uses modular programming. Programmed subroutines are available, either for purchase or with the payment of royalties.

WALK-THROUGH A technical review of a newly designed program or system. The review is conducted by interested parties such as programmers, systems analysts, users, and/or auditors. Program walk-throughs are conducted by peer programmers to

detect program errors. In a walkthrough, people play the role of devil's advocate in reviewing another person's/team's effort.

WAN (Wide Area Network) Any network extending more than a few miles. It can use more than one form of message carrying.

WAP (Wireless Application Protocol) A standard used by mobile phones and other hand-held devices to access the Internet.

WIRELESS NETWORK A LAN system that does not require physical connections—information is transmitted through the air.

WORK SAMPLING Consists of a large number of random observations of predetermined tasks that an employee or group of employees perform. Data collected by the work sampling observations identifies the amount of time spent on each task.

WORKSTATION A highly intelligent terminal often found on a LAN or client/server system. Some workstations do not require floppy disk drives because data and/or programs are downloaded from a computer server.

WORM ATTACK A worm is a program that replicates itself over and over. A worm capable of penetrating networks could quickly overload the Internet.

ZIP DRIVE Drives that employ Zip disks that can store 100 to 250 megabytes of data.

INDEX

510